Routledge Revivals

Incentives and Economic Systems

First published in 1987, *Incentives and Economic Systems* is a selection of papers presented at the Eighth Arne Ryde Symposium at Frostavallen, Sweden on how institutions attempt to guide individual behaviour by manipulating the social and economic incentive system. These economic and social aspects of incentives determine 'rational' and 'irrational' behaviour by individuals and organizations across various economic systems. The essays in the volume deal with various aspects of the incentive problems and the various manifestations of such problems, along with moral and ethical issues. The essays will be an enlightening read for students of economics, policymaking and international politics.

Incentives and Economic Systems

Proceedings of the Eighth Arne Ryde Symposium, Frostavallen, 26-27 August 1985

Edited by Stefan Hedlund

First published in 1987
by Croom Helm

This edition first published in 2022 by Routledge
2 Park Square, Milton Park, Abingdon, Oxon, OX14 4RN

and by Routledge
605 Third Avenue, New York, NY 10017

Routledge is an imprint of the Taylor & Francis Group, an informa business

© 1987 Stefan Hedlund

All rights reserved. No part of this book may be reprinted or reproduced or utilised in any form or by any electronic, mechanical, or other means, now known or hereafter invented, including photocopying and recording, or in any information storage or retrieval system, without permission in writing from the publishers.

Publisher's Note
The publisher has gone to great lengths to ensure the quality of this reprint but points out that some imperfections in the original copies may be apparent.

Disclaimer
The publisher has made every effort to trace copyright holders and welcomes correspondence from those they have been unable to contact.

A Library of Congress record exists under ISBN: 0814734421

ISBN: 978-1-032-19918-4 (hbk)
ISBN: 978-1-003-26153-7 (ebk)
ISBN: 978-1-032-19943-6 (pbk)

Book DOI 10.4324/9781003261537

 Printed in the United Kingdom
by Henry Ling Limited

To the memory of Valborg Ryde who died before
the completion of this work

INCENTIVES AND ECONOMIC SYSTEMS:

Proceedings of the Eighth Arne Ryde
Symposium, Frostavallen,
26–27 August 1985

Edited by STEFAN HEDLUND

CROOM HELM
London & Sydney

© 1987 Stefan Hedlund
Croom Helm Ltd, Provident House, Burrell Row,
Beckenham, Kent BR3 1AT
Croom Helm Australia, 44–50 Waterloo Road,
North Ryde, 2113, New South Wales, Australia

British Library Cataloguing in Publication Data

Arne Ryde Symposium *(8th : 1985 : Frostavallen)*
  Incentives and economic systems :
  proceedings of the eighth Arne Ryde
  symposium Frostavallen, August 26–27, 1985.
  1. Economics 2. Incentives in industry
  I. Title   II. Hedlund, Stefan
  330.12   HB71
ISBN 0-7099-4743-7

Filmset by Mayhew Typesetting, Bristol, England
Printed and bound in Great Britain by Mackays of Chatham Ltd, Kent

Contents

List of Contributors
Preface
Introduction *Stefan Hedlund*   1

Part One: The General View
1. The Formation of Incentive Mechanisms in Different Economic Systems *Pavel Pelikan*   27
2. Incentives to Share Knowledge and Risk: An Aspect of the Japanese Industrial Organisation *Masahiko Aoki*   57

Part Two: Incentives and the Command Economy
3. Labour Incentives and Collective Wage Systems in Soviet Industry *Hans Aage*   79
4. Labour Hoarding and Attempts at Labour Saving in the Soviet Economy *Susanne Oxenstierna*   105
5. Soft Options in Central Control *Stefan Hedlund*   126
6. Economic Incentives in Soviet Pre-War Economic Thought *Pekka Sutela*   151

Part Three: Incentives in Agricultural Transformation
7. Chinese Reforms from a Soviet Perspective *Alec Nove*   181
8. Market-related Incentives and Food Production in Tanzania: Theory and Experience *Mats Lundahl and Benno J. Ndulu*   191
9. Kibbutz Efficiency and the Incentive Conundrum *Haim Barkai*   228

Part Four: Incentives and the Welfare State
10. The Share Economy: Plausibility and Viability of Weitzman's Model *D. Mario Nuti*   267
11. An Economic Theory of Workfare *Richard S. Toikka and William L. Dreifke*   291
12. British Work Incentives and the IR/DHSS Effective Tax System: An Essay Designed to Provoke Discussion *Tom Kronsjö*   315

Part Five: A Final Note
13. 'Productive' and 'Non-productive' Economic Activities: A Note on Haavelmo *Björn Thalberg*   349

Index   361

List of Contributors

Hans Aage is Associate Professor of Economics at Copenhagen University, Denmark. His main research interest lies in comparative wage and income systems.

Masahiko Aoki is Henri and Tomoye Takahashi Professor of Japanese Studies at Stanford University, USA, and Professor of Economics at the University of Kyoto, Japan. His publications include *The Cooperative Game Theory of the Firm* and *The Economic Analysis of the Japanese Firm*.

Haim Barkai is Professor of Economics at the Hebrew University in Jerusalem, Israel, and a specialist in kibbutz agriculture. His publications include *Growth Patterns of the Kibbutz Economy*.

William Dreifke is a doctoral candidate at the University of Pennsylvania, and Economist, KETRON, Inc., Malvern, PA, USA. His interests include applied econometrics, industrial organisation and labour economics.

Stefan Hedlund is Assistant Professor of Economics at the University of Lund, Sweden. He specialises in Soviet studies and is the author of *Crisis in Soviet Agriculture*.

Tom Kronsjö is Professor of Economic Planning at the Centre for Russian and East European Studies, Birmingham University, England. He is a co-author of *Trade Negotiations in the Tokyo Round: A Quantitative Assessment*.

Mats Lundahl is Professor of Development Economics at the Stockholm School of Economics, Sweden. His publications include *Peasants and Poverty: A Study of Haiti* and *Unequal Treatment: A Study in the Neoclassical Theory of Discrimination*.

Benno Ndulu is Associate Professor of Economics at the University of Dar-es-Salaam, Tanzania. He specialises in transport economics, and received his PhD from Northwestern University, USA.

LIST OF CONTRIBUTORS

Alec Nove is Professor Emeritus of Economics at Glasgow University, and a well-known international authority on Soviet and East European affairs. His publications include *An Economic History of the USSR, The Soviet Economic System* and *The Economics of Feasible Socialism.*

D. Mario Nuti is Professor of Economics at the European University Institute in Firenze, Italy, and a former Director of the Centre for Russian and East European Studies in Birmingham, England. He specialises in comparative economic systems, and in Polish economic affairs, and has written extensively on these topics.

Susanne Oxenstierna is a Research Fellow at the Swedish Institute for Social Research. She is presently working on a PhD thesis on Soviet labour market problems.

Pavel Pelikan is formerly Professor of Economics at the Universities of Toronto and Sorbonne, and is presently Research Fellow at the Swedish Industrial Institute for Economic and Social Research. His main research interests lie in the fields of economic systems and evolutionary economics.

Pekka Sutela is a Research Fellow at the Department of Economics, Helsinki University, Finland, and a specialist in the development of Soviet Economic thought. He is the author of *Socialism, Planning and Optimality.*

Björn Thalberg is Professor of Economics at the University of Lund. He has written *A Trade Cycle Analysis. Extensions of the Goodwin Model*, and is also a trustee of the Arne Ryde Foundation, which has sponsored this volume.

Richard Toikka is Deputy Area Manager at Applied Management, Inc., Silver Spring, MD, USA. He is a public policy specialist managing studies designed to improve the effectiveness of government programmes. His current projects include quality control studies of educational loan programmes and unemployment insurance.

Preface

The present volume contains a selection of papers presented at the Eighth Arne Ryde Symposium, on *Incentives and Economic Systems*, 26–27 August 1985, at Frostavallen, Sweden. During the process of editing I have received valuable help from a number of referees, who unfortunately will have to remain anonymous. In addition, however, help has also been rendered by a number of other people who can — and should — be mentioned by name. Claudio Vedovato acted as symposium secretary and thus had to perform all those little but tedious chores that are never noticed when well performed. Agnetta Kretz has drawn a number of figures and diagrams. Pia Åkerman, Jeanie Petersson and Lena Somogyi typed and retyped some of the manuscripts, while Alan Harkess and Richard Brooks did their best to brush up the English of some authors, not least that of the editor. Finally, Keith Persson has been in charge of considerable amounts of photocopying and Erling Petersson has supervised the departmental word processing system. To all of these, and above all to the Arne Ryde Foundation, without the help of which neither this volume nor the original symposium would have been possible, goes my warmly felt gratitude.

Introduction

Stefan Hedlund

'Incentive' is a word with many different connotations. To some it implies rewards for those who behave in a certain way, to others penalties for those who fail to behave in that specific way. This old issue of sticks versus carrots ought to be well known. Yet, underlying it is another and far more complicated dimension of *what* should be rewarded or penalised. Will it always be the case that individuals are faced with such incentives that the sum of their actions will produce a collectively rational outcome? If not, should we punish those who act rationally, according to the given incentives, or reward those who act irrationally? Can the latter be done?

It all really boils down to variations on the theme of the classic Prisoner's Dilemma. As Jon Elster has pointed out in his book *Ulysses and the Sirens*, humans are separated from animals by the capacity for strategic behaviour.[1] Needless to say, this capacity has made possible many of the achievements of mankind — positive as well as negative. Yet, it also stands firmly in the way of some other potential achievements. Assuming self-interest on behalf of the single individual, he will plan his behaviour in such a way that his own utility is maximised, something that will often take place at the expense of others. The problem facing the economic policy-maker is that, given such strategic behaviour, there is no guarantee whatsoever that rational behaviour by all single individuals will add up to a rational final outcome. Rather, the spectre of the Prisoner's Dilemma would lead one to believe that the reverse would be the case.

At precisely this point there is also something odd about neoclassical economic theorising, an 'asymmetrical dilemma' as it is presented by Douglass North.[2] In neoclassical theory, we simultaneously assume individual wealth-maximisation and a Hobbesian model of the state, the latter implying the imposition of rules to constrain individual behaviour, in order to produce a viable political system. However, rational action on the first count necessarily precludes rationality on the second, as it is in the 'interests of a neoclassical actor to disobey those rules whenever an

INTRODUCTION

individualistic calculus of benefits and costs dictate such action'.[3]

The threat against the viability of the state is embedded in the well-known '1/N problem'. In many instances, the cost to the individual of refraining from certain actions will be greater than the costs he might incur by committing such actions. In the case of littering, for example, the holder of an empty beer can will himself have to bear the full cost of preserving the environment by disposing of the can properly, while if he throws it out the car window that cost will be shared by all alike.

Yet we observe that most of the rules that constrain our behaviour are observed by most of the people most of the time, and not simply for fear of the police. How do we explain this seeming irrationality? North's explanation runs in terms of imposing a value system that automatically blocks simple hedonistic behaviour: 'Strong moral and ethical codes of a society is the cement of social stability which makes an economic system viable.'[4]

Of course, in a narrow economic interpretation it is indeed quite irrational to follow such moral and ethical codes, at the cost of a reduction in individual utility. Yet, as Elster observes in a later essay, it may be precisely such irrational behaviour that forms the true cement of society — a 'socially beneficial illusion' — and it 'may not be a good thing if social scientists spend too much of their time discussing such connections among rationality, morality and collective action'.[5]

Irrational or not, this issue has obvious implications for the very foundations of an economic system, something that brings us to the second part of the title of the present volume. Included in the volume are a number of essays which all deal with various aspects of incentive problems, as represented by countries with widely differing economic systems. While the root of such problems can be taken to be similar across systems, as this stems from basic human behaviour, the manifestations of the problems will differ, largely because of the moral and ethical issues hinted at above.

As soon as we move away from *laissez-faire*, which has been the general tendency, albeit to varying degrees, across the entire range of economic systems, we run into the dilemma of the primary and secondary effects of intervention. An institutional change, or the introduction of an economic policy measure, will almost inevitably carry various side-effects, in addition to the effects intended by the policy-maker. In some cases this will mean that the individual is faced with incentives to behave in a manner that in the end will be detrimental not only to others but, as the total cake shrinks, perhaps even to himself.

A long list of such examples could be made. In the market economies, various tax and subsidy schemes induce both individuals and organisations to spend time on activities that have no productive outcome, aiming merely to redistribute given wealth in one's own favour. In the centrally planned economies, the widespread absence of any reasonable labour effort is the most conspicuous manifestation of the removal of the individual's direct material interest in the outcome of his actions (in the official sphere that is).

To some extent, this type of collectively irrational behaviour can be blocked by the sort of rules mentioned above. However, as the number of such cases grows, the strain on the individual's desire to observe the rules will increase and thus the basic legitimacy of the social and economic system will come under pressure.

It is in this connection that we find an important difference between the economic systems of East and West. It must obviously be the case that rewarding those who behave 'irrationally', i.e. who observe the rules, will produce a better outcome than penalising those who behave 'rationally', by breaking them. Yet the available rewards will be exclusively in the form of social esteem and approbation, factors that will diminish greatly in value as the basic legitimacy of the system comes under pressure. There is thus a danger of a vicious spiral here, a danger which has already manifested itself in the atomisation and alienation of large sections of the citizenry of the command economies, and which may threaten to do so in some of the market economies as well, under the pressure of rising unemployment and consequent social tension.

The essays presented in this volume do not deal directly with the problems I have raised here, but each of them contains a small piece of the larger puzzle. The purpose of this brief introduction has been to hint at the existence of such a larger framework, within which governments, firms and organisations attempt to guide individual behaviour by manipulating the social and economic incentive system. In particular, the distinction between the social and economic aspects of incentives is important to make, as this determines 'rational' and 'irrational' behaviour. With this in mind, let us now proceed to the essays proper.

THE GENERAL VIEW

This first section includes two contributions that focus on the problem of incentives and economic systems from a general perspective. The similarity between the two lies in the fact that both depart from the framework of market versus hierarchy, in the sense of Oliver Williamson.[6] The problems of incentive mechanisms and incentive structures that are associated with each of these two types have of course been amply dealt with in the literature, and even a brief survey would have to be rather lengthy. Yet both chapters presented below — albeit from different angles — manage to contribute novel ideas.

In the first, *Pavel Pelikan* aims at developing a new methodology for comparing and evaluating the efficiency of incentives in different economic systems. Traditionally, comparisons have been made among constant organisational structures. most frequently as a simple dichotomy between given markets, representing the system of private enterprise, and given hierarchies, representing the system of socialist planning. Pointing to several shortcomings of the traditional approach, Pelikan proposes to recognise organisational structures as endogenously variable.[7] The typical structure of a modern economy is considered to be a mixture of both markets and hierarchies, which are to be studied in the process of their forming and reforming. Different systems are represented by the respective sets of institutional rules which govern this process. The aim is to compare alternative sets of rules according to their capacities to promote efficient structures with suitably designed incentives.

The forming and reforming of organisational structures is closely related to the allocation of tacit knowledge. This is the information which must pre-exist in the very structure of a system — such as the working knowledge of languages (codes), decision logic and abilities for learning by doing — before any other (communicable) information can be used. Tacit knowledge has several properties which distinguishes it from other scarce resources. In particular, it cannot be directly communicated within a given structure, nor can it be directly measured or compared between individuals. These properties imply that the forming and reforming of organisational structures must involve a trial-and-error search, in which two ingredients are of particular importance: entrepreneurship for the initiation of trials, and competition for the elimination of errors. The crucial question, then, is how entrepreneurship and competition are organised under alternative institutional rules.

To answer this question, Pelikan focuses on two types of organisational failures: surviving errors and absent successes. The former refers to inefficient parts of the organisational structure which have not been eliminated, and the latter to potentially efficient ones that have failed to appear. The relatively best system will be the one which suffers least from such failures.

Two simple examples illustrate the argument. Both involve a comparison with the system of 'contestable private enterprise', characterised by decentralised rights to initiate organisational trials and to eliminate organisational errors. The first comparison is made with the system of 'centralised entrepreneurship', where such rights are restricted to government agencies and their appointees, as in the case of the Soviet-type economies, irrespective of the degree of decentralised resource allocation. This system is less likely to generate successes, due to its politico-administrative selection of entrepreneurs, and also more likely to tolerate errors, due to the fact that the elimination of errors is entrusted to government agencies which are often the very authors of the committed errors.

The second comparison is made with 'market socialism', broadly defined as a market system imposing certain rules of collective decision-making and profit-sharing within each participating firm. As to surviving errors, this system can perform quite well. It can entrust error-elimination to market competition, and thus keep the trial-makers and the error-eliminators equally well separated as private enterprise. As to absent successes, however, market socialism discourages or prevents some potentially successful trials by the obligatory rules of decision-making and profit-sharing. Consequently, the correctly eliminated errors are less likely to be replaced by new trials than in private enterprise, causing lower growth and higher unemployment.

Contestable private enterprise is thus shown to have a relatively higher potential to resist organisational failures and, therefore, to form efficient organisational structures with suitably designed incentives, than both forms of socialism. To conclude his chapter, Pelikan argues that this conclusion allows for more nuances, but is more difficult to refute, than comparable conclusions from the traditional organisationally static analysis.

One thing that is pointed out at the outset of Pelikan's chapter is the fact that the market versus hierarchy dichotomy is not directly relevant to the comparison of real economic systems, since the real world will normally incorporate features of both. *Masahiko Aoki* picks up that line by extracting out of the dichotomy a third type of model — one which, although it has features in common with the two 'pure' types, also has some interesting features of its own. Aoki claims that this forms a fruitful framework for understanding

INTRODUCTION

the experience of Japanese industrial organisation.

Three important features are seen to distinguish the Japanese model from typical western organisations. First, the enterprise workshop features frequent rotation of teams of workers between different tasks, which permits *ad hoc* solutions to emerging problems. Secondly, inter-shop relations are designed to facilitate such solutions, via a system of flexible supply of tools, parts, materials, etc. from shops upstream, known sometimes as the *kanban* method. Thirdly, firms to a large extent rely on outside suppliers. In order to reduce transaction costs, a system of 'relational contracting' has emerged, as a substitute for the western practice of integration. Such contracting implies a steady, long-run relationship with a rather small number of suppliers.

All these features place great demands on the sharing of knowledge. In a conventional hierarchy, sub-units will be highly specialised and the information needed for their interaction will be intermediated by management, utilising specialised professional competence. In the Japanese firm, however, coordination will be semi-horizontal, based on transactional relationships between the sub-units, and localised knowledge will be utilised. Although the lack of centralisation precludes a first-best solution, Aoki maintains that this may be outweighed by the greater flexibility in response and the better utilisation of local knowledge. A prerequisite though, is that knowledge is shared within the workshop, between workshops and between firms. Such sharing promotes the honesty and trust necessary in this type of transactional relations.

A main question that arises concerns the incentives that will induce individuals to engage in the sharing of knowledge. In this context, another peculiar feature of the Japanese model becomes relevant: the sharing of outcome. The chapter maintains that the need to share knowledge-*cum*-outcome are not only interrelated, but also mutually reinforcing.

An important fact here is that remuneration is not specifically linked to the job, as in a western firm. Instead, the length of service together with general contextual skills and an ability to communicate with fellow employees will be important. The latter in particular will influence decisions on promotion. Furthermore, an important part of total remuneration comes in the form of bonus payments, which are made both currently and upon retirement. Both offer obvious incentives for long tenure and for the acquiring of contextual skills, as the bonuses are, at least in the long run, determined by the firm's performance.

A final problem dealt with is that which arises from the fact that the bonus system accumulates substantial individual assets within the firm, assets which are not saleable. This might have been conducive to risk-averse behaviour, but a system of inter-firm risk-sharing has been developed as a substitute for individual risk diversification. Relational subcontracting will be characterised by a sharing of profit fluctuations, which provides insurance for the permanent employees of both firms. At a higher level, corporate groupings, including banks, have similar arrangements.

By ways of conclusion, Aoki suggests two topics for application of this model. The first is the generation and diffusion of new technology, where the greater mobility of researchers in western firms stands against the sharing of knowledge-*cum*-outcome of the Japanese firms. The second is the current US–Japanese trade dispute, where the main non-tariff barrier to the Japanese market is seen to lie precisely in relational contracting arrangements. A better understanding of the specific features of the Japanese model might shed light on both these issues.

INCENTIVES AND THE COMMAND ECONOMY

From this general perspective, we now shift our focus firmly to the hierarchy end of the economic systems spectrum. Four chapters are included here, all of which deal with incentive problems in the Soviet economy, the model which in various ways has inspired the whole group of countries that (following Gregory Grossman) are normally referred to as 'command economies'.[8]

Hans Aage starts Part Two by looking at the longstanding ambition of Soviet would-be industrial reformers to improve labour productivity, via a reduction in the number of workers and/or an increase in the work effort supplied by the single individual. His approach is to construct a model that allows him to make a formal inquiry into the incentive mechanisms contained in four different bonus systems, in order to find out to what extent these have been conducive to the aforementioned two objectives.

The first example is the 1965 Kosygin reform, which brought a radical decrease in the number of plan indicators used to control enterprise behaviour. Various bonuses increased in importance, with the wage fund used as the basis for their determination. Aage assumes that both managers and workers had an interest in maximising bonus payments per worker.

INTRODUCTION

The next case is the so-called Shchekino experiment, introduced in 1967. In this instance, the enterprise was allowed to retain, for bonus purposes, whatever savings could be made by reducing labour use, provided that it did not reduce production. This system has since been widely introduced, but the net labour-saving has been small, as most of the redundant workers have been redeployed within the same factories or enterprises.

The third case relates to an important decree that was issued in 1979, following a number of experiments that were performed throughout the 1970s. Labour productivity and the share of high quality goods now became compulsory indicators, together with the condition that the firm must fulfil at least 98 per cent of contracted sales in order to qualify for any bonuses at all. The decree also introduced two novelties. First, labour productivity was to be measured in terms of 'net normative output', which resembles value-added and was clearly intended to discourage excessive materials use. Secondly, profit was substituted for the wage fund as a basis for calculating bonuses.

Lastly, the most recent experiment which was started in 1984, and which Aage views largely as an effort to implement measures introduced in 1965 and 1979. A renewed attempt was made to restrict the number of plan indicators, and a separate fund for the development of new technology was introduced. Finally, provision was made for price increases of up to 30 per cent for high quality products, and the importance of fulfilling contracts was again underscored.

A number of results — some determinate and others not — are generated via the formal analysis. Nevertheless it is interesting that Aage himself hints at the limited value of such modelling, when seen against the background of the never-ending process of negotiations and changes in plan targets. (A case in point is 'net normative output'.) His conclusions are marked by the latter observation. On the one hand, there are obvious benefits involved in being able to determine from above the objective function of firms, but on the other these benefits are constrained by the great complexity of the system. Moreover, there lies a paradox in the control mechanisms, in that they are successful in hampering initiative but surprisingly impotent in stifling 'anti-social' behaviour. The core of the problem remains: the practice of fixing rules for everything is not conducive to efficiency, nor does limited personal responsibility help in this matter.

Susanne Oxenstierna reveals a similarly sceptical attitude to the importance of changes in the formal incentive structure when she discusses another of the many paradoxes in the Soviet economy: the coexistence of labour shortages and overstaffing. An important explanation of this paradox lies in past policy. The traditional Soviet growth strategy has meant a strong bias towards the installation of new capacity instead of the modernisation of existing plant. This has helped to stimulate labour demand via recruitment for the new plants and via an increased need for repair work in the old. In addition, a low priority for the mechanisation of many auxiliary operations has maintained a high level of demand for manual labour.

The consequences have been particularly noticeable in the past two decades, as the pool of available labour has become exhausted. The number of vacancies in relation to total jobs, for example, increased twelvefold in the period 1965–85. Labour shortage can thus hardly be said to be a frictional problem. Attempts have been made to curb the growth in demand, for example via a recent policy of 'workplace attestation', which aims at an increased rate of scrapping technologically obsolete equipment, via frequent surveys of existing plant. As the author rightly notes, however, such a policy requires the cooperation of enterprise managers who, for a number of well-known reasons, have every incentive to hoard and conceal.

Oxenstierna finds a major culprit in the planning system. The use of quantitative labour targets has discouraged labour-saving and encouraged inflating reported labour needs. Although regulation has varied over time, both in form and detail, it remains a fact that managers have been swift in adapting to change, in a way that consistently defies the intentions of the planners. The reintroduction of detailed regulation in 1979 is seen to have had little impact, due both to the crude nature of limits and to the reluctance to use available sanctions against uncooperative managers.

One example of the lack of fine-tuning in regulation is the wage fund, which in the 1965 'reform' was made the main instrument for controlling labour use. Managers were set a definite limit on how much they could spend on labour. Oxenstierna discusses several problems in this context. First, labour use below the set limit is no 'cost', and thus there is no incentive to economise. Secondly, the size of the wage fund is a function of planned employment, and thus there is every reason to inflate needs. Thirdly, the wage fund can sometimes be increased, which provides an incentive to increase output by using more labour rather than by improving productivity. Finally, the author also points out the further disincentives to reduce labour input that stem from the long use of the wage fund as a basis

INTRODUCTION

for calculating the size of the bonus fund.

Several attempts have been made to overcome these problems. A recent example is via so-called normative planning. This method is based on assigning norms for permitted labour cost per rouble of output, and on this count Oxenstierna would seem to be in agreement with Aage in saying that the use of 'norms' of various kinds suffers from the problem of decisions being made via negotiations rather than in accordance with economic criteria.

The main conclusion of the chapter is that all measures that have been attempted so far, to solve the labour dilemma, have been traditional within-the-system modifications. In consequence, results have been correspondingly disappointing. Increased detail of regulation increases the flow of information to the centre, by producing yet more reports that nobody has the time to read. Decreased detail offers more scope for managers to act in their own interest. The basic reasons for managerial labour hoarding have thus not been dealt with, and as long as this is the case, Oxenstierna predicts scant results from the outwardly vigorous policy of the new Soviet leadership.

The point of departure for *Stefan Hedlund* is an old observation by Alec Nove,[9] that things that seemingly go wrong in the Soviet economy may actually be the results of rational actions taken by rational individuals faced with irrational incentives. In order to try to find such a hidden rationale, Hedlund starts by examining the situation of an individual in the Soviet economy, first as a labourer and then as an enterprise manager.

In his former role, the individual will be faced with a choice between working and shirking, and incentives are shown to be such that the threat of a Prisoner's Dilemma of universal shirking can only be offset by costly supervision. As a manager, on the other hand, he will find himself in the situation of playing against the system that has been well described by Joseph Berliner and others.[10] Both cases share the same common feature in that the incentive system turns micro-rational behaviour into a macro-irrational outcome.

From this, Hedlund goes on to argue that the seeming irrationalities of the Soviet economy, that are such frequent targets of *Krokodil* satire, may actually be *tolerated* consequences of a second-best solution, where first best is blocked by overriding political objectives. To substantiate this claim, Albert Hirschman's concepts of Exit and Voice are introduced.[11] The relevance of this approach lies, on the one hand, in the psychological effects of being

INTRODUCTION

able to leave and/or protest, and on the other in the feedback that is produced by such signals. Hedlund argues that while it is obvious that the Soviet model offers neither of these options in their pure original forms, we can define 'soft' versions which may generate interesting results.

A *soft exit* is defined as a retreat within the system, the most important examples of which are agriculture's private plots and free markets. This option has two functions. In the political sense, the possibility of engaging in activities outside the state-controlled sphere will help release some discontent, and such slow seepage will be conducive to the overall stability of the system. In the economic sense, if there is a productive outcome, this will help take some pressure off the official system, which can then continue an inefficient and quiet life. The option is soft because the individual does remain within the system — at least physically. Yet it is there, to release some steam and to capture some effort.

The *soft voice* is a disguised form of expressing discontent. On the individual level it can take the form of books of complaint in shops and restaurants, and of writing letters to *Pravda*. The important thing for the individual is that he sees some immediate result: managers will have to explain, letters may be printed, etc. The important thing for the rulers of the system is that normally little will come out in the end. It is a safety-valve and little more. The voice is soft because it cannot be organised and articulated. Yet, it is there and it fills the functions of releasing some steam and of capturing some feedback.

The importance of such soft options, in Hedlund's view, is that they attenuate the conflict between political stability and economic performance. A real solution to the longstanding problem of economic stagnation would — as is well known — imply unpalatable political changes, changes that might threaten the stability and security of the system. Via the soft options, however, muddling through acquires a new dimension. During the Stalin era, tight repression had the combined ill-effects of removing feedback and of building up a strong pressure of discontent. Since then, an increasing use of the soft options has helped in capturing some feedback and in defusing some discontent, by allowing pressure to seep out at various points. Muddling through along this path may prove viable for quite some time to come.

In concluding Part Two, *Pekka Sutela* discusses the *nature* of incentives, a topic which lies at the very heart of this volume. It is a well-known fact that in the Soviet economy of today, differentiated

INTRODUCTION

material rewards form an important part of the incentive system. Yet, this has not always been the case. In the years around 1930 the issue was very much in a state of flux. In 1930, material incentives were being rapidly overtaken by socialist stimuli to work, while at the end of that decade such incentives were considered to be the 'very essence of socialist labour'. How did this change come about, and how was it rationalised in the minds of the Soviet economists of the time?

Sutela limits his discussion to the use of real income (i.e. wages and premia) for incentive purposes, and he focuses on the concept of *khozraschet*, which can be loosely translated as enterprise profit and loss accounting. To determine changes in the understanding and status of *khozraschet*, four different sub-periods are contrasted.

The *first* period is the NEP years, 1921–28, when discussions of enterprise finance and incentives were both complex and incoherent. The concept of *khozraschet* was unclear, as was the attitude taken to it. The Left was most outspoken in its critique of existing material incentives, and Preobrazhensky stated that piece-rates had 'nothing in common with communism'. Instead, socialist incentives were to be developed, via a re-education of the population aiming to create the famed 'socialist man'. Socialism was seen to be incompatible with bonuses and differentiated wages.

The *second* period is formed by the years 1929–30, which were marked by a general belief that full socialism was just around the corner, and thus that planned production and distribution would replace markets and trade. From this it followed that economic incentives were outdated. The wage form was seen as alien and irrational and was demoted to a mere accounting device. The new socialist incentives of emulation and shock work were set firmly against material incentives. Rationing and administrative distribution of labour were seen as steps towards the introduction of a fully planned economy. The existence of commodity–money relations was denied. *Khozraschet* was dying out.

The *third* period started in early 1931, when it was officially established that the introduction of *khozraschet* was of the 'utmost importance'. The prevailing interpretation of *khozraschet*, however, was in terms of accounting, and its potential incentive function was neglected. This role was instead played by wages. Collective forms of pay were to be abolished and replaced by piece rates. *Khozraschet* was associated with the remnants of capitalism, i.e. mainly the private sector in agriculture. Then, when Stalin personally came out against 'egalitarianism', others took the hint and established that there was no contradiction between material and socialist incentives, as had been previously believed. The problem of income distribution became completely subordinated to the needs of production.

The *last* period covers the years 1934–41, starting with the Victors' Congress in January 1934. Here Stalin ridiculed socialist incentives as 'leftist chatter' and declared that *khozraschet* was to be the 'basic method of socialist management'. The earlier 'non-*khozraschet*' period was explained as the work of 'wreckers'. The interpretation of *khozraschet* in accounting terms was abandoned and its incentive role firmly established. By then the Soviet economic system had been established in a form much the same as today.

It is commonly held that the role of economics during the Stalin era was more or less non-existent, and Sutela partly shares that view when he talks about 'dishonest nonsense' and 'dour commentary'. Yet, as he himself has shown elsewhere,[12] there did exist a political economy of Soviet socialism, and the present chapter is a further step towards the understanding of this neglected period.

INCENTIVES IN AGRICULTURAL TRANSFORMATION

We shall now leave the realm of the Soviet bloc proper, and turn to the experience of three countries which have each been inspired in their own special way, by the example set by the Russian Revolution in 1917. The common denominator of the three chapters in Part Three lies in their focus on the role of incentives in agricultural transformation. However, as we shall see, the three countries dealt with also differ greatly in terms of how they have been inspired and what they have chosen to make of that inspiration.

Alec Nove selects the most obvious starting point, by looking at the current Chinese reform attempts in the mirror of similar Soviet attempts in the 1960s. The basis for comparison is clear-cut. After the Revolution in 1949, the new Chinese leadership adopted the Soviet model as their own, in terms of both economic structure and Marxist-Leninist ideology. In a sense, the Chinese was an even more rigid version. There was less managerial autonomy. There was stricter labour control, and there was even a repetition of Stalin's policy of collectivisation, the latter in the form of the Great Leap Forward in 1958–60. Thus the Chinese also had their share of famine and excesses.

A striking characteristic of Chinese development is that, despite the Great Leap Forward and the Cultural Revolution, the basic features of the centralised model have remained intact. Above all, this was true of the much-criticised labour incentives. After Mao's death, discussions on economic reform quickly surfaced, and when characterising the arguments presented in that debate, Nove relies on personal impressions from a visit in 1979: 'I have heard all this before, only in Russia and twenty years ago.' He points to the great similarity with the ideas put forward by Liberman during the Soviet 1960s, and sees similar causes behind the abortive Kosygin reform of 1965 and the fate of the first wave of Chinese reforms, in 1979–81.

Another important similarity between the two cases lies in the decollectivisation attempts in agriculture. Here Nove compares the Chinese 'household responsibility system' to the Soviet experiments with autonomous work teams (the *beznaryadnoe zveno*) and finds reason to warn about a repetition of the problems that have marked Soviet experience, above all in terms of widening income differentials and consequent social tension within agriculture.

An important political issue to be raised is, of course, Moscow's appreciation of the new Chinese path. If it is successful — in the terms of, say, South Korea — then Moscow will obviously be deeply worried. Yet, Nove sees reason to question the magnitude of that threat. A fundamental reform decision has indeed been taken (in October 1984) but the decree contains a number of qualifying phrases, which might indicate hesitation or a lack of agreement on how far to go. Is the party, for example, ready to accept the emergence of an entrepreneurial class, which will 'Get Rich', *à la* Bukharin, via the market and not via party-state officialdom? The latter may obviously have a powerful political backlash.

In conclusion, Nove poses the really central question: If we are seeing a Chinese version of the Soviet NEP of the 1920s, what will the end-result be? Does the current Chinese vision of 'real socialism' incorporate elements of markets, or is the new reform wave, as Lenin once said about NEP, a way to *réculer pour mieux sauter*, a temporary retreat on the way to the proper form of socialism?

From China we move on to Tanzania, a country which has *de facto* copied many of the basic features of the Soviet model, even down to an attempt at collectivising the peasantry. While this may have been done quite inadvertently, out of common ideological beliefs rather than out of an explicit desire to go the Soviet way, the consequences pay no heed to intentions.

Mats Lundahl and *Benno Ndulu* start their chapter by showing the emergence of a rapidly deteriorating food supply problem in Tanzania, from the mid-1970s and onwards, implying mounting health risks to the population and a growing dependence on food aid. They then move on to relate this development to the main ingredients in what they call the 'traditional control model'. One of these ingredients is seen to be the belief that smallholders are unresponsive to market signals, and thus have to be guided or controlled in some way, while another is found in the belief that a monopolistic/ monopsonistic structure is the only way to promote development. Out of these two beliefs, the authors extract the rationale for the introduction of the statal and parastatal crop authorities and other agencies that by government decree replaced the private traders.

The next section of the chapter shows the backlash for poor urban consumers that resulted from this structural shift. Rapidly growing costs in the new, bureaucratic marketing structure forced the government to introduce fiscally burdensome food subsidies, and the risks involved in selling on the black (or parallel) food markets led to both high prices and a reduction in total supply.

By the mid-1970s, however, as the crisis was setting in, the Tanzanian government began to show an increasing willingness to resort to the use of price incentives in order to stimulate production, and the core of this chapter is devoted to the construction of a formal model which allows the authors to investigate the impact of various policy changes on smallholder decision-making.

The conclusion reached from this investigation is that the production of food crops is likely to increase both when the price of these crops increases in relation to the price of cash crops and industrial consumer goods purchased by the smallholder, and when the latter goods are made cheaper in terms of food and cash crops. The effect on the marketed surplus of food, however, is uncertain, although presumably the income-elasticity of food among smallholders is low enough so that the most likely outcome will be that the marketed surplus will also increase.

One feature which is not included in the model is black market sales. Throughout, the Tanzanian authorities have taken a very unfavourable attitude to private trade in agricultural produce, which has been allowed only locally and in small scale. With the drought in 1973–74, however, the pressure on the low official prices started to mount, and with rising oil prices there was not enough foreign exchange to support the official system via imports. Instead, private trade started to increase on the so-called parallel markets. As such activities are illegal, and can result in heavy penalties, prices naturally include risk premia, and in the third section of their chapter Lundahl and Ndulu proceed to investigate under what conditions smallholders can be expected to sell in these markets.

Equipped with this additional knowledge, the authors set out to review existing evidence on smallholder responsiveness to price incentives. After complementing the existing picture with econometric estimates of their own, they find nothing to indicate that the smallholder should not be responsive to incentives, regardless of whether these stem from changes in relative prices within the agricultural sector or from changes in the terms of trade between agriculture and the rest of the economy.

The policy recommendations derived consequently focus on strengthening the role of incentives and economic motivation, chiefly via increased producer prices but also via improvements in the provision of basic consumer goods. Moreover, the chapter also has strong recommendations for changes in the institutional framework, aiming at decentralisation and increased flexibility. Finally, the Tanzanian government is strongly urged to take firm action to improve the agricultural infrastructure, instead of placing emphasis on intervention and control in the micro level environment.

Against the somber evidence of incentive problems outlined in the previous chapters, *Haim Barkai* presents an upside-down world in the form of the success story of the Israeli kibbutz, a form of agricultural cooperation which was explicitly inspired by ideological beliefs taken from Russia at the turn of the century, but which would not bear fruit on Soviet soil.

The chapter starts by reviewing the 'traditional' case against this form of cooperation. In the consumption sphere, distribution of rations and free goods makes for waste in the use of wealth, while the absence of an interest rate for member savings implies a rate of dissaving which inevitably must lead the cooperative to devour itself. In the production sphere the absence of wages makes an efficient factor allocation impossible, while the 'principle of equality' removes incentives for members to work. Hence overconsumption of leisure and the inevitable demise of the organisation is implied. In theoretical terms, these arguments are flawless and yet, as Barkai goes on to show, the kibbutz is now in its sixth decade of existence, prosperous, efficient and as stubbornly as ever refusing to succumb to its 'inevitable' doom. How is this possible?

The explanation provided centres around the very specific milieu of the kibbutz. The point about the absence of formal wages, argues

Barkai, is a misconception. Efficiency can be achieved via a shadow wage, and kibbutz practice has always been striving in that direction, first via rules-of-thumb and later via more sophisticated techniques, such as linear programming, in both cases making use of information generated in the external market. Furthermore, the argument on erosion of incentives rests squarely on the assumption that increased effort by one member will not be matched by the others, an assumption which is diametrically opposed to the very nature of the kibbutz as a social organisation.

It is precisely the social aspects that form the real crux of the matter. The kibbutz can set work norms for its members, but in eliciting *effort* it will face the same problems that are discussed in a number of other papers in this volume. This motivation problem is solved partly via voluntary membership, in combination with strict screening of potential candidates, and partly via a subtle mechanism of social control, resting on social approbation for an 'honest day's work'.

However, problems do undoubtedly exist. Rising real incomes make for a greater spread of tastes, which puts pressure on the 'moneyless' distribution technique. This has been met via a greater share of 'cash endowments' (various 'points' systems) awarded to members, while the free good technique is increasingly limited to items that normally characterise a welfare state. Savings form another problem, with the majority vote being biased in favour of the present. Yet, data show that kibbutzim have high saving ratios, which is explained by the connection between high education levels and a perception of the needs of the future.

In conclusion, Barkai speculates about the possible message of the kibbutz experience. Here the special milieu once again looms large. The problem of factor allocation has been able to be solved via various shadow-pricing techniques, but this has required a pool of skilled manpower which is normally not available in Third World agriculture. Similarly, the problems of motivation and incentives have been solved via voluntariness, selectivity and a uniting exclusive ideology, features that will normally not be present in command agriculture. The kibbutz is thus likely to remain a minority phenomenon, which may provide a certain amount of inspiration in some of its aspects but is not for export *in toto*.

INTRODUCTION

INCENTIVES AND THE WELFARE STATE

So far we have devoted substantial interest to the problems of commands and incentives, and in this Fourth Part the time has come to turn to the other end of the economic systems spectrum, in order to examine the role of incentives in a market environment. In so doing, we more or less automatically find ourselves within the confines of the welfare state, where the manifestations of incentive problems are considerably different from those at the hierarchy end of the spectrum. The three chapters included here all focus on unemployment and what can be done to remove this increasingly troublesome disease of the market economies. As in Part Three, however, they adopt very different perspectives on the common problem.

In the first, *Mario Nuti* approaches the classic conflict of inflation versus unemployment. His approach, however, is not to propose yet another possible solution to this dilemma, as there has already been a number of such proposals of different kinds. The intention is instead to take issue with a recent contribution, where Martin Weitzman suggests the creation of a 'share economy'.[13] This proposal, according to Nuti, is different from its predecessors in two important respects, first in its total rejection of all forms of worker codetermination, and secondly in its 'evangelic' belief in having found a miracle cure for the plague of stagflation.

The centrepiece of Weitzman's model is the replacement of fixed wage contracts by a form of generalised sharing contract, whereby at least a substantial part of workers' earnings is made up of a stake in the performance of their enterprise. This institutional change is expected to guarantee the achievement and maintenance of full employment of labour without either inflationary pressures or sacrifices in real wages; on the contrary, the general price level would fall and real wages would increase, due to output expansion in conditions of monopolistic competition between firms. These results derive from the decoupling of the marginal cost of labour from the level of average earnings, which is implicit in the sharing contract.

Nuti's critique of this model proceeds in two broad steps, starting with the plausibility of its assumptions. First, the narrow focus on reducing money wages is seen implicitly to neglect both Keynesian and classical unemployment. Moreover, as the empirical evidence on the relation between employment and wage levels is inconclusive, it is a matter of faith that labour demand will be at least as high as supply after the switch to sharing contracts. Moreover, if an expansion of employment and real output actually takes place, the demand curves of firms will shift upwards, unless there is a zero income-elasticity of demand. This will fuel the inflation that the model was supposed to cure. The inflationary pressure will also be aggravated by the strengthening of workers' bargaining position that follows from the permanent disequilibrium in the labour market. Finally, and most importantly, Weitzman's rejection of codetermination is not only the model's sole claim to fame, Nuti also argues that it rests on 'neither evidence nor analysis, it is assertion without foundation in economics or political economy'. Weitzman's model is not one of a share economy, it is a model of a *non-voting* share economy.

If the model's assumptions can be accepted, the second stage of the critique goes on to examine its viability. For several reasons, it can be suspected of institutional instability. In the short run, there will be an incentive for mergers to arise, as firms seek to take advantage of the differences in marginal revenue products of labour between firms, that follow from the sharing contracts. As there is nothing to stop such a merger process, large monopolies will arise. In the medium run new firms will enter that are either cooperatives or non-sharing firms, and this will gradually squeeze out the sharing sector of the economy. The reason to believe that new entrants will be non-sharing is that workers will have no possibility of assessing prospective pay under a sharing contract; thus fixed wage contracts will have to be offered. Finally, and critically, in the long run the system will revert to a wage economy, as competitive pressure will tend to eliminate the sharing elements. A correct appreciation of labour opportunity costs will make firms pay the marginal cost of labour, which is nothing but the basic wage, net of the sharing component. Risk-averse workers will gladly accept this increase in security, and as the sharing element vanishes so does Weitzman's share economy. In any case, the chapter concludes, if Weitzman's model were accepted, the gradual introduction of a wage subsidy is shown to have the same beneficial effects of income sharing, without any of its drawbacks.

In the following chapter, *Richard Toikka* and *William Dreifke* examine the problem of incentives to work from a different but perhaps equally controversial angle. They depart from the US experience of various welfare programmes (from 1935 onwards) and focus on the crucial issue of the impact of such programmes on work incentives. 'Workfare' — a term which is politically more tasteful than 'welfare' — is used to define programmes featuring

INTRODUCTION

work requirements in combination with the provision of benefits.

A primary objective of such programmes is to distinguish individuals who need public assistance and are willing to work, from those who are in need of help simply due to a high preference for leisure or an unwillingness to work. An appropriately structured workfare programme would provide incentives for the former group to accept adequately paying jobs, and thus to leave the programme. A number of studies have been made estimating the impact of such programmes, but little attention has been paid to the underlying theoretical aspects of how workfare affects individual behaviour. This chapter is an endeavour in that direction.

After briefly reviewing the labour supply effects of a public transfer programme, the chapter sets out to analyse the effects of a generalised workfare programme, under two different sets of assumptions. In the first case, it is assumed that rules regarding sanctions are strictly enforced. The formal model derived is then used to investigate the impact of workfare on labour supply under three different forms of work requirement. The evidence suggests that the market wage rate will play a key role in determining the individual's choice on whether or not to participate in workfare, but the impact on labour supply is ambiguous. One important implication, which has not been widely recognised in the literature, is that labour supply may actually fall, as a result of participation in workfare.

In the second case, the assumption on strict enforcement of sanctions is removed, and instead individual expectations regarding potential penalties for non-compliance with programme work requirements are considered. Here it is shown that for individuals whose wage exceeds the implicit wage in workfare the sanction probability will become an important determinant of participation. Under perfect sanctions such individuals would never select participation. However, in the event of imperfect sanctions some of them may choose to do so. The conditions under which this will take place are derived, and the decision to cheat is seen to depend on a comparison of the expected utility of cheating with the utility of market work only.

In conclusion, Toikka and Dreifke find, first, that programme participation is negatively correlated with both market wages and the probability of facing sanctions for non-compliance with work requirements. Secondly, they find that should participation be preferred, then the impact of workfare on the supply of labour to market work may be negative, and, thirdly, that the *form* of work obligation will be important in determining effects on labour supply. Moreover, in a dynamic perspective, investment in human capital enters the picture as well, as this may induce participants to leave the programme as market wages increase. Policy-makers thus face a trade-off, between high investment costs and short-term benefits, on the one hand, and low investment costs and long-term benefits, on the other. Here the authors argue that some investment in training and job-search instruction may well be warranted, if seen against the future savings in benefit expenditure.

The third chapter in Part IV, by *Tom Kronsjö*, provides a rather striking illustration of what can happen if insufficient attention is paid to potential disincentive effects when devising benefit programmes for people hurt by joblessness. The focus of Kronsjö's attention is the impact of the current British benefit programme, administered by the Department of Health and Social Security (DHSS), in combination with Inland Revenue (IR) progressive tax rates. The results presented indicate that a wedge of quite considerable proportions has been driven between gross wages and net earnings which, according to Kronsjö, has led to the creation of a new-style poverty-trap for a large section of the more than three million British unemployed.

The empirical evidence presented emanates from tabulations made by the DHSS of marginal effective tax rates for ten representative households, of between one and two adults and zero to four children of specified ages. From these tables one can find what gross wage the head of each of the representative households will have to earn in order to have the same net amount as he would receive from the DHSS when unemployed. These calculations, however, implicitly attribute a zero value to the free time given up when accepting a job offer. As shown by Kronsjö, even a minor positive valuation of that time will drastically alter the results presented by the DHSS.

To capture this effect the concept of an acceptable gross wage (AGW) is introduced, which is defined as the gross wage that will have to be offered in order for the unemployed person to earn a specified amount over and above what he receives from the DHSS as compensation for the relinquished free time. The AGW is shown to exceed the worthwhile net amount by three to nine times, depending on the type of household, and the explanation is seen to lie in the combined tax and benefit system.

As incomes go up, an increasing number of benefits will be withdrawn and this, in combination with high marginal tax rates on incomes, makes for a very high *effective* marginal tax rate. For the representative households of the DHSS it is shown to be in the range of 70–90 per cent.

The main part of the chapter is devoted to the empirical investigation of these disincentive effects, but it also aims at sketching a possible transition into a system where the 'trap' is removed. The essence of this is the provision of a tax credit in lieu of the various benefits. The unemployed would then be faced by powerful incentives to improve their lot by taking up gainful employment, as the former wedge between the AGW and the worthwhile net amount is substantially reduced.

Kronsjö calculates the financial effects of three different levels of such tax credits, and finds that there would be considerable savings to the public sector compared to the costs of the present social policies. Assuming that employment can be found, the recommended middle-level tax credit would leave all the DHSS representative households, except those with four children, better off and in the latter case the reduction in welfare would be of minor importance only.

Whether the unemployed would actually be able to find employment, even given the lower requirements of the new system, is of course a matter of considerable dispute. To address this particular issue, however, is not Kronsjö's intention, and the chapter ends with a call for others to respond to the challenge implicit in the evidence presented, by working out more detailed recommendations as to how the present system could be revamped.

A FINAL NOTE

In concluding this volume, *Björn Thalberg* revives an old unpublished manuscript by the Norwegian economist Trygve Haavelmo, which anticipated much subsequent work on what Jagdish Bhagwati has called 'Directly Unproductive Profit-seeking (DUP) Activities'.[14] Haavelmo here distinguished between 'productive' and 'non-productive' activities, where the former was defined to have a positive impact on the total volume of goods and services produced in society, while the latter were undertaken for distributive purposes only.

Thalberg proceeds to show how Haavelmo constructed a formal model which allowed him to investigate how the individual's choice between these two activities was determined, and here he found two parameters — k and h — to be of crucial importance. The former measures the share of total production that is distributed according to productive activities — a high value indicating a low share of social transfers and public consumption — while the latter indicates the scope for various non-productive activities.

Haavelmo's finding was that the relative size of total non-productive activities will depend on the relationship between the two parameters h and k. The greater the value of h, in relation to k, and the larger the share of total production that is distributed according to rules other than productive input, the greater will be the incentive to engage in non-productive activities.

The model, argues Thalberg, reflects surprisingly well what came to happen after Haavelmo wrote his lectures, back in 1950. Both the development of important public transfer systems, and increasingly complicated rules governing taxes and subsidies, have become important ingredients in the welfare state, as have a growing propensity to engage in various 'non-productive' activities, much as predicted by Haavelmo. With his short note, Thalberg wishes to give some long due credit to Haavelmo for his foresight.

NOTES

1. Elster (1984).
2. North (1981), p. 44.
3. Ibid.
4. Ibid., p. 47.
5. Elster (1985), p. 145.
6. Williamson (1975).
7. Pelikan (1985).
8. Grossman (1963).
9. Nove (1977), p. 9.
10. Berliner (1957).
11. Hirschman (1970).
12. Sutela (1984).
13. Weitzman (1984), and further reference in the chapter by Nuti in this volume.
14. Bhagwati (1982).

REFERENCES

Berliner, Joseph (1957), *Factory and Manager in the USSR*, Cambridge, Mass.

Bhagwati, Jagdish (1982), 'Directly Unproductive Profit-seeking (DUP) Activities', *Journal of Political Economy*, vol. 90, no. 5.

Elster, Jon (1984), *Ulysses and the Sirens. Studies in Rationality and Irrationality*, Cambridge and Paris.

——— (1985), 'Rationality, Morality and Collective Action', *Ethics*, vol. 96, no. 1 (October).

Grossman, Gregory (1963), 'Notes for a Theory of the Command Economy', *Soviet Studies*, vol. 15, no. 2.

Hirschman, Albert (1970), *Exit, Voice and Loyalty. Responses to Decline in Firms, Organizations and States*, Cambridge, Mass. and London.

North, Douglass (1981), *Structure and Change in Economic History*, New York and London.

Nove, Alec (1977), *The Soviet Economic System*, London.

Pelikan, Pavel (1985), 'Private Enterprise vs. Government Control: An Organizationally Dynamic Comparison', Working Paper No. 137, Industriens Utredningsinstitut, Stockholm.

Sutela, Pekka (1984), *Socialism, Planning and Optimality. A Study in Soviet Economic Thought*, Helsinki.

Weitzman, Martin (1984), *The Share Economy*, Cambridge, Mass.

Williamson, Oliver (1975), *Markets and Hierarchies. Analysis and Antitrust Implications*, New York.

Part One

The General View

1

The Formation of Incentive Mechanisms in Different Economic Systems

Pavel Pelikan*

Traditional comparative economics identifies the capitalist or private enterprise system with markets, and the socialist or centrally planned system with a hierarchy.[1] Consequently, when assessing incentive mechanisms in these systems, attention is focused on comparing incentives within markets to incentives within hierarchies. All advantages of the market-type incentives are then treated as advantages of private enterprise, while all advantages of the hierarchy-type incentives are regarded as advantages of socialist planning or government control.

To begin my argument, I wish to claim that such an approach has two serious weaknesses. First, it is futile to seek a universally valid answer to the question of which of the two types of incentives — of markets or of hierarchies — lead to a socially more efficient behaviour. Although efforts have been made trying to demonstrate that the former are universally superior, they have not been convincing. The most vigorous arguments of this kind are based on the theories of government bureaucracy, public choice and rent-seeking.[2] Starting with the assumption that all individuals are perfectly rational opportunists, these arguments claim, in essence, that only market-type incentives can discipline such individuals to strive for social efficiency. Hierarchies are claimed to be unable to fulfil this task because they protect their participants from market competition, allowing them to hide important information about real costs. The perfectly rational opportunists are then expected to exploit such a situation in various socially detrimental ways.

There are several reasons why these arguments fail to convince the unbelievers. Empirically, it can be shown that not all people are always as perfectly rational, nor as narrowly opportunistic, as these arguments claim, thus contradicting their assumptions. Moreover, it can also be shown that reasonably efficient hierarchies, including even some government ones, do exist, thus contradicting their conclusions.[3] From the point of view of theoretical analysis, these arguments can be exposed as being deduced from the claim that no hierarchy can be made incentive-compatible, but this claim has been formally refuted — precisely under the assumption of perfect rationality.[4] When the more plausible assumption of bounded rationality is made, Williamson (1975) convincingly shows that the issue of market *v.* hierarchies has no simple solution: under some conditions it is markets, and under other conditions it is hierarchies, which can be conducive to socially more efficient behaviour.

The second weakness of the traditional comparative approach is that the issue of market *v.* hierarchies is actually of little relevance in the comparison of real economic systems. The reason is that mixtures of both types of organisations, and incentives, can be found in all major economic systems. For instance, much of the economic transactions in the developed capitalist economies is internalised within large private firms, where individuals are most motivated by hierarchy-type incentives. On the other hand, since only a part of the production tasks in any economy can be specified and sanctioned by a central plan, all real socialist systems must to some extent rely on decentralised, market-like negotiations among socialist producers, where the market-type incentives necessarily prevail. Consequently, an argument in favour of market-type incentives is not always an argument in favour of private enterprise, nor does an argument in favour of hierarchy-type incentives necessarily support the cause of socialism. Namely, the former attacks not only government bureaucracy, but large private firms as well, while the latter does not automatically imply the superiority of socialism or government control, but can equally signify that that social efficiency is to be achieved by a large capitalist firm. The false belief that the only important difference between capitalism and socialism is that between markets and a hierarchy has also led, after the correct observation, that hierarchies increasingly grow within capitalism and markets within socialism, to the naive theory about the convergence of these two systems, which overlooks the truly substantial differences between them.

In Pelikan (1985) I have suggested an organisationally dynamic approach to comparative economics which is without these weaknesses. Instead of asking whether it is markets *or* hierarchies into which a well-performing economy should be organised, this approach fully recognises that a real economy, in order to internalise properly all important externalities and efficiently exploit modern technologies of production, communication and computation, must be made of *both* markets *and* hierarchies. Rather than comparing the ways in which some *given* markets and hierarchies *function* — which is what traditional analysis has done — it turns attention to the ways in which markets and hierarchies *form and re-form*.[5] Consequently, when comparing different economic systems, the focus is placed on their ability to form and maintain a well-performing mixture of both types of organisation. The purpose of this chapter is to summarise the main points of this approach, with particular attention paid to the problem of incentives.

TOWARDS AN ORGANISATIONALLY DYNAMIC ECONOMIC ANALYSIS

The suggested approach requires some modifications and extensions of the usual conceptual apparatus of economic analysis. The most important extensions can be summarised as follows:

Organisational structures

As is usual in microanalysis — and a meaningful inquiry into the formation of incentive mechanisms must necessarily be microeconomic — the economy under consideration will be described by three categories of parameters: (i) the collection of its economic units, such as households, firms, government agencies; (ii) their behaviour, for instance, as described by their preferences, types of rationality or behavioural rules; (iii) the network of the exchange channels by which they are interrelated, indicating the directions and the varieties of permissible transactions. It is this last category which indicates the set of the markets and/or the hierarchical relations into which the units of the economy are organised. These three categories of parameters together will be called the *organisational structure* (OS) of the economy.

By definition, OS contains all the parameters which determine the functioning of the economy in terms of resource-allocation, and can be regarded as a resource-allocation mechanism in the sense of Hurwicz (1971). For the purpose of our present discussion it is important to realise that each particular form of OS contains its specific types of incentives through which the given units motivate each other to exchange certain economic information (coordination signals), and resources, within the given network of exchange channels.

In contrast to traditional analysis, which often abstracts from the internal organisation of firms and agencies, the present inquiry will often force us to recognise that internal organisation matters. In this case, we shall refine the picture of OS by considering the internal organisational structure of each unit in terms of some sub-units, such as divisions, plants, workshops and eventually individual participants.[6] The term organisational structure of a unit (denoted sub-OS) will refer to three analogous categories of parameters: (i) the collection of the sub-units constituting the unit in question; (ii) their behaviour; (iii) the network of their exchange channels. Such a network can be visualised as depicting the inside of one node in the overall network of OS.

In a similar way as OS determines the functioning of the economy, sub-OS determines the functioning of the corresponding unit. Although, in principle, all sub-OSs can be classified as hierarchies, they may still be of many different forms (e.g. more or less decentralised), using differently designed incentives (e.g. flat-rate or piece-rate wages, fixed salaries or profit bonuses).[7] In general, when organisational structures of several levels are considered, different forms may appear at different levels: for instance, a market may contain units which are classified as hierarchies (e.g. firms), and a hierarchy may contain areas which can be classified as markets (e.g. among the divisions of a firm, among the firms of a centrally planned economy).

In principle, with the help of the concept of organisational structure, the behaviour of any system can be expressed in terms of the behaviour of its constituent parts. This means, among other things, that one ultimately needs to refer to a set of some elementary subunits whose behaviour is considered basic. In social sciences, such sub-units are individuals. I shall use the term *socio-cultural environment* to denote the set of the individuals with their behavioural characteristics — e.g. as described by their tastes, values and types of rationality — who play the role of the most elementary sub-units in the economy under consideration.

It is also with the help of the concept of organisational structure that the suggested organisationally dynamic approach can be distinguished from the traditional, organisationally static analysis. While traditional analysis assumes organisational structures to be exogenously given, the main feature of the suggested approach is to recognise them as endogenously formed.

Institutional rules

In a parallel and partly overlapping way, the economy under consideration can also be described by the list of its *institutional rules* (IR), which constrain the permissible behaviour of its units in a similar way as the rules of a game constrain the permissible moves of its players.[8]

The various forms of such rules can be classified much like the forms of organisational structures — for instance, by distinguishing the market type of rules, such as tradeable property rights, from the hierarchy type, such as a certain asymmetrical distribution of rights and duties between a central (privileged) unit and different types of peripheral units.

Like the concept of organisational structure, the one of institutional rules can also be applied within an economic unit. Denoted as sub-IR, it then refers to the 'rules of the game', e.g. as specified by a firm's constitution, which constrain the permissible behaviour of the participating sub-units. Typically, IR contains some rules constraining the permissible forms of sub-IRs — such as certain parts of the labour and corporation laws which constrain the choice of the internal rules (constitution) of a firm.

While organisational statics often identifies an economic system according to the supposedly invariant OS, organisational dynamics, which recognises OS as endogenously variable, can no longer do so. Another relatively invariant concept is therefore needed which could identify an economic system whose organisational structure is changing. The concept of IR is important for organisational dynamics precisely because it can play the role of such a (relative) invariant: while OS can be changing — e.g. some units may enter or exit, or modify, within some permissible limits, their behaviour and/or their exchange channels — IR can stay constant, imposing its particular constraints on both the functioning and the changing of OS.[9]

Organisational processes and associative actions

While traditional analysis focuses on the allocational processes through which OSs function, organisational dynamics must also consider processes through which OSs form, reform and dissolve. A suitable adjective for denoting such processes seems to be 'organisational'. To visualise such processes, one may think of hierarchies and/or markets which appear, grow, replace each other, reorganise internally, merge, split, diminish or dissolve. The changing hierarchies and markets may be of different kinds and levels. For instance, the hierarchy in question may be a firm or a government agency, or only a part of a firm or an agency, or a group of firms under the control of a government agency; the market in question may appear among several hierarchies when they engage in mutual exchanges, or within one hierarchy when this becomes decentralised. While modern economic analysis, as Samuelson's foundations make particularly clear, often seeks inspiration in the paradigm of mechanics, organisational processes are intuitively closer to that of chemistry.[10]

It should be emphasised that organisational dynamics is an extension of, and not a substitute for, organisational statics. The question of how an economic system functions in terms of allocational processes is not to be put aside, but to be completed by the question of how the organisational structures which run these processes are being formed. Since both allocational and organisational processes are taking place within OS, this structure can no longer be regarded as a mere resource-allocation mechanism, but as a self-transforming (self-organising) system as well.[11]

Organisational and allocational processes are interrelated in two ways. On the one hand, the organisational outcomes — that is, the actual form of OS and sub-OSs — determine how the allocational processes will unfold, according to the above-mentioned principle that each organisational structure implies a certain allocational behaviour. On the other hand, the allocational outcomes reached — e.g. the production realised, the savings made, the credits obtained — impose constraints on how the organisational processes can subsequently continue. For instance, a sub-OS can expand only within the limits of available resources, a lack of resources possibly forcing its dissolution.

When trying to anatomise organisational processes into some well-defined micro-actions of individual units (and sub-units) — without which a good understanding of these processes would not be possible — it can be shown that there is one basic type of individual actions into which all organisational processes can ultimately be decomposed. Such actions consists in a unit (sub-unit) modifying — which includes both forming and interrupting — some exchange channels connecting it to other units (sub-units). To denote such actions, a suitable adjective seems to be 'associative'.

Associative actions are to be distinguished from the usually considered allocative actions which consist of exchanges (transactions) of resources and/or information along some already established channels — e.g. on existing markets, within existing hierarchies. While allocative actions are the elementary steps by which structures function, associative actions are the elementary steps by which structures form, reform and dissolve.

It is important to recognise that associative actions are not mere instruments in the search for higher economic efficiency, as an economist would like to see them, but may have their own specific constraints and underlying preferences. Examples of associative constraints are the limited fineness and clarity of available common languages,[12] and the limited number of persons with whom one may interact (e.g. the limited span of control); examples of associative preferences are the feelings of sympathy or antipathy for potential partners, and the wishes to be independent, to lead, or to follow. While allocative preferences can be traced to the traditionally quoted Robinson Crusoe's needs for food and shelter, associative preferences can be regarded as stemming from human needs for socal contacts. Although some rates of substitution are likely to develop between the two, they are unlikely ever to become complete because of bounded rationality and/or ethical scruples.[13]

Once the existence of associative constraints and preferences is recognised, they can be assigned places among the tastes, values and types of rationality which characterise the individuals of a given socio-cultural environment. Together, they constrain the variety of organisational structures which are feasible in this environment, and possibly also imply that some of these structures are more likely to form the others.[14]

The view that the behaviour of economic units falls into two relatively separate spheres — the formation of exchange channels, and the use of the channels formed for the conduct of specific exchanges — seems to be the key to a good understanding of the processes of economic organisation and self-organisation.[15]

The role of tacit knowledge in organisational structures and processes

Thus far, most of economic analysis has been conducted under two alternative assumptions about information (knowledge). The older one assumes away any form of scarce information: all economic units know perfectly well both the state of the world and the rational decision procedures for acting upon it. The newer one recognises that some information may be scarce, but assumes that such information is always communicable: all units can perfectly well understand and rationally act upon all perceptible signals. Although the costs of communication may have to be paid, and the initial holder of information properly motivated to send it, if this is done, any scarce information can be transferred anywhere across a given organisational structure as a pure matter of allocation, while the structure stays constant.

The problem which has been ignored in this way is the one of the information (knowledge) which must always pre-exist before any other information can be communicated, interpreted and acted upon.

To denote such pre-existing, uncommunicable information, I shall use the term 'tacit knowledge', due to M. Polanyi (1967), and employed in economic analysis by Nelson and Winter (1982). This is the information contained in the OS itself, determining the decision procedures (behaviour) of the system, including the working knowledge of languages and codes, decision logic, learning procedures.[16]

Since tacit knowledge cannot be communicated, it must be either given initially, or individually acquired through learning by doing. In the latter case, however, the initial endowment with learning procedures — themselves a part of the initially given tacit knowledge — acts as the constraint on what can be eventually learned. It seems natural to use the term 'competence' to denote the tacit knowledge which an individual actually uses at a given point in time, and the term 'talent' to denote his learning abilities. One can then say that, at any moment, the actual competence depends on experience and talents; in the long run, talents determine the limits of attainable competence.[17]

One important property of tacit knowledge, which immediately follows from its definition, is that no direct interpersonal comparison of the stocks of tacit knowledge is feasible. Not only is it impossible to measure accurately the stocks of another person's tacit knowledge, but people may not even be able to measure (be fully conscious of) their own stocks: it is quite frequent that one overestimates or underestimates one's own competence and talents. Consequently, whenever information about such stocks is needed, only indirect methods for estimating their states can be used. There seems to be only two such methods. One consists in using different contests (competition, tournaments) where the success of the contestants is positively correlated with their possession of certain types of tacit knowledge.[18] The other method is to rely on qualified guesses made by some selected individuals on the basis of incomplete, and possibly secondary, evidence. The point to retain is that if such guesses are to be qualified — that is, positively correlated with reality — their makers must be endowed with much of certain specific tacit knowledge themselves (e.g. to have the 'knack' to recognise another person's talents, or a lack of talents, under possibly misleading appearances).

With the introduction of the concept of tacit knowledge, an important piece of the puzzle fits into place. Namely, the dividing line between allocational and organisational processes corresponds to the dividing-line between communicable and tacit knowledge. It is only through organisational processes that tacit knowledge can be acquired and handled, and it is only in organisational structures that it can be stored and made utilisable. It is the tacit knowledge contained in an organisational structure that determines how well, or how poorly, communicable information will be used by that structure.

THE FORMATION OF INCENTIVE MECHANISMS AS AN ENDOGENOUS PROCESS

With the help of the proposed concepts, the ways in which organisational processes unfold within different economic systems will be examined. The focus will be on the incentive mechanisms which appear within the organisational structures formed by these processes.

Self-organisation and entrepreneurship

The proposed concepts lead to the following view of the formation of organisational structures. Under *any* institutional rules — no matter how much centralisation or decentralisation they might impose on the allocational process — much of the detailed shape of organisational structures is inevitably determined by decentralised self-organisation of *all* of its units: each of them contributes to some degree to the formation of at least those exchange channels where it is directly involved. This is not to say, however, that self-organisation is egalitarian. In fact, a profound asymmetry between two types of roles is implied. Namely, some of the units (sub-units) must play the role of entrepreneurs, taking the initiative of proposing specific channels to specific partners, while others stay less active, limiting themselves to accepting, modifying or rejecting the channels which have been proposed. The entrepreneurs, characterised by particular combinations of their allocative and associative preferences — which is what makes them respond to certain conditions by taking the initiative — can be said to supply the initial organisation projects, around which markets or hierarchies can form. Of course, the resulting structures may develop, under the inevitable influence of self-organisation, into a somewhat different shape than what these projects appeared to indicate. They are nevertheless crucial, for without them no organisational process would ever be initiated.[19]

The question now is how self-organisation and entrepreneurship will be constrained by different types of institutional rules. For instance, the rights to act as entrepreneur may be differently centralised or decentralised, the permissible organisational projects may be required to satisfy different conditions, and different agents may have different rights to join, modify, exit or block the organisational project of other agents.

It should be noted that this view need not contradict the paradigm of equilibrium analysis, for organisational processes can very well be interpreted as a part of the adjustment processes chasing a general equilibrium. Adjustment processes can be regarded as consisting of two interconnected stages: the usually studied functional adaptations of a given structure, e.g. through various cobweb processes; and the presently examined organisational processes modifying the structure itself, e.g. by creating and reorganising markets and hierarchies.

It is during the organisational stage of the adjustment process — that is, as long as this process requires creation or reorganisation of markets and hierarchies — that entrepreneurship appears as an essential input. It thus finally gains the status of a scarce resource — the status which it has been denied all along by traditional analysis for the simple reason that its social returns at equilibrium are strictly zero. In contrast, organisational dynamics not only recognises the social value of entrepreneurship as positive, but even indicates that, when in short supply, entrepreneurship takes on some of the characteristics of a public good. Namely, without a sufficient supply of entrepreneurship, not enough organisational processes would be initiated, leaving the structure of the production sector under-developed and/or maladapted to the prevailing environments. For instance, some potential markets might not fully develop, or not form at all, leaving large numbers of potentially diligent workers involuntarily unemployed, far from their most preferred bundles of work efforts and consumption goods for which the availability of *all other* resources should allow. Clearly, in such a situation, the social returns to entrepreneurship can easily exceed the private returns.

The present view of entrepreneurs as organisers should now be compared with the two main existing views: that of Schumpeter (1934) who focuses on the role of entrepreneurs as technological innovators, disturbing a general equilibrium ('circular flow'); and that of Kirzner (1973), for whom entrepreneurs are the discoverers of economic opportunities, helping the economy approach an equilibrium. Because entrepreneurs are regarded here as catalysing the adjustment process, the present view is obviously much closer to Kirzner's. While I am far from underestimating the importance of technological innovations, I propose to classify them, in a Knightian spirit, as belonging to the technical dimension of production, exogenous to economic analysis. Although each discovery of a new product and/or a new production technique is fully reognised as shifting the potential equilibria of the economy to a new locus, such discoveries can be regarded as made by some specialised producers, such as scientists or engineers. Entrepreneurs — who may, of course, be the same persons as the scientists or engineers — can then be regarded, in agreement with Kirzner, as pure users of such discoveries, with the task of pushing the economy towards a corresponding new equilibrium, away from the old one.

There is, however, one point on which the present views come close to Schumpeter's. Since entrepreneurs are defined as the designers of organisational projects and the initiators of organisational processes, they are regarded as creators, innovators or at least problem-solvers, which is closer to the status which Schumpeter gives them. The qualification, of course, is that for Schumpeter, the creations and innovations are above all technological, while here they are purely organisational. For Kirzner, in contrast, entrepreneurs simply respond to some pre-existing opportunities without much creative contribution of their own, their main advantage over the other agents being their greater alertness.

Incentives for resource-allocation *v*, incentives for entrepreneurs

Following such a dual view of economic behaviour, incentives can be divided into the two corresponding dimensions: the usually studied incentives for resource-allocation, including incentives for truthful information about resource-allocation, and the less often considered incentives for organisation, including incentives for entrepreneurship. Of course, the two dimensions are not unrelated, since incentives for resource-allocation (e.g. the profit incentive) usually play an important role among the incentives for entrepreneurship. Yet, as the above discussion about the relative independence of associative preferences suggests, there are also other incentives for which people engage, or do not engage, in organisational processes. This is one of the reasons why such a dual view of incentives may be useful. A second reason is that this view corresponds to the distinction between endogenous and exogenous variables: incentives for resource-allocation are formed endogenously, as an integral part of the endogenously formed OS, while incentives for entrepreneurship more directly depend on the prevailing IR — in particular, on certain property rights — which is assumed, within the framework of organisational dynamics, to be exogenously given.

Most of the existing literature on incentives is limited to incentives for resource-allocation, examined from an organisationally static point of view. One example is the literature on incentives for truthfulness in hierarchies, and on the principal agent problem.[20] Another example is the treatment of the incentive problem by Williamson (1975, 1985). This example is more relevant to our discussion than the former for two reasons. First, Williamson recognises human rationality as bounded, which corresponds to our recognition of the scarcity of tacit knowledge. Second, his systematic use of the market *v.* hierarchies comparative approach is an important step towards organisation dynamics. Namely, by comparing hierarchies with markets, rather than treating each type of organisational structure separately, important indications can be obtained as to when it would be potentially efficient to transform a market into a hierarchy (e.g. through vertical integration) or vice versa, even if the question of when and how such a transformation will actually take place is not addressed.

Without trying to duplicate such studies, what organisational dynamics does is to point to some of their limitations and to situate them in a broader context. One implication of our argument is that the detailed form of the incentives for resource-allocation actually used in a real economy must be regarded as a product of endogenous organisational processes, which must have been projected and initiated by endogenous entrepreneurs and modified through the inevitable self-organisation of all the participants concerned. For instance, one may think of the incentives effectively at work within a firm, which are the result of both the design and the implementation of long-term employment contracts. This means that an organisationally static theory can at best state certain general principles which apply to entire classes of incentives. It cannot, however, predict very precisely which particular incentives will appear in a particular situation and how well or poorly they will actually work. The point to be emphasised is that details which no theory can comprehend can be very important: different entrepreneurs can apply the same theoretical principle in a clumsy or ingenious way, with very different outcomes. While the communicable knowledge of a theory may be useful to designing incentives, it cannot be sufficient. The actual efficiency of the incentives for resource-allocation within a real economy is also, and sometimes above all, determined by the tacit knowledge of endogenous entrepreneurs.[21]

To illustrate this idea, consider the two main questions studied by Williamson: When can a hierarchy successfully internalise a part of a market? How big can it become before losing its comparative advantage? The factors which Williamson points out and examines — such as limited spans of control, opportunistic behaviour, bounded rationality, informational asymmetry, side-effects of selective intervention — undoubtedly play an important role in determining the answer to these questions, yet they cannot predict, by themselves, how large an efficient hierarchy can actually become in any given economy. The obvious reason is that all such factors can only indicate the *potentially attainable efficiency* of market and hierarchies, while the *actually attained efficiency* will also depend on the tacit knowledge of the entrepreneurs who happen to initiate the formation of the market and hierarchies in question. Clumsy entrepreneurs may fail in building an efficient hierarchy of any size where the most talented ones may succeed in organising and maintaining surprisingly large efficient hierarchies, securing the cooperation of their participants by ingeniously designed and sensibly implemented incentive mechanisms, with an important role played by organisational innovations.[22]

On the one hand, organisational dynamics thus sets limits to what an organisationally static theory can say about incentives for resource-allocation in different economic systems. On the other hand, by introducing the tacit knowledge of entrepreneurs as an additional factor to be considered, it enlarges the inquiry by some new, more roundabout questions, such as: How are the candidates for the role of entrepreneurs recruited? In which contests will they have to succeed? Which type of tacit knowledge is favoured by these contests and how is it relevant to the task of designing well-performing incentive mechanisms? Which incentives will motivate people to become candidates and to succeed at these contests? In other words, organisational dynamics submits that theory itself cannot solve the problem of incentives for resource-allocation in all relevant details and, therefore, calls attention to the question of how the people who *can* do so are attracted, selected and given the opportunity to act.

It is according to the answers to the above questions that organisational dynamics compares different economic systems, dealing with the two previously discussed dimensions of incentives. As already mentioned, the incentives for entrepreneurship are directly defined by IR, in the form of certain property rights, such as the rights to the proceeds of entrepreneurship, and the distribution of responsibilities in case of adversity among entrepreneurs, labour, creditors and customers. As to the incentives for resource-allocation, the influence of IR is less direct, although not less important. On the one hand, IR defines the limits of admissible types of markets and hierarchies, including admissible types of incentives, e.g. by prohibiting slavery, or by imposing certain forms of profit-sharing. On the other hand, by defining the incentives for entrepreneurship and the conditions under which entrepreneurs are selected and given the opportunity to act, IR also has much responsibility for the quantity and the quality of the entrepreneurs who will assume the task of designing, within the defined limits, the actual incentives for resource-allocation and, thereby, for the quality of these incentives themselves.

The preferences for entrepreneurship

The responsibility of IR is, however, limited by the fact that the outcomes of any economic process, including the formation of incentive mechanisms, depend not only on the general rules which channel the process, but also on the behaviour of the actors who run it. One may think of the outcomes of a game which depend not only on its rules, but also on the quality of its players. This means that one cannot compare different economic systems (forms of IR) without also taking into consideration the socio-cultural environment where they are applied.

It seems that a brief discussion of people's preferences concerning entrepreneurship can expose most of the socio-cultural parameters which are of importance for the present discussion.

Obviously, the problem of preferences is complementary to the problem of incentives since, in order to become an effective motivational force, an incentive must always interact with some corresponding preferences within the agent who is to be motivated. As follows from earlier discussion, both the allocative and the associative preferences will play an important role in determining the preferences for entrepreneurship — that is, the conditions under which different individuals would volunteer to become entrepreneurs.

The allocative preferences concern the traditionally quoted desire for material gain and require no comment. The associative preferences contribute to the motivation of the potential entrepreneurs by making them appreciate their gains (losses) in terms of social contacts, such as the status gained, the friends and/or the enemies made, the admiration and/or the envy provoked. Moreover, these preferences also influence the subjective costs of entrepreneurship. For instance, a shy person will find these costs much higher than someone who enjoys taking the initiative and leading others.

The rewards for, and the costs of, entrepreneurship depend not only on the associative preferences of the entrepreneurs themselves, but also on the values concerning entrepreneurship of the population at large. On the one hand, these values determine the social esteem, or the hostility, which a successful entrepreneur will attract, thus contributing to his rewards. For instance, if a successful entrepreneur is admired, the need for material incentives to entrepreneurship may be lower than if he were dispised. In the latter case, he would clearly have to be offered an additional material compensation. Moreover, entrepreneurship would then be made particularly attractive for the morally deviant individuals who care little about social disapproval. On the other hand, these values influence the objective costs of entrepreneurship by determining some important socio-cultural parameters, such as the general standards of honesty and loyalty, on which the costs of setting up and running economic organisations depend. For instance, these costs are obviously lower in a culture where such standards are high than in a culture where cheating one's employer is regarded as a moral duty towards one's family and/or the working class.

The point to be retained is that different socio-cultural environments may exhibit substantial differences in the preferences for entrepreneurship. Consequently, they can substantially differ in the supply of potential entrepreneurs for different lines of economic activities (e.g. simple trade *v.* complex manufacturing *v.* industries with high moral hazards, such as investment and insurance), with an important impact on the attained economic development and social welfare. The importance which organisational dynamics thus ascribes to the contents of people's preferences is one of the points where it substantially departs from traditional analysis. According to traditional views, the contents of people's preferences do not matter. Provided that certain formal conditions of transitivity and connectivity are met, a Pareto-efficient equilibrium can be defined for any particular contents. Organisational dynamics, in contrast, shows that the content of certain preferences is crucial for the very formation of the resource-allocation mechanisms (organisational structures) without which the system could not work and no equilibrium could thus be approached.

PRIVATE ENTERPRISE IS LIKELY TO FORM MORE EFFICIENT INCENTIVE MECHANISMS THAN OTHER ECONOMIC SYSTEMS

While organisational statics has been unable to determine which economic system contains the most efficient incentive mechanisms, we shall now see that organisational dynamics has some more conclusive results to offer.

What kind of social welfare?

In principle, each economic system can be regarded as working with certain efficiency towards a certain type of social welfare. Therefore, different systems can be evaluated according to either their efficiency, or the kind of social welfare they tend to achieve, e.g. as imputed from the final demands they effectively satisfy.

To compare types of social welfare is a thorny problem which can easily be confused by differences in the tastes, values and ideologies of the comparers. However, as suggested by Nelson (1981), much of this problem can be avoided by focusing on the system of production, while leaving the question of the contents and the distribution of final consumption largely open. If one system of production can be shown to be superior to another for a wide range of types of social welfare, a valuable result is reached. While different comparers may continue to disagree, within this range, as to which type of social welfare should be strived for, they must now at least agree that in any case, production should be organised according to the former systems rather than the latter.

As I show in Pelikan (1985), this approach strengthens the cause of the private enterprise system of production, for it disconnects it from the value-laden questions of consumer sovereignty, individualistic society and philosophical liberalism. More precisely, government — no matter how democratic or undemocratic, wise or unwise it might be — is left to determine much of the final demands which production should meet, e.g. in terms of public goods, merit goods, employment, growth, environmental protection. If one can then show that *even under these conditions*, a good system of production must be of the private enterprise type, one disarms all the critics of this type of system who accuse it of meeting the wrong final demands.

It is this approach which will be adopted here. When speaking of the relative efficiency of incentive mechanisms contained in different economic systems, I shall have in mind their respective capacities to induce people into socially efficient (non-wasteful) production activities *vis-à-vis* some largely unspecified final demands.

Organisational failures

Organisational processes in any single economic system are difficult to model, since much of their course and outcomes depend on the entrepreneurs who happen to appear, and on the ideas that these entrepreneurs happen to have — both of which any positive theory must regard as largely stochastical variables. As the following reasoning will suggest, it is nevertheless possible to obtain, by relatively simple means, a fairly good idea of how different systems compare with each other as to their respective capacities to channel organisational processes towards the formation of efficient organisational structures with efficient incentives.

To begin, recall that organisational processes are to use tacit knowledge in order to handle some other tacit knowledge, without anyone reliably knowing how such knowledge is distributed.

Consequently, they cannot avoid having the character of a trial-and-error search. A suitable model of organisational processes thus appears to be the one which decomposes them into two interwoven stages: generation of organisational trials and elimination of organisational errors.[23]

Such a trial-and-error model of organisational processes implies two types of potential organisational failures which would cause poorly performing organisational structures to appear:

(i) *surviving errors*, denoting cases of defective error-elimination which tolerates the presence of some errors, for lack of detection or for lack of effective elimination.
(ii) *absent successes*, denoting cases of defective trial-generation which prevents some potentially successful trials from materialising, or cases of defective error-elimination where some of such trials are eliminated by mistake.[24]

The idea to be followed is very simple. Different economic systems will be compared according to their relative capacities to avoid these two types of organisational failure. If system A proves more resistant to at least one of these types, and no less resistant to the other, than system B, we can then conclude that A will form *relatively* better organisational structures, with more efficient incentive mechanisms, than B.

The inferiority of centralised entrepreneurship

Let me first compare two types of economic systems: *contestable private enterprise*, which is defined here as decentralising the rights to initiate organisational trials and to eliminate organisational errors over both established units and potential newcomers (open decentralisation);[25] and *centralised entrepreneurship*, defined as restricting the rights to conduct these two kinds of activities to government agencies and their appointees. It may be useful to emphasise once more that centralised entrepreneurship need not at all imply centralised resource-allocation. The central entrepreneur might very well try to imitate markets by setting up relatively independent units and letting them decide about their current production and even compete with each other as can be illustrated by the example of the Hungarian economy. From an organisationally static viewpoint, such markets may be indistinguishable from private enterprise markets.

The first conclusive result can now be obtained in the form of the following proposition: *In comparable circumstances, centralised entrepreneurship is likely both to generate fewer successful organisational trials and to tolerate more surviving errors — thus forming less efficient organisational structures and incentive mechanisms — than contestable private enterprise.*

There are three joint reasons to justify this proposition. The first, relevant to trial-generation, consists of two simple steps. First, it is to be noted that only contestable private enterprise is potentially able to take advantage of all the talented entrepreneurs present (but more or less hidden) in a given socio-cultural environment. On the other hand, centralised entrepreneurship restricts the rights to initiate organisational trials to government officials, selected through politico-administrative contests.

Second, in order to see that such a restriction effectively prevents some of the potentially feasible good trials from materialising, it must be shown that government cannot succeed in concentrating all the talented entrepreneurs into its agencies, and in promoting them to sufficiently high positions where they would have the decision authority to initiate organisational trials. This can be done by pointing to the fact that the politico-administrative contests, through which government officials are selected and promoted, are relevant to another type of tacit knowledge (e.g. the talent of winning political support, the art of pleasing one's superiors) than that needed for organising efficient productive arrangements. Although some individuals might be talented at both, the distribution of these two types of tacit knowledge is unlikely to be perfectly correlated. This means that centralised entrepreneurship is bound to stifle the effective supply of successful trials by requiring all entrepreneurs to first succeed at the wrong contest, where some of the good ones will fail, or not even try, while some mediocre ones may excel.[26]

The second reason, relevant to error-elimination, begins by noting that the ultimate criterion for distinguishing organisational successes from organisational errors is their respective ability to perform. Although preliminary judgements by qualified guesses are also possible, and some people may be quite talented at making them, such judgements are, by their nature, unreliable. The units which make such guesses (e.g. market analysts, investors, planners) may themselves be successes or errors, and their ability to guess correctly must also be subjected to error-elimination.

In order to show that contestable private enterprise performs better than centralised enterpreneurship in localising and eliminating organisational errors on the basis of their insufficient performance, one can refer to the 'exit vs. voice' argument due to Hirschman (1970). Only contestable private enterprise decentralises the effective authority of error-elimination to the dissatisfied units (sub-units) which are directly affected by insufficient performance of other units. This authority is ultimately exercised through 'exit' from the sphere of the entrepreneur whose organisational errors caused such a dissatisfaction, and a tentative 'entry' into the sphere of an alternative entrepreneur, with the legal possibility for the dissatisfied unit to become an entrepreneur itself. On the other hand, in the industries or economies where entrepreneurship is centralised, no such exit is possible, for no alternative entrepreneurs are allowed to show their talents. The dissatisfied units are limited to 'voice', such as complaints addressed to a supervising agency, belonging to the sphere of the same central entrepreneur, which may be unable to understand and/or unwilling to listen to them. Clearly, such an arrangement is prone to let more errors survive for longer periods of time than what contestable private enterprise would tolerate.[27]

The third reason is relevant to both trial-generation and error-elimination. Contestable private enterprise, by making both these dimensions openly decentralised, has the exclusive potential to keep the trial-makers and the error-eliminators well separated from each other. In this way, each trial can be provided with a jury of independent error-eliminators, different from its authors (e.g. an entrepreneur facing his investors and customers). In contrast, centralisation or closed decentralisation of these two kinds of activities necessarily brings the trial-makers closer to the error-eliminators. Consequently, error-elimination is bound to lose some of its independence to the detriment of its quality.

The systems with centralised entrepreneurship, which have thus been proved to be inferior to contestable private enterprise, contain several categories of real systems. The most important ones are the Soviet type of socialism where centralised entrepreneurship embraces most of the entire production, the Swedish style of welfare society where government acts as an institutionally priviledged entrepreneur for most of the production of merit goods and services, and the French version of planning where government is a priviledged entrepreneur for organising exchanges of economic information and the elaboration of economic forecasts. It is worth repeating and emphasising that organisational dynamics does not claim that these systems lack *the potential* to accommodate efficient organisational structures and incentive mechanisms. Traditional analysis has been quite successful in showing — and on this point it is not to be challenged — that ingenious organisational structures with efficient incentive mechanisms are theoretically conceivable for all these systems.[28] What organisational dynamics does claim is that systems with centralised entrepreneurship suffer from inherent weaknesses in their organisational processes which make such structures and mechanisms unlikely to be *actually* generated and preserved against deterioration.

The inferiority of market socialism

Economic systems based on market socialism need not, at least in theory, make use of any central planning, and not even of centralised entrepreneurship. They can make room for a wide variety of markets under the condition of all production units, or at least all production units over a certain size, apply certain rules of collective decision-making and profit sharing within their sub-OSs. I shall now show that contestable private enterprise is superior to these systems as well.

Let me first emphasise that the point is not to examine the impact of such internal rules on the performance of a given firm. This impact may sometimes be quite beneficial indeed: examples of successful firms in market socialism are not impossible to find, and even in the private enterprise system one can find firms which have developed variants of such rules voluntarily, to their obvious advantage. Rather, the focus is again on the organisational processes which generate and maintain organisational structures across the entire production sector, and on the organisational failures from which they are likely to suffer, if such rules are obligatory for all firms.

As to surviving errors, market socialism need not, if not interfered with by arbitrary political decisions, perform worse than contestable private enterprise. Obviously, the mechanism of exit can work on socialist markets with the same force as on capitalist markets. Also, market socialism can keep trial-makers reasonably well separated from error-eliminators, thus preserving the necessary independence of error-elimination to a comparable degree as private enterprise.

It is on the side of absent successes that the decisive weakness of market socialism can be located. This type of system is bound to stifle the supply of potential successes for at least two reasons. First, the obligatory rules of collective decision-making and profit-sharing necessarily act as a constraint which discourages or prevents some, possibly important, organisational trials where such rules would be unsuitable, thus decreasing the stream of new trials in comparison with private enterprise, *ceteris paribus*.

Second, the quantity of risk capital and/or the quality of its allocation will necessarily be lower in market socialism than in private enterprise. One consequence of imposing the rules of collective decision-making and profit-sharing on the capital market is that specialised investors are virtually prevented from appearing, which will limit the supply of risk capital to self-financing, with the well-known efficiency losses, and to banks organised by government, likely to suffer from the earlier exposed failures. Consequently, some potentially successful new trials will be prevented from materialising for lack of resources.

Market socialism thus leads to a disadvantageous combination of a relatively good error-elimination with a relatively poor trial-generation. The effect will be that the rightly eliminated errors are less likely to be replaced by new successful trials than in private enterprise. The organisational structure of production is thus likely to stay chronically underdeveloped, causing a higher level of involuntary unemployment than what contestable private enterprise would achieve in comparable conditions.

The present unemployment level in Yugoslavia, which is higher than in the comparable capitalist countries, seems to illustrate well the present argument. On this point, the Soviet-type socialism has a certain 'advantage': its surviving errors (wasteful production units), instead of being eliminated, can purposefully be dimensioned so as to keep everyone busy.

CONCLUDING REMARKS

Organisational dynamics thus allows us to reach a difficult to refute conclusion: *Contestable private enterprise is superior to both centralised entrepreneurship and market socialism in that it is most likely to form better organisational structures with more efficient incentive mechanisms.*

It is easy to verify that this conclusion is more difficult to refute than the parallel conclusion based on the theories of public choice and government bureaucracy. Namely, none of the objections to these theories which were mentioned in the introduction can be used against the present argument.

As to its assumptions, the present argument fully recognises that different individuals can be differently intentioned and differently rational, thus having no quarrel with the objection that not all people are perfectly rational opportunists. Instead, the individual behavioural characteristics which will eventually prevail within an economic system are claimed to depend largely on the system itself, in particular on the type of the contests (selection) which the system implies.

As to its deductions, the present argument is not built on the incorrect claim that hierarchies are bound to be incentive-incompatible. On the one hand, the problem of incentives is recognised as possibly aggravated by the problem of tacit knowledge, which shows that hierarchies are threatened not only by competent egoists but possibly also by incompetent altruists. On the other hand, both these problems are regarded as very difficult but not quite impossible to solve. Consequently, large efficient hierarchies are not claimed to be deterministically infeasible, but only very difficult to find and keep among the vast majority of similarly looking but poorly performing variants.

In this way, the present argument is made fully resistant to all theoretical and empirical evidence presenting cases of successful hierarchies and/or failing markets. All such cases can easily be accommodated, for what is claimed is not that markets are necessarily better than hierarchies, but only that the system of contestable private enterprise is likely to obtain a better performing mixture of markets *and* hierarchies than any other system.

The accusation of sweeping too widely does not apply to the present argument either. By focusing on the genesis of organisational structures rather than on their static appearance, this argument makes a clear distinction between government hierarchies and private enterprise hierarchies. Government hierarchies are not criticised for being hierarchies, but for being the fruit of centralised entrepreneurship. This is claimed to be the reason why these hierarchies are less likely to become and stay efficient than apparently similar private enterprise hierarchies which have formed and survived under the system of contestable private enterprise.

Two qualifications are necessary, however, in order to avoid possible misinterpretation of these conclusions. First, it should be emphasised that the present argument has been limited to the system of production, while the question of which final demands should be satisfied has been left open. This means that this argument should not be interpreted as defending some extreme forms of *laissez-faire*. *A priori*, government has not been disqualified from conducting a wide array of policies outside the production sector, e.g. concerning final consumption, general work conditions and environmental protection. Even some highly paternalistic or welfare-type economies may thus be given good marks in the present comparison, provided they allow private enterprise to compete in the production of whatever merit goods government might wish to be consumed. Moreover, as I show in Pelikan (1985), government may also be allowed, and indeed required, to intervene directly in production, in order to protect the contestability of markets, and to increase the supply of entrepreneurship if this proves to be insufficient.

Second, the term 'contestable private enterprise' refers to an entire category of economic systems which may still differ from each other in many important aspects. Therefore, the property of belonging to this category should be regarded as necessary, but not sufficient, for a successful economic system. What I claim is that without contestable private enterprise — that is, without institutional rules which make room for contestable markets — efficient organisational structures and incentive mechanisms are unlikely to appear and survive. On the other hand, I do not claim that any system of contestable private enterprise must necessarily be successful. For instance, systems of this category which are too tolerant to predation, or too inhospitable to entrepreneurs by over-protecting creditors and/or consumers and/or labour, would likely suffer from high level of absent successes, thus failing to develop efficient organisational structures. Much research is still needed to determine in detail all the properties which would enable an economic system to develop efficient organisational structures in a given socio-cultural environment. Far from knowing how to find such a system, all I claim is that it would be futile to search for it outside the category of contestable private enterprise.

NOTES

* The Industrial Institute for Economic and Social Research, Grevgatan 34, S-114 53 Stockholm, Sweden. I wish to thank Gunnar Eliasson, Bruno Frey, Stefan Hedlund, Albert Hirschman, Richard Nelson, Claes Wihlborg, Oliver Williamson and Milan Zeleny for valuable comments. I owe a special debt to Bengt-Christer Ysander for long inspiring discussions which helped me greatly in understanding and expressing many of the problems examined. Steve Turner deserves special thanks for his thoughtful editorial

assistance which much improved not only the form but also the content of my argument. I also thank Margit Faijersson for her careful word-processing of the text. None of them is responsible for the remaining errors and the views expressed.

1. The terms 'market' and 'hierarchy' are used here in the sense of Williamson (1975). Hurwicz (1971) is an example, formally impeccable, of such a simplified application of the markets vs. hierarchies dichotomy to the comparison of economic systems.

2. The basic references are Niskanen (1971), Buchanan and Tollison (1972), and Buchanan, Tollison and Tullock (1980).

3. A critical survey of these arguments attacking their assumptions and conclusions is in Greffe (1981).

4. An ingenious solution of the incentive-incompatibility problem was proposed by Groves (1973), and elaborated in the context of central planning by Loeb and Magat (1978).

5. Reference should be made to the famous quotation from Schumpeter (1942; 1976 edn: p. 84): 'the problem that is usually being visualised is how capitalism administers existing structures, whereas the relevant problem is how it creates and destroys them'. The present argument will not, however, be limited to capitalism, but will embrace different economic systems, and different types of incentive mechanisms within them.

6. In this respect the present argument comes close to modern transactional analysis, in particular as developed and applied by Williamson (1975).

7. An example of classification of hierarchies at the firm level is in Williamson (1975) who distinguishes three types: U-form, M-form and corrupted M-form. At the economy level, a parellel classification of hierarchies in terms of centralisation and decentralisation can be found in discussions on economic reforms in the socialist economies (see e.g. Nove, 1977).

8. This concept has appeared in economic literature under different names, such as 'general rules' (Hayek), 'economic constitution' (J. Marschak, Buchanan), 'economic regime' (Hurwicz), 'property rights' (Demsetz), 'institutional framework' (a generally used term). Since the term 'rules' is sometimes also employed in the sense of 'behavioural rules', describing the actual behaviour of a unit, it may be useful to underline the difference between the two alternative uses of this term: 'institutional rules' have the meaning of *constraints* imposed on the space of variants of 'behavioural rules'.

9. In a loose but illuminating biological analogy, the relationship between the institutional rules and the organisational structure of an economic system could be compared to the one between the genotype and the phenotype of a living organism: the genotype stays constant, while channelling both the functioning and the organising of the phenotype.

10. The closest economic literature has come to dealing with such processes is in the writings on coalition formation, the design and the implementation of long-term employment contract, and the dilemma 'exit or voice' as elegantly stated by Hirschman (1970).

11. In this way organisational dynamics closely relates to the newly

developing theories of self-organisation and autopoiesis. Zeleny (1980) is probably the best reference for a survey of these theories and their applications in the social sciences.

12. The impact of this constraint on the feasibility of centralised economic systems is examined in Pelikan (1969).

13. It seems that the influence on human behaviour of associative preferences, relatively independent from allocative preferences, might help to explain some of the bureaucratic costs and distortions in large hierarchies which Williamson examines (1985, Ch. 6). The explanation offered would be that the participants of a large hierarchy perceive much more sharply and directly the associative outcomes of their actions — such as the personal relationships formed, the power and status gained — than their contribution to the allocational gains or losses of the entire hierarchy. On the other hand, even if a market is also frequently used for satisfying some associative preferences — such as making and maintaining social contacts, exchanging news — the allocative and associative outcomes can be quite symmetrically perceived and easily compared. Indeed, each market participant feels rather directly the relationship between the social intercourse enjoyed and the deals made.

14. Biology offers an interesting term for denoting such a constraint, namely, the constraint of morphogeny (Gould and Lewontin, 1979). This term was coined in a discussion which is likely to have important implications even in the social sciences. The general argument is that, contrary to what the neo-Darwinian orthodoxy implies, natural selection is not the only determinant of the forms of life, and need not lead to their optimal adaptation to the environment. The reason is to be sought in the limited organisational possibilities — the inherent constraint of morphogeny — of the material of which living organisms are made (cf. the inherent properties of atoms constraining the feasible forms of crystals). In other words, adaptation is not to be regarded as unbounded optimisation in terms of parameters exclusively given by the environment, but rather as optimisation under the constraint of morphogeny — that is, limited to the structures which are feasible, given the constituent parts. If this constraint is strongly binding, it may determine more features of the resulting structures than what is determined by the selective pressures of the environment. In economic literature, Alchian (1950) was very close to expressing this idea when he emphasised that selection is always limited to the set of *actually tried* alternatives. Clearly, it is the constraint of morphogeny which marks the outer limit of such sets. This means that some forms of organisational structures may never appear as the candidates for selection — such as perfectly profit-maximising firms, or optimally planning socialist economies — simply because of the limited perceptual, communicational, computational and moral capacities of the individuals who are to constitute them. Moreover, different cultures at different levels of development are likely to imply different sets of potentially feasible organisational structures — that is, different constraints of morphogeny.

15. Strictly speaking, this is not a complete view of the dynamics of economic systems, for it assumes that the institutional rules which constrain both these spheres of behaviour are exogenously given and constant. In order to develop this view further, IR should also be recognised as possibly

evolving, e.g. through changes of legislation and/or custom. This type of dynamics, appropriately denoted as 'institutional', would pay attention to yet another sphere of units' behaviour — namely, their proposing, accepting or refusing changes of IR. While keeping open the possibility for such an extension of analysis, the present chapter is limited to organisational dynamics, examining the respective ways of different *given* IRs to channel organisational processes, and thereby to form OSs of different qualities.

16. A simple computer analogy may help to clarify this concept. As is generally known, one distinguishes between 'software' information which a computer can receive by its inputs, including both data and certain programs, and the 'hardware' information, embedded in its construction. The latter consists of built-in programs and parameters, which is what must be contained in the structure of any information processing system, in order to enable it to receive and act upon a certain software. Intuitively, 'software' corresponds to communicable information which can be handled by allocational processes, and 'hardware' to the tacit knowledge which must pre-exist within the organisational structure running these processes, which must be handled by organisational processes.

17. This indicates a way in which the traditional theory of human capital, which assumes this capital to be homogeneous, could introduce considerations for non-homogeneity, and thus avoid the criticism raised by Ysander (1978).

18. The competition referred to here is of the dynamic type whose main task is to reveal information which could not be revealed otherwise, as recently studied, in a slightly different context, by Nalebuff and Stiglitz (1983).

19. The paradigm of biology gives here the right intuition: an entrepreneur more closely resembles the enzyme in a biochemical reaction than the constructor of a machine. The believers in self-managed socialism who expect the theories of self-organisation to support their beliefs should note that even a cooperative, administered in the most democratic way once it has been formed, required an entrepreneur to initiate its formation.

20. See e.g. Groves (1973) and Ross (1973).

21. In other words, the problem of incentives is seen here as a *design problem* in the sense of Simon (1969), which a positive theory can help clarify but not fully solve. Similarly as no chess manual can tell how to become a chess master, no positive theory of incentives can tell how to design and implement a high-quality incentive scheme for a specific group of people in a specific environment. And similarly as there is no other way to tell excellent chess players from the mediocre ones than by letting them play a tournament, the present argument claims that there is no other way to recognise the talented designers of incentives than through competition (contests) and selection.

22. While the works in the Schumpeterian tradition often treat technological and organisational innovations together, the present approach makes a clear distinction between the two and focuses on the latter (cf. p. 37).

23. Obviously, this is nothing more than one possible way of describing the well-known logic of a general evolutionary process without an omniscient creator. For instance, Schumpeter (1942) denotes trial-

generation as 'innovation' or 'creation', and error-elimination as 'destruction'. Modern writers, such as Nelson and Winter (1982), often use the biological terms 'mutations' and 'selection'. The presently proposed terminology seems to have the advantage of being intuitively transparent in various economic problems, while clearly marking that the discussion is not about social-Darwinism or sociobiology.

24. As Professor Hirschman has pointed out to me, it is much easier to observe empirically the first type of failure than the second. While this is undeniably a drawback of the suggested concept, I believe that we must learn to live with it, for the poorer observability of the second type of failures does not at all imply lesser losses imposed on the economies which suffer from them. One way in which we can try to cope with this drawback is to replace some empirical observations by mental experiments and logical deductions. More precisely, we can try to deduce the fate which a hypothetical talented entrepreneur would meet in different economic systems, and thus discover which systems are more likely to suffer from absent successes than others. In this way we can clearly distinguish the cases when the lack of talented entrepreneurs is due to the socio-cultural environment, from the cases when the system itself would make it difficult for talented entrepreneurs, even if they were abundant, to make themselves useful.

25. The concept of contestable private enterprise is closely related, but not identical, to the one of contestable markets as introduced by Baumol, Panzar and Willig (1982). To recall, such markets are defined by zero costs of both entry and exit. In contrast, contestable private enterprise only provides the necessary institutional framework for the formation of such markets, by not imposing any institutional constraints on either entry or exit. The actual formation of such markets may, however, be impaired for various other reasons, such as positive costs of entry or scarcity of entrepreneurship.

26. An interesting study of the differences between private enterprise and government concerning their ways of running selection processes (contests) is in Forte (1982).

27. A part of Hirschman's argument is, however, that 'exit' should not be too easy, for it discourages 'voice', which he sees as an important tool in attempts to save failing organisations. It is therefore important to stress that this is no argument in favour of centralised entrepreneurship. As he emphatically notes, if 'exit' is impossible, there are no incentives to listen to 'voice'. Moreover, Hirschman's argument seems to be biased in favour of 'voice', because it does not consider the alternative of 'entry' — that is, the formation of new organisations replacing some of the current ones. But as soon as the possibility of 'entry' is considered, 'exit' appears less alarming. The value of 'voice' then depends on the talents (abilities to learn) of the failing organisations as compared to the talents of the potential newcomers: obviously, one should not waste too much effort on 'voice' for an organisation which cannot adapt, if new, better organisations could appear in its place.

28. The argument that economic analysis cannot attribute any substantial advantage of private enterprise in comparison with some alternative systems is advanced by Nelson (1981). In Pelikan (1985) I qualify

this argument by showing that it is true only as long as economic analysis is limited to organisational statics, while quite a different story can be disclosed by organisational dynamics.

REFERENCES

Alchian, A.A. (1950), 'Uncertainty, Evolution and Economic Theory', *Journal of Political Economy* 58: 211–22.

Baumol, W.J., Panzar, J.C. and Willig, R.D. (1982), *Contestable Markets and the Theory of Industry Structure*, San Diego: Harcourt Brace Jovanovich.

Buchanan, J.M. and Tollison, R.D. (eds) (1972), *Theory of Public Choice*, Ann Arbor: University of Michigan Press.

——— Tollison, R.D. and Tullock, G. (eds) 1980), *Towards a Theory of the Rent-Seeking Society*, College Station, Texas: A & M University Press.

Forte, F. (1982), 'The Law of Selection in the Public Economy as Compared to the Market Economy', *Public Finance* 27: 224–45.

Gould, S. and Levontin, R. (1979), 'The Spandrels of San Marco and the Panglossian Paradigm: a Critique of the Adaptationist Paradigm', *Proceedings of Royal Society Ser. B.* 205, 581–98.

Greffe, X. (1981), *Analyse Economique de la Bureaucratie*, Paris: Economica.

Groves, T. (1973), 'Incentives in Teams', *Econometrica* 41: 617–31.

Hayek, F.A. (1967), *Studies In Philosophy, Politics, and Economics*, Chicago: University of Chicago Press, and London: Routledge and Kegan Paul.

——— (1973), *Law, Legislation and Liberty*, Chicago: University of Chicago Press, and London: Routledge and Kegan Paul.

Hirschman, A.O. (1970), *Exit, Voice, and Loyalty: Responses to Decline in Firms, Organisations and States*, Cambridge, Mass.: Harvard University Press.

Hurwicz, L. (1971), 'Centralization and Decentralization in Economic Processes', in *Comparison of Economic Systems*, A. Eckstein (ed.), Berkeley: University of California Press.

Kirzner, I.M. (1973), *Competition and Entrepreneurship*, Chicago and London: The University of Chicago Press.

——— (1981), '"The Austrian" Perspective on the Crisis', in D. Bell and I. Kristol (eds) *The Crisis in Economic Theory*, New York: Basic Books.

Loeb, M. and Magat, W.A. (1978), 'Success Indicators in the Soviet Union: The Problem of Incentives and Efficient Allocation', *American Economic Review* 68: 173–81.

Nalebuff, B.J. and Stiglitz, J.E. (1983), 'Information, Competition, and Markets', *American Economic Review* 83: 278–83.

Nelson, R.R. (1981), 'Assessing Private Enterprise: an Exegesis of Tangled Doctrine', *The Bell Journal of Economics* 12: 93–111.

——— and Winter, S.G. (1982), *An Evolutionary Theory of Economic Change*, Cambridge, Mass: Harvard University Press.

Niskanen, W.A. (1971), *Bureaucracy and Representative Government*, Chicago: Atherton Aldine.

North, D.C. and Thomas, R.P. (1973), *The Rise of the Western World*, Cambridge: Cambridge University Press.
Nove, A. (1977), *The Soviet Economic System*, London: Allen and Unwin.
Olson, M. (1982), *The Rise and Decline of Nations*, New Haven: Yale University Press.
Ordover, J.A. and Willig, R.D. (1981), 'An Economic Definition of Predation: Pricing and Product Innovation', *Yale Law Journal* 91.
Pelikan, P. (1969) 'Language as a Limiting Factor for Centralization', *American Economic Review* 59: 625–31.
―――― (1985), 'Private Enterprise *vs.* Government Control: An Organizationally Dynamic Comparison', Working Paper No. 137, Industriens Utredningsinstitut, Stockholm.
Polanyi, M. (1967), *The Tacit Dimension*, Garden City, N.Y.; Doubleday Anchor.
Ross, S. (1973), 'The Economic Theory of Agency: The Principal's Problem', *American Economic Review*, 63: 134–9.
Schumpeter, J. (1934), *Theory of Economic Development*, Cambridge, Mass: Harvard University Press.
―――― (1942), *Capitalism, Socialism and Democracy*, New York: Harper and Row; Harper Colophon Edition, 1976.
Simon, H. (1969), *The Sciences of the Artificial*, Cambridge, Mass.: MIT Press.
Williamson, O.E. (1975), *Markets and Hierarchies: Analysis and Anti-trust Implications*, New York: Free Press.
―――― (1981), 'The Modern Corporation: Origins, Evolutions, Attributes', *Journal of Economic Literature* 19: 1537–68.
―――― (1985), *The Economic Institutions of Capitalism*, New York: Free Press and London: Collier Macmillan.
Winter, S.G. (1971), 'Satisficing, Selection, and the Innovating Remnant', *Quarterly Journal of Economics* 85: 237–61.
Ysander, B.C. (1978), 'Homogeneity in Education', in *Learning and Earning: Three Essays in the Economics of Education*, National Board of Universities and Colleges, Stockholm: Liber.
Zeleny, M. (ed.) (1980), *Autopoiesis, Dissipative Structures, and Spontaneous Social Orders*, AAAS Selected Symposia Series, Boulder, Col.: Westview Press.

2
Incentives to Share Knowledge and Risk: An Aspect of the Japanese Industrial Organisation

Masahiko Aoki

In neoclassical economics, two types of information (allocational) mechanisms have been studied in earnest: the market mechanism and the hierarchy. Each of these mechanisms is supported by, and in turn reinforces, respective incentive structures of competitive and administrative rewards. Each mechanism has inherent resource misallocation problems motivated by its associated incentive structure. Problems that arise within the context of the market mechanism have been analysed in detail in the market failure literature, while problems that arise in the context of a hierarchy have been analysed within the theoretical framework of the principal-agency relationship. But the two information incentive pairs, albeit intended as theoretical prototypes, do not seem to exhaust important classes of information-incentive combinations. I submit that there is another important theoretical prototype: that of information-*cum*-outcome-sharing.

This chapter argues that this third type, although mixed with the other two in practice, is indeed important in a certain industrial context. Specifically, I submit below that some aspects of Japanese industrial organisation can be understood better by referring to the third prototype. For this purpose, this chapter begins with a description of some stylised facts about Japanese industrial organisation which cannot comfortably rest with the traditional dichotomy of the market and the hierarchy. The chapter then formalises the observed stylised facts into a theoretical information-systematic model and discusses how that information system is supported by a unique incentive structure. This information system operates on the basis of information sharing of participants, and incentive-wise is supported by outcome- and risk-sharing among the participants.

SOME STYLISED OBSERVATIONS

Workshop

In a typical workshop of a Japanese factory, individual workers are graded into a number of promotional classes depending on their years of employment and general skill qualifications, and are paid accordingly. However, the assignment of workers to particular jobs is not as rigid nor as specified as under the Anglo-American job classification schemes stipulated in collective agreements. Particularly when unforeseen events occur (such as the breakdown of machines, unexpected absenteeism, unusually high defective rate, emergence of bottlenecks, etc.), remedies are often sought *ad hoc* in the workshop, without exclusively relying upon the specialised services of engineers, maintenance men, relief workers, inspectors, and the like. This *ad hoc* and informal nature of job assignments has been developed into a formal job rotation scheme, typically observed in the auto and steel industries. The scheme is succinctly described by Koike (1984).

In this scheme, a team composed of experienced as well as inexperienced workers is allotted to a cluster of jobs and it is the task of the sub-foreman, who leads the team, to rotate members among the jobs. The rotation of jobs occurs monthly, weekly or even twice daily depending on the conventions of the shop. In many cases, an inexperienced worker may be assigned to a relatively difficult job alongside someone more experienced. This practice facilitates an intergenerational transmission of skills. The rotation of jobs can be understood as a means to make workers familiar with various aspects of the work process, thereby enhancing the team's on-the-spot problem-solving capability.

In sum, within the workshop organisation of the Japanese factory, the achievement of efficiency through collective knowledge-sharing within the team is given greater emphasis than the development of specialised, yet compartmentalised, skills in individual workers.

Inter-shop coordination

The production, procurement and sales activities of the firm are carried out separately by the various shops and departments. The outcome of the activities of each operational unit are normally affected by unpredictable and uncertain factors, such as a shift in consumer taste, machinery malfunctions, delays in the delivery of materials, etc. In order to achieve cost-efficiency, the activities of the various shops and departments must be coordinated in response to those events as they happen. One way of doing this is for management to centralise information concerning emergent events, and utilising professional knowledge concerning the whole work process, devise a solution which is compatible with the organisational purpose. This centralised solution is then decomposed into specific directions to relevant shops and departments, and is expected to be implemented there as directed. The method normally operating within the western firm is essentially of this kind.

In a typical large Japanese firm, a somewhat different coordinating mechanism seems to be operating, as exemplified by the well-publicised *kanban* system of the Toyota factories. The term *kanban* refers literally to a card in a plastic envelope, used for ordering materials, tools, parts or finished goods from immediate upstream shops or suppliers. The order must be fulfilled at a specific time of the day or the following day to minimise the need of in-process inventory. Therefore, this system is sometimes referred to as the 'zero inventory method'. In this system, inter-shop coordination is performed not through a centralisation of information and computation, but rather through a horizontal flow of information and mutual adjustment of activities between neighbouring shops. While one could argue that a lack of centralisation might hinder the achievement of a 'first-best' solution, in practice the *kanban* system has contributed greatly to cost reduction in auto and other industries by reducing inventory, discovering defects and bottlenecks quickly, allowing for rapid adjustment of product lines to changes in the consumer market, and reducing managerial personnel, etc.

It should be pointed out that in order for the *kanban* system to be workable, it is critical that neighbouring shops share information concerning relevant technology and emergent events. Otherwise strategic haggling by each shop to take advantage of the ignorance of other shops in an effort to save its own effort expenditures, etc. may hinder the achievement of overall efficiency. I shall come back to this point later.

Relational contracting

Another important characteristic of Japanese industrial organisation is found in the supplier–manufacturer relationship. The degree of integration of the Japanese firm is normally low when compared to that of the western firm. For instance, a joint US–Japan study of the auto industry estimates that, in the United States, 45 per cent of a car's purchased value is provided by primary manufacturers and their wholly-owned subsidiaries, the rest being provided by outside suppliers. This compares to about 25 per cent made in-house for Japanese manufacturers.[1] On the other hand, Japanese primary manufacturers normally maintain stable long-run relationships with a relatively small number of suppliers rather than enter into spot market transactions with suppliers chosen from a relatively large number of competitors. We may call this long-term relationship *relational contracting*, in contrast to spot contracting.

Often cited as the reason for integration is the reduction of transaction costs caused by the opportunistic and strategic behaviour of separately owned sellers and buyers when either must make transaction-specific investments. But excessive integration may be accompanied by its own economic costs — for example, those caused by the removal of 'high-powered market incentives' (Williamson) and increasing information handling in an administrative framework. On the other hand, there may be less opportunistic and strategic behaviour under non-integration if both parties share information regarding emergent events and how these might affect each other's technological conditions. Both parties may then reciprocate cooperative behaviour as need based on shared knowledge.

Two major types of relational contracting exist in Japan. One type is between two large manufacturers, such as between a steel manufacturer and an auto manufacturer. A variant of relational contracting of this type is found between a financial institution, such as a bank and an insurance company on the one hand, and a non-financial company on the other. The other type is between a relatively large manufacturer and a relatively smaller supplier. This relationship is customarily referred to as the subcontracting relationship and the latter agent as the subcontractor.

Two types of *corporate groupings* emerge from these two types of relational contracting. One is a group of major companies connected to each other directly or indirectly through a transactional network and/or connected to common member bank(s) through relational contracting. The other is a group of subcontractors and subsidiaries connected to a primary, parent company. The former group is formalised by the formation of the President Club of member companies. The second group is formalised by the association of cooperating companies (*kyoryoku kigyo kai*) of a major company. Neither organisation is a legal entity like a corporation, but is socially visible by explicit membership. There are six major President Clubs in Japan, and almost all major non-financial companies organise their own associations of cooperating companies.[2]

The first type of groupings have their genesis in the old *zaibatsu* groups which were consolidated by family-owned holding companies and managed by professional managers loyal to the families. Those old *zaibatsu* connections undoubtedly still provide the basis of mutual trust in spite of the outlawing of holding companies and purging of *zaibatsu* managers in the Post-War Reform. Even though transactional relationships between member firms in this type of grouping may not be as coherent as in the case of the second type of grouping (except for a bank and non-financial company), the exchange of knowledge concerning general business conditions and new business opportunities mutually relevant to member firms seems to be still the most important function of the President Clubs.

In the second type of groupings, the relationship between the primary manufacturer and the subcontractor is normally forged only through a long-term trial-and-error process. Those subcontractors who cannot consistently meet cost and quality standards are denied further relational contracting, while promising subcontractors are given assistance in terms of funds, technological know-how, etc. and nurtured to be effective members of a group. Mutual efforts for research and development between prime manufacturer and subcontractor may be cited as conspicuous evidence for mutual trust and knowledge-sharing existing between them.[3]

I have described certain stylised facts about Japanese industrial organisation at different levels: the shop level, the firm level and the inter-firm level. I should now like to extract a common feature from them from an informational systematic point of view and discuss what type of incentive structure can support such an informational system. My hope is to clarify the *raison d'être* of this information system in terms of efficiency, in contrast to the prototype market and hierarchy.

THE SHARING OF KNOWLEDGE

What is the most important common characteristic of the above stylised facts about the Japanese industrial organisation? I consider it the ability to adapt to unexpected day-to-day events and to coordinate activities swiftly, based on knowledge-sharing among relevant operational units as opposed to hierarchical control over specialised jobs.

Let us look into this particular feature more systematically from the informational-systematic theory point of view. First, look at the internal structure of the firm — on the shopfloor as well as between shopfloors — and compare the information-handling mechanism operating there with the conventional model of hierarchical information-handling. In doing so, let us remember that our focus is only on the mechanism associated with operational adjustments, leaving aside the important dynamic process of strategic decision-making such as for investment and R & D.

In the conventional model of a hierarchy, constituent units (individuals or shops) of the system are supposed to be specialised in a particular type of knowledge, and the flow of information between constituent units necessary to accomplish the organisational goal is supposed to be intermediated only by a superordinate (the foreman or the management). The superordinate receives information from subordinates and monitors necessary information at the subordinate level. On the basis of that information he computes signals to be transmitted to the subordinates, usually in the form of quantity directives (such as assignments of organisational resources, output directives, etc.). A possible informational advantage of this pure hierarchy (the tree structure) is the centralisation of information which is necessary in order to compute a set of activities for constituent units so that the organisational goal may be achieved. A centralisation of information and computation is not costless, however, as I shall comment on shortly.

In contrast, some aspects of the information system of the Japanese firm may be characterised by semi-autonomous and localised problem-solving, as well as semi-horizontal coordination. I have formulated this idea into a rigorous mathematical model elsewhere (1986), but without going into detailed technicalities, the essential idea may be described as follows.

The whole system is composed of small groups of constituent units (say, teams or groups of shops) connected by transactional relationships. Suppose that the organisational goal is also decomposed into sub-goals accordingly. (I shall discuss shortly how this decomposition is related to the incentive structure.) Those constituent units within a subgroup exchange information horizontally, as new events reach them, and compute jointly relevant transactional quantities necessary for the approximation of the sub-goal under changing environments. Those constituent units are possibly ignorant of, or at most able to utilise only partially, information regarding events occurring outside the subgroup. The lack of centralisation of information and computation means that the resulting transactional plan will not be the first best, but it may be able to outperform the hierarchical system in other respects: the first-hand response to unexpected events (shocks) may be faster by saving on information exchange time, and on-the-spot knowledge may be utilised more precisely and usefully.

The performance of this *semi-autonomous problem-solving cum semi-horizontal coordination* seems to depend critically upon two factors: the degree of the ability of constituent units within subgroups of the system to understand jointly mutually relevant technology, and the appropriateness of decomposition of the organisational goal to sub-goals of subgroups. In connection with the first factor, one may note that the practice of 'lifetime' employment at the Japanese firm is a device to serve precisely the purpose of facilitating team-oriented learning-by-doing.

Relational contracting (corporate grouping) lies somewhere between complete integration and the market, and shares some common aspects with each of them in its information-systematic characteristics. But there are contrasting aspects as well. If we contrast corporate grouping with the neoclassical model of complete integration, a similar observation as concerning the semi-autonomous problem-solving *cum* semi-horizontal coordination on the one hand, and the pure hierarchy on the other hand, may be tenable. That is, the neoclassical model of complete integration may be modelled as the pure hierarchy, whereas informational exchange among members of corporate groups may be characterised as the semi-autonomous problem-solving and semi-horizontal coordination. Information is less centralised in the corporate group than in the hierarchically-structured, integrated firm. In the case of the subcontracting relationship, there is a certain degree of centralisation of information and computation on the side of the prime manufacturer, but that degree is still limited, especially when the subcontractor possesses transaction-specific knowledge not readily available elsewhere. The possible advantages of this semi-horizontal subcontracting relationship *vis-à-vis* hierarchical integration would be quick adaptation to external shocks and the precise local utilisation of knowledge, although it has its own shortcomings, as noted already, resulting from the lack of centralisation.

If relational contracting is contrasted with the market on the other hand, the former may be characterised by the specificity of knowledge involved in the relation. In the market-place, private knowledge concerning preferences and technologies of individual agents are summarised and aggregated in the form of prices before being utilised socially. Price signals are anonymous. In contrast, in a system of relational contracting, quantities and prices are normally negotiated as a pair, or very often a quantity specification proceeds and price is negotiated on the basis of quantity specification (see Asanuma, 1985). In this bilateral negotiation, a certain degree of mutual knowledge-sharing concerning each other's characteristics (technology and/or preference) seems necessary if an efficient outcome is to result and if the relationship is expected to continue. This is in contrast to the market mechanism in which the only socially shared information is in the form of prices.

What incentives lead to the extensive utilisation of relational contracting in Japan? In other words, what incentives promote the sharing of knowledge not available in a pure market setting? Are the incentives operating under relational contracting expected to lead to a more efficient outcome than under the pure hierarchy or the pure market? If so, under what conditions?

THE SHARING OF OUTCOME WITHIN THE FIRM

If a semi-autonomous, semi-horizontal information system based on knowledge-sharing can perform better than the hierarchy and the market under certain conditions, the sharing of the outcome (surplus of revenues over costs) among the bearers of the system would be an important incentive. Further, sharing of the outcome would motivate the bearers to promote conditions favourable to the better performance of the system as a whole. Since an important condition for bettering the performance in the semi-autonomous, semi-horizontal information system is the sharing of knowledge among constituent units, one may say then that the sharing of knowledge and the sharing of outcome are dual to each other.

First, consider the remuneration scheme for individual employees in the firm. As already mentioned, the payment to the worker is not specifically linked to his job, as in the western firm. Rather, he is paid according to his years of service to the firm as well as to the skills and knowledge he has obtained, which need not be specifically related to a narrowly defined job but relevant to effective participation in the semi-horizontal coordination mechanism. The ability to communicate with fellow employees, for example, is a skill that is taken into account in promotional decision-making.

Also note should be taken of the fact that the biannual payment of bonuses and the lump-sum compensation payment at the time of mandatory retirement constitute very important components of remuneration to employees.[4] The bonus payment is not, as is often misunderstood by western observers, simply current profit-sharing. The yearly bonus adjustment is synchronised more with the base salary/wage and its amount is relatively inelastic to the business fluctuations of current profit. Therefore, the employee regards a substantial portion of his bonus as part of his salary/wage payment and not as profit-sharing. However, if the firm's profit remains low for consecutive accounting periods, it is expected that the amount of bonus relative to base salary/wage will be adjusted downwards, if not in proportion to profit. To determine how much of the bonus payment is regarded as permanent income and how much is regarded as transitory income requires a careful statistical study. But I conjecture, tentatively, that there is a statistically significant correlation between the average performance of the firm over a period of years and the average amount of bonus paid to the employee.[5]

The correlation between the profit performance of the firm in the long run and the amount of retirement lump-sum compensation payment is more dramatic. According to a survey, the lifetime employee of a large firm receives a lump-sum payment worth more than three years' salary/wages at the time of compulsory retirement.[6] Reserves for retirement compensation can be accumulated within the firm free of tax up to 40 per cent of the total composite obligation, under the assumption that every employee retires at the end of the accounting period. The reserves are recorded as a liability of the company and used at the discretion of the management. In fact, they constitute a non-negligible source for non-taxable internal funds.[7] Although the employees' claim for retirement compensation has priority over any other claim (including taxes at the time of the company's reorganisation under bankruptcy law), if the company actually does go bankrupt, the employees may not be able to collect the full amount of quasi-contractual retirement compensation. This contrasts with the western case in which pension benefits are funded outside the employing company and are often transferable and free of firm-specific risk.

The above observation may entertain the following hypothesis: A part of the employee's lifetime compensation is linked, in the long run, to the performance of the employing firm and involves sharing in costs of, as well as returns to, investments in firm-specific skills and knowledge. The cost is partly borne by the firm in the form of financial expenditures as well as efficiency losses due to the training of inexperienced workers in the context of teamwork, and partly borne by the employee in the form of lower compensation at the beginning of his career within the firm. As the employee accumulates more knowledge and skills relevant to the operation of the semi-autonomous, semi-horizontal information structure of the firm, benefits accrue to him in the form of seniority premium and retirement compensation.

In order to promote knowledge-sharing relevant to the operation of the semi-autonomous, semi-horizontal information structure, and in order to discourage the earlier exit of the employee, the age profile of the salary/wage scale is steeper than the age profile of accumulated skills and knowledge. The employee's skills and knowledge may be ranked according to the degree of his contribution to team-work and the semi-autonomous problem-solving by the team. These involve not only skills specific to a particular job, but also involve a wider understanding of the whole context of the job and the ability to communicate effectively with other members in a team. In this sense then, it may be said that the Japanese employee is paid according to his 'contextual skills'.

The compensation scheme, as described above, would certainly make the employee more conscious of the company's overall performance, particularly its long-run viability and competitiveness, than under the competitive scheme in which the rate of remuneration to individual employees is determined in reference to the market rate. The compensation scheme also provides appropriate incentives for the employee not only to develop a specific skill, but also to participate cooperatively in the semi-autonomous, semi-horizontal information structure, particularly to share knowledge useful for its efficient operation. But I should probably anticipate the following questions from neoclassically trained economists: if the remuneration of the employee is partly linked to the company's performance, will it not yield a free-rider problem? Even if just one employee shirks, will it not noticeably be recognised as reducing the productivity of teamwork? Consequently will everybody not be induced to shirk and, as a result, be trapped in the Prisoner's Dilemma of poorer collective performance?

Okuno (1984) advanced a hypothesis that mutual monitoring by employees and the 'ostracism' of a shirker from the team is the important monitoring mechanism in the Japanese firm, and he built an elaborate game-theoretic model on this assumption to prove that mutual monitoring is effective for forestalling the Prisoner's Dilemma. Since the contextual skills are acquired over a long period of time at various jobs, the evaluation of employees can be conducted on a long-term basis by a large number of superordinates. The long-run evaluation of subordinates by multiple superordinates, together with the reciprocal evaluation of superordinates by subordinates for the effectiveness of their leadership, may be interpreted as having an element of mutual monitoring. Considering the degree of knowledge-sharing built into the Japanese firm, it seems reasonable to conclude that such 'mutual monitoring' is, in fact, relatively effective in preventing shirking compared to job-specialisation schemes.

The remuneration schedule which increases over time makes the cost of shirking in mid-career extremely high.[8] One possible problem with this incentive scheme is that employees who have failed to advance may be induced to shirk towards the end of their career, because their shirking, even if known, may not affect their quasi-contracted end-of-period benefits, including retirement compensation, in the normal course of affairs. In the Japanese firm, however, seniority rights as regards lay-off are not institutionally established as in the American unionised firm, and it is often senior employees who are the most vulnerable to lay-off, when needed. This practice may have the effect of mitigating the incentive of senior employees to shirk.[9]

THE SHARING OF RISK IN RELATIONAL CONTRACTING

Granted that the dual sharing of information and outcome reinforce each other within the firm level, this structure creates one problem: The very fact that the employee's wealth can be accumulated only gradually during his 'life-time' association with the firm, specifically in the form of a potential claim for retirement compensation, implies that a substantial portion of his wealth is not saleable at his discretion until the last stage of his career, which is the time of his mandatory retirement. Thus a substantial portion of his wealth is strongly associated with the company's performance. This non-saleability condition might make the manager and the employee of the firm behave in a risk-averse manner, unless there is an alternative mechanism compensating for the lack of risk-diversification on the capital market by individuals according to their own risk preferences. How is this non-diversification problem dealt with in the Japanese economy? In connection with this problem, I shall now discuss the incentive scheme operating in the context of relational contracting.

The sharing of outcome is also prevalent in relational contracting. In the subcontracting relationship, as an excellent field study by Asanuma (1985) shows, the price of intermediate goods supplied by the subcontractor is fixed for a certain period of time, while the quantity of goods supplied is adjustable depending on the current market condition of the final products of the primary manufacturer. Price is negotiable at regular intervals, normally twice a year. When the demand for the final products of the primary manufacturer fails to meet expectations, the price of intermediate goods supplied by the subcontractor may be adjusted, even upwards, to cover fixed costs incurred in transaction-specific investments committed by the subcontractor. In this way, the profit fluctuation may be borne by both parties. In such cases, the traditional stereotyped notion that the primary manufacturer utilises the subcontractor as a business-cycle buffer does not seem to be warranted.

The dual aspects of the subcontracting relationship have respective incentive effects. On the one hand, the market-relationship aspect of the subcontracting relationship provides quasi-market incentives for both parties not available in complete integration. On the other hand, its sharing aspect gives incentives for the joint profit-maximisation necessary for the efficiency of corporate grouping as a whole. Further, relational contracting provides insurance for the relative stability of the earnings of the participating firms.

Through this mutual insurance scheme, the permanent employees of member firms may be protected, albeit incompletely, from firm-specific risk. In other words, the inter-firm risk-sharing can be substitued for individual risk diversification on the capital market to the extent that risk characteristics of member firms are different. In the subcontracting relationship, risk characteristics of the subcontractor and the primary manufacturer may be highly correlated. But the primary manufacturer may diversify its product portfolio, and to that extent its risk cost may be relatively smaller. In such a case it will become an optimal arrangement for the parent company to absorb more fluctuation of income from a certain sub-class of products, guaranteeing more stable income to subcontractors in general, and extract a larger proportion of the resulting savings on risk costs as a sort of insurance premium.[10]

There is also a positive incentive for subcontractors to be technologically progressive. Risk-sharing among risk-averse companies (or risk-averse subcontractors and a risk-neutral primary manufacturer) generates a surplus (savings or risk costs in terms of higher expected utilities across firms) which is not possible under the competitive market mechanism. This surplus can be distributed between participating firms depending on their bargaining powers. The bargaining power of each, in turn, depends upon the potential damage that it can inflict upon the other party by withdrawing cooperation. Therefore, the subcontractor can extract greater profits by developing its own technological expertise not readily available elsewhere. Thus there is considerable motivation for the subcontractor to be technologically progressive. In fact, Japan ranks the highest in the adoption of programmable numerically-controlled machines, and more than half of those machines have been introduced by relatively small subcontractors.[11]

In addition to the opportunity for product-diversification, some larger firms enter into an implicit mutual insurance agreement with other major firms by the intermediation of major banks. In corporate grouping centring on so-called 'major' banks, member firms mutually own stock in other member firms. Specifically to be noted is that, in Japan, banks are allowed, albeit to an upper limit of 5 per cent, to own stock in non-financial corporations, and bank holdings actually account for a substantial portion of inter-firm holdings. Mutual stockholding not only provides the mutual bonds necessary for the maintenance of relational contracting, but also provides reserves which can be cashed by other member firms in case of financial difficulty. Corporate grouping thus provides an ultimate security to constituents of member firms, including the employees.

This function of corporate grouping is dramatically exemplified in the case of the bailing out of Toyo Kogyo Co., the maker of Mazda, from possible bankruptcy in the late 1970s. This company, run by a founder who had an ingenious engineering mind but exhibited a somewhat authoritarian attitude, had lost out in the highly competitive market mainly because of a failure to elicit employees' incentives. In contrast to Chrysler's case, the government's role was minimal in its turnaround, and the assistance of the

Sumitomo group, headed by the Sumitomo Bank to which the company belonged, was essential. The assistance of the group included not only the provision of emergency funds, but also the dispatch of a management team from the Sumitomo Bank and exclusive purchases of Mazda cars by member companies. After the turnaround, the management was turned over again to career-long employees promoted from within.[12] In contrast to the case of Toyo Kogyo, the recent bankruptcy of Ohsawa Shokai, a trading company, was unavoidable since it had not insured itself, by relational contracting, with a major bank.

There is significant evidence, however, that the bargaining power of banks has been eroding, in general, *vis-à-vis* other non-financial companies. This phenomenon has been occurring since the 1970s when non-financial companies gained competitive positions by diversification of their product portfolios, while banks have been under increasing competitive pressures from other financial institutions domestically as well as internationally.[13] The strengthening of the financial viability of some non-financial companies tends to make the risk-sharing function of corporate groups somewhat redundant, and there are signs of a gradual erosion of group coherence. Yet, for those member companies whose competitive positions are not strong enough, the ultimate insurance through relational contracting with banks is still deemed important. Nakatani's econometric study (1984) indicates that member companies of major corporate groups pay higher interest rates on the average than independents, while the former's performance tends to be poorer in terms of the average level of profit and growth. It may be added that relatively successful member companies are beginning to assume a more independent character, relying on themselves for investment financing, project organising, risk-bearing, etc.

One may still wonder, if corporate grouping provides the last resort insurance, whether it has negative incentive effects on the constituent firm. Particularly, since mutual stockholding in a member company by other member companies ranges on the average somewhere between 15 and 30 per cent in the six major corporate groupings, those member companies may be regarded as being effectively insulated against unfriendly takeover by outsiders. How then can the management of member companies be motivated to be competitive? Comfortably protected from the stockmarket discipline, are they not motivated to indulge in the collusive exploitation of their monopolistic positions?

It appears that competition in product markets, rather than the stockmarket, has played a key role in disciplining management against inefficient conduct, at least to date. Prior to gaining a competitive edge in international markets, those successful companies in such industries as steel, auto, electric machinery and electronics manufacturing had experienced fierce competition in corresponding domestic markets. Incumbents in those markets were contested by important new entries such as the Sumitomo Metal Manufacturing Co., Kawasaki Steel Manufacturing Co., Honda Co., Japan IBM, etc.

In this connection, it is interesting to note that corporate grouping played an important role in making Japanese markets more contestable in the 1950s and 1960s rather than the converse. In that era, the major corporate groups, which were more coherent under the stronger leadership of member banks, considered it imperative for their viability to include in their group a firm from every promising market so that they would not be forced to be dependent on other groups. Under this premise, member companies of each corporate group made concerted efforts to make it easier for each other to gain entry or to form new joint ventures, whenever there seemed to be potentially growing markets. This is what some people call the 'one set-ism' of corporate groups.[14] In addition, there was significant competition from independents who did not affiliate with any of the major corporate groupings. According to any conventional measure, the rate of market concentration of Japanese industry has in general been declining since the 1960s.[15]

Contrary to the stereotypical view that the paternalistic and enlightened government bureaucracy prepared a well-designed strategy for the penetration of Japanese industries into international markets and that Japanese companies followed in collusion, the government bureaucracy often feared 'excessive competition' in domestic markets in steel, auto and other industries brought about by private competition among corporate groupings and independents, and on some occasions even tried, in vain, to restrain new entries.

CONCLUDING REMARKS

I have described some important aspects of Japanese industrial organisation in terms of the informational structure, explained the supporting incentive structure, and characterised the essential feature as knowledge *cum* outcome (risk)-sharing. This information incentive pair is somewhat different from the neoclassical norm of the market and the hierarchy. I am not yet able to say anything definite about the macroscopic welfare implications of information- and outcome-sharing with the same rigorousness of neoclassical welfare analysis. But it still seemed worthwhile to present a consistent story of the Japanese model, if it exists, and to show that it 'works'. Hoping that this brief review has accomplished a first small step towards it, I should like to conclude by suggesting two contemporaneous, yet unresolved, issues associated with this rather unique model.

The first issue is whether or not the Japanese model is consistent with the rapid generation and diffusion of new technology and, if so, how. Conventional wisdom suggests that the system of lifetime employment is detrimental to the mobility of researchers, and thus hinders rapid technological diffusion. This theory, combined with another conventional notion that spin-offs of new venture businesses aided by the venture capital market are decisive vehicles for innovation, argues that the Japanese industrial organisation is not conducive to technological innovation without the government's active involvement.[16]

There is an alternative theory,[17] however, which holds that excessive mobility of researchers, such as is the case in the US, may result in premature leakage of research results from firms which have financed expensive research efforts. Being fearful of the possibility that quitters 'free-ride' on firm-financed innovative efforts, the firm may resort to the compartmentalisation of research activities within the firm, hindering inter-firm communication. On the other hand, under the lifetime employment system, mobility of researchers among firms is low. Japanese firms routinely encourage inter-firm mobility of personnel, however, and one might argue that the Japanese firm, therefore, actively encourages communication between the research and development department and the production department. This would facilitate the systemisation and development of potentially useful knowledge acquired through the production experience. A good case in point would be the biotechnology industry in Japan, which has come to include traditional food-processing companies striving to adapt their excellent food and amino acid fermentation techniques to the screening and breeding of new micro-organisms which have been genetically modified through the use of recombinant DNA. This may be contrasted with the western case, where the leaders in biotechnological innovation are university researchers with a more basic science orientation. Will this difference in approach to research and development between Japan and the West have any bearing on the performance characteristics of research and development? This is the first unresolved issue.

The second issue concerns the compatibility of the Japanese model with the international economic order. Japan is now among the most liberal countries in terms of tariffs, so most international criticism against the 'closedness' of Japanese markets is now directed towards non-tariff barriers. Aside from governmental regulations and licensing procedures, the practice most often cited by foreigners as a non-tariff barrier is nothing but relational contracting, or the long-term business association, among Japanese firms. We have seen that relational contracting in Japan has developed both as an efficient informational structure based on knowledge-sharing and as a risk-sharing device which supports the 'lifetime' employment system. On the other hand, the neoclassical dichotomy of market-hierarchy seems to be the consequence of the emphasis on specialism in the West. That is, specialisation and standardisation of jobs results in a relatively homogeneous competitive market for each job, on the one hand, and requires the integration of specialised jobs as a specialised function of management, on the other.

Thus there seems to be two different approaches to knowledge: knowledge-sharing, underlying the Japanese model, and specialism, underlying the neoclassical dichotomy of the market-hierarchy. In my opinion, the current trade dispute between the West and Japan may not be ultimately resolvable until we find a way to symbiose and/or synthesise the two approaches. As the Japanese firm becomes truly multinational, will it be able to adapt itself to diverse cultural environments? Will there be any aspect of the Japanese model from which the western firm can learn to increase its efficiency? Will the development of information technology assist the process of symbiosis and possible synthesis? These are but some of the questions which have emerged from the comparative analysis of Japan and the West.

NOTES

1. See Cole and Yakushiji (1984), pp. 153–4; also Aoki (1984b), pp. 26–7.
2. For the two types of corporate groupings, see the introductory chapter of Aoki (1984b).

3. For joint research and development between the prime manufacturer and the subcontractor, see a series of works by Asanuma summarised in (1985).
4. See Aoki (1984b) Chapters 1, 5 and 11 for the bonus scheme and the retirement compensation (*taishoku-kin*) scheme.
5. See Ishikawa and Ueda (1984) for a statistical decomposition of bonuses to the transitory component and the permanent component.
6. A survey of retirement compensations done by the Institute of Research in Labour Administration in 1979.
7. See Aoki (1984b), Chapter 1.
8. This is nothing but a familiar point raised by Lazear (1979) and others.
9. I owe this point to Philip Branson.
10. See Aoki (1984b), appendix to Chapter 7; and Aoki (1984a), Chapter 2.
11. An unpublished survey by the Ministry of International Trade and Industry.
12. A fascinating account of the cause of the decline of the Toyo Kogyo Co. as well as the role of the Sumitomo group in its resurgence, may be found in Pascale and Rohlen (1983).
13. See Aoki (1984b), Chapter 5.
14. See Miyazaki (1976).
15. See Uekusa (1982).
16. Such a viewpoint is expressed by Saxonhouse (1984).
17. This view is articulated by Kenney (1984).

REFERENCES

Aoki, M. (1984a), *The Cooperative Game Theory of the Firm*, Oxford: Oxford University Press.
—— (ed.) (1984b), *The Economic Analysis of the Japanese Firm*, Amsterdam: North-Holland.
—— (1986), 'Horizontal vs. Vertical Information Structure of the Firm', *American Economic Review*.
Asanuma, B. (1985), 'The Organization of Parts Purchase in the Japanese Automotive Industry', *Japanese Economic Studies*, Summer, 32–53.
Cole, R.E. and Yakushiji, T. (1984), *The American and Japanese Auto Industries in Transition*, Center for Japanese Studies, University of Michigan.
Ishikawa, T. and Ueda, K. (1984), 'The Bonus Payment System and Japanese Personal Savings', in Aoki (ed.) (1984b), 133–92.
Kenney, M. (1984), 'Some Observations of the Structure of the U.S. and Japanese Biotechnology Industries', Ohio State University, mimeo.
Koike, K. (1984), 'Skill Formation Systems in the US and Japan: A Comparative Study', in Aoki (ed.) (1984b), 47–75.
Lazear, E.P. (1979), 'Why Is There Mandatory Retirement', *Journal of Political Economy*, 87, 1261–84.
Miyazaki, Y. (1976), *Sengo Nihon no Kigyo Shudan (Corporate Groups in*

Post-War Japan), Nihon Keizai Shinbun.
Nakatani, I. (1984), 'The Economic Role of Financial Corporate Grouping', in Aoki (1984b), 227-58.
Okuno, M. (1984), 'Corporate Loyalty and Bonus Payments: An Analysis of Work Incentives in Japan', in Aoki (1984b), 387-41.
Pascale, R. and Rohlen, T.R. (1983), 'The Mazda Turnaround', *Journal of Japanese Studies*, 9, 219-63.
Saxonhouse, G. (1984), 'Industrial Policy and Factor Markets: Biotechnology in Japan and the United States', mimeo, University of Michigan.
Uekusa, M. (1982), *Industrial Organization* (in Japanese), Chikuma-Shobo.
Williamson, O.E. (1985), *Economic Institutions of Capitalism*, New York: Free Press.

Part Two

Incentives and the Command Economy

3
Labour Incentives and Collective Wage Systems in Soviet Industry

Hans Aage

INCENTIVE MECHANISMS

Although the Kosygin reform of 1965 could rightly be characterised as abortive or as a 'reform that never was',[1] the official belief in its basic rationale has nevertheless persisted, namely that decentralised decision-making could be substantially improved within the existing planning system by means of well-designed incentives and economic responsibility. There is a line of continuity from Kosygin's complaint, that '*Khozraschet* is largely of a formal character',[2] to Brezhnev's dictum: 'The economy must be economical — that is dictated by the times',[3] and to Gorbachev's recent call for 'introducing full *khozraschet*, and on this basis, for enhancing the responsibility, as well as the interest, of the collective and of the individual worker, for the final results of work.'[4]

The concept of *khozraschet* dates back to the NEP period. It means 'economic accounting', and for enterprises and other economic units operating according to *khozraschet*, it implies that money expenditures should be covered by revenues. But the exact content of the principle remains obscure.

During this twenty-year period a variety of measures with the aim of strengthening *khozraschet* have been discussed, implemented more or less, and abandoned again. Only some of these will be considered here.

The incentive mechanisms considered below deal with Soviet industry, management (certain input and output decisions) as well as workers (everyday work effort), and material incentives (wages and bonuses from the material incentive fund) exclusively. However, the bonus-making mechanism is simplified very much in the models. As summarised by Bornstein,[5] this mechanism:

has a number of elements: (1) 'fund-forming' indicators, results regarding which secure the allocation of money to the material incentive fund; (2) a 'base' indicator, some measure of enterprise activity to which it is deemed appropriate to relate the size of the material incentive fund; (3) a set of coefficients (normatives) expressing, as a percentage of this 'base', the amount to be paid to the material incentive fund for a given result on each fund-forming indicator; (4) 'fund-correcting' indicators, performance regarding which can reduce the payments to the material incentive fund otherwise due from the combination of the first three elements; (5) the source of money for the material incentive fund; and (6) the rules for the disbursement of the material incentive fund among the personnel of the enterprise.

Furthermore, rules differ considerably between industries and between enterprises. These differences are neglected, as well as points (4) and (5) in the quotation above, and the description of the other elements is simplified.

The main focus of analysis is effects upon labour productivity, which has been of major concern to Soviet economic policy. But the most important determinant of labour productivity is not considered, i.e. fixed capital formation. According to investigations by Cohn,[6] capital productivity is declining in both major western economies and in the USSR but more so in the USSR, whereas the USSR is close to the western mainstream concerning increases in labour productivity which are positive but diminishing.[7] The productivity determinants considered are the number of workers in the enterprise and the effort supplied by each worker,[8] which are decided by the enterprise management and the individual worker, respectively. The interaction between these two types of decision-making is studied by means of simple, formal models. The basic assumptions are as follows:

1. The enterprise produces one output (Q) using labour (L) and capital (K) as inputs, according to the production function

$$Q = Q(L,K); \quad Q_L > 0, \quad Q_K > 0; \quad Q_{LL} < 0,$$
$$Q_{KK} < 0; \quad Q_{LK} > 0$$

(cf. the list of symbols below).

2. Total labour (L) equals the number of workers (n) multiplied by the effort (ℓ) supplied by each worker:

$$L = n\ell$$

3. All workers are identical with regard to utility functions and supply the same type of effort.

4. Workers choose effort (ℓ) individually in order to maximise utility (U), which depends on income (y) and effort (ℓ):

$$U = U(y,\ell); \; U_y > 0, \; U_\ell < 0; \; U_{yy} \leq 0, \; U_{\ell\ell} \leq 0;$$
$$U_{y\ell} \leq 0$$

5. The utility function (U) is assumed to take the form[9]

$$U(y,\ell) = y - V(\ell), \; V_\ell > 0, \; V_{\ell\ell} > 0$$

and then the marginal rate of substitution (MRS) becomes equal to the marginal utility of leisure (possibly during working hours), which becomes independent of y:

$$MRS = -U_\ell(y,\ell)/U_y(y,\ell) = V_\ell(\ell)$$

6. The effort (ℓ) of each worker influences income (y), but only by increasing total bonus (B), which is shared equally. There is no direct payment according to the individual amount of effect (ℓ). Therefore, ℓ is interpreted as 'effort', not as 'hours worked'.

7. Management chooses the number of workers (n) in order to maximise bonus per worker (B/n) or some other expression of income per worker. Management takes the response of workers concerning effort (ℓ^*) into account.

8. The bonus function, its parameters as well as input and output prices are exogenously given policy variables. It is assumed that plans are fulfilled, so that side conditions and 'fund-correcting' indicators, like output mix, minimum output etc. can be neglected. The interplay between production and the planning process is neglected, and the analysis is purely static and limited to one period.

However, this partial analysis reflects some essential traits of the collective wage system based on bonus-sharing. The results could be interpreted as the optimal input and output levels, which the management would have in mind during the planning process.

The symbols used are as follows: first and second derivatives are indicated by one or two subscripts, respectively, i.e. $\partial Q/\partial L = Q_L$, $\partial Q_L/\partial K = Q_{LK}$, etc. Individual workers are referred to, when necessary, by subscripts i.

$$Q = Q(L,K) \text{ output}$$
$$L = n\ell \text{ labour input}$$
$$n = \text{ number of workers}$$

LABOUR INCENTIVES AND COLLECTIVE WAGE SYSTEMS

ℓ = level of effort supplied by each worker
K = input of capital and raw materials
p = output price
r = rent
w = wages per worker
W = wn wages fund
π = $pQ - W - rK$ profits
B = bonus
y = $w + B/n$ total income per worker
U = $U(y,\ell) = y - V(\ell)$ utility for the typical worker
α, β, a, b = weights of fund-forming indicators in bonus functions

The bonus-sharing models are based on two assumptions:

(i) bonuses are shared equally, and there is no proportional payment for individual effort;
(ii) each worker maximises utility individually, while considering that other members' supply of effort is unaffected by his own choice: $dL/d\ell = 1$. This defines a Nash-equilibrium.

These assumptions are supposed to be the most relevant, but for the purpose of comparison, the alternative assumptions are considered as well:

(i') individual effort is remunerated proportionally;
(ii') effort is decided upon collectively, i.e. it is taken into account in the maximisation that workers are identical and choose identical levels of effort. In this case $dL/d\ell = n$ should be applied when $U(y,\ell)$ is maximised with respect to ℓ. Effort levels are identical in any case, but this is not taken into account when each worker chooses his ℓ individually.

In the case of simple income-sharing, maximising utility with respect to ℓ gives the following results under the four alternative sets of assumptions:

Income-sharing *without proportional payment* means:

(1) $\quad y_i = w + \pi/n$

and the first order conditions for maximum utility with respect to ℓ are:

(2) $\quad V_\ell = \frac{1}{n} pQ_L \quad$ individual maximum: ℓ is too small

(3) $\quad V_\ell = pQ_L \quad$ collective maximum: Pareto-optimum

Income-sharing *with proportional payment* means:

(4) $\quad y_i = w + (\pi/L)\ell_i$

and the first-order conditions for maximum with respect to ℓ are:

(5) $\quad V_\ell = \frac{1}{n} pQ_L + \left(1 - \frac{1}{n}\right)\frac{\pi}{L}$

individual maximum: ℓ is too big

(6) $\quad V_\ell = pQ_L \quad$ collective maximum: Pareto-optimum

In both types of payment system a collective decision fulfils the condition for Pareto-optimum for the group of workers. Individual decisions entail that ℓ is too small in the case without proportional payment (because each worker ignores that other workers contribute to the common bonus), and that ℓ tends to be too big in case with proportional payment (because the marginal effort not only gives a maginal product but also an increased share of the product already produced), i.e. ℓ is too big if $pQ_L < \pi/L$, and this condition is usually assumed to be fulfilled.[10]

In the Soviet collective wage systems considered below, this simple income-sharing is replaced by more or less complicated bonus-sharing schemes.

THE KOSYGIN 1965 REFORMS

There were several elements in these renowned reforms: abolition of the regional *sovnarkhozy* and restoration of economic ministries and Gosplan, setting-up of the central supply agency Gossnab, introduction of a capital charge of normally 6 per cent, more credit financing of investment and wholesale trade, based on contracts between enterprises.[11]

But the interest here is in the recasting of the managerial incentive system. Among the large amount of compulsory plan indicators in use only nine were retained: value of sales, output mix, total wages fund, profits, profitability as a percentage of capital, payment to and from the state budget, centralised investment, introduction of new technology, material supply. The fulfilment of most of these targets are necessary conditions for obtaining bonus; but two (usually sales and profitability) are 'fund-forming indicators' in the sense that the size of three newly-established funds were proportional to these two indicators. Besides the bonus fund considered here there were also a fund for social needs and housing and an investment fund. Before 1965 gross output (the notorious *val*) and cost reductions were the most important success indicators.

For managers bonus from the bonus fund may amount to 50–60 per cent of basic salary, and

> there are indications that originally the bonus fund was supposed to be used primarily for rewarding managers and engineering staff who, more than other groups, influence the performance of enterprises. Apparently, due to pressure from manual workers the authorities abandoned this intention.[12]

Workers increased their share of the bonus fund from 35 per cent in 1967 to 49 per cent in 1975, and in 1973 the share of premia in workers' wages were 15 per cent, of which 10 per cent originated from the wages fund and 5 per cent from the bonus fund.[13] The share of premia has increased since to about 25 per cent. Based on this evidence it is assumed that management as well as the workers wishes to maximise bonus per worker.[14]

Although bonus should be paid out of profit, the size of the bonus is computed as a percentage of the wages fund.[15] This percentage depends on the two basic fund-forming indicators — sales and profitability — and the parameters of the bonus function. Actually growth of sales was used, but this can be neglected in the one period model:

(7) $\quad B = \alpha wnpQ + \beta wn\pi/K$
$\quad U(y,\ell) \quad$ w.r.t. ℓ, by each worker
$\quad$ max B/n w.r.t. n, by management, given the chosen ℓ^*

The reason for introducing the wages fund ($W = wn$) in the bonus formula is, of course, to reduce differences in bonus per worker due to differences in capital-intensity of firms (e.g. the few workers in a hydropower plant might earn very high profits per worker). But it may also give rise to peculiar input choices of firms, to be seen below. It could be argued that the wages fund total (W) should be fixed, rather than the wages per worker (w) as in the optimisation problem below, which shows the optimum number of workers (n) opted for by the enterprise during the planning process.

The assumption is that there is a sequence of decisions more or less influenced by management, and at least it seems more reasonable to assume that management chooses n for fixed K than the other way round.[16]

Bonus-sharing without proportional payment of effort means that

(8) $U(y,\ell) = w + B/n - V(\ell)$

(9) $B/n = \alpha wp\, Q(L,K) + \beta w[pQ(L,K) - wn - rK]/K$

and *individual maximisation* of utility yields the first order condition

(10) $V_\ell(\ell) = wp\left(\alpha + \dfrac{\beta}{K}\right) Q_L(n\ell,K)$

$$\text{individual maximum: } \frac{dL}{d\ell} = 1$$

For comparison the condition for collective maximisation is also stated

(11) $V_\ell(\ell) = wp\left(\alpha + \dfrac{\beta}{K}\right) nQ_L(n\ell,K)$

$$\text{collective maximum: } \frac{dL}{d\ell} = n$$

Compared to simple income-sharing (2) it appears that the presence of the term nw in the bonus function (7) mitigates the sharing effect and makes the income-sharing Pareto-optimum possible even under individual maximisation (10). If the supply of effort is decided collectively, it pays to supply still larger amounts of effort in order to exploit the system (cf. (11)). The condition (10) gives the implicit response function:

(12) $\ell^* = \ell^*(n,K,w,p,\alpha,\beta)$,

$\ell_n^* < 0,\ \ell_K^* \gtreqless 0,\ \ell_w^* > 0$

$\ell_p^* > 0,\ \ell_\alpha^* > 0,\ \ell_\beta^* > 0$

Given this individual response function *management maximises bonus per worker*

(13) $B/n = \alpha wpQ(n\ell^*,K) + \beta w[pQ(n\ell^*,K) - wn - rK]/K$

with respect to n, and the first order condition becomes:

(14) $w = \left(\dfrac{\alpha}{\beta}K + 1\right)(n\ell_n^* + \ell^*)\, pQ_L(n\ell^*,K)$

The response function ℓ^* tends to reduce the demand for labour, and the form of the bonus function (7) tends to increase labour demand.

If $(n\ell_n^* + \ell^*)$ is small enough, but still positive, i.e. a strong individual response ℓ_n^*, then labour demand may be low compared to cost-minimisation without individual response, i.e. $\ell_n^* = 0$ and $w = \ell^* pQ_L$. This may put a brake on the growth of B/n, which is otherwise unbounded from above, when K and L are increased for fixed K/L.[17]

The first condition for maximum B/n with respect to K is

(15) $\quad r + \dfrac{\pi}{K} = \left(\dfrac{\alpha}{\beta} K + 1\right) p(Q_K + Q_L n\ell_K^*)$

For $\alpha = 0$ and $\ell_K^* = 0$ this shows the tendency towards using too little K, because profitability, not profits is maximised, just as maximising income per worker in labour managed firms means that too little labour is used. If $\ell_K^* = 0$ is assumed, then (14) and (15) yields:[18]

(16) $\quad \dfrac{Q_L}{Q_K} = \dfrac{w}{(r + \pi/K)(n\ell_n^* + \ell^*)}$

which differs from the usual condition for technically efficient capital–labour ratios. The term π/K means that the enterprise would prefer less capital-intensive input combinations compared to a cost-minimising enterprise, and if π/K differs between firms, then in fact the firms with the highest profitability would prefer the less capital intensive input combinations.

For fixed K the condition (14) gives the optimum number of workers as an implicit function n*, and some statements are possible concerning the sign of the first derivatives (if all second derivatives of ℓ^* are assumed equal to zero):

(17) $\quad n^* = n^*(K,w,p,\alpha,\beta)$
$\quad\quad\quad n_K^* > 0$ if $\ell_K^* = 0$; $n_w^* < 0$ if $\ell_w^* = 0$, $n_p^* > 0$
$\quad\quad\quad n_\alpha^* > 0$, $n_\beta^* < 0$ if $\ell_\beta^* = 0$

THE SHCHEKINO METHOD

As mentioned above, it may not be justified to consider the wages fund as varying depending on the number of workers. However, the effects of a fixed wages fund are analysed below as a model of the experiment introduced at the Shchekinskij chemical combine in Tula province in April 1967. The combine was granted a fixed wages fund and the right to reduce the number of workers, allowing remaining workers to benefit from the consequent savings, provided that output was not reduced:

> The experiment quickly yielded positive results. By 1970 it was deemed to have 'saved' roughly 1000 men of the original workforce of around 7000, labour productivity had risen by 114%, output by 87%, wages had fallen from 12% to 8% of unit costs, profitability had risen from 6.8% to 19.1% and average wages had risen by 8% above the planned increase, with 50% of the workers benefitting.[19]

This reduction in manpower implies a 17 per cent wage increase rather than the actual 8 per cent. In fact, only 30–55 per cent of the savings were distributed, not the maximum of 90 per cent allowed, and the wages fund was changed administratively contrary to the provisions. This may be due to the obligation for managers to account for any savings distributed in terms of specific types of productivity gains. This obligation could counteract the possibility that the experiment was merely rewarding past inefficiency.[20]

Intuitively it seems evident that fixing the wages fund provides an incentive for reducing the number of workers. However, productivity should also be increased, and a look at the possible ways to do this makes things less obvious. In the framework used here labour productivity could be increased by increasing effort (ℓ), by increasing the amount of other inputs (K), or by changing the production function (Q), and the first of these is considered in the model (18) which is identical to the model (7), except that the wages fund (W) is fixed:

(18)
$$B = \alpha WpQ + \beta W\pi/K$$
max $U(y,\ell)$ w.r.t. ℓ, by each worker
max $(B+W)/n$ w.r.t. n, by management, given the chosen ℓ^*.

In this system of 'bonus plus wages fund-sharing' income per worker becomes

(19) $$y = (B+W)/n = \left(\alpha + \frac{\beta}{K}\right)pW\frac{1}{n}Q(n\ell,K)$$
$$+ \left[1 - \beta\left(\frac{W}{K} + r\right)\right]W\frac{1}{n}$$

and the first-order condition for *individual maximum utility* with respect to ℓ, and the implicit response function ℓ^* become:

LABOUR INCENTIVES AND COLLECTIVE WAGE SYSTEMS

(20) $\quad V_\ell(\ell) = pQ_L(n\ell,K)\left(\alpha + \dfrac{\beta}{K}\right)\dfrac{W}{n}$

(21) $\quad \ell^* = \ell^*(n,K,W,p,\alpha,\beta)$

$\quad\quad\quad \ell^*_n < 0,\ \ell^*_K \gtreqless 0,\ \ell^*_W > 0$

$\quad\quad\quad \ell^*_p > 0,\ \ell^*_\alpha > 0,\ \ell^*_\beta > 0$

For given n and W the response ℓ^* is the same as (10), but the response to changes in n is much stronger in (21). The condition for *management maximisation of (B+W)/n* with respect to n, given the response ℓ^*, becomes:

(22) $\quad \dfrac{\pi}{n} + \dfrac{1}{n}\dfrac{K}{\beta}(\alpha pQ+1) = \left(\dfrac{\alpha}{\beta}K+1\right)(n\ell^*_n+\ell^*)pQ_L$

(cf. (14)) and in this case very little can be said about the signs of the first derivatives of the implicit function n* giving the optimum number of workers.

It is not straightforward to evaluate whether optimal ℓ^* and n* obtained from (20) and (22) differ from those obtained from (10) and (14). Some light may be thrown on this by considering two specific situations.

First, starting in an optimum (ℓ^*,n^*) according to (10) and (14) and keeping ℓ^* fixed at this level, will it then be profitable for management to reduce n, when the Shchekino system is introduced? Writing (14) and (22) in the form

(23) $\quad W = \left(\dfrac{\alpha}{\beta}K+1\right)(n\ell^*_n+\ell^*)pnQ_L$ from (14)

(24) $\quad \pi + \dfrac{K}{\beta}(\alpha pQ+1) = \left(\dfrac{\alpha}{\beta}K+1\right)(n\ell^*_n+\ell^*)pnQ_L$ from (22)

it appears that if $d(nQ_L)/dn > 0$, then the value of n satisfying (24) will be less than the value satisfying (23), if

(25) $\quad \pi + \dfrac{K}{\beta}(\alpha pQ+1) < W$, which by means of (18) gives

$\quad\quad \dfrac{B+W}{W} < \beta\dfrac{W}{K}$

The Shchekino enterprise will try to reduce n (and output as well) if the bonus fund is small relative to the wages fund. The tendency to reduce n is strengthened if it is taken into account that reducing n increases ℓ, which increases bonus.

Second, starting again in optimum according to (10) and (14), it could be asked whether introducing the Shchekino system makes it possible for workers to improve utility by reducing n and increasing ℓ while keeping output constant, i.e.

(26) $\quad dQ = Q_L n d\ell + Q_L \ell dn = 0$ or
$\quad\quad d\ell = - \ell/n\, dn$

Then $d\ell > 0$ will improve utility if (cf. (18) and (19)):

(27) $\quad dU = -(\alpha+\dfrac{\beta}{K})pWQ\,\dfrac{1}{n^2}\,dn - \left(1-\beta\left(\dfrac{W}{K}+r\right)\right)W\dfrac{1}{n^2}\,dn$

$\quad\quad - V_\ell d\ell > 0$, or

$\quad\quad (B+W)/n > \ell V_\ell$

Utility could be increased by reducing n, increasing ℓ and keeping Q constant, if n is small, B and W are large and the marginal utility of leisure (V_ℓ) is small. If the initial values of ℓ and n is an optimum according to (10) and (14), then the condition (27) becomes

(28) $\quad \dfrac{B+W}{W} > \dfrac{\beta}{K}\,\dfrac{\ell w}{(n\ell_n^* + \ell^*)}$

where ℓ^* is the function defined by (10) and (12). The conclusion is that specific conditions must be fulfilled, if introducing the Shchekino system should make reductions in n and increases in utility possible (cf. (25) and (28)). If the number of workers is cut, clearly the effect is to make production more capital intensive in the first place at least.[21]

The Shchekino experiment was a success — as experiments usually are — and although the positive effects faded (the combine starting to fail on major plan targets in the mid-1970s) the system was imposed across Soviet industry, more than half of the industrial labour force now being involved in some variant of the system. A decree of April 1978 gave all enterprises the right to adopt the method, which was modified during the 1970s. In 1971 it was specified that distribution of savings in the wages fund was contingent upon a rise in labour productivity.[22]

This is closely related to the modifications of the incentive system in 1979 and to the 1984 experiment. A separate experiment beginning in July 1983 in the design departments in five Leningrad enterprises is a direct continuation of the Shchekino method. The enterprises are granted a fixed wages fund and some freedom as to the distribution of savings, but it is supposed that remaining staff should be remunerated according to their individual labour contribution, and in one factory it was stipulated that supplements should be no less than 25 roubles (average monthly wage for industrial technical staff is 221 roubles[23]) and that they could only be given to the best 70 per cent of staff.[24] Substantial cuts in staff of 8–15 per cent ensued but so far the Soviet labour laws, which make assignment to a new job a condition for most lay-offs, as well as the persisting labour shortage, have prevented reabsorbing redundant personnel from being a problem. In Shchekino itself most surplus employees were redeployed within the enterprise itself, which was enlarged at the same time.

However, in an article subtitled 'How to Develop the Shchekinskij Method'[25], economics professor G. Popov has proposed a system of redundancy as a consistent development of the Shchekino method. It includes unemployment benefit, resembling Scandinavian-type systems except for the fact that the 'unemployed' are obliged to work in jobs assigned by the state in order to receive the benefit. Enterprises should be entitled to lay off workers without finding a new job for them and to retain saved wage cost except an amount corresponding to the minimum wage of 80 roubles a month, which is less than half the average monthly wages. This amount should be paid to the state, and the state in turn should guarantee a job for everyone but only at this statutory minimum wage of 80 roubles.

> Of course, people who for a certain time do not work in their specialities will receive only the minimum wage established by law. And when, some time later, they get 'normal' workplaces they will, one would think, keep a tight grip on them and try to do a good job. . . . A strict measure? Perhaps. But it's inevitable, I think. . . . A clear distinction must be made between the right to work and the right to a certain wage level.[25]

THE 1979 DECREE

The incentive system of 1965 underwent a sequence of more or less experimental changes during the 1970s. In 1971 sales increases and profitability were supplemented by output and productivity as the main fund-forming indicators. In 1977 the indicators were changed again; labour productivity and the share of high quality goods in output became obligatory, and in addition each ministry could choose one or two of the following four indicators: output (in some cases profits), profitability, reductions in costs and introduction of new technology. Several other indicators were important, especially output mix, and contract fulfilment. Besides, counter-planning was strengthened in 1971, and the formation of associations (*ob'edinenija*) from 1973.[26]

In July 1979 a widely published resolution[27] initiated some major modifications of the planning system — the phrase reform was carefully avoided — including more detailed material planning and the introduction of a so-called enterprise 'pass-port', a greater role for Gosplan, new industrial wholesale prices from January 1982, dissemination of the brigade organisation of work, delivery of finished product as measure of construction activity — as well as modifications of the incentive system.

The main fund-forming indicators should be productivity and quality mix of output, with fulfilment of delivery contracts as a fund-correcting indicator, 98 per cent (97 per cent in a few cases) fulfilment being the condition for receiving any bonus.[28] Only the first of these is explicitly analysed by the model (29) below due to difficulties of quantification, and according to the new rules productivity was supposed to account for 50 per cent of the material incentive fund.[29] In addition, two genuinely new elements were introduced into the incentive system.

First, labour productivity should be measured in terms of 'net normative output' (NNO) in order to eliminate the incentive to produce outputs with excessive material contents inherent in the former gross output measure. The NNO is close to the concept of value-added and consists of wage and social insurance cost plus profit, not computed as actual outlays, but as a coefficient ('normative') multiplied by gross output, in order to prevent the temptation to boost labour input. This is checked, not by market competition but by the negotiations with planning authorities about normatives. The interests of management in these negotiations and in production decisions when normatives are fixed are clearly different, and it could be argued that output is more relevant as the fund-forming indicator in (29) than productivity.

Second, bonus is computed as a percentage of profit which replaces the wages fund as the base indicator. In order to avoid too big differences in bonus per worker between enterprises, the percentage is differentiated and apparently chosen in order to adjust the planned bonus fund to the size of the wages fund. This does not necessarily invalidate the principle of the model (29), but its interpretation is dubious.[30]

(29) $\quad B = \alpha\pi(pQ-rK)/n$
max $U(y,\ell)$ w.r.t. ℓ, by each worker
max B/n w.r.t. n, by management

Income per worker becomes

(30) $\quad y = w + B/n = w +$
$\alpha[p^2Q^2 - (wn+2rK)pQ + rK(wn+rK)]/n^2$

and worker maximisation of utility and management maximisation of bonus per worker as above yield the conditions for optimum effort (ℓ) and number of workers (n), respectively, as given by (31) and (33):

(31) $\quad V_\ell(\ell) = \alpha\dfrac{1}{n^2}(2\pi+wn)pQ_L$

(32) $\quad \ell^* = \ell^*(n,K,w,p,\alpha)$

The signs of the derivatives of ℓ^* are not easily determined as the right-hand-side of (31) does not depend in a predictable way on ℓ, especially not for $2\pi+wn > 0$ as indicated by (31).

(33) $\quad (n\ell_n^*+\ell^*)pQ_L = (pQ-rK)/n > w$ for $\pi > 0$

Compared to (14) and (22), (33) shows that in the case of no individual response ($\ell_n^* = 0$) the labour demand of the enterprise will be lower than for a profit-maximiser, provided that profits are positive. The effect of individual response is uncertain.

Considering the negotiations procedure for establishing net output normatives it is understandable that one Gosplan economist in a discussion in *Pravda* concluded: 'None the less, the main operative index right now is the volume of sold output, and the fulfilment of contractual commitments, as rightfully stated here, still plays a minor role'.[31]

THE 1984 EXPERIMENT

The experiment was decreed in July 1983[32] to begin in January 1984, lasting one year and covering 5 per cent of industry with the purpose of amplifying the role of production associations and enterprises in drafting plans and increasing their economic responsibility. Some of the measures were elaborated by a recent decree, which stressed the role of technological progress and extended the 'new conditions for economic activity' of the experiment to apply permanently to all industrial enterprises from January 1987.[33]

Most of the provisions are not very different from the 1965 and 1979 changes and may be considered a new attempt at carrying out these earlier intentions without applying any genuine new means. The main measures introduced by the experiment are: an attempt at — once again — limiting the number of plan indices; a fund for development and new technology to be used at the discretion of the enterprise; stable normatives for the wages fund and for retained profit, throughout the five-year plan; opportunities for using credits for 90 or 120 days (60 days at present) at no more than 20 per cent interest;[34] opportunities for management to use savings in the wages fund for additional incentive payments, especially for designers and research personnel who may receive up to three months' extra pay;[35] and further spread of the contract brigades.

Speeding of scientific advances in industry is pursued by various measures:[36] establishment of large research enterprises and *ad hoc* research groups; creation of free reserves in plans to be used for the production of new types of equipment and materials; introduction of the position of general designer; new quality evaluations (goods that are not classified as either superior or first-quality will be subject to removal from production within at most two years); high-quality goods may receive a 30 per cent incentive price mark-up, and products subject to removal a 15 per cent discount to be subtracted from (to a maximum 20 per cent) the material incentive fund; fulfilment of assignments for technological development is included among the most important indices for enterprise performance and for the results of socialist competition, and if these assignments are not fulfilled bonuses for executives are to be reduced by at least 25 per cent.

The main success indicators are: (1) output sales volume, subject to product mix stipulations; (2) fulfilment of contractual obligations (15 per cent extra as bonus, but subtraction of 3 per cent for each per cent breach of contract);[37] (3) fulfilment of assignments for development of technology; (4) increases in labour productivity; (5) cost reductions and savings of energy and raw materials;[38] and (6) value of exports.

For management, contract fulfilment appears to be the most important condition for obtaining bonus,[39] but product quality also looms large. The existing rules provided for a price mark-up for quality goods corresponding to 50–100 per cent of normal profits.

The new price mark-up is up to 30 per cent of the price, a very strong incentive to meet quality standards, or if that is not possible, to simulate quality improvements and apply various other improving techniques.[40]

The intentions concerning contract fulfilment and product quality are not only difficult to accomplish but also to describe in quantitative terms (and supposedly partly for the same reasons). Therefore, the model (34) only considers output and productivity as fund-forming indicators. These are the indicators mentioned by Aganbegyan in an article asserting the superiority of 'progressive' income-sharing contract brigades paying 10–12 per cent capital charge compared to the experiment. Some examples of numerical coefficients are given in the article:

When the plan for output deliveries is 100% fulfilled, the enterprise's material incentive fund is increased by 15%.

The basis of the experiment is the achieved wages fund, which increases — at enterprises of the Ministry of the Electrical Equipment Industry, for instance — by 0.35% for each percentage point of increase in normative net output.[41]

Under the Shchekino-system productivity gains had to take the form of labour force reductions in order to increase payment, because the total wages fund was fixed. In the experiment the wages fund is increased by (often) 35 per cent for each percentage point increase in normative net output, but it still pays to obtain productivity increases by reducing the labour force because in this case 100 per cent of the savings accrue to the enterprise, not only 35 per cent[42] (disregarding the fact that actually only about 50 per cent of the savings were distributed in the Shchekino system). It is illuminative that in the recent, closely related wage regulations in Poland the coefficient is not 0.35, but 0.50 and in some cases 0.80, and that there are rules for progressive taxation of wages fund increases in excess of these limits with tax rates increasing to 400 per cent.[43]

With the planned[44] wages fund as the base indicator, the model becomes:

LABOUR INCENTIVES AND COLLECTIVE WAGE SYSTEMS

(34)
$$W/n = a\overline{W}(pQ-rK) + b\overline{W}/n$$
$$B = \alpha\overline{W}pQ$$
max $U(y,\ell)$ w.r.t. ℓ, by each member
max $(B+W)/n$ w.r.t. n, by management, given the response ℓ^*

Profits has been abolished as the base indicator (cf. the 1979 decree (29)). Even if a = b, average wages will not be proportional to labour productivity. According to the provisions a and b correspond to values of 0.35 and 1.00, respectively, if measured in terms of percentage changes.

Under this 'bonus plus wages fund-sharing' income per worker becomes:

(35) $$y = (B+W)/n = \overline{W}\left[\left(\frac{\alpha}{n}+a\right)pQ - arK + \frac{b}{n}\right]$$

(cf. (9), (19), (30))

Worker-maximisation of utility and management-maximisation of bonus plus wages per worker as above yield the conditions for optimum effort (ℓ^*) and number of workers (n*) respectively as given by (36) and (37):

(36) $$V_\ell(\ell) = \overline{W}\left(\frac{\alpha}{n}+a\right)pQ_L(n\ell,K)$$

(37) $\ell^* = \ell^*(n,K,\overline{W},p,\alpha,a,b)$
$\ell^*_n < 0$, $\ell^*_K > 0$, $\ell^*_{\overline{W}} > 0$, $\ell^*_p > 0$
$\ell^*_\alpha > 0$, $\ell^*_a > 0$, $\ell^*_b = 0$

(38) $$(b+\alpha pQ)/n^2 = \left(\frac{\alpha}{n}+a\right)(n\ell^*_n+\ell^*)pQ_L$$

The sign of the first derivatives of the implicit function n* defined by (38) are indeterminable. Instead, the effects of parameter changes are considered for two specific problems.

First, how do they influence the profitability of expanding Q and n in the same proportion? In this case

(39) $$\frac{d(Q/n)}{dn} = \frac{1}{n^2}(nQ_L(n\ell^*_n+\ell^*) - Q) = 0$$

and using this in (35) it appears that y increases for increasing proportional n and Q, if

(40) $apQ > b/n$

95

so a large value of b tends to reduce n (and Q proportionately) in this case.

Second, how do parameter values influence the inclination of workers to produce the same output with fewer men (n) and more effort per man (ℓ)? In this case

(41) $dQ = Q_L n d\ell + Q_L \ell dn = 0$ or
  $d\ell = -\ell/n \, dn$

and $d\ell > 0$ will improve utility, if: (cf. (34) and (35)):

(42) $dU = -(\alpha pQ+b)/n \, dn - V_\ell d\ell > 0$ or
  $\alpha pQ + b > \ell V_\ell$

The possibility of increasing utility by reducing n and increasing ℓ with constant Q is more likely if α, p, b and Q are large, and effort and the marginal utility of leisure (V_ℓ) are small.

The new incentive scheme seems to be an improvement. Profit is no longer the base indicator, and the wages fund is itself adjustable. But the problem remains that the effort to economise on the use of labour creates an incentive to substitute materials, equipment and other inputs for labour, even if output is measured as 'net normative output' which is itself a normative (labour outlay per unit of gross output) to be negotiated and settled in advance. It is also a question whether the resulting income inequalities between enterprises will in fact be tolerated by the authorities.

Most likely, these changes of indicators in otherwise traditional bonus functions will have only marginal effects upon incentives and efficiency. However, other more promising changes of the incentive system are currently being introduced, i.e. the dissemination of the brigade system in industry and in agriculture as well, which tends to stimulate individual effort and to reduce the number of workers.[45]

INCENTIVE PROBLEMS

At first sight it should be an evident advantage for central authorities to be able to influence or decide the objective functions of enterprises rather than being forced to operate with objective functions as unchangeable side conditions. But this possibility entails problems of its own.

First, as amply demonstrated by the preceding overview, objective functions tend to be still more complicated. It has been a declared aim of all the changes to simplify the incentive system. After the July 1979 decree about twenty plan indicators were approved, compared to 8–10 in the 1965 reform. Despite assertions that profit and product mix would suffice as plan indicators, there is evidence that the number of indicators is actually growing — to 59 compared to 18 ten years ago in one case.[46] No wonder that Soviet specialists are complaining:

> The procedure for forming incentive funds and the system of awarding bonuses to personel have become significantly more complicated. The direct link between the results of a collective's work and the size of material incentives has either been lost or is so complex that it has sometimes become hard to understand not only for rank-and-file workers or engineers but even for enterprise managers. The detailed spelling out of control by increasing the number of indicators certainly does not strengthen plan discipline; rather, it broadens the field for the manipulation of reports, gives an enterprise additional pretexts for citing 'objective causes', and ultimately leads to 'adjusting the plan' to fit actually achieved results . . .[47]

The effects of the bonus scheme is further complicated by frequent interference from purely administrative decisions: plans are changed (even after the end of planning period), inputs are directed to priority sectors, prices are arbitrary.

> Large numbers of instructions, explanations and restrictions of every kind have accumulated over the years. As a result, a manager who has been entrusted with an enterprise that produces hundreds of millions of rubles' worth of output can't make flexible use of a sum amounting to a few hundred rubles, especially where wages are concerned. These restrictions lead to a decline in initiative, sometimes to indifference, and usually to a search for detours.[48]

These facts also impose serious limits on the value of the kind of formal analysis undertaken here,[49] which omits central features of the administrative process: that future plans are affected by current output, that plans depend on information delivered by enterprises (and bonuses as well due to counter-plan incentive schemes), and that inputs (and therefore also outputs and bonus) depend directly on the output plan.

The second problem of objective functions not chosen by the enterprises themselves is the problem of enforcement. The notorious efficiency problems in Soviet industry despite plenty of strong material incentives, is not only due to general apathy, alcoholism and other 'degradation of tissue',[50] but also due to 'soft budget constraints'[51] for management, and the general security of working life for workers, which is, broadly speaking, one of the remarkable achievements of 'real existing socialism'. Although there are many administrative regulations they do not, oddly enough, effectively secure discipline on the part of the workers:

> More often than not one faces the paradoxical situation in which the possibility of working people taking any initiative is reduced to zero by innumerable administrative restraints while the scope for anti-social behaviour remains wide.[52]

Recent measures have stressed the strengthening of discipline and contain elements of what Berliner[53] has labelled 'reactionary' reform (i.e. more discipline) as well as some 'radical' elements (i.e. market mechanisms in planning), but few 'liberal' (i.e. private business, as in Hungary), and apparently the whole reform appears rather 'conservative' (i.e. no changes). The Novosibirsk report frankly discussed the problems of the wage incentive and the interests of different groups that may block any reforms together with a harsh critique of the type of worker fostered by Soviet socialism.

> The common qualities of the worker whose personality was shaped under the recent five year plans are a low labour and produciton discipline, an indifferent attitude to work, a poor quality of work and a poor appreciation of it as a means of self-realization, social inertia, a well-pronounced consumer mentality and a low code of morality.[54]

> Logically the group most interested in a transition to economic methods of management would be the leading officials of 'head' enterprises (associations) whose authorities are to be much expanded, as well as the rank and file workers, engineers and technicians who would be able to realise their talents more fully under the new conditions, work more efficiently, and earn higher wages . . .
> In contrast the more inert and less skilled group of older

workers are afraid that they would have to pay a high price for somewhat broader rights and higher incomes in terms of more intensive labour and enhanced responsibility for the results of their work. This is not to the liking of many of them, especially as the productive relations that have been in effect for a number of decades have tended to foster the kind of passive worker who sticks to the maxim: 'Why should I care? It's no concern of mine'.[55]

These are hard facts that point to two conclusions, concerning what might be called 'the social relations of a planned economy'.[56] First, the idea of fixing rules for everything is contrary to efficiency, which requires that some persons are entrusted with power to the best of their judgement and are personally responsible for the outcome. Second, limited personal responsibility implies limited efficiency as well. Directors and workers are only rarely sacked, and economic results are subject to soft budget constraints, negotiations, evasive behaviour and concealment of information. According to the rules, bonuses should be earned and deserved by the efforts of the workers themselves. There is no possibility of the big jackpot whether earned, unearned or due to sheer luck, and this means the absence of a strong motivating force.

But bureaucracy also has its advantages, namely to protect ordinary workers against the highhandedness and whims of employers, to prevent abuses of power, and to limit unemployment, inequality and other nuisances of the market mechanism for those who do not succeed in market competition.

There seems to be no easy solutions to these incentive problems involving efficiency, social justice and welfare, and it is, for example, not at all evident that complete carrying out of the widespread slogan that 'earnings must be earned'[57] would mean an unambiguous improvement.

NOTES

1. Nove in Nove and Nuti (1972), p. 354.
2. Kosygin in his report to the Central Committee of the CPSU, 27 September 1965. *Ekonomicheskaya Gazeta* (29 September) no. 39: 2–9. Translation in *The Current Digest of the Soviet Press* 17 (13 October 1965, no. 38): 1–15.
3. Brezhnev in his 1981 report to the 26th Congress of the CPSU; cf. *Documents and Resolutions of the 26th Congress of the Communist Party*

LABOUR INCENTIVES AND COLLECTIVE WAGE SYSTEMS

of the Soviet Union, Moscow, 23 February–2 March 1981 (Moscow: Novosti, 1981), p. 54.

4. Gorbachev at the meeting at the Central Committee of the CPSU, 8 April 1985 on *Initsiativa, organizovannost', effektivnost'*, preceded by Gorbachev and attended by enterprise managers, brigade members, *kolkhozniki* and others. Cf. *Ekonomicheskaya Gazeta* (April 1985, no. 16): 3–5. For an historical account of the concept of *khozraschet*, see Pekka Sutela's contribution to this volume.

5. Bornstein (1985), p. 17. See also Nove in Nove and Nuti (1972), p. 356.

6. Cohn (1982), p. 173.

7. Therefore, the decline in the growth rate of labour productivity is hardly more 'alarming' in the USSR than in the West (cf. Rutland, 1984, p. 347). But the level of labour productivity is considerably lower in the USSR, where it is 'over 55 per cent' of the US level, according to Soviet estimates. (*Nar. Khoz.*, 1983, p. 59). It should be mentioned that laying off 10 per cent of the labour force as unemployment, which occurs in the West but not in the USSR, has some positive effects upon labour productivity.

8. Both of these are sources of potential improvement. There is, for example, considerable overmanning in Soviet firms, often 50–70 per cent compared to western firms using the same technology (Gomulka, Nove and Holliday, 1984).

9. Cf. Ireland and Law (1982), p. 58.

10. Sen (1966), especially pp. 365–6.

11. Nove, in Nove and Nuti (1972), pp. 354–5; and Kosygin, ibid., pp. 319–34. Conyngham (1982).

12. Adam (1980), pp. 359–60; cf. also pp. 357–62

13. Freris (1984), p. 152; cf. also pp. 143, 151–6; Adam (1980), p. 360; Kunel'ski (1981), pp. 76, 177–8.

14. Not the total bonus, as in Martin's (1976) models; cf. Bonin (1976); Conn (1979); Ireland and Law (1980). See also the contribution by S. Oxenstierna in this volume.

15. I.e. the base indicator in the quotation from Bornstein above is the wages fund, and the money source is profits.

16. As assumed by Martin (1976), p. 218; cf. Freris (1984), p. 52; Wiles (1977), p. 38.

17. Ireland and Law (1980), p. 35.

18. Cf. Bonin (1976); Freris (1984), pp. 59–61; Martin (1976), p. 233.

19. Rutland (1984), p. 348.

20. Rutland (1984), pp. 349–53.

21. Rutland (1984), p. 352, where also more long-run effects are considered.

22. Rutland (1984), pp. 348, 349, 350, 352.

23. *Nar. Khoz.* (1983), p. 393.

24. *Pravda*, 2 December 1984, p. 2.

25. *Pravda*, 27 December 1980, p. 3.

26. Adam (1980), especially p. 354, where an explicit bonus function is given.

27. Hanson (1983); Bornstein (1985); *Postanovlenie*, 12 July 1979; *Sovershenstvovanie* . . . (1980, 1982); Belkin *et al.* (1980); Petrov and

Pazychuk (1982).
28. Hanson (1983), pp. 4,6; Bornstein (1985), p. 16.
29. Hanson (1983), p. 7; Freris (1984), pp. 137–8.
30. Bornstein (1985), pp. 9, 11, 14, 17, 20; Freris (1984), pp. 17, 68; Hanson (1983), p. 5.
31. *Pravda*, 17 March 1983, p. 2. Translation from *The Current Digest of the Soviet Press* 35 (13 April 1983, no. 11): 9.
32. *Postanovlenie*, 25 July 1983; cf. Berliner (1984); Aage (1984).
33. *Postanovlenie*, 12 July 1985.
34. Busjatskaya (1983).
35. Zajkauskas (1983). The new decree apparently limits these payments to two months' extra pay.
36. *Postanovlenie*, 12 July 1985; cf. also the decree of 27 August 1983. *Ekonomicheskaya Gazeta* (September 1983, no. 36) : 5.
37. Busjatskaya (1983).
38. *Ekonomicheskaya Gazeta* (March 1985, no. 13) : 15 and (April 1985, no. 14) : 11.
39. *Postanovlenie*, 12 July 1985; *Pravda*, 17 December 1984, p. 1.
40. *Postanovlenie*, 12 July 1985; Berliner (1984); Bergson (1978), pp. 13, 24; Hanson (1983), p. 5.
41. S. Aganbegyan in *Trud*, 28 August 1984, p. 2. Translation from *The Current Digest of the Soviet Press* 36 (3 October 1984, no. 36) : 1–4. Productivity is mentioned in general terms in the new decree (*Postanovlenie*, 12 July 1985), and was the subject of a decree of 1 September 1983 (*Pravda*, 3 September 1983).
42. Cf. Dmitriev and Rajkhel'son (1984), pp. 53–4. Detailed methods for wages fund computation are found in *Ekonomicheskaya Gazeta* (January 1984, no. 3) : 15.
43. Baka (1984).
44. Actually, Dmitriev and Rajkhel'son (1984), p. 54, proposes to use the corrected wages fund as the base. Now, the base is corrected only if productivity decreases.
45. For a discussion of the mechanisms of the brigade system, see Aage (1982; 1985).
46. G. Kulagin in *Pravda*, 12 July 1983, p. 2; cf. *Pravda*, 17 March 1983.
47. G. Kulagin in *Pravda*, 12 July 1983, p. 2. Translation from *The Current Digest of the Soviet Press* 35 (10 August 1983, no. 28) : 1, quoted by Bornstein (1985), p. 18; cf. Rutland (1984), pp. 347–56.
48. V. Trapeznikov in *Pravda*, 7 May 1982, pp. 2–3. Translation from *The Current Digest of the Soviet Press* 34 (2 June 1982, no. 18) : 1–4.
49. Alec Nove in *Soviet Studies* 37 (April 1985, no. 2) : 276; Cave and Hare (1981), pp. 165–74; Freris (1984), pp. 70, 145.
50. Drewnowski (1982), pp. 77–86.
51. Kornai (1980), pp. 195, 202, 235–66, 389–97, 524.
52. *Novosibirsk Report* (1983), p. A11.
53. Berliner (1983).
54. Novosibirsk (1983), pp. A23.
55. Ibid., A16.
56. Cf. Aage (1984), pp. 17–21, 29, 32–4.

57. 'Zarabotnaja plata dolzhna byt' zarabotannoj', cf. e.g. *Pravda*, 2 December 1984, p. 2.

REFERENCES

Aage, H. (1982), 'Labour Allocation in the Soviet Kolkhoz', *Economics of Planning*, vol. 16, no. 3.
―――― (1984), 'Econonomic Problems and Reforms: Andropov's 15 Months', *Nordic Journal of Soviet and East European Studies*, vol. 1, no. 2.
―――― (1985), 'Labour Incentives and Decision Making in Soviet Agriculture', Paper presented at the III World Congress for Soviet and East European Studies, Washington, D.C., 30 October–4 November.
Adam, J. (1980), 'The Present Soviet Incentive System', *Soviet Studies*, vol. 32, no. 3.
Baka, W. (1984), 'The Essence of the New Principles of the Functioning of the Economy (An Outline of the Whole System According to the Present Legal States of Affairs)' (in Polish), *Rzeczpospolita*, 7 June. (Supplement *Reforma Gospodarcza*, pp. 1–4.)
Belkin, M.I., Volkonskii, V.A., Pomanskij, A.B. and Shapiro, A.D., (1980), 'Modelirovanie vozdejstviya khozyajstvennogo mekhanizma na pokazateli raboty predprijatiya', *Ekonomika i Matematicheskie Metody* 16 (May, no. 5) : 880–92.
Bergson, A. (1978), *Productivity and the Social System — the USSR and the West*, Cambridge, Mass.: Harvard University Press.
Berliner, J. (1983), 'Planning and Management', in A. Bergson and H.S. Levine (eds), *The Soviet Economy Toward the Year 2000*, London: Allen & Unwin.
―――― (1984), 'Economic Measures and Reforms under Andropov', in NATO, Economics Directorate (ed.), *The Soviet Economy after Brezhnev*, Brussels, NATO.
Bonin, J.P. (1976), 'On Soviet Managerial Incentive Structures', *Southern Economic Journal*, vol. 42, no. 3.
Bornstein, M. (1985), 'Improving the Soviet Economic Mechanism', *Soviet Studies*, vol. 37, no. 1.
Busjatskaya, L. (1983), 'Ekonomicheskij eksperiment v mintyazhmashe', *Planovoe Khozyajstvo*, no. 10.
Cave, M. and Hare, P. (1981), *Alternative Approaches to Economic Planning*, London: Macmillan.
Cohn, S. (1982), 'Sources of Low Productivity in Soviet Capital Investment', in US Congress, Joint Economic Committee (ed.), *Soviet Economy in the 1980's: Problems and Prospects* (2 vols), Washington: US Government Printing Office.
Conn, D. (1979), 'A Comparison of Alternative Incentive Structures for Centrally Planned Economic Systems', *Journal of Comparative Economics*, vol. 3, no. 3.
Conyngham, W.J. (1982), *The Modernization of Soviet Industrial Management. Socio-economic Development and the Search for Viability*,

Cambridge: Cambridge University Press.
Dmitriev, Yu. and Rajkhel'son, E. (1984), 'Pervye itogi raboty po-novomu', *Planovoe Khozyajstvo*, no. 8.
Drewnowski, J. (ed.) (1982), *Crisis in the East European Economy*, London: Croom Helm.
Freris, A. (1984), *The Soviet Industrial Enterprise*, London: Croom Helm.
Gomulka, S., Nove, A., and Holliday, G.D. (1984), *East-West Technology Transfer*, Paris: OECD.
Hanson, P. (1983), 'Success Indicators Revisited: the July 1979 Decree on Planning and Management', *Soviet Studies*, vol. 35, no. 1.
Ireland, N.J. and Law, P.J. (1980), 'Incentives and Efficiency in the Kosygin Reforms', *Journal of Comparative Economics*, vol. 4, no. 1.
―――― and ―――― (1981), 'Efficiency, Incentives and Individual Labor Supply in the Labor-Managed Firm', *Journal of Comparative Economics*, vol. 5, no. 1.
―――― and ―――― (1982), *The Economics of Labour-Managed Enterprises*, London: Croom Helm.
Kornai, J. (1980), *Economics of Shortage*, Amsterdam: North-Holland.
Kunel'skij, L.E. (1981), *Zarabotnaja plata i stimulirovanie truda. Sotsial'no-ekonomicheskij aspekt*, Moscow: Ekonomika.
Martin, J.M. (1976), 'Reforms and the Maximizing Behaviour of the Soviet Firm', in J. Thornton (ed.), *Economic Analysis of the Soviet Type Systems*, Cambridge: Cambridge University Press.
Narodnoe Khozyajstvo SSSR v 1983 g. Moskva: Finansy i Statistika 1984.
Nove, A. and Nuti, D.M. (eds) (1972), *Socialist Economics*, Harmondsworth: Penguin Books.
Novosibirsk Report (1983), Analysis of the Soviet economic system prepared by the Academy of Sciences, Siberian Branch in Novosibirsk, presumably by T.I. Zaslavskaya, and leaked to Western journalists in Moscow in July–August 1983. Cf. *The New York Times*, 5 August 1983 and *Osteuropa* 34 (January 1984, no. 1).
Petrov, A. and Pazychuk, E. (1982), 'Iz opyta planirovaniya raboty predpriyatiya', *Planovoe Khozyajstvo*, no. 2.
Postanovlenie (1979), 'Ob uluchshenii planirovaniya i usilenii vozdejstviya khozyajstvennogo mekhanizma na provyshenie effektivnosti proizvodstva i kachestva raboty', *Ekonomicheskaya Gazeta* (12 July, no. 32).
Postanovlenie (1983), 'O dopolnitel'nykh merakh po rasshireniyu prav proizvodstvennykh ob''edinenij (predpriyatij) promyshlennosti v planirovanii i khozyajstvennoj dejatel'nosti i po usileniyu ikh otvetstvennosti za resul'taty raboty', *Ekonomicheskaya Gazeta* (25 July, no. 31).
Postanovlenie (1985), 'O shirokom rasprostranenii novykh metodov khozyajstvovaniya i usilenii ikh vozdejstviya na uskorenie nauchno-tekhnicheskogo progressa', *Ekonomicheskaya Gazeta* (12 July, no. 32).
Rutland, P. (1984), 'The Shchekino Method and the Struggle to Rise Labour Productivity in Soviet Industry', *Soviet Studies*, vol. 36, no. 3.
Sen, A.K. (1966), 'Labour Allocation in a Cooperative Enterprise', *Review of Economic Studies*, vol. 33, no. 96.

Sovershenstvovanie khozyajstvennogo mekhaniszma (1980, 2nd edn), Moscow: Ekonomika.

Sovershenstvovanie khozyajstvennogo mekhaniszma: Sbornik dokumentov (1982, 2nd edn), Moscow: Ekonomika.

Wiles, P. (1977), *Economic Institutions Compared*, Oxford: Basil Blackwell.

Zajkauskas, B.A. (1983), 'Eksperiment v otrasli', *Planovoe Khozyajstvo*, no. 11.

4
Labour Hoarding and Attempts at Labour Saving in the Soviet Economy

Susanne Oxenstierna*

Labour hoarding is a longstanding practice in Soviet enterprises.[1] Many attempts have been made to curb this tendency, especially since the late 1970s. The fundamental incentives of the economic system, however, seem to persist in generating hoarding instead of efficient use of labour.

The basic reasons for labour hoarding (as well as hoarding of other inputs), may be summarised by three distinguishing characteristics of the Soviet economic system: (1) plan fulfilment is the prime concern of Soviet managers, as this is what makes them successful in the eyes of their superiors. Traditionally quantitative indicators, especially output targets, have been attributed more importance than qualitative aspects of enterprise activities (e.g. labour productivity), in the evaluation of the enterprise's overall performance. Further, failure to obtain inputs is not an acceptable excuse for failure to fulfil the plan. (2) Plan targets are set 'from the achieved level', a method that provides the enterprise with a strong motive for not economising on labour. Improved labour utilisation in one period will call for further improvements in the next, and the enterprise will have trouble in fulfilling and overfulfilling its future output and productivity targets. As the criterion of success is to perform better in relation to previous periods and the plan, i.e. better than the level achieved, no incentive is provided for efficient resource usage in absolute terms. Thus, in order to survive in the long run, the enterprise has to keep 'hidden reserves'. (3) The necessity of keeping reserves within the enterprise is reinforced by the notorious supply uncertainties to which Soviet enterprises are exposed. By keeping surplus labour, the enterprise gains in flexibility when the right materials are not delivered on time, if at all. Thereby it is possible to meet planned output levels of 'storming' at the end of the month, and to engage part of the workforce in dwarf-shops, producing the tools, components, spare parts, etc. needed. Like storming, the self-supporting tendency is a widespread phenomenon, and adds to the inefficient labour utilisation in the economy as a whole, as this small-scale production is much more costly in terms of labour, than the corresponding production in specialised industries.

Many other factors make it rational for Soviet managers to hoard labour: high costs of hirings and firings; difficulties to obtain labour on the external labour market because of increasing labour shortages; managers' pay-scale being linked to the number of workers employed; the habit of local authorities to summon up workers from the enterprises for work on various civil projects, and in agriculture during the harvest season, to name a few examples.

This chapter discusses how the central authorities act against the pressure for surplus labour from below and the reasons for the limited success of these attempts. This topic cannot be satisfactorily dealt with without considering the allocation of capital, which is the basic determinant of the number of officially sanctioned jobs within the enterprise, and we start by reviewing the effects of Soviet investment policies on labour utilisation.

CAPITAL EXPANSION AND INEFFICIENT LABOUR USAGE

Looking back at the 1920s, we are reminded that in those days labour, especially unskilled labour, was a comparatively abundant resource in the Soviet economy. Instead, capital shortage was a main impediment to the policy-makers aiming at transforming Russia into an industrialised nation in the shortest possible time. The strategy chosen at the time of the first five-year plan (FYP), implied expansion of the production apparatus rather than making it more efficient, and resource mobilisation rather than resource allocation. Thereby the industrialisation drive also made it possible to attain another urgent goal, full employment. In 1930 unemployment was finally eliminated according to official Soviet sources.[2] This may of course be questioned considering western contemporary definitions. There is evidence of search and frictional unemployment in the USSR as elsewhere. Guesstimates of frictional unemployment rates, for the non-*kolkhoz* labour force, range between 0.4 and 3.3 per cent.[3] From this, and the fact that the growth of jobs in the socialist sector has been at least equal to, and has usually outstripped the growth of the able-bodied population,[4] it may be concluded that unemployment is a marginal problem in the Soviet Union.

The survival of the extensive investment pattern into the present day has several negative effects on both labour and capital utilisation. The major part of investments (around two-thirds) is still directed to new projects, instead of being used to re-equip and modernise existing capacities.[5] The low replacement share has resulted in fixed capital being retained in service twice as long, on the average, as in the major market economies.[6] Apart from this being an explanation for the negative capital productivity rate during the past 20 years, it has a negative impact on labour allocation. New jobs are constantly created and increasingly hard to fill. For instance, during 1976-79 more than one million new jobs in industry stood vacant.[7] Another source reports that a survey of the investment plans put forward in some ministries for 1981-85 revealed that these implied increased capacities that would raise planned employment in the subordinated enterprises by 15 per cent.[8] How the new jobs were to be manned had not been considered. At the same time, manpower is tied up in obsolete, low-productivity production units. Old equipment requires more repairs than new, which forces the enterprises to keep a considerable number of people in maintenance work. In 1977, repair of machinery engaged 'several million workers', 18 per cent of industrial wage workers.[9]

Another aspect of investment policies, originating in the historical scarcity of capital and relative abundance of unskilled labour, is the practice of mechanising basic production processes to the neglect of auxiliary functions (repair work, loading, unloading, etc.). As a result the ratio of basic to auxiliary workers is low (1 to 1) in the Soviet union, compared to other industrialised countries (2 to 1).[10] It is recognised nowadays, that investments in auxiliary operations are far more efficient than investments in basic operations — in terms of labour, one million roubles invested in the former releases 4-5 times more workers than in the latter. Yet, only 20 per cent of the investment resources directed to re-equip existing enterprises is used to mechanise auxiliary work.[11] According to the Central Statistical Office (TsSU SSSR), the amount of people in many auxiliary functions increased absolutely between 1959-72, in some cases more than two times.[12] The high percentage of auxiliary works also accounts for a large share of manual labour, which in 1979 engaged 40.1 per cent (compared to 41.5 per cent in 1975) of all workers in industry and over 50 per cent in construction and agriculture.[13] Although one might argue that, 'A part of the explanation for the slow reduction in the use of manual labour lies in the proclivity of managers to hold labour in reserve to meet emergencies; in the interim, the workers must have job titles and something to do',[14] one has to consider what possibilities the managers have for releasing these workers, even if they wanted to, when no equipment is available to replace them. During the 10th FYP (1976–80), ministries producing labour-saving techniques fulfilled their plans for those items by only 42–68 per cent.[15]

Thus, inefficient labour use is largely a result of an investment pattern established during a period when the prerequisites for economic development were very different from today's. The principle of extensive growth has since become a fundament of the Soviet model. Efficient resource allocation and utilisation are hard to achieve within this framework.

Labour shortage

Taking into account that the labour supply prospects for the 1980s and 1990s are the tightest ever,[16] it is quite evident that by proceeding along these lines, the Soviet leadership will have no problem in maintaining full employment. However, the efficiency losses implied by the traditional investment pattern have attracted more serious attention in the light of the increasing labour shortage resulting from the stagnating labour supply on the one hand, and the constant growth of jobs on the other.

The question of the nature and dimension of the Soviet labour shortage is problematic. First of all, it is not evident what the 'shortage' should be related to. It is hardly enough to state that the labour requirements, put forth by the enterprises, generally exceed the labour demand estimated by Gosplan. (For the previous FYPs this figure has been reported to be around 2.5–3.5 million people.)[17] What this divergence does reflect is that central planners do not know what the actual labour requirements are and that the enterprises may well inflate their labour demand. It does not provide us with a clear idea of either the economic significance of labour shortage or its actual dimension. A more sophisticated approach, that would tell us if labour shortage has real economic meaning, is to look at whether labour has become the binding constraint on output or, in other words, has output become more sensitive to variations in labour inputs? This sort of evidence is provided by

Table 4.1 The degree of labour shortage (vacant workplaces as a percentage of the total amount of workplaces)

1965	1970	1975	1980	1985
1%	4.9%	7.3%	9.9%	12.2%

Source: Baryshnikov and Malmygin (1983), p. 39.

Weitzman's estimations of output elasticities in Soviet industry 1950–1978.[18] According to these, output elasticity with respect to labour has increased (from 0.52 in 1965, to 0.73 in 1978), and the elasticity of substitution of capital for labour is low (0.5). This suggests that an increasing labour shortage has a depressing impact on output and, thus, represents a real economic problem. Conclusions based on this kind of macro-model are, however, never beyond dispute, and this case is no exception.[19]

The most straightforward way to evaluate Soviet labour shortage is to look at the difference between the number of jobs filled, and the number of workers available. This, however, is not without difficulties, as neither figure is known for the USSR. Table 4.1 shows some Soviet estimates of a related measure; the number of vacant workplaces as a percentage of their total amount. How the figures were arrived at is not clear from the source. It is also unclear as to what parts of the economy they relate, but probably they refer to industry only.

Assuming that these figures reflect, at least roughly, the development of the number of vacancies, and thereby the degree of labour shortage, it seems that the shortage is not a negligible problem; it deserves the attention it has been receiving in Soviet press and economic literature for several years. The figures above are not adjusted for the number of unemployed job seekers, but given the low rate of unemployment in the Soviet economy, the shortage of workers can hardly be dismissed as a frictional phenomenon. A more serious problem is to what extent the vacant jobs represent productive ones. That is, are all these vacant workplaces necessary to keep up output growth? And, related to this, have the enterprises financial means to cover the potential wage costs related to them? Most probably, the magnitude of the labour shortage suggested in Table 4.1 is largely explained by the bulk of jobs being attached to capital items well beyond retirement age. This, however, does not make the problem less 'real', or serious, as there is no effective mechanism that guarantees that workers are allocated to their most productive use.

Attempts at labour-saving

Labour shortage has forced policy-makers to consider ways of decreasing the excessive demand for labour. Besides the general directives to give priority to the modernisation of existing capacities and the mechanisation of manual works, which have so far shown unsatisfactory results, the authorities are now beginning to introduce measures aiming directly at the elimination of technologically obsolete equipment. One such measure is 'workplace attestation'.[20] Henceforth, all Soviet enterprises in the material sphere of production are supposed to conduct a survey (repeated at least twice during each five-year period) of their equipment, and of the workplaces associated with each item of capital stock. Directives on the broad implementation of this scheme were published in 1985,[21] but several experiments have been undertaken since the beginning of the 1980s.[22] The idea of workplace attestation is, of course, to push scrapping of obsolete equipment, to cut back the officially sanctioned jobs within the enterprise, and thereby to improve the efficiency in labour allocation, both between enterprises and within each enterprise. It will also provide a means to obtain information on what the actual labour demands of the enterprises are, to what extent existing jobs are manned, and to give the central planners an idea of the number of workplaces in the country as a whole, as well as of their distribution over regions. The lack of such data in the past has neither prevented central planners from drawing up labour balances, nor regulating enterprises' labour demand in detail. Not surprisingly the effectiveness of central controls in this area has been very limited.

Workplace attestation is an attempt to increase central controls over demand for labour, but it is hard to see how the scheme will succeed in its objectives, as it requires the cooperation of the enterprise managers. For them, the dominant incentive is still to hoard labour, and the central planners can hardly process enough information to see whether the attestation has been properly carried out. There are already newspaper reports of managers having falsely reported completion of the attestation process.[23] Who is going to check on the immense number of reports coming in when workplace attestation is implemented on a broad scale? This is an ever-present problem.

Institutional obstacles to labour-saving

Apart from the incentives generated by the economic system, some characteristics of the Soviet labour market make workplace attestation and other labour-saving attempts unattractive to enterprise managers. Like capitalist firms, Soviet enterprises have costs related to hirings and firings, which makes it rational to keep a certain labour reserve.

Labour is not an administratively allocated input in the USSR, and recruitment of workers is a matter almost entirely left to the enterprise to deal with on its own. Organised forms of placement contribute only marginally, the main type of organised placement being the various ways of placing graduates from different levels of the education system in specific jobs. The enterprises recruit around 80 per cent of all hirings themselves, with little assistance from the labour exchanges. (See Table 4.2.)

The insignificant role played by the labour exchanges (job placement bureaux) in the placement of workers is partly explained by their being few. In 1980 there were around 600, which is more than before, but quite marginal when viewed in combination with the fact that more than 20 million people (excluding *kolkhoz* peasants) change jobs every year.[24] The use of labour exchanges has been said to produce positive results, especially in reducing the time workers spend between jobs. For the enterprise the exchanges are not only essential as recruiters of workers, but also as information collectors and spreaders, a helping hand most Soviet enterprises lack today.

The difficulties associated with dismissals also make enterprise managers reluctant to fire redundant workers. Soviet labour legislation reflects a strong commitment to full employment, and requires that the enterprise finds alternative employment for the employees it intends to dismiss. The factory trade union must be satisfied that there are valid reasons for reductions of staff, and it seems that a worker who finds himself dismissed on false grounds has a fairly good chance of winning his case, if applying to the People's Court.[25]

Thus, institutional characteristics of the Soviet labour market do not promote enterprise managers' willingness to release redundant workers. The difficulties and uncertainties related to the recruitment of labour make it preferable to have a supply of workers in reserve in case a need should arise. Dismissals are associated with legal obstacles. These burdens placed upon the enterprise, reinforce its reluctance for labour-saving.

Table 4.2 Share of different forms of placement in the RSFSR, 1980 (percentage of total hirings)

Organised recruitment (*orgnabor*)	0.7
Resettlement of families in agriculture	0.2
Recruitment of young people through Komsomol (*obshestvennye prizyvy*)	2.8
Placement of graduates from vocational schools (PTU)	9.3
Placement of graduates from higher education	1.9
Placement of graduates from special secondary education	3.0
Transfers between enterprises (*perevod*)	3.8
Hiring by the enterprises themselves	77.8
of which with assistance of job placement bureaux	9.7
Residual	0.5
Total	100.0

Source: Kotlyar *et al.* (1983), pp. 45–6.

PLANNING AND INCENTIVES

We now turn to the traditional central instruments used to control enterprise demand for labour: quantitative labour targets and the planned wages fund. We also consider the implications of the rules governing the size of the Material Incentive Fund (MIF) which, since the 1965 reform, has been the principal source of cash bonuses to management, for the input decisions of the enterprise. Both plan directives concerning labour and the rules of the MIF have been subject to many changes over the years, and we discuss the possible effects of these for the enterprise's motivation to economise on labour.

Quantitative labour targets

Before the 1965 reform, the enterprise was given four centrally fixed labour-related targets: the total wages fund (the sum at the enterprise's disposition to cover labour costs during the plan period, i.e. a planned wages budget), the number of workers to be employed broken down into categories, an average wage, and labour productivity. Under the reformed system, the enterprise was simply to be given its wages fund and the rest of the labour indicators were to be planned by the enterprise independently, i.e. they were not to be confirmed by superior organs.[26]

The deregulation of labour was in line with the general aims of the reform. The enterprises were to be granted more freedom in decision-making in order to promote efficiency in the economy. Only eight principal plan targets were retained. Highest priority was still attributed to the output target, now in terms of the volume of sales, but the inclusion of profits and profitability (the ratio of profits to capital) among the principal indicators was a signal to pay more attention to the cost side of production and to efficiency.

The abolition of the labour quotas meant that the enterprises were now able to hire what labour they needed when necessary. This discretion was thought to improve labour utilisation. With the quotas the enterprises had had strong incentives not to reduce their workforce, as this would mean that the quota was reduced and the enterprise would be in trouble in case of unanticipated events. To insure themselves, as high quotas as possible were negotiated for, and extra workers hired, whether needed or not, to hold the job titles.[27]

The rationale behind the abolition of growth of labour productivity as a centrally fixed target is more obscure. One argument might have been the distortions caused by how labour productivity was measured. Usually the indicator was expressed as gross output in value or physical terms, thus rewarding the use of expensive materials or, for instance, excessive weight. On the whole it seems that the reformers were primarily concerned with capital productivity; profitability was entered among the centrally confirmed plan targets, the size of the MIF was conditioned upon this indicator, and a capital charge was introduced. Capital productivity eventually did improve with the reform, while labour productivity began to slow down in the early 1970s. This is reflected in Table 4.3.

It is hard to say to what extent the lack of a centrally fixed labour productivity target did contribute to the slowdown in this indicator. In any case, the planners responded to it by reintroducing growth of labour productivity as a compulsory, centrally confirmed indicator in 1971.[28] Labour productivity also became one of the 'fund-forming' indicators of the MIF.

During the 1970s, the idea that the enterprises would make better decisions when granted more flexibility and relieved of excessive central control, has been successively substituted by the idea that improvements in the economic mechanism have to be attained by centralisation and improved planning. The 1979 decree proposes a considerable increase in the amount of centrally fixed targets, and a stronger control of the efficiency indicators in the evaluation of the enterprise's activities.[29] Many of these measures were adopted in

Table 4.3 Labour and capital productivity (average annual percentage increase)

	Productivity of social labour	Capital productivity in social production
1961–65	5.6	−2.4
1966–70	6.8	−0.3
1971–75	4.6	−1.9
1976–80	3.2	−2.6

Source: Pachomov *et al.* (1984), p. 32.

the 11th FYP (1981–85). Again labour is regulated in detail, and the enterprises were assigned at least four labour targets from above: a wages fund normative, or a total wages fund, labour productivity growth, a limit on the maximum number of workers to be employed, and tasks for the reduction of manual labour.[30]

The introduction of limits on the number of workers reflects dissatisfaction both with labour productivity and the economic levers — the wages fund and the MIF — in restricting the enterprise's labour demand. A Soviet labour specialist claims that the introduction of limits was necessary because, 'At present there is no effective mechanism to make economic organs interested in fulfilling their production plans with a minimum of labour required.'[31] The efficiency of the limits in restricting the enterprise's workforce as far may, however, be questioned. First of all, if a limit is at all assigned by a ministry, it is set as a branch indicator, without sufficient consideration of the availability of manpower in the region where the enterprise is situated. Local labour market organs are asked for agreement only in cases of increases in the limits, or when employment in new enterprises is planned. As a result, the limits are not restrictive enough and enterprises often cannot 'fulfil' their labour plans, because local labour supplies fall short. Many enterprises operating with a workforce below their quotas still manage to fulfil their production plans, which indicates that limits have a far weaker impact on labour utilisation than the actual availability of manpower. Secondly, even when the limits are effective (i.e. less than the labour supply available to the enterprise) they are often not perceived as binding constraints by the enterprise managers. The sanctions designed to impede managers from overstepping their labour limits (e.g. reductions in their bonuses) are often not used by the ministries, if other aspects of the enterprise's performance are satisfactory.[32] Thirdly, the use of quantity constraints reintroduce the pre-reform motives to hoard labour.

The wages fund

In the 1965 reform, the principal instrument for controlling enterprise employment, would be indirect, through the allocation of money for wages. There were proposals to abolish this target also, but these were considered 'premature', and Kosygin stated that the main reason for not taking this step was to guarantee 'The necessary balance between the quantity of consumer goods manufactured and the population's purchasing power', the latter being determined 'in large measure by the [total] wage fund'. In the future, when we are able considerably to expand the production of consumer goods and accumulate necessary reserves of these goods it will be possible to abolish the system of pre-determining the wage fund for enterprises.[33] Since then, no further proposals have been made in this direction; instead several attempts have been made to improve this instrument, as its deficiencies hamper attempts to curb labour hoarding and to raise labour productivity.

The problem of making the wages fund an effective means of control has many sides. First of all, the fact that the enterprise is assigned a wages budget, instead of being forced to cover labour costs (as well as other costs) from revenues, implies that labour is no 'cost' in the traditional sense as long as wage payments are below or equal to this budget. That is, there is no incentive for the enterprise to reduce staffing to press down wage costs below the budget level. This lack of incentive to reduce staffing (and costs in general), the Soviet enterprise shares with many budget financed public agencies in the West. Despite this, one might argue that the central authorities could set the wages fund 'low enough' to force down the enterprise's labour costs, and thereby their workforce. A major reason for not doing this is that wages are not only costs but represent incomes and incentives to work to the population. The Soviet state has a comparatively strong influence over wage distribution, as basic wages for all occupational groups are set centrally.[34] However, the fact that a considerable share of the take-home wage is paid in the form of bonuses (paid out of the wages fund) on top of the basic wage and depends on the performance of the worker and the enterprise makes it impossible to determine what wages fund is exactly necessary for the enterprise. The principle that Soviet citizens should be paid according to their work input and a strong belief in the impact of wages on work effort and productivity make the planners bound to listen to the enterprises' claims concerning their wage costs.

A second major problem with the planned wages fund, is that its size has been conditioned by the number of workers employed in the enterprise. Up to 1981, the planned wages fund was determined by multiplying of the planned number of employees by the average wage (excluding bonuses from the MIF).[35] That is, the larger the planned number of employees the larger the wages fund, and vice versa. Bachurin, Deputy President of Gosplan, remarks that this practice of planning the wages fund 'induces the enterprises to decrease their indicators of production growth in order to overfulfil the plan and thereby get additions to the wages fund. Enterprises that plan a higher productivity and decrease their workforce seldom do not get into trouble: often their wages fund is not enough. Therefore many enterprises inflate their planned labour requirements in order to acquire bigger wages funds.[36] This malpractice is also motivated by planning from the achieved level: cutbacks in the workforce in one period, will call for further reductions in the future, and result in a smaller wages fund. The motives for keeping on extra workers, that were hoped to be reduced, by the abolition of central regulation of the number of workers employed, in the 1965 reform, were thus essentially kept alive by the regulation of the wages fund. As will be seen below, the significance of a large wages fund on the size of the MIF was another incentive not to reduce the number of employees.

The quotation above points at a third weakness of the wages fund as a constraint on employment: the wages fund might be increased above its planned level under certain conditions. This obviously provides the enterprise with an incentive to increase output by employing more workers rather than by raising productivity, when able to choose between these alternatives.[37]

Several attempts have been made to overcome these shortcomings in regard to the wages fund. One of these is the so-called 'Shchekino model' where the enterprise is assigned a fixed wages fund which does not vary with the number of workers employed. At least 50 per cent of reduced wages costs, resulting from dismissals of redundant workers, may be used to increase the wages of the remaining personnel. This experiment, first launched in 1967, has proved quite successful in raising labour productivity in enterprises where adopted. Most of the released workers have, however, been redeployed within the same factory.[38]

Another measure is the introduction of normative planning of the wages fund, adopted by around 25 ministries for the running FYP period.[39] The essence of this method is that instead of being assigned a total wages fund (based on the planned number of employees and the average wage), the enterprise gets a normative for labour costs per rouble of output. The normative should be stable for the five-year period and is disaggregated over the separate years in a regressive manner, i.e. labour costs per rouble of output should decrease over the FYP. In this way, the size of the wage budget becomes conditioned on the volume of output (or more precisely sales), which means that the enterprise has to produce more, not just increase the number of workers, in order to get a larger wage fund. Of course, this looks very similar to past practices, when additions to the workforce and subsequently to the wages fund could be attained by overfulfilment of output targets. The labour cost norms should, however, restrain the traditional tendency of output being boosted to the neglect of labour productivity. The main problem, so far, is the setting of reasonable normatives from the start, which has resulted in their being frequently changed. This instability, as well as the idea that the normative should decrease during the five-year period, makes it reasonable to question whether the positive effects on labour productivity expected from this measure, will materialise. There is also a strong motive for the enterprise to keep the normative as high as possible, in order to avoid too great a reduction in the next plan period. Thus, the new method will probably not succeed in effecting any radical change toward better labour utilisation. 'Too many' workers is still not costly to the enterprise, as long as wage costs are kept within the stipulated norm.

There are some suggestions for imposing a 'real' labour cost on the enterprise by introducing a wage fund tax, which would be deduced from the enterprise's profit. Various forms of wages funds and labour taxes, exist in other Socialist countries, but so far, the reluctance to let Soviet enterprises pay for the use of labour has prevented even experiments in this direction.[40] One argument against such propositions is that labour costs vary considerably between branches, and that a tax would affect the various branches very unevenly. In 1980, the average share of labour costs was 14.8 per cent in industry, but varied between the extremes 1.6 (cotton cleaning) and 37.9 per cent (logging).[41] A labour tax would raise costs dramatically in the latter case, but have a very marginal impact on costs and employment in the former. Also, industries with low profitability would get in trouble, specifically if their labour costs are comparatively high. The Soviet source concludes that the introduction of a labour tax would require a reconstruction of the whole price system if these sectors are to be able to cover their costs,[42] and such a reform can hardly be anticipated.

A more moderate proposal is to let the enterprise pay for increases in staff over the previous year.[43] This would, however, lead to a situation whereby enterprises that are not overstaffed from the beginning are penalised, while enterprises having an internal labour reserve are unaffected, if a need for extra workers suddenly arises.

Like other propositions, aiming at strengthening the restrictions and sanctions preventing enterprises from overstepping their labour quotas, wage funds, or wage cost normatives, this suggests that the intention is not to make the enterprise pay the full cost of labour, but only to restrain increases in the number of workers employed compared to the 'achieved level'. Thereby the margin of slack in labour utilisation may fall, or is at least kept constant, but no incentive is provided for efficient use of labour *per se*, as only improvements in labour utilisation compared to planned and previous levels are rewarded. 'Hidden reserves' is a prerequisite for achieving such results.

The material incentive fund

The increased importance attributed to labour-related targets during the 1970s, and in the 11th FYP, is also reflected in the rules governing the size of the material incentive fund. In the 1965 version, no special incentive was provided this way to use labour more efficiently. The general formula for determining the planned MIF was originally[44]

(1) $MIF_p = (aX_p + bR_p)W$

where X_p is the planned percentage growth in sales (sometimes replaced by profits) over the previous period; R_p, planned profitability (the ratio of accounting profits to capital); W, the wages fund of the current year; a,b, norms of deductions set by the ministry. The actual MIF was dependent on the MIF_p and actual performance compared to planned with regard to the 'fund-forming' indicators, sales and profitability

(2) $MIF_a = MIF_p + (k_x a(X_a - X_p) + k_R b(R_a - R_p))W.$

The subscript a denotes the actual value of a variable: k_x and k_R

are norms taking on different values whether the plan is fulfilled or not (k = 1 for exact fulfilment, k > 1 when underfulfilled, k < 1 when overfulfilled). Their purpose is to provide the enterprise with an incentive to adopt high plan targets instead of overfulfilling lower ones, and a disincentive to acquire a high MIF_p by adopting high targets and then underfulfil the plan. Besides the fund-forming indicators, the size of the MIF was conditioned on a set of 'fund-correcting' indicators, which, if not fulfilled, could reduce the payments out of the fund.

From (1) and (2), it is evident that a large wages fund produces more bonuses than a small one. This was, in fact, one intention behind the bonus scheme, introduced in order to prevent big divergences in bonus per worker in different industries, which might have occurred if the MIF had instead been directly related to profits. However, the drawbacks of this practice soon became apparent. Increases in wage cost would automatically result in increases in the bonus fund, and the wages fund became more crucial to the size of the MIF than the fund-forming indicators. For the 9th FYP (1971–75) the MIF was related to the actual wages fund achieved in 1970. According to Soviet estimates, the retention of the current wages fund for each year as the base, would have resulted in 50 per cent of the (estimated) increase in the MIF for the five-year period being caused by increased wage costs.[45] Nevertheless, the use of the wages fund in the bonus formulas, throughout the 1970s, continued to act as a disincentive to reduce staffs. Soviet observers, in their retrospective analyses of the past incentive rules, conclude that 'under these conditions any decrease in the number of personnel, resulting from improved utilisation of labour, and the resulting reduction in the planned wages fund would be directly reflected as a decrease in the incentive funds'.[46] For the 11th FYP (1981–85), this practice was finally abolished (at least in the instructions for how to determine the MIF), and the size of the fund was instead related directly to profits.

There are several studies of the implications of the 1965 bonus schemes on the input and output decisions of the enterprise.[47] If we assume that the enterprise manager tries to maximise the MIF, it might be seen quite intuitively (from expressions (1) and (2)) that the labour demand of the enterprise will be between that of a profit-maximiser and an output-maximiser. Formal results show that this is true as long as growth of sales and profitability are both positive, and also that under these conditions the enterprise will choose a more labour-intensive technique than would a profit-maximiser.[48]

The impact of letting the wage fund vary with the number of employees is also highlighted by this kind of exercise. The 'wage fund effect' will produce a positive term that should be added to the value marginal product in the first order condition.[49]

The inefficient labour–capital combination, implied by the 1965 bonus schemes, was slightly adjusted by the introduction of labour productivity as a fund-forming indicator, in the early 1970s. It seems, however, that this change did not succeed in outweighing the effect of the inclusion of sales in the formulas. For the 11th FYP, changes in the rules determining the MIF were more radical. Sales and profitability were not among the obligatory fund-forming indicators. Instead, the obligatory indicators were growth of labour productivity and the share of high-quality goods to total output.[50] Compared to the 1965 bonus schemes, these rules provide the enterprise with incentive to improve labour utilisation and raise labour productivity. The actual effect on decision-making at the enterprise level, however, depends on the degree to which labour productivity and other quality indicators succeed in dominating the traditional quantity indicators in the evaluation of the overall performance of the enterprise. Even if this might be achieved if the new bonus rules remain stable over a longer period,[51] the other traditional reasons for inefficient labour usage remain — for instance, planning and evaluation 'from the achieved level', supply irregularities, labour shortage, and the risk of having to release parts of the workforce for tasks outside the enterprise temporarily — and continue to provide managers with incentives for labour-hoarding.

CONCLUSIONS

What then are the prospects for curbing labour hoarding in the Soviet economy? As described above, all measures introduced so far are traditional and represent adjustments within the centrally administered system. A common element in most of these attempts is the increase of central control over staffing at the enterprise. Workplace attestation is such an example, and would, if it did work, promote a more efficient allocation of labour both between and within enterprises by decreasing labour-hoarding associated with obsolete equipment. The prospects of this attempt ever succeeding, however, are gloomy. As remarked by Hanson,[52] the attestation process bears many similarities with the 'passportisation' of enterprises, required by the 1979 decree. This too was intended to supply more accurate information on available capacities and their utilisation. The common problem with these attempts is that they increase the information overload on central planners, and tend to create but a new stream of reports from below, which nobody has the time to check. Further, this kind of remedy does not alter any of the basic reasons for Soviet managers to keep surplus labour, and the hoarding tendency will, thus, remain. It follows that the potential efficiency gains that are nevertheless implied by the measure will not materialise.

It is hard to envisage that the reintroduction of quantitative labour targets would lead to any such improvements of efficiency, even in theory. Like other plan indicators, they contribute to maintaining the *status quo*, and do not promote reallocation of labour inputs to where they are most productive. They suffer from all traditional drawbacks of Soviet planning, exemplified by the difficulties to set effective 'limits'; the built-in incentive, present in a centrally fixed labour productivity target, not to reveal hidden reserves, in order to make it possible to perform better than the achieved level, also in future periods, etc. On the other hand, if there are plan targets for other aspects of enterprise performance, there have to be ones for labour too, if this aspect should not be entirely neglected by the enterprise managers, when they decide what course of action to take.

Which parts of the plan that the centre wishes the manager to pay special attention to is also transmitted by the rules determining managerial bonuses. These have been subject to repeated changes since 1965, and now reflect a much stronger concern for labour productivity, and other qualitative indicators, than previously. The effects of these changes on enterprise behaviour, however, are hard to predict. The use of ordinary analytical techniques does shed some light,[53] but to what degree the theoretical results reflect what is actually going on in Soviet reality remains an open question. It is for instance, not quite evident that the idea that bonuses express what the centre considers important, is best described by assuming that the enterprise managers maximise the bonus formulas, which is what western scholars are apt to do. Even if this assumption is partly valid, other influences and constraints on Soviet micro-decision-making should be taken into account, if the input decisions of the Soviet enterprise are to be properly studied.

Finally, the problems of making wage costs a binding constraint on labour demand point at the weakness of financial constraints in general on Soviet producers. The fact that Soviet enterprises are not bound to cover their expenses from a competitively-earned revenue, is a feature that distinguishes them from capitalist firms. This difference is as crucial as the distinction between plan and market or plan fulfilment versus profit-maximisation, when Soviet enterprise behaviour is compared to that of western enterprises. The prerequisites for making Soviet enterprises genuinely self-financing are not met in the Soviet economy. This would, for instance, require 'real' prices, i.e. prices that are not primarily accounting units, and therefore fixed over longer periods, but prices that reflect opportunity costs and are free to vary. This also invalidates the possibilities of dealing with excess labour demand by 'fiscal' policies, e.g. by imposing a wages fund tax on the enterprise. Under present conditions, such an attempt would probably just add to the mass of imperfections already there, without changing enterprise behaviour in any radical way.

We cannot say that the attempts made to improve labour utilisation in the Soviet economy will necessarily all fail. Presumably, they represent what is feasible within the Soviet economic model, which is strongly constrained by political considerations. The measures might decrease the degree of labour-hoarding, although they do not represent any final solutions to the problem. For this, a change in the economic system is required, providing the enterprises with the motivation to economise on labour (and other inputs), which is usually provided by a competitive environment. Despite the new wind in Soviet economic policies under the new leadership, such as systemic reform cannot be expected in the near future.

NOTES

* Research for this chapter has been financed by the Bank of Sweden Tercentenary Foundation. I am indebted to Hans Aage, Pieter Boot, Stefan Hedlund, Mario Nuti, Pavel Pelikan, Ann-Mari Sätre, Eskil Wadensjö, Lars Werin and participants of the labour market seminar at the Swedish Institute for Social Research, for comments on an earlier version of the paper. I would also like to thank Eva Carlsson and Anne-Maj Folmer-Hansen, who have typed and retyped the manuscript.

1. See e.g. Berliner (1957), pp. 178–81.
2. Narkhoz (1980), p. 87.
3. Aage (1985), p. 2. See also Hanson (1985a), p. 5.
4. Kotlyar *et al.* (1983), pp. 28–9.
5. Ibid., p. 23.
6. Cohn (1982), p. 170.
7. *Kommunist* 19/1980. See also Pachomov *et al.* (1984), p. 23.
8. Malmygin (1982), p. 60.

9. Schroeder (1982), p. 8.
10. Ibid., p. 7.
11. Kostin (ed.) (1979), pp. 128-9.
12. Ibid.
13. Bachurin (1982), p. 35.
14. Schroeder (1982), p. 8.
15. Bachurin (1982), p. 35.
16. See e.g. Schroeder (1982), p. 18.
17. See e.g. Kostin (ed.) (1979), p. 154.
18. Weitzman (1983).
19. For comments and discussion of the results, see Aage (1985), pp. 24-6, and Hanson (1985a), pp. 10-11.
20. This section draws on Hanson (1985b), where a detailed presentation and discussion of the measure is given. See also Hanson (1985a).
21. Joint decree by the USSR Council of Ministers and the Central Council of Trade Unions, published in *Pravda*, 12 September 1985.
22. Gorelov *et al.* (1982).
23. Hanson (1985b).
24. See e.g. Chapman (1982), pp. 5, 8.
25. Berliner (1976), pp. 158-63; Godson (1984), p. 121.
26. Kosygin (1965), p. 30.
27. Berliner (1976), pp. 166-7.
28. Rutland (1984), p. 358. According to Ryabushkin and Dadashev (1981), p. 101, the year was 1972.
29. 'Ob uluchshenii planirovaniya i usilenii vozdejstviya khozyajstvennogo mekhanizma . . .', *Postonovlenie*, 12 July 1979.
30. See e.g. Rutland (1984), p. 359.
31. Kotlyer *et al.* (1983), p. 32.
32. Ibid., pp. 32-4.
33. Kosygin (1965), p. 29.
34. For a detailed discussion of the Soviet wage system, see McAuley (1979) Ch. 8; Kirsch (1972).
35. Gosplan (1975), pp. 114-16.
36. Bachurin (1977), p. 286.
37. See Adam (1973), p. 88.
38. See further Rutland (1984), and Aage in this volume.
39. See Rutland (1984), p. 359.
40. Markov (1980), p. 75.
41. Narkhoz (1980), p. 153.
42. Kunelskij (1981), pp. 36-7.
43. Ibid.
44. The formulas are simplified. See further Ellman (1972), Ch. 8.
45. Drize and Sidorova (1975), pp. 5, 12.
46. Ryabushkin and Dadashev (1981), p. 97.
47. See references given in Aage in this volume.
48. See e.g. Martin (1976), and Aage, this volume.
49. See Martin (1976). The same result is obtained in the first model presented by Aage (ibid.) if total bonuses, instead of bonuses per worker, are chosen as the enterprise manager's maximand.
50. 'Osnovnye polozheniya ob obrazovanii fonda material'nogo

pooshchreniya ... v 1981-1985 godach v promyshlennosti', *Ekonomicheskaya Gazeta*, nos. 15 and 17, 1980. For a summary and discussion of the new rules, see Freris (1984), Ch. 6.

51. For the 12th FYP (1986-90) the rules for the MIF have again been changed. The size of the MIF is now to be conditioned on the MIF of the previous year. Only one fund-forming indicator is to be used, either unit cost of production or profit. Labour productivity is to be used as a fund-correcting indicator. If labour productivity growth does not at least equal average growth 1981-85 the MIF should be reduced. 'Fond material'nogo pooshchreniya na dvenadtsatuyu pyatiletku', *Ekonomicheskaya Gazeta*, no. 8, 1986.

52. Hanson (1985a), p. 18, and (1985b).

53. See Aage, this volume, op. cit.

REFERENCES

Aage, H. (1985), 'Unemployment: Lessons from the Socialist Countries', Paper presented at the Seminar on Unemployment, Danish Social Science Research Council. Rønne, 26-8 September.

Adam, J. (1973), 'The Incentive System in the USSR: The Abortive Reform of 1965', *Industrial and Labor Relations Review*, vol. 27, no. 1, October.

Bachurin, A.V. (1977), *Planovo — Ekonomicheskie metody upravleniya* (2nd edn), Moscow.

—— (1982), 'Problemy ulucheniya ispolzovaniya trudovykh resursov', *Planovoe Khozyajstvo*, no. 1.

Baryshnikov, Yu. and Malmygin, I. (1983), 'Sbalansirovannost' rabochikh mest i trudoyykh resursov: problemy, opyt regulirovaniya i stimulirovaniya', *Sotsialisticheskij trud*, no. 9.

Berliner, J.S. (1957), *Factory and Manager in the USSR*, Cambridge, Mass.

—— (1976), *The Innovation Decision in Soviet Industry*, Cambridge, Mass.

Chapman, J. (1982), 'Market and Administration in Improving Labor Allocation in the USSR', Paper presented at AAASS Meeting, Washington D.C. 17 October.

Cohn, S.H. (1982), 'Sources of Low Productivity in Soviet Capital Investment', in US Congress, Joint Economic Committee (ed.), *Soviet Economy in the 1980s: Problems and Prospects*, Washington, D.C.

Drize, I.D. and Sidorova, Zh. I. (1975), *Obrazovanie pooshchritel'nykh fondov na predpriyatiyakh*, Moscow.

Ellman, M. (1972), *Soviet Planning Today*, London.

Freris, A. (1984), *The Soviet Industrial Enterprise*, London.

Godson, J. (1984), 'The Role of the Trade Unions', in Schapiro, L. and Godson, J. (eds), *The Soviet Worker* (2nd edn), London.

Gorelov, N. *et al.* (1982), 'Organizastiya ucheta rabochikh mest i obespechenie ikh sbalansirovannosti s trudovymi resursami', *Planovoe Khozyastvo*, no. 3.

Gosplan (1975), *Tipovaya metodika razrabotki pyatiletnego plana proizvodstvennogo obedinenya (kombinata), predpriyatiya*, Moscow.

Hanson, P. (1985a), 'The Labour Shortage and Soviet Economic Policy', Paper presented at the Third World Congress for Soviet and East European Studies, Washington D.C., 30 October–4 November.

—— (1985b), 'Work-Place Attestation: Attempts at Labour Saving in a Labour-Hoarding Economy', *Radio Liberty Research*, RL 316/85.

Kirsch, L.J. (1972), *Soviet Wages: Changes in Structure and Administration since 1956*, Cambridge, Mass.

Kostin, L.A. (ed.) (1979), *Trudovye Resursy SSSR*, Moscow.

Kosygin, A. (1965) 'On Improving Management of Industry, Perfecting Planning and Enhancing Economic Incentives in Industrial Production', *New Methods of Economic Management in the USSR*, Moscow.

Kotlyar, A.E. et al. (1983), *Zanyatost' naseleniya: izuchenie i regulirovanie*, Moscow.

Kunelskij, L.E. (1981), *Zarabotnaya plata i stimulirovanie truda*, Moscow.

Malmygin, I. (1982), 'Sbalansirovannost' rabochikh mest i trudovykh resursov', *Planovoye Khozyajstvo*, no. 8.

Markov, V.I. (1980), *Oplata truda v sisteme upravleniya ekonomikoj razvitogo sotsializma*, Moscow.

Martin, J.M. (1976), 'Economic Reform and the Maximising Behaviour of the Soviet Firm', in Thornton, J. (ed.), *Economic Analysis of the Soviet-Type System*, Cambridge.

McAuley, A. (1979), *Economic Welfare in the Soviet Union*, Madison, Wins.

Pachomov, Ju. N. et al. (1984), *Ekonomiya truda: Formy osushchestvleniya i puti uskoreniya*, Kiev.

Rutland, P. (1984), 'The Shchekino Method and the Struggle to Raise Labour Productivity in Soviet Industry', *Soviet Studies*, vol. 36, no. 3, July, pp. 345–65.

Ryabushkin, T.V. and Dadashev, A.Z. (1981), *Trudovye resursy i effektivnost' proizvodstva*, Moscow.

Schroeder, G.E. (1982), 'Managing Labour Shortages in the Soviet Union', in Adam, J. (ed.), *Employment Policies in the Soviet Union and Eastern Europe*, London.

Weitzman, M. (1983), 'Industrial Production', in Bergson, A. and Levine, H.S. (eds), *The Soviet Economy: Toward the Year 2000*, London.

5
Soft Options in Central Control

Stefan Hedlund*

The topic of this chapter can best be illustrated by the use of an example. Everyday life for a Soviet dogcatcher is governed by the need to meet specified plan targets; in this case to catch X number of stray dogs. He who has seen stray dogs on the outskirts of Moscow, however, realises that dealings with them will definitely not be without danger; Soviet food shortages affect man and beast alike. It is thus natural that the dogcatcher will seek an easier way to fulfil his plan target, and such options will of course always be available.

In private gardens pet dogs run loose. Happily wagging their tails, they allow themselves to be caught and delivered according to plan. The dogcatcher is happy. His superiors are happy. The owner of the pet dog (i.e. the consumer) may be unhappy, but can we realistically expect the dogcatching bureaucracy to upset their plan just to keep a simple dogowner happy? Of course not! The fact that everybody would be better (or at least not worse) off if the stray dogs were kept off the streets and the friendly dogs remained in the gardens, is a fact that is anomalous to the system.

This chapter attempts to identify the existence of such 'soft options' in the Soviet economy, options that are Pareto-inferior but at the same time logical consequences of the economy's incentive system. The latter point is of particular importance. To a casual observer, it would be all too easy to brand the Soviet economic system as highly irrational, given the numerous and officially reported examples of waste and misallocations. Yet, we must be careful to differ between micro- and macro-irrationality.

It is an underlying assumption in our argument, that Soviet citizens act in a highly rational manner at the micro-level. Indeed, their behaviour may be even more rational than in some western market economies, where greater personal welfare may allow a more lax attitude towards finding the best decision in each given situation of choice. It is when all the actions taken by the single individuals are aggregated to form the macro-system that the problems start. Irrespective of which economic system we choose, there can never be a guarantee that aggregated micro-actions will produce a macro-rational outcome.[1] The most celebrated illustration of this fact is of course the Prisoner's Dilemma, to which we shall return below.

The difference between the market-type systems of the West and the hierarchy-type systems of the East, is that from an economic perspective the latter have a higher tendency to produce macro-irrational outcomes. Our aim below will be to seek an explanation for this tendency in terms of the supremacy of politics over economics. The seeming economic irrationality will then be seen as a second-best solution, which is conditioned by political preferences regarding the functioning of the economy.

The soft option that was presented above, in relation to the dogcatcher, will be sought in two quarters. First, we shall look at the individual as a labourer, and then consider him in the role of enterprise manager. In both cases, we shall focus on the incentives that govern his behaviour, and we shall see how these incentives induce him in both instances to diverge from the path that would lead to a rational outcome at the macro-level. There is, however, also an important difference between the two, in the interpretation of the soft option.[2] In the former case, the individual does have a real choice between hard and soft options, while in the latter case, this does not hold in the same sense. For the enterprise manager, the soft option has become the only one possible. We shall return to this distinction below.

In the fourth section of the chapter, we shall bring together the soft options and investigate their impact at the *system* level, arguing that far from being control failures, these are subtle ingredients in a model designed to promote political stability. In the final section, we shall examine this argument against the background of economic reform and the current campaigns for improved discipline, to see what prospects there may be for success along the road taken by the new Soviet General Secretary, Mikhail Gorbachev.

WORK OR SHIRK?

Inefficiency, shirking and low labour productivity have long been notorious problems for the Soviet economy. To some extent this can be explained by demoralisation and disillusionment with the promises of the workers' state. In this section, however, we shall attempt to find a structural explanation, couched in a simple game-theoretic approach to the economy's incentive system.

A crucial point in the discussion of incentives to work is the question of *numéraire*. In much of the existing literature on incentives in collective organisations, the focus is on the supply of *hours* by the individual member.[3] In practice, this may not be a very fruitful approach. First, the decision on hours is largely determined by institutional constraints. Secondly, it has little to do with observed inefficiencies regarding the actual supply of labour.[4]

A better way would be to study the *effort* expended by the individual at work. Here there should be considerable scope for individual choice and the link to overall system efficiency is obvious. We shall, however, also indirectly cover two cases of a variable supply of hours: unauthorised absence and moonlighting. The former can be interpreted as an extreme case of a low supply of effort and the latter as a second economy activity. Our overall contention thus is that the main problem lies not in insufficient *hours* but in insufficient *effort* being supplied to the socialised sector.[5] We shall identify three different cases.

Case 1: Cooperation

Assuming that the individual employee is required to work a specified number of hours, and that no alternative employment opportunities exist, his only choice will be in deciding on the amount of effort to be put into each hour worked. In simple game-theoretical terms, this can be shown in a choice between two strategies: work and shirk. Assuming that all individuals are identical and faced with identical choices, there will be four possible combinations of strategies between individual i and the remaining block of N-1 individuals. These are summarised in the pay-off matrix in Figure 5.1.[6]

If all individuals decide to work conscientiously, maximum collective benefit will be derived (10,10). This outcome, however, is threatened by the classic Prisoner's Dilemma. For the single individual, the best position would be for him to be lazy and for everyone else to work hard (12,6), and given the assumption of identical individuals the outcome will be global shirking (7,7). This,

Figure 5.1 Case I Pay-off

		N-1 Individuals	
Individual i		Work	Shirk
Work		10,10	6,12
Shirk		12,6	7,7

incidentally, is not far removed from an intuitive picture of the working of the Soviet economy.

Whether or not the Dilemma will actually materialise hinges on the size of the membership in the group (the number of employees) and on their mental framework, or 'collective consciousness'. If the membership is small and collectively inclined, an implicit contract to work hard would be spontaneously forthcoming. The best real-life illustration of this would be the Israeli *kibbutzim*, where diligent labour is forthcoming without formal material incentives. The *kibbutz* also provides an example where the assumption of identical individuals can be relaxed. There it has been possible to absorb a certain number of 'shirkers' within the larger group of 'workers', whilst preserving the viability of the system.[7]

However, returning to the general case, as soon as we leave the small group and allow the membership to grow, the organisation will come under strain from two sides: on the one hand, the incentive for the individual to shirk will be strengthened, as the negative consequences of his activities will be shared among a larger group, and on the other, the supply of 'conscious' individuals to the organisation will become exhausted, thus necessitating the recruitment of progressively more shirk-prone members. Both these factors will work to erode the collective spirit and thus to produce the Dilemma outlined in Figure 5.1.[8]

So far we have assumed implicitly that there is a connection between labour effort and labour remuneration, to be determined via the incentive system. If, however, we take into account that payments to labour are made according to fixed scales and that single firms will not be allowed to go bankrupt, then we have, for all practical purposes, severed the link between effort and reward at the firm level, as deficits will be covered out of the government budget.[9]

In this case, the incentive to shirk will become very strong indeed. Losses will not be borne by the organisation but by the entire population and the cost to the single individual of his shirking will thus be proportional to his share in the total population, which in the Soviet case is a small number indeed. Increased effort, on the other hand, will lead to a reduced indebtedness for the organisation, the benefit of which is hardly perceivable to the individual. The concept of loyalty to the organisation will in this case have little meaning to the single member.

The fact that most Soviet pay is according to piece-rates — which would seem to imply a powerful incentive — can now be reduced to minor importance. The incentive is simply to turn out quantity, not quality. The classic example here is the tractor driver, whose assignment is to plow X number of hectares.[10] By shallow ploughing he will increase speed, save fuel and reduce wear. The latter effects will increase his bonus while the former will provide increased leisure. The negative impact on harvest yields will be shared by all alike and can thus be ignored, if the group is sufficiently large. The obvious conclusion from this discussion is that there is a strong need for supervision, so let us now turn to that case.

Case II: Supervision

The pay-off matrix in Figure 5.2 illustrates the case where no voluntary contract to work conscientiously is forthcoming and where the state instead has to resort to compulsion and supervision. Strategy 'work' reflects perfect supervision, which effectively precludes shirking, whereas 'shirk''' and 'shirk'''' reflect decreasing effectiveness of supervision.

Two things should be observed in this case. First, supervision is a costly matter. It requires manpower to be withdrawn from productive uses, which depresses the maximum possible pay-off to the economy. This has not been reflected in the matrix, which is an expanded version of the matrix in Figure 5.1. Secondly, the actual outcome will vary greatly between firms, depending on the tasks to be carried out. For example, in branches where tasks are clearly defined and their spatial distribution is narrow, it may be possible to reach the pay-off (10,10) at little cost in terms of supervision. It is hardly a coincidence that Stakhanov was a coalminer. He had no place to hide and the results of his labour were easily monitored.

However, as spatial distribution and the complexity of production grow, the effectiveness of supervision is reduced. The extreme case is agriculture, where it is impossible to watch every man working in the fields and where the results of shirking only show up at harvest

Figure 5.2 Case II Pay-off

	N-1 Individuals		
Individual i	Work	Shirk'	Shirk''
Work	10,10	6,12	3,13
Shirk'	12,6	7,7	4,8
Shirk''	13,3	8,4	5,5

time, when no individual guilt can be assigned.[11] Cases I and II are similar with regard to the Prisoner's Dilemma. Without supervision, pay-off will fall from (10,10) to (7,7), to (5,5), and so on.

Given the costs of supervision, however, we cannot automatically assume it to aim for (10,10) (unless supervision is assumed to be considered as good *per se*, in which case its cost will be ignored, or at least played down).[12] Since returns to supervision will decline, there will be some optimal level where the extra effort elicited at the margin is just offset by the extra cost of supervision. Moreover, this optimal level will be different between different sectors of the economy, depending on the nature of work performed. In sectors that are difficult to supervise — such as agriculture — it will be better to allow some shirking. If it were possible to construct a 'supervisability' index for the economy, this might correlate well with observed labour productivity.

Case III: Second economy

Let us now relax the assumption on the absence of alternative labour options. This implies that the disutility of effort is no longer the only cause for shirking. We can take one step further by recognising that time may have an alternative use than just simple leisure. This alternative we shall define as work on a private plot or as various second economy activities, the important thing being that time has a productive alternative use, beneficial to the individual. In the pay-off matrix below, we have omitted the supervision problem, for simplicity, and the assumptions are as per Case I.

The importance of considering alternative labour options is twofold. First, opportunity costs of working for the socialised sector will increase, and thus incentives to shirk will be strengthened. Second, hostility to compulsion and supervision will increase if there are lucrative alternative uses for time and effort. The consequences

Figure 5.3 Case III Pay-off

	N-1 Individuals	
Individual i	Work	Shirk
Work	8,8	4,10
Shirk	10,4	9,9

of these two effects will be somewhat different but they will act to produce the same end result: a reduced supply of effort to the socialised sector.

The effect of demoralisation is reflected in the fact that the 'work–work' pay-off is reduced to (8,8), and the existence of alternative options is reflected in the increased returns to shirking. As the example in Figure 5.3 has been constructed, alternative activities are so rewarding that the Prisoner's Dilemma has disappeared. The pay-off from global shirking is larger than that from global work. Here there is no way of producing a voluntary contract to work conscientiously for the socialised sector. Moreover, any attempt to impose such a contract will lead to an overall reduction of efficiency in the system, by increasing labour hostility.

Here we have the basis of a vicious spiral. To increase the total pay-off from the socialised sector, supervision must be intensified. This will lead to an increased diversion of labour from productive uses and to an increased demoralisation of the remaining workers, as alternative activities become relatively more attractive. Both these forces will act to depress further the total pay-off in the socialised sector, and the government will be tempted to respond by further tightening supervision and control, etc.

This model agrees well with actual developments during the Stalin era. Preoccupation with control and extraction rather than with incentives and production led to serious economic stagnation. More interestingly, Stalin's successors maintained the core of the model in the sense that control continued to dominate incentives. The attempt to improve labour performance via increased wages thus came to capture the worst of two possible worlds: labour costs rose, but the result was only more hours, not more effort. Strong income effects may even have led to a reduction in hours.

The soft option is the hole through which the administrative control system squeezes labour effort. It will be argued below that the failure of plugging this hole makes up a part of a social contract, designed to politically pacify the Soviet citizenry.

MEETING PLANS BY BREAKING LAWS

If we now turn from the individual's behaviour as a labourer and let him take on the role of an enterprise manager, we enter a striking paradox of the centrally planned economy. If central planning had worked in the way it is presented, there would have been no point in focusing interest on the enterprise manager. He would simply be a cog in the machinery, obeying orders for his behaviour as laid down in the plan. Yet we observe that a considerable amount of interest is directed at precisely this level. How is this to be explained?

It is a trivial point to note that the actual working of a real-life planned economy such as that of the Soviet Union is far removed from both the official presentation and from the model of optimal socialism along the lines of Oskar Lange. A question of greater interest is to find out where, on the line between planner and worker, the plan goes out of joint. It is in this respect that the enterprise manager takes on an important function. No doubt there are numerous problems involved, both in formulating the plan and in passing it down through the bureaucracy. However, it is at the enterprise level that paper directives are to be turned into goods and services. Thus, it is at this level that we shall now focus our attention.

Playing games

The comprehensive nature of decisions to be taken at the centre creates a need for information that is of considerable magnitude. This information will need to be supplied from below, and here the manager finds himself in a situation where he must decide on *what* information to supply. From the pioneering works of Joseph Berliner and others we are well aware that his incentives are strongly biased in favour of withholding and distorting information.[13] Figure 5.4 will be used to illustrate this situation.

For simplicity's sake, we assume an enterprise that produces one output with one variable input. Output (y) is measured along the vertical axis and input (x) along the horizontal, with F(x) showing y as an increasing function of x. In a world with perfect information, the planners would be familiar with the shape of this production function and could thus determine how much input would be needed at each level of planned output. An optimal plan target for the

Figure 5.4 The manager's safety zone

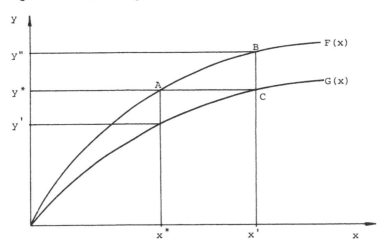

enterprise could be to produce y* with an allocation of x*. Will this materialise in the real world?

To a Soviet manager, the world is a highly unsafe place. His income and career prospects are both tightly linked to plan fulfilment, and more specifically to fulfilling the *output* plan.[14] Yet, there is little he can do to influence his environment, and he will thus strive to get as safe a starting point as possible, known in Russian as *strakhovka*. This is best done via concealing the production function, i.e. by inflating needs on the input side, or by understating production possibilities on the output side.

In terms of Figure 5.4, this can be interpreted either as an offer to produce y' with the given amount of resources, x*, or as an offer to meet the set target y* with a higher allocation, x', or as a combination of the two. What it means, in essence, is that the manager only reveals part of his production possibilities, corresponding to the production function G(x), which at all points lies below F(x). Assume (y*, x') is chosen. Here the game commences.

If the planners accept this information as correct, the manager will have secured for himself a safety zone corresponding to the area ABC, which can be used in two ways. Either he can use the 'extra' resource allocation to produce y'', thus overfulfilling the plan. This will bring bonus payments. Alternatively, he can decide to meet the **output target y*** and hoard (or trade) the extra resources. This will bring safety.

The choice of strategy will largely depend on the actual circumstances, but there are a few general rules. First, the output target is of pre-eminent importance. If only the output plan can be met, other shortcomings will be forgiven. As it was succintly put in a recent article in *Izvestia*: 'Some authorities take a more favourable view of managers who violate even that authority's own directives, than they do of those who fail to fulfil the plan.'[15] In the process of target fulfilment, even clear violations of the law may be forgiven the successful. It is a well-known fact, that a successful manager must engage in various kinds of shady activities on a daily basis, simply to cut the crude corners of real-life central planning. The official attitude is that of the ostrich. Here is *Izvestia* again: 'Are we aware of these activities? Naturally. Only, sometimes we choose not to see them'.[16]

The focus of the manager's activities is thus clearly defined. However, it would not be wise for him to make an all-out effort to increase output. It is not the absolute *level* of output that counts, but the level of output in relation to the plan. Here enters the practice of so-called *ratchet planning*.[17] Not only is the enterprise manager under constant pressure to fulfil the plan, his superiors are also subject to the same constraints. Thus, when they see a possibility of raising the target for some enterprise they will gladly do so, whereas demands for reductions will largely have to be ignored. This is the 'ratchet' effect, and it constitutes a severe constraint on the manager's behaviour. Whenever he overfulfils his plan, he will have revealed spare capacity and this can only lead to upward target revisions. (Of course, during the plan period obviously impossible targets will be revised downwards, but it is hardly a wise course to bank on being bailed out in this way.)

That such continuous revision of plan targets is still a practice has been amply documented by Eugene Zaleski,[18] and others have taken this as grounds for challenging the entire concept of a 'planned' economy in the Soviet Union.[19] This is not the place to pursue that discussion. Of greater interest are the inefficiencies resulting from the inherent bias in the risk/reward structure.

First, it is obvious that there is dynamic inefficiency, since a manager will always tend to choose to replicate existing technology rather than introduce new methods.[20] This can be illustrated by the Russian word for introducing new techniques, *vnedrenie*, which has connotations of substantial resistance to push.

Secondly, there will also be static inefficiency. To a large extent this is due to external factors, but the negative consequences of the system of planning and control tend to be augmented rather than remedied by managerial behaviour. The incentives to inflate some indicators and to deflate others, to hoard some inputs and to waste others, etc, all make for a distorted utilisation of given resources.

Finally, the game that results from the incentives to conceal and distort may be taken as an illustration of what Jagdish Bhagwati has called 'directly unproductive profit-seeking (DUP) activities'.[21] Real resources are spent on activities that have no productive outcome, the only aim of the game being to shift burdens on to someone else and to secure as quiet as possible a life for yourself. The deadweight loss is obvious.

The various aspects of this game have been amply described elsewhere, however, and we shall not pursue them further here. We shall be content with having established substantial and system-related inefficiencies. It will be argued below that these form part of a second-best solution, where economic efficiency is sacrificed to achieve political stability. Before we proceed to that discussion, however, we shall return briefly to the distinction between the two types of soft options, hinted at in the beginning of the chapter. From what has been presented above, it is obvious that the manager does not have a real choice. He must choose the soft option, both for his own good and for the good of the system. Yet, identifying it does have a certain importance, and to understand this we shall make a small digression into its wider implications.

The system strikes back

A necessary prerequisite for the elimination of those inefficiencies that emanate from the environment of the enterprise, i.e. the system of planning and control, would be to permit a greater scope for managerial decision-making, in order to allow decisions to be made where the relevant information is available. Most discussions of economic reform also incorporate some form of decentralisation proposals. We can be far from sure, however, that such a change will actually be welcomed by those concerned.

As we have seen above, in the general case, labourers as well as managers have to make a choice between playing hard and playing soft, i.e. between obeying the formal rules or taking the soft option. As we have presented the case, the choice is almost a foregone conclusion. Under a reform regime, however, the situation would be different. Rules and sanctions would be more than mere window-dressing. Would this influence behaviour towards playing hard and aiming for efficiency, or would the soft option continue in force?

The real crux of the matter, when discussing economic reform, is precisely the absence of effective sanctions. If changes that aim at improving efficiency are to be successful, they must incorporate some means of punishing those who break the rules. Here lies a problematic conflict that has been captured by János Kornai, when he speaks of a contradiction between the requirements of economic efficiency and what he calls 'socialist ethics'.[22] The former requires the elimination of weak units, whereas the latter requires the protection of the weak by the strong.

Kornai supplies evidence from the Hungarian reform experiments started in 1968 (the New Economic Mechanism (NEM)) which indicates that it was precisely the absence of hard rules and sanctions that constituted perhaps the major obstacle. His own attitude to the need for sanctions is captured in a pointed question: 'Are *negative* economic incentives — the fear of failure, and of individual material and moral loss — dispensable?'[23]

NEM provided enterprise managers with a wide scope for independent decision-making, but many preferred to stick to the old practices. An overriding reason for this was the conflict between the demands of efficiency and ethics. The former demands that firms be allowed to retain profits, the latter that they be redistributed. The former requires bankruptcy for inefficient firms, the latter that employment should be guaranteed. The former says that firms should make decisions on investment, the latter that social considerations should dominate, etc.

Hard rules imply winners and losers, but under a socialist regime it is all too easy for the latter to invoke 'socialist ethics' and call for protection. As the expected rewards to risk-taking will diminish with increased protection for the losers, the system will drift back to the old soft regime. This is seemingly what happened in Hungary.[24]

The importance of the soft option in the case of the enterprise manager is thus twofold. On the one hand, it has the negative — and seemingly unavoidable — consequences that were outlined above. More importantly, however, in social terms it also tends to become institutionalised over time, as shown by Kornai, so that soft behaviour becomes a substantial obstacle to reform proposals that aim to improve efficiency. Let us now proceed to see if we can find any positive features of these soft options, to counterbalance the negative aspects that have been outlined above.

SOFT OPTIONS

Economic reform in the centrally planned economies has long been a rather elusive concept. From time to time, there have been spurts of activity, usually highly over-publicised in the West. There lies a danger of making a false analogy here. Given the serious state of the Soviet economy in the 1980s, the logical thing to do in a western framework would be economic reforms and liberalisations. If we add to this the good humoured, almost western, image of the new Soviet leader, Mikhail Gorbachev, the conclusion is almost foregone.

Yet, the underlying assumption that the Soviets are serious in their talk about striving for economic efficiency may be mistaken. It may be part of an unattainable *first-best* solution. As an alternative, let us try to outline a *second-best* solution that incorporates economic efficiency as a desirable (supportable) component.

The core problem is that in striving for political stability it has been necessary to suppress many of those economic mechanisms that would promote efficiency. There is thus nothing in the model to arrest decline, once started, something that is amply borne out by the long trend of economic stagnation during the Brezhnev era. If no recuperative mechanisms can be introduced, there would seem to be nothing to prevent the model, not from collapse but from a very slow — and stable — submersion into the sea. Yet, it shall be our contention that there are indeed a number of such recuperative — or moderating — mechanisms, and in so doing we shall draw heavily on Albert Hirschman's concepts of *Exit, Voice and Loyalty*.[25]

The seminal idea for Hirschman's book was gained from a study of the state railway system in Nigeria. In spite of the fact that this was subject to private competition, it continued to operate in a grossly inefficient manner. Somehow, the healing powers of competition had been suppressed, and it was Hirschman's contention that the reason for this was to be found in different types of individual reactions to decline and poor performance. The existence of an alternative meant that those who could have exerted a positive influence via protesting (*voice*), chose instead to leave (*exit*). Thus the railways were left to continue an unimpeded, inefficient but quiet life.

Now, it is obvious that the Soviet model offers neither voice nor exit, in the narrow sense of Hirschman. It is, however, possible to identify modified versions of these strategies, options that offer a pragmatic compromise between reform and repression, in the all-out sense.

A soft exit

It is a basic tenet of a centrally planned economy that all important choices should be made at the centre. Since there are no competing options, consumers cannot vote with their feet and there is no point in talking about exit in the formal sense. However, as we saw in the first section of this chapter, the individuals can choose to exit from the *official* system in two important ways: they can switch into the 'private' sector, and they can reduce their supply of effort to the socialised sector. In both cases, however, they are still in a limited sense within the confines of the official system and we shall thus term these options 'soft' exits.

The problem observed by Hirschman was that the existence of a private alternative eased the pressure on the monopolist — by offering exit to those most prone to voice — and thus allowed him to continue an inefficient but quiet life. To Hirschman this was bad. To the bureaucrats of the Soviet *nomenklatura* it must surely be good. The existence of the private plots eases pressure on the official farm system. The existence of private markets eases pressure on the official distribution system, and the existence of a number of other private options (of varying legality) fill the same function with respect to their official counterparts. If all such private options were suppressed, the pressure on the official system would surely rise to a critical level.

The tolerance of these private activities for *political* rather than *economic* reasons is also borne out by the numerous — and seemingly irrational — restrictions that prevent them from efficiently utilising available resources. The alternative must not become an efficient one, but remain a mere safety valve.

A similar situation can be identified with respect to the behaviour of the enterprise manager. As we saw above, his daily activities are characterised by playing against the system, again in a seemingly irrational fashion. If managers were compelled to act strictly according to the rules (the hard option), the planning system would come under severe strain as a result of its many imbalances and inconsistencies. By allowing exit into various illegal practices, however, such pressure is reduced and the system can continue to pride itself of being a centrally planned economy. We have also documented above the official ostrich-like attitude to the various forms of such illegal activities.

The common denominator of these two versions of soft exit is that they combine taking pressure off the official system with actually being productive (private goods being produced and the performance of enterprises being improved). We can, however, also identify a third version where there is no productive outcome, merely a reduction of pressure.

In a strictly repressive system, labour productivity will be very low. Workers have no motivation to exert themselves, and there is a limit, as was shown above, to what can be achieved via supervision. For this reason, serfdom and slavery have long since been abolished in the West. Yet, in the Soviet model, it is impossible to allow the type of individual freedom that is an integral part of the western system. Another mode has to be sought and this has been a very successful one, in the 'second-best' sense.

The soft exit at this level represents a social contract between the rulers and the ruled that 'allows' the individual to engage in a broad range of illegal and semi-legal activities, as well as to go slow. The essence of this contract is captured in the anecdote about the man who said he was forced to look for a new job, because his house needed a new roof and the place where he was currently employed did not produce roofing materials. By creating an illusion for the individual that he can 'beat the system' via his own cunning, he is compensated for the fact that he is deprived of both exit and voice in the formal sense. Drunkenness and laziness, together with various shady activities, become the pillars of this social contract.

So far the possibilities of exit within the system. Let us now proceed to examine the opportunities that exist for voice, for criticising and possibly improving the model.

Soft voice

An excellent example of the range and limits of voice is found in the realm of economic theory. Economic theorising during the Stalin era was reduced to 'a general, closed and scholastic study of the socialist forms of ownership'.[26] The construction of an 'economic theory of socialism' and the practice of central planning was not found to be consistent with economic research in any constructive sense. Stalin's own personal attitude is reflected in his statement that matters of economic policy should be reserved for the political leadership: 'To include problems of economic policy in political economy would be to destroy it as a science.'[27] Yet, during the years after Stalin's death, it became increasingly obvious that economic reconstruction was needed and that this in turn demanded economic theorising of a different calibre than quoting Marx and Lenin. The traditional 'theory' was in a shambles and a pragmatic solution was found. This, we shall claim, represented a 'soft voice'.

When the curtain fell in the late 1920s, some economists managed to escape and hibernate in the less political realm of mathematics, and during Khrushchev's thaw they represented a new force, with an astounding message. The mathematical school focused on optimality, efficiency and scarcity, and utilised tools that were sheer heresy to the traditional school. The proposed model for a 'System of Optimally Functioning Socialist Economy', showed remarkable similarities with the models for optimal socialism that are associated with the names of Oskar Lange and Abba Lerner.[28] The striking difference between the traditional and the mathematical schools was that while the former was preoccupied with emphasising *differences* between socialist and 'bourgeois' economies, the latter tacitly used those very same tools.[29]

In practice, the mathematical school never came to have much influence on the running of the economy. It has been shown, on the one hand, that models for input–output and linear programming became closed loops, largely outside the planning system; and on the other, that the proposed theory may not even have been internally consistent.[30] We can thus advance several explanations for the lack of success, and data deficiencies were not the least of these.

Of greater interest, however, is to explain why it was allowed to grow. At its peak, the Central Economic-Mathematical Institute (TsEMI) was of quite respectable size, and over the years a fair amount of serious research has been conducted there. Two benefits have been derived from this development. First, those economists that might have rocked the boat, by criticising the traditional theory from within, were given their own sandbox to play in. This, more properly, should perhaps be put under the 'exit' heading. Secondly, their work did represent voice, against the traditional model. Representatives of the traditional school were forced to enter into (at times heated) polemics and this must undoubtedly have produced important demonstration effects regarding the most serious shortcomings of the prevailing theory. Some of the healing powers of voice were preserved. Just as in the case of private activities, however, strict ideological control was maintained and no open challenge to the traditional system was ever permitted.

It is not only among academics, however, that we can identify soft voice. Everyday life for the Soviet citizen offers a number of different ways of voicing dissatisfaction. At the most basic level, there is the book of complaints, which is kept by shops, restaurants, etc. In this book the dissatisfied customer can enter his complaints in writing, and the manager in charge is obliged by law to reply and explain, within a given period of time. At a somewhat higher level, we find the same opportunity in the form of writing letters of complaint to the press. Again, the culprit will have to answer for his behaviour, albeit not by law.

These channels for voice can be interpreted in two ways. First, there is the obvious mechanism of feedback, which is in line with Hirschman's original concept of voice. Although this type of complaint can probably in most cases be brushed aside with a stereotype explanation that shifts the blame, it cannot be entirely disregarded. Particularly in the case of letters to the press, there may be danger. If *Pravda*, say, decides to follow up on something by dispatching a journalist to investigate, then the culprit may suddenly find himself in deep water.

In general, however, complaints that originate from the consumers carry only minor importance. No doubt it is the case that when serious complaints are voiced at the *Pravda* level, the true source of the complaint should be sought at the top political level, rather than amongst the grassroots. In this way, it is possible to criticise a general problem by selecting a scapegoat. Those guilty of similar practices will undoubtedly get the message, and maybe some improvement will result.

The second way of interpreting these complaints is of greater importance to our line of argument. By offering institutionalised foci for complaint, the citizens are given an outlet for frustration that might otherwise build up a dangerous pressure of discontent. The fact that the *ultimate* result of such complaints will be meagre is of minor importance, since the *immediate* result is clearly visible. As those attacked are obliged to respond and explain, the individual's feeling of impotence will be reduced, and maybe he will also feel a certain satisfaction about having got his own back at the system. This should apply not only at the grassroots level, but also to various specialists and managers, who are frequently allowed to complain about absurdities in the daily life of central planning.

A highly illuminating illustration of the individual's chances of creating a nuisance is found in a book by Vladimir Bukovsky, which relates his own experiences as a Soviet political prisoner.[31] Inmates in prisons and camps had a right to send a specified number of letters of complaints about their conditions of confinement, and the proper authority was obliged to reply, within a given period of time.

Needless to say, no bureaucrat cherishes having piles of letters of complaint brought to his desk every morning (the inmates had plenty of time for writing), and in a number of cases, complaints did lead to action being taken against prison officials, simply to stop the torrent of complaints.

The reason why we have chosen to call these possibilities of complaint 'soft' voice, is that there are strict limitations on their type, number and forms. It will obviously not be possible to organise and articulate voice, in the way it is done in a western society. Yet, the option is there, and no doubt it fills an important function, releasing some steam and capturing some feedback.

So far we have been discussing options for exit and voice for the ruled. Let us now turn to the rulers, and in doing so we shall introduce another concept of Hirschman's: that of loyalty.

LOYALTY

When discussing the situation of the Soviet power elite — the *nomenklatura* — it is far too easy to focus on fringe benefits and the desire for an easy life. Simply providing these for those who obey the rules can hardly be seen as the desired mechanism for generating stability. We need to look for more subtle mechanisms and these can be found in the role of the Communist Party and its ideology.

A highly interesting feature of Hirschman's book is that he brings up the problem of the loyalty of individuals to the organisations that they belong to, the point being that loyalty will be strengthened via higher costs for entry and exit. An individual who has paid a high price in some sense to enter an organisation will put up with problems longer than one to whom entry was more freely available. He will prefer voice to exit and, as Hirschman sees voice as a recuperative mechanism, loyalty is good.[32]

This model would seem to be eminently well suited to an explanation of the workings of the *nomenklatura*. The historical experience of purges and in-fighting is the starting point and stability is the desire. Providing power, prestige and material benefits will make a party career attractive but it will not eliminate in-fighting. High costs of entry and exit, in combination with an active ideology, will achieve this objective.

What to a western ear may seem like empty regurgitation of dogma is definitely a serious matter to a Soviet official. It is required of him not only that he should be familiar with Marxist-Leninist ideology in a passive way, but also that he should be able to practise it actively. He must know the code, and this is where we are approaching the stability mechanism.

Stability of the Soviet mark precludes open debate, which means that policy must be shaped in silence, under the wrap of the party's monolithic surface. Here, ideology and loyalty to the system are important constituent parts. The strict adherence of all officials to what is currently the officially accepted version of ideology makes it possible to shape a collective will. Ideology serves as a mechanism for both inclusion and exclusion, as those who do not conform will be branded heretics and expelled. The high demands placed on officials to practice the ideology can be seen as a cost that has to be paid to remain in place. In Hirschman's model, this will increase loyalty to the system.

In this way, it has been possible to phase out the need for terror, and replace it by a more subtle mechanism of control. The ideology-loyalty mechanism is superior to simple terror in two ways. First, it is more conducive to political stability, since it builds on an active socialisation (loyalty) of the members in the *nomenklatura*, while Stalinist terror aimed at passive socialisation (fear). Secondly, it is also better suited to form an effective economic policy, since it allows for more voice and thus more feedback regarding the consequences of various policy measures. Stalinist policy-making may have more power to push decisions through a dense bureaucracy, but only at the price of becoming crude and ill-suited to deal with complex issues. *In toto* then, over time the Soviet leadership has acquired quite an interesting degree of subtlety in running their fief, and it is in this perspective that their achievements should be viewed, rather than making comparisons with western governments. Let us now pull together the various strands of our argument.

CONCLUSION

In concluding this chapter, we shall return to *Exit, Voice and Loyalty* as presented in a later essay by the same author.[33] Here, Hirschman concentrates at the state, or system, level, arguing that there must be some limitations on the practice of exit and voice. There must be a *ceiling*, since excessive voice will lead to disruption and excessive exit to disintegration. Similarly there must be a *floor*, since too low levels of exit and voice will eliminate important feedback mechanisms about performance, and thus remove potential checks on decline. In this perspective states and organisations are seen to navigate between the Scylla of disruption/disintegration and the Charybdis of deterioration, to use Hirschman's metaphor.

Now, it is obvious that the model created by Stalin was devoured by Charybdis, but what became of that which grew out of Khrushchev's thaw? One thing to note here, is that a prolonged use of repression will dam up powerful forces which, if suddenly released, might spill over into critical levels of voice as well as exit.[34] Thus, during de-stalinisation the distance between floor and ceiling was very narrow and the risk of avoiding the whirlpools of Charybdis only to be captured by the arms of Scylla was substantial.

The course chosen by Stalin's successors shows an awareness of this fact, at least once the initial shock of 1956 was over. It was necessary to keep the system as close to the floor as possible without the use of Stalinist type repression. As Hirschman points out, however, if you reduce repression this will necessarily lead to increased voice or exit, or both.[35] You can't have your cake and eat it too. Is there a way out of this dilemma? It has been the purpose of this chapter to show that there may well be a solution.

The solution to the dilemma lies in the soft options. By creating a number of 'reservations' into which dissatisfied individuals can retreat, two important benefits are gained. On the one hand, the level of voice is reduced within the official system, which promotes the desired stability, and on the other, since the exit is soft, part of the energy released can be channelled back in productive uses. Further, by allowing limited — or soft — voice, some feedback is preserved in this respect as well, parallel with ostracising the most voice-prone from the system all together.

Finally, and perhaps most importantly, the existence of the soft options and the absence of hard rules and sanctions of the market type, have two important effects that are both related to the *nomenklatura*. They create a basis for the feudal privilege system, by making all actors dependent on each other in a way that would not be possible under either a market or a terror regime, and they create loyalty to, or a feeling of safety with, the system of negotiations and lobbying, which effectively precludes the formation of alternative routes for voice aggregation.

This model has shown itself remarkably able to defy all prophecies of doom and gloom, securing political stability in the face of ever-more serious economic stagnation. At the same time it has also succeeded in slowing down stagnation to a mere crawl. Whatever its merits in these respects, however, the long-term prognosis for the economic viability of the Soviet model remains sombre and it is here that Gorbachev's campaigns for discipline and against corruption become of interest. Needless to say, such campaigns are necessary to trim the worst outgrowths of the soft options, but at the same time discipline cannot be taken too far. This would mean challenging the very foundations of the model, which in essence rest on allowing a number of illegalities. A serious crackdown would mean breaking the social contract with the labour force, and it would mean paralysing large sections of production that depend on precisely these illegal activities.

Gorbachev does represent something new in Soviet development, in the limited sense that he is reaching for a middle way between liberalisation and repression — the ceiling and the floor in Hirschman's terminology. He is playing for high stakes, however, since if he fails, the backlash of expectations built up via powerful speeches may cripple him. Muddling through has acquired a new dimension of intensity, but one wonders how many more third ways there can be in the never-ending Soviet search for panaceas that postpone the eventual need to face the real dilemmas of the economy? Maybe the youngest Soviet leader since Stalin will come up with an answer to that question.

NOTES

* Thanks are due to Professors Albert Hirschman and Alec Nove for comments and criticism on an earlier version of this chapter. Generous financial assistance from the Bank of Sweden Tercentenary Foundation is also gratefully acknowledged.

1. Indeed, it is probably not safe to assume rational action even at the micro-level. As Jon Elster has pointed out, sometimes it is necessary to delude individuals out of taking their own narrowly rational decisions, as 'irrationality rather than duty may be the cement of society, a socially beneficial illusion, like Voltaire's God. It may not be a good thing if social scientists spend too much of their time discussing . . . connections among rationality, morality and collective action' (Elster, 1985, p. 146).

2. I am indebted to Alec Nove for drawing my attention to this distinction. Consistency between the behaviour of the dogcatcher and the enterprise manager, for example, would require the former to catch large and heavy dogs rather than nice ones (if his plan were in tons), the point being that while the soft option in the former case is bad, in the latter it is imperative. If all managers were to choose the hard option, i.e. to play by the formal rules, the system would collapse.

3. This can sometimes produce absurd results, such as when Dwight

Israelsen, in a formally correct model, shows that the Soviet *kolkhoz* not only produces stronger incentives to work than both pure communes and private firms, but also that these incentives are further strengthened with the growth in size of the *kolkhoz* (Israelsen, 1980). Otherwise, common knowledge has it that it is precisely the lack of incentives that is the main problem to the *kolkhoz*, and that this problem grows as the *kolkhoz* expands.

4. It is a well-established fact that Soviet labour is inefficiently utilised. Western estimations indicate that Soviet enterprises employ 50–70 per cent more workers than western firms with comparable technology (OECD, 1984). See also Oxenstierna (1985).

5. With respect to the *kolkhoz* system, Hans Aage finds that there is an incentive, 'not necessarily to work efficiently, but only to work long hours' (Aage, 1980, p. 143).

6. Dennis Chinn uses a similar approach to study household decisions on work effort in Chinese agricultural production teams. His interest, however, is chiefly directed at exploring various forms of remunerative systems (Chinn, 1980).

7. On the kibbutz, see further Barkai (1977). The consequences of allowing for different behaviour between members in the organisation have been analysed by Cameron (1973).

8. See further Hedlund (1985) on this process of erosion and eventual breakdown of the pure forms of cooperation.

9. One example of this can be found in the development of the Soviet *kolkhoz* system. While gross *kolkhoz* income fell from 22.8 to 19.6 billion roubles in the period 1970–80, at the same time wage payments increased from 15.0 to 18.6 billion, or from 66 to 99 per cent of *gross* income (Suslov, 1982, p. 27). All other costs will then in some way be covered out of the state budget, since no bankruptcy is allowed.

10. There exist in the literature a number of similar illustrations, but this may be one of the best known. Its origin is Yanov (1968). See also further Yanov (1984), pp. 19–22.

11. This is dealt with in Bradley and Clark (1972). Yanov (1984), p. 19, describes the essence of the problem: 'To discover those who are lying drunk under their tractors, or who have driven to the bazaar in their trucks during working hours, is relatively easy. But how is the depth of plowing to be measured for each tractor driver? How is one to check the speed at which he drives the tractor?'

12. Such a case can be found in a passage in a short story by Yuri Chernichenko, which tells us about the party boss who arrives from Moscow to investigate why the region is falling behind the harvest plan. His solution is to send communists to watch over and be personally responsible for all work on the fields: 'A thousand combines? Then — a thousand plenipotentiaries! If two thousand are needed, we will send them too!' (Chernichenko, 1965, p. 206). This reflects a period in Soviet development where control was an end and not a means.

13. E.g. Berliner (1957); Granick (1954).

14. It is not known what share of managerial incomes that is made up of bonus payments, but evidence presented by Andrew Freris suggests it may be over one-fifth (Freris, 1984, p. 151).

15. *Izvestia*, 24 January 1985.
16. Ibid.
17. Berliner (1957), pp. 78–9.
18. Zaleski (1980).
19. Wilhelm (1985).
20. This fact has long been known, even to the Soviets. In 1957, an article in *Zvezda* had the following to say: 'Innovation implies risk and, as in all gambling, you need capital. Risk, however, also implies the possibility of loss, does it not? Yet, if a manager is given capital, just let him take a gamble — and not win!' (*Zvezda*, no. 5, 1957, p. 156).
21. Bhagwati (1982), p. 990.
22. Kornai (1980).
23. Ibid., p. 153.
24. Ibid., pp. 151–2 claims that around two-thirds of the gross profits of firms were taxed away and that no complete liquidation of firms occurred under NEM. Not even after the oil-price explosion were any Hungarian firms subjected to the hard rules of the market: 'the strong and the weak, the active and the passive, the innovative and the incompetent all survived the storm'.
25. Hirschman (1970).
26. This was written by Soviet academician Arzumanjan in 1964. Quotation taken from Sutela (1984), p. 77.
27. Stalin (1952), p. 171.
28. The role and contents of this school have been analysed in Sutela (1984).
29. The recognition of the need for a 'collectivist' model to use the same economic tools as a free-market economy goes back to Barone (1908) and Pareto (1909).
30. See Birman and Tretyakova (1976) on the use of input–output techniques in the Soviet Union. The feasibility of the new theory is discussed by Sutela (1984).
31. Bukovsky (1978).
32. See further Hirschman (1970), Ch. 7. He also devises a way of empirically testing the assumption on the relation between loyalty and costs of entry and exit.
33. Hirschman (1981), p. 224.
34. Development in Poland in 1976–81 is an obvious example of this.
35. Ibid., p. 227. An interesting illustration of this is the example of Cuba, where Fidel Castro was able to reduce the intensity of repression by allowing substantial exit to Miami.

REFERENCES

Aage, Hans (1980), 'Labour Allocation in the Soviet Kolkhoz', *Economics of Planning*, vol. 16, no. 3.
Barkai, Haim (1977), *Growth Patterns of the Kibbutz Economy*, Amsterdam: North-Holland.

Barone, Enrico (1908), 'Il ministerio della produzione nello stato collettivista', *Giornali degli economisti*. Reprinted as 'The Ministry of Production in the Collectivist State', in von Hayek, Friedrich (1935), *Collectivist Economic Planning*, London.

Berliner, Joseph (1957), *Factory and Manager in the USSR*, Cambridge, Mass.

Bhagwati, Jagdish (1982), 'Directly Unproductive Profit-Seeking (DUP) Activities', *Journal of Political Economy*, vol. 90.

Birman, Igor and Tretyakova, Albina (1976), 'Input–Output Analysis in the USSR', *Soviet Studies*, vol. 28, no. 2.

Bradley, Michael and Clark, Gardner, M. (1972), 'Supervision and Efficiency in Socialized Agriculture', *Soviet Studies*, vol. 23, no. 3.

Bukovsky, Vladimir (1978), *To Build a Castle. My Life as a Dissenter*, London.

Cameron, Norman (1973), 'Incentives and Labor Supply on Soviet Collective Farms: Rejoinder', *Canadian Journal of Economics*, vol. 6, no. 3.

Chernichenko, Yuri (1965), 'Russkaya pshennitsa', *Novy mir*, vol. 41, no. 11.

Chinn, David (1980), 'Diligence and Laziness in Chinese Agricultural Production Teams', *Journal of Development Economics*, vol. 7, no. 3.

Elster, Jon (1985), 'Rationality, Morality and Collective Action', *Ethics*, vol. 96, no. 1.

Freris, Andrew (1984), *The Soviet Industrial Enterprise*, London.

Granick, David (1954), *Management of the Industrial Firm in the USSR. A Study in Soviet Economic Planning*, New York.

Hedlund, Stefan (1985), 'On the Socialisation of Labour in Rural Cooperation', in Lundahl, Mats (ed.), *The Primary Sector in Economic Development. Proceedings of the Seventh Arne Ryde Symposium. Frostavallen, August 29–30, 1983*, London and Sydney.

Hirschman, Albert (1970), *Exit, Voice and Loyalty: Responses to Decline in Firms, Organizations and States*, Cambridge, Mass. and London.

——— (1981), *Essays in Trespassing. Economics to Politics and Beyond*, Cambridge.

Israelsen, Dwight (1980), 'Collectives, Communes and Incentives', *Journal of Comparative Economics*, vol. 6, no. 4.

Kornai, János (1980), 'The Dilemmas of a Socialist Economy: The Hungarian Experience', *Cambridge Journal of Economics*, vol. 4, no. 2.

OECD (1984), *East–West Technology Transfer*, Paris.

Oxenstierna, Susanne (1985), 'Labour Shortage in the Soviet Union: Planning and the Soviet Enterprise', Swedish Institute for Social Research, *Meddelande*, No. 5.

Pareto, Vilfredo (1909), *Manuel d'économie politique*, Paris.

Stalin, Joseph (1952), *Ekonomicheskie problemi sotsialisma v SSSR*, Moscow.

Suslov, I. (1982), 'Kolkhozy v sisteme narodnogo khozyaistva', *Voprosy ekonomiki*, vol. 53, no. 12.

Sutela, Pekka (1984), *Socialism, Planning and Optimality. A Study in Soviet Economic Thought*, Helsinki.

Wilhelm, John Howard (1985), 'The Soviet Union has an Administered, not a Planned, Economy', *Soviet Studies*, vol. 37, no. 1.

Yanov, Alexander (1968), 'Spor s predsedatelem', *Literaturnaya gazeta*, 7 August.
────── (1984), *The Drama of the Soviet 1960s. A Lost Reform*, Institute of International Studies, Berkeley, Cal.
Zaleski, Eugene (1980), *Stalinist Planning for Economic Growth 1933–52*, Chapel Hill, North Carolina.

6

Economic Incentives in Soviet Pre-War Economic Thought

Pekka Sutela*

The incentive system of the classic Soviet-type economic system has often been described in the literature.[1] Whatever classic Marxism may have thought about work motivation under socialism, Soviet labour was typically stimulated by (often progressive) piece-rates and progressive premia, linked to such 'success indicators' as fulfilling and overfulfilling the enterprise plan on gross production and production costs. Other incentives and sanctions ranged from honorary titles to capital punishment.

This chapter does not aim to contribute to this literature, but addresses another question. How did Soviet economists of the 1930s see economic incentives? More specifically: how did they — if at all! — rationalise and explain the radical change that took place in official Soviet thinking in a very short period of time? As late as 1930 it was still argued that old material incentives would soon give way to new socialist incentives. Less than ten years later, with an officially declared socialism in the Soviet Union reliance on material incentives was explained to be the essence of socialist labour. Such a *volte face* had to be addressed somehow, one is tempted to argue.

That such a question has been raised so seldom is part of a more general neglect. Soviet economic thought of the 1930s has attracted only scant attention among later scholars, although there are some exceptions.[2] Most of what Soviet economists wrote under Stalinism was dour commentary on the pronouncements of the leader, or extolled the virtues of Soviet industrialisation, but this is not the whole story, as I have described elsewhere.[3] Soviet socialism can be seen as the main twentieth-century attempt at a social revolution at least partly inspired by a social doctrine. What was the interaction between Bolshevik doctrine, pre-revolutionary society and post-revolutionary social and economic agenda? This question is well

151

worth asking, even if the impossibility of answering it in any definite sense should be admitted at the outset. This chapter argues that the question of economic incentives provides a good starting point for approaching this bundle of thorny questions.

The discussion that follows is limited to ideas concerning the use of real income as an economic incentive within state-owned industry. Of all the components of income — wages, premia, access to goods, social benefits — only the first two will be discussed in detail. Even here, the position of premia will be paramount, as these are connected with another fundamental question of Soviet socialism: the position of enterprises as profit-and-loss accounting units (*khozraschet*).

The next section sketches the classic socialist thinking on work motivation; then the development of the Soviet incentive system of the 1930s is outlined. A discussion on the main phases of evolving Soviet thinking on the subject follows. A short summary and evaluation concludes. The preliminary nature of this chapter should be emphasised: only a beginning has been made here at surveying a wide literature.

CLASSICAL SOCIALIST THINKING ON WORK MOTIVATION

As Lenin and other Bolsheviks complained after the Revolution, their doctrinal heritage was of little help in tackling the post-revolutionary economic problems. What they did not say was that, in fact, this heritage was a handicap. Marx has stressed that both his theory and his method were only applicable to capitalist society.[4] As later Social Democrats needed something to say about their final goal, they developed an evolutionary picture of socialism as present-day trends freed from the barriers set by capitalism. Relying on a nineteenth-century view of organisation as a mechanistic and deterministic hierarchy, Karl Kautsky offered a characteristic picture of socialism:

> In a socialist society, which is after all just a single giant industrial enterprise, production and wages must be exactly and in a planned way organized, just as they are organized in a modern large industrial enterprise.[5]

The same metaphor was later used by Lenin.

There was some development in Social Democratic thinking by

the twentieth century. In 1878 August Bebel claimed that planning would be a task for accountants. By comparing the available labour force and means of production with the needs of the population, necessary production would be readily seen, and 'with a little experience the task soon becomes child's play'.[6] Presumably, there would not be any specific problems of incentives, as in socialism 'The gratification of personal egoism and the promotion of commonweal go harmoniously hand in hand and coincide'.[7] Kautsky, on the other hand, writing in the early years of this century, saw both the need and the possibility for motivating workers by using a formal wage system.[8] This change, perhaps, reflects Marx's well-known 1875 distinction between socialism — with distribution according to work done — and communism proper, with distribution according to needs. This distinction, however, was only seldom invoked in pre-1917 socialist literature. Even in the Soviet 1920s, Marx's socialist distribution principle, so evidently including the idea of material incentives, was, it seems, hardly mentioned.

Russian Bolsheviks took the common Social Democratic image of future socialism as given. This is apparent in Lenin's *State and Revolution* as well as in Bogdanov's *Red Star*, the only major Utopia written by a former Bolshevik leader.

Later the Russians closely studied the German war economy, which strengthened their belief that the future really belongs to a centralised and demonetarised non-market economy. Perhaps the most lyrical depiction of this philosophy of administration is in Bukharin and Preobrazhensky's *The ABC of Communism*:

> The main direction will be entrusted to various kinds of bookkeeping offices or statistical bureaus. There, from day to day, account will be kept of production and all its needs; there also it will be decided whither workers must be sent, whence they must be taken, and how much work there is to be done. And inasmuch as, from childhood onwards, all will have been accustomed to social labour, and since all will understand that this work is necessary and that life goes easier when everything is done according to a prearranged plan and when the social order is like a well-oiled machine, all will work in accordance with the indications of these statistical bureaus. There will be no need for special ministers of state, the police and prisons, for laws and decrees — nothing of the sort.[9]

THE DEVELOPMENT OF MATERIAL INCENTIVES

While the future depicted by *The ABC of Communism* was thought to be behind two or three post-revolutionary generations, such ideas were a factor behind war communist policies in 1918–21. The use of work-books and the existence of a centralised supply of consumption goods were hailed as steps towards a demonetarised economy. The use of force and compulsion — also of forced labour — were explained as being immanent to socialism.[10] Soon, however, such socialist utopias had to be relegated to a more distant future, and the time of New Economic Policy followed.

In early NEP, most enterprises were guided in deciding what to produce primarily by the market and by the profit motive rather than by direct orders of the government. The 1923 statute of the trusts affirmed that they 'operate on the principles of commercial accounting [*kommercheskii raschet*] with the purpose of earning a profit'. But the scope of the controls exercised by the central authorities over the trusts gradually increased. The change was also reflected in the new statutes of 1927 which omitted the prescription that trusts operated 'with the purpose of earning a profit'. Instead, the statute declared that trusts operated 'on the principles of commercial accounting in conformity with planned tasks'. In practice, Soviet historians affirm, after 1927 these principles of commercial accounting were implemented only formally, if at all.[11]

Two tendencies clashed over the principles of wage-setting. Over time, and with increasing central planning, the one favouring wage-differentials in the name of efficiency won over the other tendency favouring equality in the name of socialist ideals. Most workers were on piece-rates while those on time-rates generally received incentive payments or bonuses of one kind or another. Such payments were often progressive. But interestingly, the share of fixed wage-rates in total pay was increased in the late 1920s for the purpose of enhancing the planning of the total wage fund.[12]

As early as 1918 Lenin had campaigned for the use of such progressive elements of capitalism as Taylorism, piece-rates and 'bourgeois specialists'. These specialists were usually given a personal salary reflecting the value of their scarce abilities. This, as well as their employment in general, was widely resented as contradicting socialist ideals.[13]

It is in fact unclear how far monetary income differentials increased under NEP as compared to the years of the civil war. Lampert concludes that such increases did not happen 'to any great extent'.[14] Compared to the 1930s, this decade still was a period of egalitarian incomes.

The Soviet industrialisation drive of 1928-32 underwent several phases, each of which was also reflected in the status of *khozraschet*.[15] The first phase (1928-summer 1930) was one of 'increasingly over-ambitious planning for rapid industrialisation, coupled with support for financial stability in words and inflation in deeds'. The provisions of the 1927 statute on trusts on commercial accounting were not implemented. Neither were those of a December 1929 Central Committee resolution that emphasised the importance of *khozraschet* for associations (*obyedineniya*, equivalent to the later *glavk*) as well as for enterprises. This phase was later characterised as a 'new non-*khozraschet* period', when 'the principle of *khozraschet* [was] dying out in associations' and any attention to it was often treated as 'an indicator of a right-wing deviation'.[16] Even in late 1930, many associations were planning 'a total liquidation of the system of contract relations. Gosplan declared a liquidation of contracts on investments'.[17] With practically no *khozraschet*, wages were the only form of incentives used.[18]

In autumn 1930 economic policies were entering a new phase. Financial stability was now emphasised in deeds too. To standardise the financial relations of enterprises and the state it was decided in September 1930 that enterprises should pay their contribution into the state budget in two forms. In addition to the turnover tax, they were to give over into the budget any profits that remained after the share of the enterprise was deducted. Such regulations, however, could have little importance as long as the enterprises were given credit automatically according to the plan. It was finally decided to give credit only according to production in early 1931. At the same time, a vigorous campaign for financial stability (*khozrachet*) and — since the summer of 1931 — incentive wages, was underway.

The policy of increasing wage differentials together with the continuing unrealistic planning contributed to increasing costs and inflation until about 1933. Then, greater realism in planning finally prevailed, combined with a determined effort to stabilise costs and halt inflation. Success is this respect finally led to the abolition of food rationing in 1934-35. The Soviet economic system, very much as we still know it, had come into being. From 1931, all the forms of material incentives enumerated above were in use.

1. *Wages*. Under NEP, most workers had been on piece-rates. This

proportion declined towards the end of the 1920s, and various forms of collective payments were introduced, often from below, in 1929–30. Egalitarian 'production communes', which shared their income evenly and sometimes had an elected brigade leader, were one form of this. After Stalin's June 1931 speech against egalitarian tendencies, such collective payment systems were suppressed. Brigades with individual book-keeping and progressive piece-rates were seen as the appropriate form of incentives. Overwhelming as piece-rates shortly became, they were never total.

2. *Premia*. Premia were paid mostly to white-collar workers. This increased their incomes significantly, but one may wonder about the incentive effects. First of all, the incentive part of profits was allocated on the association level, quite independently of the production results of enterprises and shops. Furthermore, as the division of the enterprise's share of profits was not regulated by strict rules, most of it went to non-productive construction. Individual incentive payments out of profit were in fact very rare.[19] And anyway, taking the 'free remainder' of the profit into the state budget as well as the irrational and uncertain environment of the enterprises make any profit-maximisation hypothesis seem unreal.

After various adjustments in the incentive fund mechanism, a Manager's Fund was decreed in 1936. To facilitate profit-seeking behaviour, it was decreed to direct 4 per cent of planned profits but 50 per cent of above-plan profits into it. Half of the fund was to be used for housing construction. The other half was to be divided — in unspecified proportions — into financing other services, rationalisation outlays and bonuses.[20] According to Granick this fund did become very important for managers, not, however, as a source of housing investment and premia for workers, but as a reservoir of uncontrolled money for investment and other production needs.[21]

On the average, executives' incentive payments in 1940 made up 11 per cent of their total earnings. These premia were dependent upon 'success in fulfilling and overfulfilling the plan'. The meaning of this phrase varied over time and circumstances, but gross production was the overwhelming success indicator. It was supplemented with numerous other indicators, among them production costs, in changing combinations. This makes analysing the managers' decision-making very difficult. Berliner concludes, however, that 'most of the decisions by managerial personnel may be explained by the desire for premia'.[22]

3. *Access to goods*. Men are presumably interested in their real, not

nominal pay. Food was rationed from 1929 to 1934–35 and the availability of goods was, especially after 1931, perhaps as important an incentive as were wages.[23] In fact, Voznesenskii saw this as *the* incentive for workers in 1931:

> for the individual worker, the premium for overfulfilling the production plan must be a priority supply of consumption goods, and, vice versa, the sanction for a systematic and malicious failure of fulfilling the plan is change into supply according to the second category.[24]

In fact, even stronger medicines against 'laziness' were prescribed. A 1932 decree 'on discipline now authorised not just dismissal of the transgressor — but depriving him and his family, on the spot, of the ration cards and evicting them from their lodgings'. In 1938 social security payments were also added to the strategy, and finally in 1940 indiscipline was made subject to criminal prosecution.[25]

In fact, rationing is a poor incentive, being rigid and arbitrary. Derationing was greeted as strengthening the rouble as well as *khozraschet*. Rationing was said to have weakened material incentives. It was now seen as a form of egalitarianism — *uravnilovka*.[26] Gatovskii, furthermore, was very explicit in setting the role of the rouble in relation to consumption goods market equilibrium. He argued that from the incentive point of view higher prices were preferable to disequilibrium. Certainly this was a point worth making, especially given the 1930s doctrine of a long-term declining tendency of prices, but in fact Gatovskii's point was *ex post*: derationing had been connected with huge price rises.

4. *Social benefits*. Provision of social consumption had earlier been egalitarian, but after 1931 even schooling, social insurance, etc. were made part of the fight 'for a maximal stimulation of shock work' and against the high turnover of the labour force.

PERSPECTIVES FOR MATERIAL INCENTIVES DURING NEP

The previous section gave an outline of the incentive system. We can now turn to our basic question: how did Soviet economists understand the system? It seems appropriate to divide the time under consideration into four sub-periods: 1921–28, 1929–30, 1931–33 and 1934–41. This section concentrates on the first sub-period.

As economic discussions generally, those concerning enterprise finances and incentives were both complex and incoherent in the 1920s. Marxists saw profits as an essentially non-socialist element of the transitional economy. An ambiguous distinction was often made between commercial accounting (*kommercheskii raschet*) and economic accounting (*khozyaistvennyi raschet* or *khozraschet*). When the distinction was finally codified in the early 1930s, the former was taken to mean profit-maximisation under a market regime, while the latter referred to enterprises under central management.[27] Though with accounts of incomes and costs, *khozraschet* enterprises either did not strive for profits or did that just as a by-product of fulfilling their plans. That this distinction had been an ambiguous one is shown, for instance, in the fact that while some economists equated *khozraschet* with accounting, others saw planning and *khozraschet* as opposites.[28]

The Left Opposition, in particular, contrasted existing incentives to the proper socialist ones. Preobrazhenskii insisted that the NEP wage system, that is piece-rates, 'has nothing in common with socialism, and cannot have'. Citing Marx's opinion about piece-rates being adequate for capitalism, Preobrazhenskii claimed that they made 'it possible to extract everything possible from individual, bourgeois stimuli to labour'. As a social arrangement, piece-rates were backward compared to the stage Soviet society in general had attained. Going over first to a combination of individual and collective payment and then 'to payment of the collective worker' instead of payment to the individual worker for an individual piece of work would take time, Preobrazhenskii admitted: 'The socialist incentives to labour do not drop from heaven, they have to be developed through prolonged re-education of human nature . . .'[29]

Preobrazhenskii pointed out that technological developments restricted the possible use of individual piece-rates. The main point for him, however, was the priority of collective incentives:

> The moment when collective incentives become predominant in the working class compared with individual incentives, is a great moment in the building of socialism, none less important for the future than the socialisation of the means of production was.[30]

It is interesting that Marx's socialist distribution principle seems to have been largely neglected when discussing the future socialism during the 1920s.[31] Wages were typically seen as a form of the value of labour-power, and income distribution was hardly given the status of a problem separate from reproduction in general.

An authoritative 1930 criticism of earlier wage theories distinguished between three variants. One was 'Menshevik-mechanistic': wages are a reflection of the value of labour-power. Two were 'bourgeois'. One was a Tugan–Baranovskian social theory of distribution while the other linked wages to the productivity of labour. The author of the criticism, L. Mekhlis, who thus did not find any correct wage theories in the earlier literature, did admit that rising productivity makes rising wages possible under socialism. The main point, however, was to insist that wages were planned so as to facilitate a high tempo of industrialisation and a rising proletarian standard of living.[32]

WITHERING AWAY OF MATERIAL INCENTIVES?

In 1929–30 Soviet leaders seem to have been thinking that the country actually 'was rapidly becoming fully socialised and moneyless, and that planned production and distribution were replacing the market and trade'.[33] There was uncertainty whether the present stage could still be called NEP.[34] One proposal was to see it as a synthesis of NEP and war communism.[35] The question was finally resolved by Stalin himself in June 1930:

> In going over to the offensive along the whole front, we are not yet abolishing NEP, for private trade and capitalist elements still remain, commodity turnover and the money economy still remain. But we are certainly abolishing the initial stage of NEP, and developing its following stage, the present stage of NEP, which is the last stage.[36]

NEP was thus connected with private trade, capitalist elements and commodity–money relations. On the other hand, Stalin stressed that NEP had been introduced for the victory of socialism over capitalist elements.[37] The economists generally interpreted all this to mean that NEP and thus commodity–money relations would remain until all production would be socialised so that no private trade remained.[38] This interpretation had been authored by Stalin in February 1930. He then said that NEP would be eliminated 'when we have the possibility of arranging economic links between town and countryside via product exchange, without trade with its private turnover.[39] This view was generally accepted at the time. It has even been incorporated into the 1928 programme of Comintern.[40]

But just a few years later Stalin was to condemn such talk as 'Leftist chatter', and in his *Sochineniya* the text has been changed, as Davies notes.[41] Among Soviet historians of economic thought, Bogomazov for one cites the revised version.[42]

But if private production was so crucial for the existence of money and trade, was there no trade within the state sector? This quesiton was debated in 1929–31. Kozlov, a future leading political economist, had argued in 1929 that money within the state sector was not really money, but close to 'labour coupons', mere 'nominal accounting units'.[43] Another young economist, Gatovskii, regarded such a view as being leftist. But even he claimed that transactions between state enterprises were already essentially an exchange of goods and not trade.[44] Gatovskii thus in fact also equated trade with private trade.

If full socialism thus was generally seen to be just around the corner, it was also natural that economic incentives were seen as becoming old-fashioned. They were accused of halting growth, and the declining share of piece-rates was welcomed.[45] The wage-form itself was seen as being alien to the Soviet economy, irrational in the new conditions but necessary until the end of NEP.[46]

The new socialist stimuli of socialist emulation and shock-work were not seen as functioning together with material incentives. On the contrary, these two sets of stimuli were firmly set against one another.[47] Wages were adopting a new role, that of a technical device in accounting.[48] And as in the times of war communism, the rationing of consumption goods was welcomed as a step towards the planned socialist distribution.[49] So was the administrative distribution of labour.[50] At this time, shock-workers' brigades with individual payment were still seen as the basic form of organising work. But several economists insisted that arrangements of a more collectivist character, like the egalitarian production communes mentioned above, were not to be discouraged. They might not be the best possible form of incentives, but at least with highly conscious workers they would and should be allowed to develop.[51]

The fate of *khozraschet* in general was first discussed by I. Boev in 1929. He started with the provisions of the 1927 statute on trusts, which made lowering production costs a target to be stimulated materially. But, Boev argued, with existing tight planning such a stimulus could not possibly function. It was not generally possible to lower production costs from the level stipulated in plans. Therefore, any stimuli to be used should be connected with fulfilling the plan, not with profit-making. Stimuli of the latter kind 'do not, in our opinion, correspond with the growth of planning and socialist orientation in our economy'.[52]

Boev was soon challenged by Dukor. *Khozraschet* was not to be equalled with profit-seeking, he argued. In fact, *khozraschet* primarily meant 'a certain' independence of enterprises, already seen in capitalism and 'probably' remaining in socialism even while markets or money would disappear.[53] If Boev had given a narrow interpretation of *khozraschet*, Dukor's definition was wide. Both denied the existence of commodity–money relations in socialism.

INTRODUCING *KHOZRASCHET*

Even if 1929–30 was retrospectively called 'the new non-*khozraschet* period', *khozraschet* was not officially forgotten even then.

After the December 1929 resolution mentioned above, the summer 1930 XVI Party congress complained that *khozraschet* had not been introduced in all enterprises.[54] A new campaign for currency stability and *khozraschet* was launched in autumn 1930. It was said that industrial supply had been excessively centralised, contract relations largely dismantled (which contributed to quality deterioration), all cost accounting often neglected, etc. Many plans went unfulfilled and costs soared. All this made *khozraschet* 'particularly timely', Voznesenskii commented.[55]

This was the background for the First All-Union Industrial Conference in early 1931. Of the wide audience, only one speaker called for the war communist measures of the utmost centralisation. Ordzhonikidze gave the conference the key-note saying that introducing *khozraschet* was now of utmost importance. Control by customer enterprises over the supplying enterprises by withholding payments was to be the way of improving supplies.[56] Molotov insisted that without having *khozraschet* at the different levels of the economic hierarchy, from factories to associations, it would be impossible to bring about 'the order needed'. He also set the historical limits of *khozraschet*:

> *Khozraschet* means that we still work in the conditions of NEP, that we still haven't passed NEP . . . because NEP still exists, *khozraschet* cannot be bureaucratically 'called off'. On the contrary, *khozraschet* is an indispensible method of management in state industry. Forgetting this leads to effects, serious for socialist construction.[57]

During the next few months an avalanche of articles appeared, propagating with very small variations the present attitude toward *khozraschet*:

1. At the present stage, *khozraschet* is a most important (*vazhneishaya*) method of planning and management in state-owned industry.
2. *Khozraschet* is, primarily, a method of comparing costs and productive results in monetary terms, of ensuring profitability and of struggling for the fulfillment and overfulfillment of the *promfinplan*. Decreasing production costs is the major specific goal of *khozraschet*.
3. *Khozraschet* allows for enterprise independence and initiative within the frame of the plan, especially with regard to contract relations. The relativity of this independence was always stressed and nobody seems to have envisaged a model of indirect centralization. S. Birman, one of the most emphatic proponents of enterprise independence, also wrote: 'It is clear that the Soviet enterprise cannot, for example, only produce what is profitable to it, but it must produce what the planned economy demands from it'.[58]
4. In the moneyless socialism monetary *khozraschet* will be replaced by a proper socialist method of accounting and control, using labour-time units.
5. The previous neglect of *khozraschet* had some serious consequences.[59]
6. In June 1931 Stalin added a fresh emphasis by stressing that *khozraschet* was essential so as to get more resources from heavy industry for its own development.[60] It was also in 1931 that Soviet trade — that is, socialised trade using money as the unit of account — was reintroduced into official pronouncements. This amounted to a revision of previous doctrine. Stalin had, after all, said in 1926 that creating the economic basis of socialism meant organising the relations between town and countryside on the basis of direct exchange of products.[61]

The Soviet textbook on the history of the political economy of socialism is correct in pointing out that to a large degree this amounted to a formal accounting interpretation of *khozraschet*.[62] Indeed, the 1930 edition of the standard textbook of Lapidus and Ostrovityanov had stated that commodity–money relations in general exist because they 'help us in carrying out accounting in our state enterprises'.[63] *Khozraschet* was often seen as a method of reducing production costs within a given plan: the elaboration of incentive problems was neglected and even the much-emphasised contracts could have no effect worthy of mention under conditions of unrealistically high plan targets and the resulting high-shortage economy. *Khozraschet*, then, was taken as a method of trying to fulfil unrealistic plans. But then this was a period when the existence of economic laws in the Soviet economy was generally denied. Economic laws were first equated with plans and then with the policies of the proletarian dictatorship.[64]

Noting that in 1931 *khozraschet* was restricted to NEP, R.W. Davies writes:

> This attribution of the notion of *khozraschet* to the remnants of capitalist economy, given the vast size of socialist industry and the importance attached to *khozraschet*, is a striking example of the incongruous lag of theory behind economic practice: 1931 was designed as the year of 'the completion of the foundations [fundament] of the socialist economy', but these foundations did not include *khozraschet*.[65]

This question, as it sheds much light on the evolving thinking of the Soviet economists, may warrant more comment.

It is true, of course, that NEP was generally explained by the existence of a private peasant sector. Thus the causation went: the non-socialist sector to NEP to *khozraschet*. It was argued that even the multi-sector transition economy was one whole. The state sector therefore had to be influenced by the existence of the private sector.[66] Given the miniscule size of the private sector this explanation naturally was a poor one. It was also used in arguing for the speedy abolition of *khozraschet*.[67] But the causation had also been seen — implicitly at least — to run the other way, too. This is what Butaev had to say about *khozraschet*, money and contracts in early 1931: 'Transition from them to socialist distribution will mean the liquidation of NEP on the whole and totally.'[68]

Thus there were two emphases. One could *either* see NEP fundamentally as the policy of abolishing classes *or* define it as the use of commodity–money relations. In the former case, abolishing the private sector would lead to socialism, which would by definition be moneyless. In the latter case, introducing 'socialist accounting' would signal the end of NEP. Here, commodity–money relations were the cause of NEP; in the former case, they were its effect.

Also, when the prerequisites of abolishing commodity–money

relations were listed, abolishing the private sector was usually accompanied by organizing *'polneishchii uchet'*.[69] This, of course, looks like a mere technical problem, but it also clearly foreshadows the basic 1940s explanation for the existence of the law of value in socialism: heterogeneous labour and the necessity of material incentives with scarcity.[70] In 1951 Stalin announced another explanation, the existence of two forms of property, thus reviving in fact the old doctrinal legitimation for NEP, though in a new function!

The basic explanation thus was that commodity–money relations and *khozraschet* were a result of the private sector. If the causation was sometimes seen to go the other way, the state sector specific reasons — that is, reasons not reflecting the existence of the private sector — for *khozraschet* were not spelled out clearly. Probably Gatovskii came closest to being explicit.[71] He criticised his own 1930 views for failing to see that 'elements of commodity' also existed in the interrelations of state-owned enterprises. These elements were caused by the 'certain independence' of the enterprises. Real socialist accounting would presuppose not only the abolishing of private production and trade, but also abolishing commodity shortage and 'a political, economic, organisational, technical and cultural overhaul of the apparatus of exchange, distribution (and) accounting, [as well as] mastering the school of *khozraschet* and Soviet trade'.

Others also insisted that state sector-specific reasons for *khozraschet* existed. In implicitly criticising Voznesenskii, Greblis said that those who connect *khozraschet* only with relations with the peasantry were wrong. *Khozraschet* was also needed within the state sector.[72] Neither Gatovskii nor Greblis has a real theory to offer. But such views did postpone the time of abolishing *khozraschet*. They no doubt made it easier later to accept the continuing existence of *khozraschet* even after NEP.

Second, even if *khozraschet* was not among the 'foundations of the socialist economy', in 1931 it certainly was part of 'the completion of the foundations of the socialist economy'. In 1929–30 going over to socialism was thought to imply a stepwise dissolution of *khozraschet*. In 1931, 'dialectically', abolishing *khozraschet* was to happen through its strengthening. It was argued that in an economy that was basically planned and socialist, though it also had elements of *'stikhiya'*, commodity–money relations no longer had a capitalist essence. They were tools of planning still possessing some traits of *'stikhiya'*. Therefore, what was in practice necessary was also made ideologically possible: to use *khozraschet* maximally in the interests of the socialist economy.[73] Whether one finds such dialectical dogma convincing or not, this argument also made the acceptance of socialist *khozraschet* easier at a later time.

It was never said during this period that *khozraschet* would exist in socialism. Gatovskii was, in 1931, among the first to stress Marx's socialist distribution principle and the need for material incentives in socialism, but even he insists that these incentives are a wholly different thing from *khozraschet*, which is a monetary form.[74] Davies rightly notes an ambiguity in Kuibyshev of 1932:

> Communism does not emerge at once, it is a result of the intensive effort of millions of people liberated from capitalist exploitation. It is therefore impossible to go over to direct product exchange, to the abolition of sales, trade, the rouble etc. For the present stage of socialist construction, for the period of the second five-year plan, such slogans on 'abolition' are merely a left-wing phrase, which is undoubtedly of an anti-Bolshevik nature.
>
> The economic prerequisites of socialism as the first phase of communism are such that Soviet trade, and the rouble, and the *khozraschet* necessarily retain their significance.[75]

This left it unclear whether the 'economic prerequisites' of socialism were themselves a part of socialism or not. But on the other hand, in June 1930, Stalin had asserted that the Soviet Union had already entered the period of socialism.[76] Logically, and the point was made in economic literature, money, *khozraschet*, etc. were being strengthened in the period of socialism.[77] Arguing, as Stalin had done, that the country was at the same time both in the last phase of NEP and in the first phase of socialism, had made the distinction between transitional society and socialism a very vague one indeed. This is Gatovskii's conclusion from 1932:

> NEP will remain right until the building of classless society, certain remains of the methods of NEP (for instance, the Soviet monetary form) will apparently still be used also some time in the conditions of the classless socialist society.[78]

Even earlier Borilin had insisted that there were many transitional stages on the road to a 'developed socialist society', which Borilin (unlike much later Soviet theorists) seems to set equal with communism:

There is no doubt that in socialism itself there will still exist an amount of transitional forms till the final abolishing of classes in the country, when the higher phase of communist society will be reached.

The point of view of Right and 'Left' opportunists that entering socialism means the liquidation of money, markets, material poverty, the disappearance of class division, etc. has nothing to do with Marxist-Leninism.[79]

Economists like Gatovskii and Borilin were in fact trying to lengthen the transition period. For them, it was not a sudden rupture (as was argued by Krivitskii in 1930 and 1931, criticising Gatovskii), but a period with many stages. This period, Gatovskii especially argued, could also be the object of a specific theory. At the same time these writers quite obviously were trying to argue that the abolition of commodity–money forms would be premature in the foreseeable future, even though that future already belonged to the period of socialism.

These arguments were not very conclusive, and the fact remains that the prevailing accounting interpretation of *khozraschet* left little room for thinking about incentives. The accounting approach was criticised by some economists. One of them was Ginzburg. He included such material incentives as piece-rates and premia among the main principles of *khozraschet*.[80] This connection was also stressed by those writing about *khozraschet* on the shop and brigade level.[81]

Ginzburg defined *khozraschet* as a unity of planning on one hand and the operative and property-right independence of economic units on the other hand. This independence is implemented through economic contracts which, Ginzburg argued, require 'equivalent' relations between the unit in question and 'all other enterprises, organizations and persons'. This is a truly remarkable 1931 argument, as it is clearly equivalent to Nemchinov's theorising in the 1960s about a *khozraschet* economy.

The status of *khozraschet* brigades was widely discussed in 1931.[82] Many economists saw that to be effective, *khozraschet* had to be introduced on all levels of economic management. While some looked upon brigade *khozraschet* as a mere form of socialist emulation, others, like the economic journalist M. Birbraier, gave it more prominence.[83] For him brigade *khozraschet* was an instance of democratic centralism. It presupposed that the brigade became 'to a certain extent . . . a part of the management' of the enterprise. The idea has a definitive flavour of self-management, made more probable by Birbraier's prominence as a proponent of reform in 1932–33,[84] but Birbraier also stressed the limits to the independence of *khozraschet* brigades. They should not be made materially responsible for fulfilling contract obligations, as this would turn brigades into cartels. Basic sanctions were to be stipulated in the collective agreement, and *khozraschet* contracts were to be stimulated morally and by premia.

Birbraier also had another interesting proposal. *Khozraschet* brigades were showing the amount of excess personnel in industry. To encourage efficiency, all the wages saved by cutting the workforce should be allocated to the brigade concerned. This is an explicit 1931 proposal for the Shchekino method, but then, of course, the same idea had already been accepted once in 1921.[85]

If the incentive role of *khozraschet* was generally neglected, the incentive role of wages was not. Stalin's 1931 'Six Conditions' speech had called for strengthening *khozraschet*, but primarily it was an attack against egalitarianism, *uravnilovka*. Egalitarianism was leading to a higher labour turnover and diminished workers' interest in higher qualifications. Referring to Marx and Lenin, Stalin called for distribution according to work done. *Uravnilovka* was thus both anti-Marxist and anti-Leninist.[86]

Writers like Yampolskii added the smaller print.[87] Material incentives were not in contradiction to socialist incentives (as had been earlier thought). Increasing the intensity of work must not be opposed. On the contrary, Yampolskii asserted: 'in socialism a rise in the intensity [of work] does not wear out the worker, but leads to the harmonious development of the socialist worker'. In socialism, naturally, the intensity of work would be higher than in capitalism. Following an obvious hint from Stalin,[88] Yampolskii also called for a differentiated distribution of social benefits. Collective forms of pay, especially production communes, were to be abolished.[89] Individual accounting and individual pay with progressive piece-rates and progressive premia were the best way of increasing productivity. Therefore they must also be adopted, Yampolskii insisted. To think otherwise was to be a 'Trotskyist-minded element and Leftist deviationist'.

There is really little to add to Soviet 'wage-theory' during the 1930s. Piece-rates were extolled, and the idea of equal pay was condemned as 'mere Kulak demagogy'.[90] Socialist equality merely meant the abolishing of classes, and the struggle against all other interpretations of equality was counted among the most important tasks of class-struggle.[91] The need for such propaganda undoubtedly existed, as totally different interpretations of equality had always been a central piece of socialist ideology. As late as 1931 Gatovskii took it to be self-evident that income distribution would be more even in socialism than in capitalism and totally egalitarian in communism.[92] In 1932 *Partizdat* still published a book connecting piece-rates and NEP and contrasting them with socialist stimuli. Such views were deplored as common in party *agitprop*.[93] The counter-argument to them was partly to define away all questions of income distribution and work organisation. It could be bluntly asserted that income distribution as a specific problem did not exist: it was totally subordinated to the needs of production.[94] And as to work organisation, its essence naturally was in the social ownership of means of production. As the latter was socialist, so must the former be. A contradiction between the two could thus only exist in Trotskyist imagination.[95]

SOCIALISM WITH MONEY

R.W. Davies has argued that the Soviet economic system was 'not fully formed as late as the end of 1932'.[96] Advocating significant changes in the economic mechanism was still possible. Realistic planning, market-clearing prices, a wide use of markets, incentives for efficient investments and a decentralised supply system were all defined in the Soviet press. The discussion surveyed in this chapter also partly reflects such debates. Gatovskii was a leading advocate of Soviet trade and also pointed out the disincentive effects of rationing.[97] He also argued for a heightened influence of the trading system on production in socialism: 'This especially means the active influence of the trading system on large-scale state industry'.[98] Above, we already met with the proposals of men like Birbraier and Ginzburg. All of these proposals had a non-accounting interpretation of *khozraschet* as their core.

Even then, the existence of commodity–money relations and of *khozraschet* in socialism could only be decreed by Stalin. He finally did that in January 1934, at the XVII Party Congress, claiming that there was still:

> Leftist chatter circulating among one section of our officials to the effect that Soviet trade is a past stage, that we need to establish direct product exchange, that money will soon be

abolished, since it has turned into simple accounting units.

It is of course ridiculous and amusing that these people, who are incapable of organising the simplest aspect of Soviet trade, should chatter about their readiness to organise the more complex and difficult business of product exchange . . . These people, who are as far from Marxism as the sky is from the earth, evidently do not understand that money will still remain with us for a long time, until the completion of the first stage of communism — the socialist stage of development. They do not understand that money is an instrument of bourgeois economy which Soviet power has taken into its own hands and adapted to the interests of socialism so as to develop Soviet trade to the utmost, and thus prepares conditions for direct product exchange.[99]

In the meantime, the importance of *khozraschet* had been continually emphasised, even if only parts of the proposals aired in the press had been adopted. But only Stalin's speech made it possible to call *khozraschet* an 'indispensible element of socialist reproduction'.[100] The former orthodoxy, shared by Stalin as well as others, was now condemned 'Leftist' and 'non-*khozraschet* period' was said to have been the work of wreckers.

Since the mid-1930s *khozraschet* has been regarded as a central feature of the socialist economy. This can be seen in plans for a textbook of the political economy of socialism.[101] These plans also included an important related point by admitting the existence of necessary and surplus labour in socialism and thus providing grounds for handling the category of profits. This division had been denied till quite recently.

A 1940 textbook, officially accepted for university use, called *khozraschet* 'the basic method of managing socialist enterprises',[102] while Turetskii called it 'a principle of socialist economising'.[103]

The problem of why *khozraschet* was a feature of socialism does not seem to have been directly addressed. This is hardly surprising, as the accepted wisdom of the time was that all economic laws were the result of government policies. (This, in fact, was what Stalin also implied in 1934.) *Khozraschet* thus existed just because 'Soviet power' had decided that it would be useful 'as the form of interesting enterprises in fulfilling and overfulfilling the plan, thus developing productive forces and preparing for the going over into communism'.[104]

It is interesting to note that the existence of money was not seen as the reason of *khozraschet*. On the contrary, Kronrod argued, the existence of *khozraschet*, that is the fact that 'social means of production [have been] allotted to separate socialist economic enterprises, working on the basis of a unified national economic plan' makes exchange necessary.[105] Another explanation stressed that socialism is not communism. Work was not people's first life-necessity and there still were differences between different kinds of labour. Therefore, a monetary (and not labour-unit) control over the amounts of work and consumption was necessary. Thus money and *khozraschet*.[106]

These two explanations are in fact precursors to those explanations that have been later given to the law of value in socialism, the latter one in the 1940s and the former one in the 1950s.

Khozraschet has always been an elusive concept. By 1940, its definition generally consisted of control by the rouble (including monetary accounting), of a source of accumulation and — what was most emphasised — of the basic method of managing socialist enterprises 'materially interesting collectives in fulfilling and overfulfilling the given *promfinplan* in terms of quantity, quality, assortment, schedule and costs of production'. It meant both rights and obligations.[107]

It seems that every Party congress emphasised the task of strengthening *khozraschet*. Economists had welcomed the derationing of food markets. They also welcomed the price rises in heavy industry in 1936, bringing profitability nearer. But the economists also put forward further proposals. The problems of using gross production as the main success indicator were well known. In fact, there was a 1937 decision of using 'finished and complete production' instead of it.[108] Some economists called for more fundamental changes. Strazhevskii claimed that 'the question of reorganizing the whole *khozraschet* incentives system of the enterprises has ripened already along ago'.[109] He disapproved of having the difference between (possibly too high) planned costs and actual costs as a success indicator, and proposed net profit as the indicator, accompanied by some resource use norms. Furthermore, he insisted that 'Such circumstances must be created in which *every* worker of an enterprise . . . would be vitally (through the wage system) interested in the uninterrupted bettering of the economy and finances of the enterprise.' This would come about, Strazhevskii argued, by having all the employees, including white-collar workers, on piece-rates.

Another champion of the importance of profit as a success indicator was Turetskii.[110] He also criticised the use of antiquated 1926–27 prices in planning, called for relevant relative prices with as few subsidies as possible and wanted more prominence for inter-enterprise contracts. The last point, of course, is the usual call for greater enterprise independence. As Gatovskii put it in 1935, *khozraschet* should mean that 'petty tutelage over the work of enterprises and shops fall off'. Instead of petty tutelage, 'economic accounting, monetary wages, delivery prices become those economic levers which give economic management flexibility and operativeness'.[111]

For the last time before the war, discussion about the rights of enterprises flared up in late 1940. A notable contributor was A. Birman.[112] He points out the irrationality of using 1926–27 prices, deplores the low profitability of key industries as well as the deficiencies of financial control and notes that in some branches the Director's Fund was only a few roubles per employee. Birman calls for more rights for economic managers, especially in distributing the given wages fund. Such proposals, modern as they sound, were naturally doomed to failure in the war economy of 1941.

CONCLUSION

In conclusion, it is obvious that not only had the Soviet economic system got its present form by the mid-1930s but many of the proposals for reforming and streamlining first aired at that time still sound quite familiar. It is clear that economic theory was not a guide in the birth of the system. As R.W. Davies puts it, 'the adaptation of theory to the new situation of the 1930s was slow, confused and piecemeal'.[113] We have tried to show some of this process above.

Obviously, much of Soviet economic literature was dishonest nonsense. Thus, Krivitskii must have known the real attitude of workers to progressive piece-rates when he wrote that piece-rates were an 'excellent school of socialist work attitude', convincing workers of the harmony of individual and social interests.[114] The literature surveyed in this chapter does not allow any judgement as to how representative people like Birman, Turetskii and Strazhevskii were in the late 1930s. But it is obvious that if Molotov really forbade the economists' discussion on prices,[115] some of them did not listen to him. But on the other hand, an Institute of Economics 1940 list of recommended topics of dissertations does not include prices, profits and *khozraschet*. Wages, credit and monetary circulation were present.[116]

Finally by the late 1930s *khozraschet* was firmly treated as an economic category of socialism. Opinions to the contrary[117] can best be seen as reflecting the fact that *khozraschet* was not seen as an objective economic law of socialism. No objective economic laws of socialism whatsoever were recognised till 1941, when Stalin declared the existence of the law of value in Soviet socialism.

NOTES

* This chapter was written while visiting the Centre for Russian and East European Studies, University of Birmingham. The financial assistance of the Finnish Cultural Foundation is gratefully acknowledged.
1. Berliner (1957); Granick (1954); Nove (1958).
2. Davies (1977; 1982; 1984); Bogomazov (1983), pp. 134–59; *Istoriya* (1983), pp. 366–430; Širokorad (1977), pp. 163–99.
3. Sutela (1984).
4. Ibid., pp. 17–22.
5. Kautsky (1974), p. 167.
6. Bebel (1954), p. 461.
7. Ibid., p. 469.
8. Kautsky (n.a).
9. Bukharin and Preobrazhensky (1969), p. 118.
10. Cohen (1975), pp. 88–96; Day (1973), Ch. 2.
11. Avdakov and Borodin (1973), pp. 63–6.
12. Carr and Davies (1969).
13. Bailes (1978), Ch. 2.
14. Lampert (1979), p. 135.
15. Davies (1977; 1982).
16. All citations in Davies (1977), p. 12.
17. Ginzburg (1931), p. 111.
18. Bogomazov (1983), p. 135.
19. Ibid., p. 135.
20. Ibid., pp. 136–9.
21. Granick (1954), pp. 169–71.
22. Berliner (1957), p. 73.
23. Lampert (1979), p. 142.
24. Voznesenskii (1931), p. 48.
25. Lewin (1982).
26. Neiman (1935); Gatovskii (1935).
27. Voznesenskii (1931).
28. *Istoriya* (1983), pp. 394–5, Veisbrod in Preniya (1930).
29. Preobrazhenskii (1965), pp. 192–4.
30. Preobrazhenskii (1975), p. 89.
31. *Istoriya* (1983), pp. 366–70.
32. Mekhlis (1930).
33. Davies (1977), p. 3.
34. O novoi (1930).
35. Veisbrod in Preniya (1930).

36. Stalin (1937), pp. 388-9.
37. Ibid., p. 388.
38. Rylskii (1930).
39. Voprosy (1930).
40. Bogomazov (1983), p. 144.
41. Davies (1977), p. 6, note 1.
42. Bogomazov (1983), pp. 152-3.
43. Kozlov (1929).
44. Gatovskii (1930a).
45. Smit (1930).
46. Kats (1931); Mekhlis (1930); Krivitskii (1931).
47. Kats (1931); Kraval (1929).
48. Kuznetsov (1931).
49. Gatovskii (1930b).
50. Kuznetsov (1930).
51. Pavlov (1930).
52. Boev (1929).
53. Dukor (1929).
54. *Vsesoyuznaya* (1941), p. 419.
55. Voznesenskii (1931).
56. Kontrolnye (1931).
57. Osnovnye (1931).
58. Birman (1941).
59. Greblis (1932); Butaev (1931a); Ginzburg (1931), Khavin (1931).
60. Stalin (1937), p. 463.
61. This point is still cited in Butaev (1931b).
62. *Istoriya* (1983), p. 403.
63. Cited in Bogomazov (1983), p. 140.
64. Sutela (1984), pp. 54-9.
65. Davies (1977), p. 7.
66. See, for example, Ostrovityanov (1931).
67. Voznesenskii (1931).
68. Preniya (1931).
69. Ostrovityanov (1931).
70. Sutela (1984), p. 65.
71. Gatovskii (1931a).
72. Greblis (1932).
73. Ostrovityanov (1931).
74. Gatovskii (1932a).
75. Cited in Davies (1977), p. 9.
76. Stalin (1937), p. 432.
77. See, for example, Rabinovich (1931), pp. 61-2.
78. Gatovskii (1932a).
79. Borilin (1931), p. 147.
80. Ginzburg (1931).
81. Voznesenskii (1931); Greblis (1932).
82. Bogomazov (1983), pp. 184-90.
83. Birbraier (1931).
84. Davies (1984).
85. Belousov (1983), p. 91.

86. Stalin (1937), pp. 448–66.
87. Yampolskii (1931).
88. Stalin (1937), pp. 452–3.
89. Also Leibman and Raisov (1931).
90. Meerzon (1932), p. 126.
91. Leontyev (1934).
92. Gatovskii (1931b).
93. Meerzon (1932).
94. Rozenberg (1932).
95. Gubareva (1933).
96. Davies (1984).
97. Gatovskii (1931a), especially p. 40.
98. Gatovskii (1932b).
99. *Vsesoyuznaya* (1941), pp. 552–3.
100. Gatovskii (1935), p. 45.
101. Borilin (1937).
102. *Ekonomika* (1940), p. 526.
103. Turetskii (1940), p. 17.
104. See Notkin (1939).
105. Kronrod (1940); also Plotnikov (1938).
106. Gatovskii (1935), Miroshnikov (1935).
107. *Ekonomika* (1940), pp. 526–30.
108. *Istoriya* (1983), p. 407.
109. Strazhevskii (1936).
110. Turetskii (1939; 1940).
111. Gatovskii (1935), p. 54.
112. Birman (1941).
113. Davies (1977), p. 6.
114. Krivitskii (1936).
115. See Arzumanyan (1964).
116. Ot Instituta (1940).
117. *Istoriya* (1983), p. 409; Davies (1977), p. 7.

REFERENCES

Arzumanyan, A. (1964), 'O razvitie ekonomicheskoi nauki i ekonomicheskogo obrazovaniya v SSSR', *Izvestiya Akademii Nauk*, no. 9.

Avdakov, Yuri K. and Borodin, V.V. (1973), *Proizvodstvennye obyedineniya i ikh rol v organizatsii upravleniya Sovetskoi promyshlennosti (1917–1932gg)*, Moscow.

Bailes, Kendall (1978), *Technology and Society Under Lenin and Stalin*, Princeton, N.J.

Bebel, August (1954), *Die Frau und das Sozialismus*, Berlin.

Belousov, R.A. (1983), *Istoricheskii opyt planovogo upravleniya ekonomikoi SSSR*, Moscow.

Berliner, Joseph (1957), *Factory and Management in the USSR*, Cambridge, Mass.

Birbraier, M. (1931) 'Khozraschet v rabochei brigade', *Problemy ekonomiki*, no. 6.
Birman, A. (1941), 'Nekotorye problemy ukrepleniya khozyaistvennogo rascheta v promyshlennosti', *Problemy ekonomiki*, no. 1.
Birman, S. (1931), 'Promfinplan i khozraschet', *Puti industrializatsii*, no. 8.
Boev, I. (1929), 'Evolyutsiya ponyatiya khozrascheta', *Puti industrializatsii*, no. 8.
Bogomazov, G.G. (1983), *Formirovanie osnov sotsialisticheskogo khozyaistvennogo mekhanizma v SSSR v 20–30-e gody*, Leningrad.
Borilin, B. (1931), 'Vstuplenie v periodu sotsializma i zavershenie postroeniya fundamenta sotsialisticheskoi ekonomiki', *Problemy ekonomiki*, nos. 4–5.
—— (1937), 'O predmete i prepodavanii politicheskoi ekonomii sotsializma', *Problemy ekonomiki*, no. 3.
Bukharin, N. and Preobrazhensky, E. (1969), *The ABC of Communism*, Harmondsworth: Penguin Books.
Butaev, K. (1931a), 'K desyatiletiyu nepa', *Problemy ekonomiki*, no. 3.
—— (1931b), 'SSSR zavershaet postroeniya fundamenta sotsialisticheskoi ekonomiki', *Problemy ekonomiki*, no. 1.
Carr, E.H. and Davies, R.W. (1969), *Foundations of a Planned Economy 1926–1929, Vol. One*, London.
Cohen, Stephen, F. (1975), *Bukharin and the Bolshevik Revolution*, New York.
Davies, R.W. (1977), 'The Emergence of the Soviet Economic System 1927–1934', *CREES Discussion Papers, Series SIPS*, no. 7.
—— (1982), 'Models of the Soviet Economic System in Soviet Practice, 1926–1936', in *L'industrialisation* (1982).
—— (1984), 'The Socialist Market: A Debate in Soviet Industry', *Slavic Review*, vol. 42, no. 2.
Day, Richard B. (1973), *Leon Trotsky & the Politics of Economic Isolation*, Cambridge.
Dukor, G. (1929), 'O nepe, konstruktivnom periode, khozraschete i oshibkakh tov. Boeva', *Puti industrializatsii*, no. 13–14.
Ekonomika sotsialisticheskoi promyshlennosti (1940), Pod red. Granovskogo i Markusa, Moscow.
Gatovskii, L. (1930a), 'O prirode menovykh svyazei na novom etape', *Planovoe khozyaistvo*, no. 5.
—— (1930b), 'Rekonstruktsiya khozyaistva i voprosy snabzheniya', *Bolshevik*, nos. 19–20.
—— (1931a) 'O kharaktere Sovetskoi torgovli na sovremennom etape', *Problemy ekonomiki*, nos. 7–8.
—— (1931b), 'O zadachakh teorii Sovetskogo khozyaistva', *Problemy ekonomiki*, no. 1.
—— (1931c), 'Sovetskaya torgovlya na sovremennom etape', *Bolshevik*, no. 11.
—— (1932a), 'O nekotorykh voprosakh teorii Sovetskogo khozyaistva', *Problemy ekonomiki*, no. 8.
—— (1932b), 'O Sovetskoi torgovle', *Vestnik Kommunisticheskoi Akademii*, nos. 7–8.

―――― (1935), 'O Sovetskom ruble i Sovetskoi torgovle', *Problemy ekonomiki*, no. 2.
Ginzburg, L. (1931), 'O khozraschete', *Sovetskoe gosudarstvo i revulyutsiya prava*, nos. 5–6.
Granick, David (1954), *Management of the Industrial Firm in the USSR*, New York.
Greblis, A. (1932), 'Voprosy khozyaistvennogo rascheta v sotsialisticheskoi promyshlennosti', *Problemy ekonomiki*, no. 1.
Gubareva, O. (1933), 'Review of Eskin: Sotsialisticheskie formy truda', *Problemy ekonomiki*, no. 3.
Istoriya politicheskoi ekonomii sotsializma (1983), Leningrad.
Kats, V. (1931), 'Otnosheniya raspredeleniya pri kapitalizme i v SSSR', *Problemy ekonomiki*, no. 8.
Kautsky, Karl (n.a.), *Die Soziale Revolution*, Berlin.
―――― (1974), *Erfurtin ohjelma*, Helsinki.
Khavin, I. (1931), 'Kreditnaya reforma i khozraschet', *Problemy ekonomiki*, nos. 4–5.
Kontrolnye tsifry na 1931 god i zadachi khozyaistvennykh organizatsii (1931), Doklad tov. Ordzhonikidze, *Za industrializatsiyu* 2.2.
Kozlov, G. (1929), 'K voprosu o prirode deneg i zakonov denezhnego obrashcheniya v SSSR', *Planovoe khozyaistvo*, no. 8.
Kraval, I. (1929), 'O sotsialisticheskom sorevnovanii', *Bolshevik*, no. 15.
Krivitskii, M. (1930), 'K problemam ekonomiki perekhodnogo perioda', *Problemy ekonomiki*, no. 9.
―――― (1931), 'K voprosu ob ekonomike perekhodnogo perioda', *Problemy ekonomiki*, no. 1.
―――― (1936), 'V borbe za proizvoditelnosti truda', *Problemy ekonomiki*, no. 5.
Kronrod, Ya. (1940), 'Za tvorcheskuyu diskussiyu, protiv skholastiki', *Problemy ekonomiki*, nos. 11–12.
Kuznetsov, A. (1931), 'Voprosy organizatsii truda v 1931 godu', *Bolshevik*, no. 2.
Lampert, Nicholas (1979), *The Technical Intelligentsia and the Soviet State*, London.
Leibman, Yu. and Raisov, A. (1931), 'Aktualnye problemy truda na sovremennom etape', *Bolshevik*, no. 12.
Leontyev, A. (1934), 'Sotsializm v SSSR', *Problemy ekonomiki*, no. 3.
Lewin, Moshe (1982), 'Social Relations within Industry', *L'industrialisation*, op. cit.
L'industrialisation de l'URSS dans les années trente (1982), Paris.
Meerzon, D. (1932), 'K voprosu o sotsialisticheskoi kooperatsii truda', *Problemy ekonomiki*, no. 8.
Mekhlis, L. (1930), 'Voprosy teorii zarplaty v SSSR', *Bolshevik*, nos. 3–4.
Miroshnikov, I. (1935), 'O Sovetskikh dengakh', *Problemy ekonomiki*, no. 3.
Neiman, G. (1935), 'Obmena kartochekh, razvertyvanie tovarooborota i ukreblenie rublya', *Problemy ekonomiki*, no. 1.
Notkin, A. (1939), 'Ot sotsializma k kommunizmu', *Problemy ekonomiki*, no. 5.
Nove, Alec (1958), 'The Problem of "Success Indicators" in Soviet

Industry', *Economica*, vol. 25, no. 1.
O novoi etape nepa (1930), *Problemy ekonomiki*, nos. 4-5.
Osnovnye predposylki i vypolnenie khozyaistvennogo plana (1931), Rech tov. Molotova, *Za industrializatsiyu* 12.2.
Ostrovityanov, K. (1931), 'Plan i stikhiya na raznykh etapakh nepa', *Problemy ekonomiki*, no. 3.
Ot Instituta Ekonomiki (1940), *Problemy ekonomiki*, nos. 5-6.
Pavlov, A. (1930), 'Borba za pyatiletku i sotsialisticheskaya organizatsiya truda', *Bolshevik*, no. 17.
Plotnikov, K. (1938), 'Dengi v SSSR', *Problemy ekonomiki*, no. 5.
Preniya po dokladu L.M. Gatovskogo (1931), *Planovoe khozyaistvo*, no. 4.
Preniya po dokladu t. Borilina (1931), *Vestnik Kommunisticheskoi Akademii*, nos. 5-6.
Preobrazhenskii, E. (1965), *The New Economics*, Oxford.
—— (1975), *UdSSR 1975* (Ot nepa k sotsializmu), Berlin.
Rabinovich, Ts. (1931), 'Referat no dokladu t. Borilina', *Vestnik Kommunisticheskoi Akademii*, no. 4.
Rozenberg, D. (1932), 'Menovaya kontseptiya v razlichnykh ee variantakh', *Problemy ekonomiki*, nos. 4-5.
Rylskii, M. (1930), 'Ob odnoi opasnoi teorii', *Problemy ekonomiki*, nos. 4-5.
Širokorad, L.D. (1977), *Die politische Ökonomie des Sozialismus in der UdSSR während der Uebergangsperiode*, Berlin.
Smit, M. (1930), 'Nezatukhayushchie tempy', *Problemy ekonomiki*, no. 3, pp. 3-15.
Stalin, I. (1937), *Voprosy leninizma*, Izd. desyatoe, Moscow.
Strazhevskii, B. (1936), 'Rentabelnost, finansy, khozraschet predpriyatiya i sistema zarplaty sluzhashchikh', *Predpriyatie*, no. 7.
Sutela, Pekka (1984), *Socialism, Planning and Optimality*, Helsinki.
Turetskii, Sh. (1939), 'O khozyaistvennom raschete', *Planovoe khozyaistvo*, no. 1.
—— (1940), *Sebestoimost i voprosy tsenoobrazovaniya*, Moscow and Leningrad.
Voprosy sverdlovtsev i otvet tov. Stalina (1930), *Pravda* 2.2.
Voznesenskii, N. (1931), 'Khozraschet i planirovanie na sovremennom etape', *Bolshevik*, no. 9.
Vsesoyuznaya Kommunisticheskaya Partiya (bolshevikov) v resolyutsiyakh i resheniyakh syezdov, konferentsii i plenumov TsK, Chast II, 1925-1939 (1941), Moscow.
Yampolskii, M. (1931), 'Voprosy zarabotnoi platy na sovremennom etape', *Problemy ekonomiki*, no. 6.

Part Three

Incentives in Agricultural Transformation

7
Chinese Reforms from a Soviet Perspective

Alec Nove

My only qualification for writing this chapter are two visits to China (in 1979 and 1983), and some detailed knowledge of Soviet attempts at economic reforms. I shall set out here some impressions and comparisons: what were the similarities and the differences between two countries at very different levels of development, which, while accepting Marxist-Leninist ideology, have drifted far apart politically? One recalls the case of Yugoslavia, in the aftermath of the quarrel between Stalin and Tito; the quarrel did not have any economic cause, but led to a search for a new economic model different from the Soviet, after a period of which Tito's Yugoslavia had copied the Soviet planning system.

The Chinese Communists also took the Soviet system as their model after they seized power. Industry was nationalised, a system of central planning and administered material allocation was introduced, and extended in practice even to urban local and cooperative industry. In a sense the system provided for even less managerial autonomy than did the Soviet, in that the entire profit was transferred to the state budget. Before my visit in 1979, I had imagined that the provinces exercised some significant power over the allocation of resources, but this proved not to be the case: they only had (limited) power over a portion of production in excess of the (central) plan. As for rural (commune) industry, in the places I visited it was either working as subcontractors to state enterprises, or making tools, clothes, etc. for the use of the members of the farm. Labour was rigidly controlled, attached to their place of work and unable to move without permission.

Mao was conscious of the damaging crudities of Stalin's policy towards the peasants ('drain the pond to catch the fish'), but felt constrained to impose collectivisation. Then came the drastic and highly damaging Great Leap Forward years (1958–60), with communes, backyard foundries, wildly excessive plans and serious famine. This clearly was China's equivalent to the sufferings of the Soviet peasantry in 1931–33. It is beyond the scope of this chapter to speculate why Mao instigated or allowed a repeat of the very thing that he was apparently anxious to avoid. A combination of Great Leap excesses and natural disasters (in China: in what proportion?) led to catastrophe, which expressed itself as follows so far as the pig population was concerned (figures in millions):

Table 7.1 Reductions in pig population in China and the USSR

China		USSR	
1957	145.9	1928	26.0
1961	75.5	1932	11.6

Source: *Statistical Yearbook of China* (1981), p. 165;
Sotsialisticheskoye stroitelstvo (1936), pp. 242–3, 354.

Human losses were substantial too, there being famine in both countries. In both countries, 'many people came to associate cooperation and particularly collectivisation not with mutual prosperity but with permanent sacrifice and belt-tightening', to cite Mark Selden's remarks on China's experience.[1] Of course, recovery followed, and there was a shift in China towards the triple-tier structure of commune, brigade and team, with greater toleration of peasant private plots and sideline activities. These were threatened for a time during the Cultural Revolution, but evidence is strong that this had no disastrous effects in the villages. This can be seen both from the absence of famine and from the fact that pig numbers showed a modest but significant upward trend. There were pressures to limit free markets, and also to relate rewards more to the large brigade than to the small team, and I still heard reference to this controversy in 1979. Two issues which also caused strong feelings were low state procurement prices and the relative effectiveness of labour incentives, of which more in a moment.

There was nothing in the USSR corresponding to the commune of 1958–59, but a number of reorganisations had profound effects on management. True, in 1950 began a move to amalgamate the small *kolkhozy*, of which there were some 250,000, into much larger ones, multiplying their average size by about five, and thereby changing what had been the equivalent of one village into much larger and more complex units. Also at this period Khrushchev spoke of the so-called 'agro-cities' (*agrogoroda*), modern urban-style settlements into which the peasants were to be moved, but these plans attracted criticism and were shelved. They were not revived under that name when Khrushchev became party chief, but there was a move in the direction of converting some *kolkhozy* into state farms (*sovkhozy*), and also the abandonment of small hamlets which were seen as having no future (*neperspektivnye*), which continued also under Brezhnev. In the late 1950s we saw the first experiments with the autonomous work groups (*beznaryadnye zvenya*). Other changes highly relevant to the present-day situation occurred in the early 1970s: the creation, or the extension of the functions of various 'service' organisations: *selkhoztekhnika* was charged increasingly with repairs and transport as well as supplying industrial inputs to farms, while fertiliser and pesticides became the responsibility of *selkhozkhimiya*, irrigation and drainage of still other state organisations. These obeyed their own hierarchical superiors, fulfilled plans in value (or tons, or whatever), and were not under the authority of the farms. This, plus the long-notorious fact that local party and state organs repeatedly interfered with management, considerably weakened the effectiveness of managerial stimuli given that the final outcome depended so greatly on actions of units they did not control.[2] Costs (and subsidies) rose very sharply during the 1970s.

Before returning to agriculture, let us look again at *industrial* planning. My Chinese colleagues, in 1979, expressed the opinion that the 'Soviet' centralised model remained intact having been disorganised and not having been replaced by the Great Leap Forward and the Cultural Revolution. Similarly, while every five year plan since the first was abandoned soon after it was adopted, the role of five year plans remained (nominally) unchanged. Labour incentives (or lack of them) were much criticised, because pay of management and workers alike was quite unrelated to results (even though there was considerable inequality). After Mao's death, discussions on economic reform quickly surfaced. The best account I know in a western language of these discussions of the actual reforms adopted in 1979 is a series of papers by the French scholar Yves Chevrier, notably 'Les politiques économiques de la démaoisation, 1977–1982'.[3] The controversies related to the need to decentralise and to make greater use of the price and market mechanism and material incentives, and also to the industrialisation strategy to be followed (heavy versus light industry, the import of foreign technology, etc.). The state of the debates as I encountered them in 1979 may best be summarised by citing my reply to a question put to me at the Embassy lunch at the end of my stay about the economic reform discussions: 'I have heard all this before, only in Russia and twenty years ago.' Many of the proposals were indeed very similar to the first wave of Soviet reform ideas, such as those of Liberman: give the management greater autonomy, reduce the number of obligatory plan indicators, etc. They therefore suffered from precisely the same defects; one cannot solve problems by reducing the number of plan indicators, especially if the principle of an obligatory output plan is retained and prices are unrelated to supply, demand, use-value or scarcity. In fact in China, as in the USSR, prices were neither designed nor intended to fulfil an 'active' function, and a sizeable proportion (some said 30 per cent) of China's industrial goods were produced at a loss. Failure of a reform based on such half-baked principles (or the inevitability of the failure of gradualness) showed up in the abortive Soviet reform of 1965, and can be studied in the fate of the initial wave of Chinese reforms in 1979–81. This was complicated by the emergence of shortages of producers' goods, due to an excessively sharp reduction in output (especially of machinery and equipment) in 1980–81, corrected in 1982, and by strains occasioned by a much needed but expensive increase in agricultural prices, which in turn led to the abandonment of the ambitious development plan ('small leap forward') adopted in 1977–78 ('a period of readjustment' was announced). As one Chinese economist said to me (in 1979): 'a 25 per cent increase in incomes of 800 million peasants, even from a very low level, requires a major change in our priorities if we are to supply the goods they will wish to buy; it would be simpler if there were not as many as 800 million!'

Also it was found (as in the USSR) that incentives are one thing, stimulating efficiency and quality quite another. Thus a bonus for output measured in tons stimulates waste of metal; pay for area ploughed can reward shallow and ineffective ploughing, and so on.

Returning in 1983, the industrial planning situation was still confused, with marked local variations. In Sichuan (the former fief of Premier Zhao Ziyang) much was being said about retained profits, and of freedom to buy and sell those inputs and outputs which were not subject to administrative controls, and devolution to urban complexes. In Shanghai, however, output was still subject to the central plan, though some profits would be retained. Major changes have indeed affected the cooperative and above all the private sectors. Petty private enterprise (craftsmen, small traders) has been legalised. The biggest changes of all are in the villages, with *de facto* decollectivisation (of which more below). This has produced a series of potentially dangerous contradictions. Side by side with a still largely centralised large-scale industry with its still surviving organisational deficiencies, with the partial retention of administered material allocation, we now have what Chevrier calls 'the appeal of the non-state economy, which reinforces market incentives and the second economy', which 'stimulates the productivist and disorganising pressures at the grass-roots, in town and in country'.[4] He, and also some Chinese colleagues, warn of the social tensions to which all this can give rise, further complicated by the setting-up of enclaves which are attracting foreign investment.

In the Soviet Union too there is consciousness of the inadequacy of the inherited system of centralised planning, and the failure of the 1965 reforms has stimulated a number of schools to devise more coherent alternatives. Changes introduced in 1979–81, however, did nothing to achieve any effective decentralisation. On the contrary, the net effect was to weaken the profit motive and to increase the number of and scope of centrally-imposed targets, indicators, norms.

The Soviets have not followed the example of China (and Hungary) by legalising petty private enterprise, nor have urban producers' cooperatives (abolished in 1961) been resurrected — yet.[5] The rejuvenated leadership of Gorbachev is attempting some major planning and management reforms, but this is not the place to speculate about them. What might be seen in China as their version of NEP, corresponding to China's backward economy, must seem inapplicable to the USSR, and not only for ideological reasons (though much benefit might be obtained from legalising small enterprises, especially in the services sector).

Here the contrast may be due to some very different national characteristics and experience. The Chinese are not only remarkably skilled craftsmen, they are also extremely able traders and businessmen, as their outstanding performance in Singapore, Hong Kong, Taiwan, Malaysia and Indonesia amply demonstrates. It may be argued that before 1949 the biggest obstacle to economic development in mainland China was disorder (foreign invasion, warlords, banditry, etc.). Mao re-established order, but for ideological reasons frustrated and persecuted private business. Deng and his comrades are well aware of the achievements of the overseas Chinese, and indeed are trying to attract their capital and know-how to China. By contrast, Russian business enterprise before the Revolution was not particularly distinguished, with a big role played by non-Russian capital and entrepreneurs. So in these respects it is not surprising that the two countries, though both anxious to improve efficiency, seem to be following rather different paths.

Directly relevant to their theme, however, is the change that has taken place in both countries in agriculture. Needless to say, the level of development and natural conditions are very diverse, and the optimum solution to the problems of management and labour incentives must be different too. Yet, as also in industrial planning, despite everything there are some common features, both in terms of defects and in the possible remedies.

The shift in China from collective work, whether organised by a brigade or a team, to the 'household responsibility system', is evidently a quite fundamental change in what Marxists call the relations of production. Subject to meeting the contracted compulsory delivery quota, the family is left to organise its own labour, and is encouraged to produce more for own consumption or for sale. Evidently, this makes for more effective incentives, and motivates the peasant not only to work but to work well. As already mentioned above, and as Soviet experience amply proves, one can pay people well, but the incentives can have perverse effects: thus the Soviet tractor-driver in a collective or state farm is paid in relation to area ploughed, and can increase his income by ploughing shallow (and get a further bonus for saving fuel!). A recent *Pravda* article[6] referred to a noxious flea which attacks flax; previously the farm had the necessary insecticide, now it is with a separate organisation, *selkhozkhimiya*, and by the time they arrive the fleas are all over the field, the flax is damaged — and the insecticide squad get a bonus for high labour productivity!

The Soviet equivalent of the household responsibility system is clearly the contract brigade or the so-called *beznaryadnoye zveno*, or autonomous work-gang. After twenty years of experiment and ups and downs, at long last this line of attack on the incentive problem was blessed by the Politbureau and announced — by Gorbachev, then still in charge of agriculture — in March 1983. On the face of it, the resemblance to the Chinese solution is clear, except that the group is usually not a family (sometimes it *is*; *Pravda* did refer to *semeinye zvenya*). Zaslavskaya expressed her evident delight that such family groups were spreading.[7] The numbers involved vary from roughly 6 to 30. A field, a crop rotation, livestock, are handed over to the group, which organise their own work and are paid by results, carrying out all the consecutive and/or complementary operations, which eliminate the need for outside supervision (thus the tractor-driver is directly interested in ploughing to the required depth).

In contrast with China, where the effect on production seems to have been both rapid and positive, this reform has run into many difficulties in the Soviet Union. The fact that Soviet agriculture relies much more heavily on industrial inputs makes the whole system much more dependent on supplies (of machines, spare parts, fertiliser, etc.), and these are notoriously unreliable. Also payment has become dependent on a complicated set of conditions: there are imposed norms for material utilisation and fuel, cost plans, etc., which greatly complicate the apparently simple 'payment by results'. Also state and *kolkhoz* management can still issue orders to send members of these groups to do other jobs. Furthermore, payment by results, in so far as it is operative, causes much tension within the farms, since differentials can become excessive, causing management arbitrarily to amend the contracted payments. There is still much to be worked out. Much is also still wrong with the co-ordination of different tasks, despite (or because of?) the creation in 1982 of a new hierarchy to operate the 'agro-industrial complex' — as the above example of fleas in the flax illustrates.

Excessive income differentiation is emerging as a problem also in China. Indeed it was excessive before the reform, thus 11.5 per cent 'basic accounting units' (teams) in 1981 distributed less than 40 yuan, while 15.7 per cent distributed over 150 yuan.[8] 'Income distributed to commune members' averaged 56.79 yuan in Gansu province, as against 177 in Shanghai and 203 in Beijin, and these provincial averages conceal much differentiation *within* each of these provinces. Current policy directly and consciously encourages the emergence of a stratum of 'rich peasants'. Yet, as I was told by a local official near Nanking in 1983, 'no one grows rich by growing grain', and those designated or allowed to be rich were raising ducks, or providing transport services.

How much of the income differentiation is due to hard work, and how much to what the various families are permitted to do? And what of necessary communal work, e.g. on irrigation? What effects on labour supply will there be if many transfer their efforts to making profits through trade? Will not existing regional inequalities be exacerbated?

The latest reports from China are both encouraging and disturbing. There is a highly positive response to material incentives, so much so that the peasants are eager to deliver produce to the state (at the new and higher prices) in greater quantities than the state procurement agencies can handle! What is less satisfactory is not only that inequalities are becoming more extreme, with little being done to redress them, but the village poor might well suffer hardship because there are now fewer provisions for the support of the economically weak.

Finally, what of inflation? There is a clear need to bring prices, both retail and wholesale, into line with the requirements of the reform, in town and village, and to reduce the subsidy burden (which is also immense in the Soviet Union, owing to repeated increases in prices paid to farms, while prices of basic foodstuffs have remained unchanged for 23 years). At the same time the tight control in China over urban wages and peasant incomes is being loosened, and market-oriented private and cooperative enterprise is being legalised. If the higher incomes are not to be a source of frustration, a sizeable rise in prices there must be, and indeed this is already taking place. Again, a possible source of social tension and political backlash. It is a fear of such tension and backlash that is restraining the Soviet leaders from decreeing much needed increases (especially for livestock products).

Finally, it is sometimes said that the 'Chinese NEP' might have a profound effect on the prospects of Soviet reform. Maybe. But those who believe this tend to have a possibly too rosy view of what is happening and will happen in China. It is not yet clear that the reform movement there has succeeded. If it does, if China gets onto the rapid-growth path of such countries as Japan, South Korea and Taiwan, then indeed Moscow will be deeply concerned. But it is too soon to assert confidently that China is on that path. Yes, they have adopted in October 1984 what looks like a fundamental reform decision. Thus the central committee decision[9] does indeed advocate the 'test of direct judgement by consumers in the market place, so that only the best [enterprises] survive', speaks of the desirability and need of 'competition', advocates a radical reform of the price system, seeks to 'extend the decision-making powers of enterprises owned by the whole people', and so on.

However, a careful reading of the document reveals a number of qualifying phrases, perhaps reflecting lack of agreement in the top leadership about how far or how fast to go in the direction of 'marketising' the state sector of industry. Can the party really contemplate the long-term emergence of an entrepreneurial class, albeit as managers of state industry, whose incomes and success indicators would be derived from the impersonal market and not from party-state officialdom? Might officialdom itself become corrupted? Some rather fundamental principles of ideology and power are involved, and there is some evidence of doubt and hesitation. Thus one has in the above-mentioned decision such phrases as: 'because of China's rather undeveloped commodity production at the present stage, it is necessary to stimulate commodity production and exchange', but also 'there have to be guidance, regulation and administrative control through planning'. In an unpublished paper, Chevrier rightly notes that central controls have not been abandoned, at least over large-scale industry, despite talk of a 'socialist commodity economy'; he and others cite a phrase attributed to Chen Yu, who uses the analogy of the cage and the bird. Yes, management's wings must be freed, but within a (larger) cage, for otherwise the bird will fly away. This analogy is applicable also to the Soviet Union, where there is the same concern to liberate the energies and enterprise of management from petty tutelage and excessive regulation (Gorbachev spoke of this several times), but at the same time keeping control. Are these aims compatible?

A more fundamental question arises, and this chapter will end by putting it. If what we are seeing is a sort of 'Chinese NEP', then what is its outcome to be? Or, to express the same thought in a different way, is *this* NEP to be a sort of *reculer pour mieux sauter*, a temporary retreat on the way leading to 'real' socialism, as the Soviet NEP is presented in Soviet historiography? Or is 'real' socialism in China intended to contain the basic features of NEP, not just 'seriously and for a long time' (Lenin), but indefinitely (for the sort of reasons advanced in my book on *Feasible Socialism?*). Another way of looking at this question is as follows. Are the Chinese introducing and strengthening the role of the market because they are still backward, because 'NEP' would correspond to their low stage of development? This is indeed the logic of such phrases, heard in China, as 'premature excessive socialisation'. But then one must recall that economic reform of a market type is advocated in the Soviet Union on the grounds that its relatively *high* level of development renders it essential, makes centralised non-market planning unworkable. So then a market is needed *both* because one is too immature or too mature to do without it. So is there any situation, other than that of a war economy, in which one *can* do without it?

NOTES

1. Selden and Lippit (1982), p. 82.
2. See Suslov (1982).
3. Chevrier (1983).
4. Ibid., p. 70.
5. Since this paper was written, there has — finally — been such a law (*Pravda*, 21 November 1986). This law, however, may well prove to be limited in its implications.
6. *Pravda*, 18 April 1985.
7. *Izvestiya*, 1 June 1985.
8. Statistical annual of China (1981), p. 203.
9. Reported in *China Daily*, 22 October 1984.

REFERENCES

Chevrier, Yves (1983), 'Les économiques politiques de la démaoisation', *Revue d'études comparatives est-ouest*, September.
Selden, M. and Lippit, V. (1982), *The Transition to Socialism in China*, Armonk, New York.
Suslov, I. (1982), 'Kolkhozy v sisteme narodnogo khozyaistva', *Voprosy ekonomiki*, no. 12.

8
Market-related Incentives and Food Production in Tanzania: Theory and Experience

Mats Lundahl and Benno J. Ndulu*

THE FOOD PROBLEM

The food problem in Sub-Saharan Africa has recently generated a great deal of concern among both policy-makers and analysts. Stagnating or declining trends in food production per capita and an increasing inability to meet shortfalls with imports has created severe problems for a number of countries. Given the precarious balance between consumption per capita and recommended food intake, this both creates a health risk and induces dependence on food aid. Furthermore, increased production fluctuations linked to the current climatic phase of lower average rainfall and higher variability, expected to last up to 2020,[1] are superimposed on the production trends. In an area where rain-fed agriculture dominates and where it is difficult to maintain adequate reserves, this increases considerably the probability of recurrent drought-related famines.

In the particular case of Tanzania, the data pertaining to this issue are somewhat shaky. On the basis solely of food imports, the country is facing a problem which has tended to become worse over time. Between 1965-72 and 1973-80 total average food imports more than tripled while on a per capita basis the figure increased two and a half times.[2] This must be seen in relation to the decline in import capacity over the last decade. As a result the dependence on food aid has increased. The share of food aid in total food imports increased from an average of 49 per cent between 1975-76 and 1978-79 to 66 per cent between 1979-80 and 1982-83. The ratio of food imports to total export revenues increased from some 4 per cent between 1966 and 1974 to more than 12 per cent in the period 1975-80. In the absence of food aid this would have required a substantial diversion of revenues from other uses. Subtracting the aid component, food imports consumed an average of some 5 per cent of export revenues between 1975 and 1981.[3]

Import figures, however, provide only part of the picture. To assess agricultural performance accurately, production figures are also required. The series for export crops indicate a downward trend. During the first five year plan (1964–69), the output of all export crops except sisal was growing. However, during the second five year plan period, up to the mid-1970s, the production of coffee, sisal and cotton declined and by the latter half of the 1970s (third five year plan) all crops except coffee and tea displayed negative growth rates.[4] The best available estimates of food crop production appear to indicate that all crops, with the exception of sorghum and millet during the 1960s and wheat and bananas/plantains from the early 1970s to the mid-1980s, displayed growth rates that exceeded the rate of growth of the population.[5] Figures relating to the average food intake indicate that a sufficient number of calories seem to be available, but that the protein intake is well below recommended standards.[6]

The main food problem concerns *marketed* quantities of food in general and preferred cereals (maize, paddy and wheat) in particular. The rural population by and large manages to feed itself, with the exception of drought years. The urban population has been growing rapidly, at the rate of 8.3 per cent during the 1970s, far exceeding the country's population growth rate of 3.3 per cent per annum.[7] Feeding this rapidly growing segment of the population requires not only increased production but also efficient marketing institutions. In the Tanzanian case, such efficiency has not been present. The officially marketed quantities of all food crops handled by the government purchase organisation have displayed large fluctuations during the entire 1970s and early 1980s. Declining trends can also be observed for rice and wheat while in the case of maize there is no trend. The official marketing network for all products has performed significantly worse in the early 1980s than during the second half of the 1970s, with recent average purchases significantly below the figures of five to ten years ago.[8]

Incentive policy instruments are a critical part of the policy package that is essential for achieving increased productivity in agriculture. It is this aspect of the effort to raise production that will be the concern of the present chapter. We shall begin by examining the underlying assumptions of the incentive system employed in Tanzania during the post-independence period. The second section deals with recent efforts towards liberalisation and an increased use of price-related measures to stimulate marketed production. The core of the chapter deals with a theoretical analysis of peasant behaviour in the Tanzanian institutional context. This is followed by an empirical examination of the extent to which the peasants respond to price-related incentives. The concluding section deals with the policy recommendations that may be extracted from the preceding analysis.

THE TRADITIONAL CONTROL MODEL

Most efforts to promote agriculture in Africa have relied heavily on direct control. The traditional control model is based on two basic assumptions regarding the behaviour of peasants and the infrastructural framework needed to break out of subsistence agriculture:

African smallholders are unresponsive to market signals. The model implicitly treats peasants as an inert mass who have to be actively directed for their own good and the good of the nation. It is believed that peasants in general pursue a survival algorithm with rather low target levels of income beyond which they are not interested.[9] Left on their own, peasant economies would be trapped at low levels of income and development. Thus, during the colonial period, conscription and taxation was used to foster commercialisation of smallholder agriculture. In the post-colonial period, coercion, exhortation, political campaigns and moral suasion have all been extensively used to promote agricultural development.

Only a monopsonistic/monopolistic integrated organisation can ensure commercial production in underdeveloped African agriculture. The logic behind this assumption is the following. Traditional subsistence agriculture will not develop cash production by itself. Given the initial lack of services and the underdeveloped state of the physical infrastructure, modernisation is only deemed to be possible through subsidisation, financed by the revenues generated via the official marketing boards, and also directly from the government budget. This type of logic thus confines the modernising agent status to statal and parastatal institutions which operate within the integrated framework.

As a result of these two assumptions, crop development agencies assume by means of direct control the central role in the agricultural development process. Institutions that are integrated either vertically around a given crop or horizontally for particular regions are typical of the traditional control model through which production factors, credit, extension, marketing and physical infrastructure are provided.

The traditional control model has also been used in Tanzania. This is reflected by the suppression of market-oriented incentives during the first fifteen years of independence and the central role that public institutions and government-controlled organisations play in directing agricultural development. A combination of vertically and horizontally integrated institutions has been employed. Crop development boards covering cotton, coffee, tea, pyrethrum and tobacco provide vertically integrated channels through which inputs are distributed for the respective crops. During the first independence decade, marketing services at the regional level were provided through government-controlled cooperatives serving as agents for the specific crop boards in the single-channel, multi-level marketing system that existed at the time. This system formed the basis for subsidisation of services out of marketing revenues. When cooperatives were abolished in 1976 and crop authorities were formed, a crop-specific integrated control system was created. The registered villages[10] became the primary agents for the crop authorities.

The deterioration in the financial performance of these institutions over the last decade has created a strong dependence on budgetary subsidies. In addition the expansion of commercialisation has generated pressures for a more flexible and timely supply of services over wider areas.[11] Several problems have arisen from the continued use of the traditional control model.

Due to the uncoordinated piecemeal support provided to specific crops or regions, the development of scientifically based agriculture and national economic infrastructure has also become fragmented. Of the 19 regions and 8000 villages in 1980, for example, only 11 regions and 815 villages were given credit services for smallholders for crop development by the Tanzania Rural Development Bank (TRDB). The vast majority of smallholders have not been able to obtain fertilisers even if they wanted to use them since over 75 per cent of all fertilisers have been provided on credit extended by the TRDB and the cotton and coffee authorities, while the remainder has been allocated to large and medium-sized private farmers and directly to statal and parastatal farms.[12] In addition extension services have been largely concentrated in areas served by crop authorities who had their own extension wings.

The traditional control model is particularly prejudiced against food production. Food has a predominantly domestic market and it is very difficult to police its marketing effectively through state monopolies. As a result, difficulties arise from attempts to provide subsidised services out of marketing revenues to producers of a particular crop. This partly explains why single-crop integrated monopolies are built around export crops where this type of marketing control and subsidisation framework is easier to implement. The marketing of food crops, in turn, is controlled via a single parastatal which does not offer any services for production development.[13]

Thus, it is not surprising that the first major effect to encourage scientifically based peasant food production came as late as 1975 with the National Maize Project and the Small Farmers' Food Crop Loan (following the severe drought of 1973-74 and the ensuring large food imports). Before then, only areas producing export crops and served by the specific crop authorities could get any support for food production.[14] This bias was also reflected in the agricultural development budget where, for example, between 1974-75 and 1981-82 only 17.3 per cent of the total was allocated to food crops (predominantly for state farms and marketing services to smallholders), the rest going to export crops and sugar producing state farms.[15]

Emphasis on the use of subsidies tied to integrated programmes for inducing commercialisation and scientifically based production has tended to stifle the incentives for utilising locally available natural fertilisers (manure and compost).[16] The profitability of farming was assumed to increase with the use of expensive subsidised chemical fertilisers whose supply was severely limited and whose distribution was costly. Increasing profitability via higher real producer prices, for all farmers rather than those who are tied specifically to the integrated programme subsidies, was not attempted. Hence, the benefits of innovation were limited to the areas served by the integrated institutions.

The existence of government monopolies and monopsonies entails a high risk of administrative malfunctions and financial problems with a concomitant deterioration in services. In combination with a poorly developed physical infrastructure, failures to provide required inputs or collect produce on time tend to lead to poor harvests and large crop losses.[17]

Confusion has also prevailed among producers regarding the

signals to be followed in relation to decisions on cultivating acreage and crop mix. Two types of signals have been sent out from the centre — one in terms of plan targets for acreage and crop mix down to the village level, the other in terms of prices set and announced by the government.[18] The two are frequently incompatible and producers have generally preferred to respond to the latter. The dual signal system creates frustration both among those who issue the signals and among those who have to follow them. In particular, the task of determining acreage and crop mix from the centre via physical plans is a hopeless one, in view of the extremely limited knowledge there of the variety of production conditions that prevail locally.

The government has attempted to control both the supply and the demand side of the food market via an administered price system. The goal has been to hold down the cost of living by maintaining low prices for food in order to limit the budgetary pressures of wage increases. The intended beneficiaries of this policy are the low-income urban dwellers who constitute the largest proportion of the urban population and for whom food comprises more than 50 per cent of their expenditures.[19] Although the government was successful in maintaining a low price level without recourse to large subsidies until 1971, the situation has changed drastically during the subsequent period. A growing urban food demand, a decline in official purchases and falling producer prices in real terms have led to shortages which increasingly could not be covered via imports.

This phenomenon had three main effects that are of interest in the present context. First, a market parallel to the official one developed, induced by the difference between the scarcity price and the official price and by the increased difficulty of effective enforcement of marketing via official channels. Secondly, the rapid increase in unit marketing costs due to the reduction of the official market share and the increase in transport and other input costs amounted to an increased subsidisation of consumers since consumer prices had been maintained at an artificially low level. Finally, the high costs of marketing outside the official system, associated with the risks of detection, have reduced the physical flow of food. Thus, the target group for government policy seems to benefit least from the subsidies, given the lack of an effective, egalitarian rationing system. Instead, access to official sources of supply is partly linked to status and connections and partly to the ability to pay for favours. In addition, consumer hawking (i.e. unofficial resale of commodities bought at official prices) effectively reduces the number of consumers paying the official price. Consequently the poor urban consumer has difficulties finding food at officially set prices and has to rely on the unofficial market where prices are considerably higher.

THE TURNING POINT

The problems connected with the traditional control model are numerous. The use of this model has frequently made the very objectives for which controls were established unobtainable. This is especially the case with food production. It is becoming increasingly clear, even to the policy makers, that there is an accelerated erosion of control as more shortages develop. Political scientists and political economists like Göran Hydén and Robert Bates have described the recent reaction of producers in reducing supplies offered for sale officially as a political reaction to a divergence of interests between the government and the urban population on the one hand, and the peasant producers on the other.[20] In economic terms, the same phenomenon may be interpreted as a rational response to incentives, based on self-interest.

Since the mid-1970s a more active use has been made of price incentives within the institutional structure of the traditional control model. After a period of rather stagnant prices, when between 1965–66 and 1973–74 nominal official producer prices for food increased by an average of 27 per cent over eight years, nominal prices were increased by 233 per cent over the next six years. Nominal prices for export crops were increased by 123 per cent over the same period. However, real producer prices of food crops, after increasing by 77 per cent between 1973–74 and 1977–78, declined sharply, by 41 per cent between 1978–79 and 1981–82,[21] as the inflation rate jumped from an average of 13 per cent for the former period to an average of 30 per cent in the latter period. During the post-1979 period, official producer prices could not keep pace with the inflation rate, and the terms of trade of the agricultural sector worsened.[22]

The active use of price as an incentive to increased production was, however, an important development since to some extent it contradicted the first assumption of the control model, that of lack of responsiveness to prices, especially in such remote areas as Ruvuma and Rukwa, where producer prices were increased significantly more than in the average case as a result of instituting pan-territorial pricing.[23] The two regions responded by increasing their marketed food surplus by 1600 per cent between 1970–75 and 1981–82.[24] These regions have also very substantially increased their use of modern inputs in food production.

At present, it would seem that the main obstacle to higher growth of production is still the declining agricultural terms of trade, together with an institutional structure that confines the increased profitability of modern input use to areas served by integrated crop development institutions. There seems to be a general consensus on the need to modernise agriculture as a basis for increased production but not on the methods to be adopted. Behavioural assumptions that view the farming household as a rational unit capable of making its own decisions, based on self-interest, tend to invoke an institutional structure that puts the farmer in control and uses more market-related incentives to attain national goals. In this case, even those who strongly believe that the peasant is working as hard as possible, given the level of technology, have to contend with the possibility that a reduction in the work effort may occur as the agricultural terms of trade continue to decline. Moreover, the possibility of adopting technological innovations depends heavily on the profitability of the innovations in question. Prices are definitely a significant factor here, together with complementary services. A more flexible institutional structure, that relies less on control and more on positive incentives, is of critical importance for production development.

It is for these reasons, particularly the encouraging trend towards putting the farmer in control, that we shall concentrate in the following sections on the micro behaviour of the producers, the characteristics of the food market and the responsiveness to market-related incentives. The success of a movement away from the traditional control model may eventually hinge heavily on the understanding of the micro aspects of the production and consumption system in rural areas.

A BEHAVIOURAL MODEL OF THE TANZANIAN SMALLHOLDER

The typical small farm household in Tanzania is of the semi-subsistence kind. It makes a series of production and consumption decisions that are interrelated. The available time is allocated between leisure, production of food and cash crops, and wage labour. Most of the non-leisure time is spent on farming, but off-farm work (for medium and large-scale farming enterprises or in urban areas) together with handicrafts and petty trade contributes almost 40 per cent of the total cash income of a typical smallholder family.[25]

The household consumes food, non-farm commodities (obtained from sales of food and cash crops) and leisure. The crops grown are produced with the aid of cleared land and labour.[26] Uncleared land is typically in abundant supply and is not leased.[27] This land is converted into cleared land with the aid of labour and negligible quantities of capital.[28] Thus, in the following, we shall not include land explicitly in the production functions, but only indirectly, via the labour variable.

The optimisation of the farm household is centred on the allocation of time between various types of income generation and leisure on the one hand, and on the choice between the consumption of different types of commodities and leisure on the other. This is a joint optimisation problem, where production and consumption are connected via the leisure variable.

The model presented below emphasises the role of price incentives for peasant behaviour.[29] The inclusion of more than one cash-earning crop (food and cash crops) and more than one consumption good (food and non-farm products) has been made in order to focus on the role of *relative* prices both on the production and the consumption side for agricultural output. It has been widely observed over the past one and a half decades in Tanzania (as we shall come back to in the last section) that changes in relative producer prices effect the crop mix. Moreover, changes in the prices of non-agricultural goods in relation to the price of farm produce ought to play an important role for the smallholder's decision of whether to dedicate his time to agricultural production, to other income generating activities or to leisure.

Now, for the formal model. The farming household derives its utility from consuming food, purchased commodities (predominantly manufactures and services) and leisure (social and cultural activities not related to production). Thus, the utility function can be specified as

(1) $\quad U = U(F, M, L_e)$

where F = food, M = purchased commodities, and L_e = leisure, in time units. This utility function has the familiar properties of positive and diminishing marginal utility for each argument, and is strictly quasi-concave, generating convex indifference surfaces.

The household produces two crops. Crop f is food that can be partially consumed on the farm and partly sold to earn cash. Crop c is a 'pure' cash crop, not consumed at all by the farm household. The production functions for these crops are

(2) $\quad q_f = q_f(L_f)$

and

(3) $\quad q_c = q_c(L_c)$

where L indicates labour. These production functions have positive and diminishing marginal productivities of labour. Thus, adding labour in a line of production does not yield a proportional increase in output. The difficulty of handling a larger enterprise (the management factor) and the increased difficulty of clearing land, assuming that the best or closest land is cleared first, makes for smaller and smaller contributions to output.[30]

The total quantity of labour available to the household is fixed at $\bar{L}$, after taking into account minimum physiological requirements for body rest and such routine activities as household care. It is also assumed that the wage rates for labour sales are given over the agricultural season. (Off-season labour sales do not compete with agricultural production. Our analysis, strictly speaking, is confined to the agricultural season.)

The household maximises its utility, subject to

(4) $\quad M = [(p_f/p_m)q_f(L_f) - F] + (p_c/p_m)q_c(L_c) + (w/p_m)L_w$

and

(5) $\quad L_e = \bar{L} - L_f - L_c - L_w$

where L_w indicates labour sales, p commodity prices and w the wage rate.

This yields the following first-order conditions:[31]

(6) $\quad U_F - \lambda(p_f/p_m) = 0$

(7) $\quad U_M - \lambda = 0$

(8) $\quad -U_{Le} + \lambda(p_f/p_m)q_{fL} = 0$

(9) $\quad -U_{Le} + \lambda(p_c/p_m)q_{cL} = 0$

and

(10) $\quad -U_{Le} + \lambda(w/p_m) = 0$

From (6) and (7) we obtain

FOOD PRODUCTION IN TANZANIA

(11) $U_M(p_f/p_m) = U_F$

In equilibrium, the marginal valuation of a unit of food is the same regardless of whether it is sold to purchase commodities or is consumed on the farm. This determines the quantity marketed and consumed on the farm, given the output of food.

Conditions (7)–(10) yield

(12) $U_M(p_f/p_m)q_{fL} = U_M(p_c/p_m)q_{cL} = U_M(w/p_m) = U_{Le}$

In equilibrium the household will allocate its labour resources in such a way that it obtains the same satisfaction from their use at the margin regardless of whether the time is used for food production, for cash crop production, for wage employment or for leisure.

Diagrammatically, the equilibrium of the smallholder family can be portrayed as in Figure 8.1. Starting in the southwest quadrant, the OA curve describes the income–leisure trade-off. Over the OB segment which, due to decreasing returns to labour, is curved, the family works in agriculture. At point B, the value of the marginal product of labour in both food and cash crop production has fallen to the point where it equals the given wage rate for outside work. After that point all further work will take place outside the farm.

Given its preferences, the household chooses the labour–leisure combination given by point C. There, the marginal valuation of leisure equals that of income (condition (12)). OD hours are spent in agriculture, DE outside the farm and the remaining EL hours consist of leisure. This yields an income of OF, measured in terms of non-agricultural goods.

Moving via the DG line in the northwest quadrant to the northeast quadrant, we find the transformation curve for agricultural production.[32] Working OD hours in the production of cash crops would yield an output of OG and working the same number of hours in food production would result in OH units being produced. Where on the GH curve the actual production point I will lie depends on the relative price of food and cash crops. In point I the value of the marginal product of labour is equal in both uses (condition (12)).

Finally, we have the southeast quadrant. Trading the entire cash crop output obtained in point I for food at the given prices p_f/p_c would yield a total food quantity of OJ (including what the household itself produces). However, the smallholder family also consumes non-agricultural goods. At the given relative price p_f/p_m, OJ units of food can be traded for OF units of purchased commodities (equal to the total income of the household). What the

FOOD PRODUCTION IN TANZANIA

Figure 8.1 The equilibrium of the peasant household

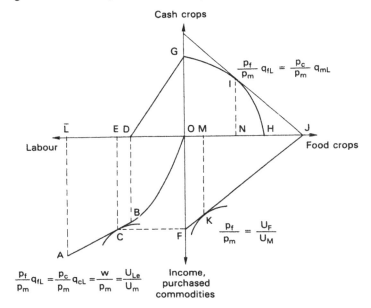

consumption bundle will actually look like depends on the preferences of the family, the ratio of the marginal utilities of the two goods being equal to the ratio of their prices (condition (11)) at the equilibrium point K. This also determines the marketed quantity of food, MN, equal to the difference (assumed to be positive throughout) between the production, ON, and the consumption, OM, of the household.

It is clear from the above description that changes in the relative price of food on the one hand and cash crops or non-agricultural goods on the other could be made subject to manipulation by the policy-makers in an effort to stimulate food production. Let us next turn to the effects of such price changes.

Food versus cash crops

First we want to find out the impact of an increase in the price of food crops, holding the price of cash crops and purchased commodities constant.

Again, we may start in the southwest quadrant, singled out in

202

Figure 8.2 An increase in the relative price of food

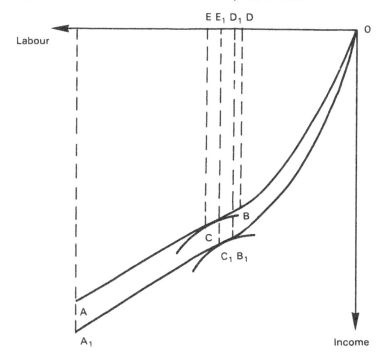

Figure 8.2. When more is obtained for a unit of food than before, the income–leisure trade-off shifts downwards in the figure, to OA_1, as the value of the marginal product of labour in food production increases. Any given number of hours worked in agriculture will yield a higher income than before. More hours will now have to be spent on food production (and consequently on farming as a whole) before the value of the marginal product of labour in that line falls to the level corresponding to the exogenously given wage rate. Point B_1 on the OA_1 schedule will lie to the left of B, and the larger the increase of the food price, the further leftwards B_1 will move.

The magnitude of the increase in p_f is an important determinant of the allocation of time between leisure and work. If the increase is large, outside employment could become an inferior alternative from the income point of view. Point C_1 could be located on the curved segment of OA_1, i.e. to the right of B_1. All the available time would then be distributed between leisure and farming. In that case, whether more or fewer hours will be worked in agriculture cannot be unequivocally determined but will depend on the relative magnitudes of the income and substitution effects. If the income effect, which increases leisure, provided that leisure is not an inferior good, is large enough, it will swamp the substitution effect (leisure becoming more expensive in terms of income). Thus, the possibility that increased food prices will make the typical smallholder family work less on the farm cannot be ruled out in this case. Point C_1 could lie to the right of B.

However, in the more realistic case where, given the higher food price, the smallholder family continues to devote some of its time to outside work, more hours will be worked in agriculture.[33] This is the case shown in Figure 8.2. Since the wage rate remains constant, B_1A_1 is parallel to BA. C_1 must lie on B_1A_1 since some hours continue to be devoted to wage labour. Thus, there will not be any substitution effect. The marginal valuation of leisure in terms of income has not changed. Only the income effect remains and, assuming that leisure is not inferior, this is positive. Point C_1 must lie to the right of point C. The number of hours worked is reduced from OE to OE_1. At the same time fewer hours are spent on wage employment (D_1E_1 against DE before) and more hours on farming (OD_1 against OD), B_1 lying to the left of B.

We may now move to the impact on the composition of agricultural production. The number of hours worked in agriculture increases from OD to OD_1. This will make the transformation curve in Figure 8.1 shift outwards. How will these additional hours be distributed between food and cash crop production? To find out, we may start by examining what would have happened if the additional hours had gone into agriculture at *given* relative food and cash crop prices, i.e. we move from the old to the new transformation curve at given prices. Therefore, we look at the movement along the new curve as the price of food crops increases in terms of cash crops.

In equilibrium, according to (12), we have that

(13) $p_f q_{fL} = p_c q_{cL}$

Differentiating (13), with p_f and p_c constant, yields

(14) $p_f q_{fLL} dL_f = p_c q_{cLL} dL_c$

Furthermore, we know that more hours than before will be worked in agriculture. Differentiating (5) yields

(15) $dL_f + dL_c = -d(L_w + L_e) > 0$

Solving (14) and (15) for dL_f and dL_c gives

(16) $\quad dL_f = -(1/\Delta)p_c q_{cLL} d(L_w + L_e) > 0$

and

(17) $\quad dL_c = -(1/\Delta)p_f q_{fLL} d(L_w + L_e) > 0$

where

(18) $\quad \Delta = p_f q_{fLL} + p_c q_{cLL} < 0$

Thus, when labour is added in agriculture at given relative prices of food and cash crops, the output of both crops will increase.

However, we started by assuming that the price of food crops increased. Differentiating (13), allowing p_f to change, but not p_c, gives

(19) $\quad q_{fL} dp_f + p_f q_{fLL} dL_f = p_c q_{cLL} dL_c$

and differentiating (5), keeping leisure and outside work constant, gives

(20) $\quad dL_c = -dL_f$

Solving (19) and (20) for dL_f and dL_c, finally, yields

(21) $\quad dL_f = -dL_c = -(1/\Delta)q_{fL} dp_f > 0$

The production point moves to the southeast on the new transformation curve, increasing the positive impact on food production, but possibly leaving the smallholder producing less cash crops altogether than he did at the outset.

Finally, let us see what will happen to the consumption of food and purchased commodities by the peasant household and to the marketed surplus of food. The former is a standard budget problem. When incomes increase in terms of non-agricultural goods, at given prices, the peasant household will demand more of both types of goods. There is, however, also the substitution effect. Increasing the price of food in terms of purchased goods makes the latter relatively more attractive. Thus, we cannot determine unequivocally what will happen with food consumption. However, in present-day Tanzania, it hardly appears as a realistic possibility that the consumption of food should fall. On the other hand, the income elasticity of demand of the peasant household for the type of food produced on the farm should be low.[34] Thus, perhaps the most likely outcome is only a small increase in food consumption. This, in turn should lead to an increase in the marketed surplus, since as we have demonstrated, the *production* of food will increase.

Making industrial consumer goods cheaper

The second parameter shift to be discussed is that of a cheapening of industrial consumer goods of the type purchased by the peasants. This analysis is analogous to the one we have already performed. In fact, provided that the outside wage does not change in terms of purchased goods, the only difference will be in the area of agricultural production. Since we have chosen to measure income in terms of purchased goods, making these goods less expensive in terms of food and cash crops is tantamount to increasing smallholder income and will shift the income–leisure trade-off in the same way as in Figure 8.2. Once again, there will be more leisure, less outside work and more hours available for working in agriculture.[35]

The second step, that of analysing the output changes in agriculture, differs from the one already discussed in that here the relative price of food and cash crops remains constant. Thus, there will only be a movement from the old to the new transformation curve at constant prices, but no reallocation along the new curve. Thus, the production of both food and cash crops will increase.

Finally, the same remarks as before apply to the consumption decision.

To conclude, our analysis shows that the production of food crops is likely to increase both when the price of these crops increases in relation to the price of cash crops and industrial consumption goods purchased by the smallholder and when the latter goods are made cheaper in terms of food and cash crops. However, the effect on the marketed surplus of food is uncertain, but the income elasticity of food is presumably low among smallholders, so that the most likely outcome is that the marketed surplus will also increase.

In the final section, we shall examine the available empirical evidence with respect to the impact of the price changes discussed above. Before we do that, however, we must take a look at a complication which was left out of the model of peasant behaviour, but which must be taken into account in the empirical section — the existence of a parallel, partly illegal, marketing channel for food crops. (The food price employed so far could be conceived of as a weighted average of official and parallel market prices.)

THE DUAL MARKETING OF FOOD CROPS

In Tanzania, the government controls the marketing of scheduled cereals (maize, rice, wheat) by setting controlled prices for both producers and consumers as well as by confining this trade to public institutions. Private trade in these cereals beyond the local, free traditional market is illegal and punishable if detected. The traditional free market, strictly speaking, is confined to limited sales by producers to individuals for private consumption. The rest is to be sold legally through official marketing channels: parastatals and cooperatives.

Although the enforcement of this arrangement was fairly successful during the pre-1973 period, it has subsequently broken down. During the earlier period, control was mainly imposed via imports during periodic shortfalls, in order to support the administratively set prices. Surpluses were either used to build up modest reserves or were exported. In any case, the controlled prices were effectively maintained and there were hardly any price differences between official and traditional markets.[36]

Beginning with the drought of 1973-74 and the first oil price shock in 1973, the growth of excess demand, together with an increasing inability to cover the shortfalls with imports, exerted upward pressure on official prices. Parallel markets started to expand beyond the traditional level. Further declines in export earnings (and hence of import capacity) coupled with an increased excess demand, especially in urban areas, increased the attractiveness of illegal trade and further weakened the efficiency of the official marketing system. This is evidenced by the declining share of scheduled cereals marketed through official channels and the growing share of unofficial marketing, currently estimated to be around 75 per cent.[37]

This development of a dual market structure has, however, not been uniform across the country. In remote high transport cost regions, such as Ruvuma and Rukwa, virtually all marketed surpluses of maize, beyond the traditional market exchanges, are sold through official channels. Since the adoption of pan-territorial pricing for scheduled crops in 1973, the producers in these remote regions have benefited from interregional subsidisation of the transport costs related to procurement. Hence, the producer prices they receive are effectively support prices which are higher than they would have been if the relevant transport costs had been deducted from the final consumer price.

Although pan-territorial pricing to producers was abolished in 1983, the principle of differentiating prices solely in terms of climatic advantage in production, thereby ignoring the impact of transport costs, has left the subsidy element that reflects the comparative disadvantage of these regions in marketing intact. The recent observation that unofficial consumer prices in these regions are most frequently lower than official prices confirms the supportive role of official prices.[38] The existence of some unofficial trade there simply reflects sporadic timing problems resulting from the availability of cash for purchases, especially during the peak of the buying season. It also reflects the difference between official producer and consumer prices of unmilled grains (which are preferred in such areas to the standardised, poor quality/high subsidy milled products from official sources). Instead of buying from the official distributor at a price which includes a marketing margin, the consumers prefer to buy directly from the producers. The fact that these two regions have substantially increased their share of official purchases of maize from 2-3 per cent prior to 1973 to 25-30 per cent thereafter[39] partly indicates responsiveness to the higher supportive prices in those regions but also reflects a reduction in the actual volume of official purchases in the more accessible regions where illegal private trade is profitable.

Statal and parastatal producers of paddy and wheat by statute have to market their goods through official channels. The share of state farm supplies in the total officially marketed volume of paddy has increased to 50 per cent.[40] Domestically, wheat is mainly produced by state farms and here again the official market dominates. The special requirements for milling wheat have also played a significant role in inducing private production to be sold via official channels that in addition undertake milling and packaging.

The pattern of the Rukwa and Ruvuma regions and the marketing of the cereals produced by state farms and parastatals, however, constitute an exception to the general rule that for preferred cereals a dual marketing structure exists. Let us now turn to the theoretical characterisation of the operations of this structure.

Official and illegal markets

The food quantities sold in the *legal* traditional markets can in principle be included in the subsistence consumption at the village level, their purpose being simply to compensate for temporary shortfalls in particular farm households. Using this approach, the *marketed* quantities of scheduled cereals are either sold via the official channels or in purely *illegal* unofficial markets. The latter type of

Figure 8.3 Official and illegal food markets

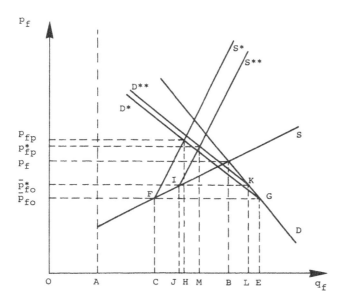

sales cannot be made without risk of detection and both buyers and sellers face a risk of penalties if the transactions are detected. This in turn makes for a higher price in the illegal market, as shown in Figure 8.3.

If trade in food crops had not been regulated, a single equilibrium price would have been established: p_f. Assuming that nothing is supplied in the market until the subsistence needs of the peasant households (OA) are covered (possibly via the traditional markets), this price is given by the intersection of the supply curve S with the demand curve D, the marketed quantity being AB.

If the government sets a price ceiling at $\bar{p}_{fo}$, an excess demand of CE will result. Should this be covered by imports, as was the case in Tanzania prior to 1973, all trade will take place in the official market. If, on the other hand, the imported quantities are too small to make $\bar{p}_{fo}$ the market clearing price, illegal trade will arise. Given the risks of detection and the penalties for engaging in illicit trade, it takes a higher price than in the uncontrolled situation to induce a given quantity to be supplied, and conversely, at each given price, less than before will be demanded. Beginning at point F, the supply curve will have a steeper slope, and beginning in point G, the demand curve will be flatter. A new equilibium will be established by the intersection of S* and D*, yielding a market-clearing price equal to p_{fp} in the illegal market, AC being the legally traded quantity and CH being provided illegally.

If imports are introduced, these will shift point F, the starting point of S*, to the right, making both the illegally supplied quantity and the price in the illegal market fall.

Increasing the official price, on the other hand, will make the supply of food crops via official channels increase, but it does not necessarily lower the price that clears the illegal market. Increasing $\bar{p}_{fo}$ to $\bar{p}_{fo}^*$ moves the starting point of the illegal supply curve from F to I, shifting S* rightwards, to S**, increasing official sales to AJ. At the same time, the starting point of the illegal demand curve moves from G to K, thus reducing the excess demand at the official price from CE to JL. In the case shown in Figure 8.3, this results in an intersection between S** and D** which gives rise to a lower equilibrium price, p_{fp}^*, than before, the illegally traded quantity being JM.

This is, however, not a necessary result. Both illegal supply and illegal demand will be reduced as a result of the higher official price. The actual outcome in terms of a rise or fall in the illegal market clearing price will depend on the relative size of these two changes.

The above provides a description of the relationship between what happens in the official market and what takes place with illegal demand and supply, at the *market* level. However, it provides no clue as to whether the individual producer will sell illegally or stay within the channels prescribed by the law. As we have stressed, the key concepts regarding the illegal market are the risks of detection and the penalty that goes with detection. The expected effective price received by a seller on an illegal transaction is

(22) $p_{efp} = (1 - \beta)p_{fp} + \beta(p_{fp} - \alpha) = p_{fp} - \alpha\beta$

where α is the loss per unit illegally sold if the transaction is detected while β is the probability that the transaction in question is revealed to the authorities (assumed, for the sake of simplicity, to be equal for all peasants). Thus, as long as the probability of detection is positive and a penalty is associated with the offence, the expected effective price received will always be less than the actual price prevailing in the illegal market.

Given the expected effective price, the peasant has to decide whether to sell in the illegal market or not. Because of the risks and penalties involved, the price that the peasant requires to sell illegally will be

(23) $p_{rfp} = \bar{p}_{fo}(1 + \gamma)$

where γ is the premium over what can be obtained by selling via the official marketing channels that the peasant requires for selling illegally. Depending on the perception of risk, γ differs between individuals. Provided that $p_{rfp} < p_{efp}$, the peasant will sell in the illegal market. Otherwise he will not, i.e. only peasants with $\gamma < (1/\bar{p}_{fo})(p_{fp} - \alpha B - \bar{p}_{fo})$ will undertake the illegal transaction. The risk premium required must not exceed the difference between the expected effective price when selling illegally and the official price, measured as a share of the official price.

Equipped with this knowledge regarding the illegal markets, let us finally look at the empirical evidence regarding the responsiveness of the Tanzanian smallholders to price incentives.

THE EMPIRICAL EVIDENCE

Several studies exist on agricultural supply response in Tanzania, ranging from those dealing with groups of crops, notably food and cash crops, to those concentrating on individual food and non-food crops. Using time series data for official purchases and prices of food and cash crops, Frank Ellis has shown that the composition of marketed production changed in the direction of more food crops between 1975 and 1979 in response to relative price changes in favour of food.[41] G.D. Gwyer and Kighoma Malima have checked supply responses for sisal and cotton, respectively, using the Nerlove model.[42] Both studies obtained significant positive price elasticities, that of cotton being 2.5. Benno Ndulu, also using the Nerlove framework, has estimated short-run supply functions for maize and paddy at the regional level, for the main surplus producing regions.[43] Statistically significant price elasticities (using relative prices), ranging from 1.5 to 7.8, were found for the various regions.

Christopher Gerrard and Terry Roe, in an econometric study of government intervention in food grain markets, have *inter alia* estimated short-run supply functions for maize and rice, covering the 1964–78 period.[44] Own price elasticities of 2.29 were obtained for both crops and the elasticities with respect to the competing crops were −1.57 and −0.81, respectively. The elasticities were statistically significant and the R^2 values were 0.53 for maize and

0.82 for rice. The low value for maize is probably due to the failure to include the effects of the weather and of the dual marketing structure in the regressions. The partial adjustment coefficients of 0.92 (maize) and 1.08 (rice) suggest fairly rapid adjustments of the quantities produced and marketed to price changes.[45] The results support the hypothesis that marketed quantities are responsive to both own and relative prices.

Knut Ödegaard has estimated the relationships between the officially marketed quantities of maize, the ratio of official real producer prices to the prices of annual, competing cash crops, the unofficial market premium (to capture market-switching effects) and the weather.[46] He obtained a relative price elasticity of 1.04 and a market premium elasticity of −0.14, both statistically significant, with an adjusted $\bar{R}^2$ of 0.71. The low elasticity with respect to the unofficial market premium is probably due to the overestimation of the unofficial market premium to producers which results when the differences between unofficial and official *consumer* prices is used. Using data on unofficial maize marketing in Rukwa, Torben Rasmussen has shown that an increase in unofficial consumer prices leads to a less than proportional increase in unofficial producer prices. However, the increase in the trade margin was proportionately greater than the rise in unofficial consumer prices.[47] Moreover, the subsidised official consumer prices have stagnated to a far greater extent than official producer prices. This leads to a further overestimation of the premium to the producers when selling in the unofficial markets. Unfortunately, given the paucity of data, the unofficial *consumer* prices are the only ones available for the type of exercise carried out by Ödegaard.

All the cited studies indicate a positive response of the marketed surplus to both own and relative price changes for individual crops and groups of crops. Nevertheless, the analysis is incomplete, for at least two reasons. In the first place, doubts have been expressed from time to time regarding the responsiveness of the *total* officially marketed production (food plus cash crops) to *general* producer price increases in agriculture, the argument being that the transformation curve does not expand outwards in the manner predicted by our theoretical model above. Secondly, our model makes a distinction between nominal food producer price increases on the one hand and changes in the overall agricultural terms of trade (the price of food and cash crops in terms of purchased goods) on the other. Disentangling these effects should be important when it comes to discussing policy measures towards agriculture. None of the empirical studies quoted above distinguishes between these measures.

Data are, however, available that permit us to fill in these gaps. Let us begin with the question of the influence of changes in the agricultural terms of trade on total officially marketed production.

The analysis covers the period 1972/73–1982/83, a timespan with a stable number of scheduled crops, avoiding the earlier years when the number of crops scheduled for official marketing changed rapidly. Moreover, the chosen decade is characterised by a rather active use of price measures, compared to the preceding one. The total marketed quantities include all cash crops and all food crops except legumes other than beans, which were only subsequently included as scheduled crops.[48] The aggregate price used is an average of official prices (lagged one year) for all crops, the weights being the respective quantities purchased officially.[49] The national consumer price index is used for definition, in order to reflect the terms of trade.

Fitting a regression line to the series of total officially marketed quantities and weighted average real producer prices (in log-linear form, to obtain the price elasticity of marketed output directly) yields

(24)   LQNTM = 0.99 + 0.88 LRPR, R^2 = 0.93
        (1.01) (5.78)   F = 122.7

where LQNTM = log of quantity marketed, LRPR = log of real producer prices, and the values within parentheses are t values.

The price-elasticity of marketed supply, although it is lower than that of the individual crops, is statistically significant at the 0.05 per cent level. The variations in the terms of trade account for 93 per cent of the variation in marketed quantity.

In view of the rather significant increases in nominal producer prices after 1974–75 (cf. above), the steep decline in total marketed quantities after 1978 seems to have been caused by the deterioration in the agricultural terms of trade resulting from the rapid increase in the rate of inflation, which jumped from a previous average of 13 per cent to 30 per cent.[50] In order to check the influence of changes in the consumer price index, the marketed quantity was regressed on nominal producer prices (PP) and the national consumer price index (NCPI), with the following result:

(25)   LQNTM = 4.85 + 0.925 LPP − 0.909 LNPCI
                    (4.36)   (−5.38)
       $R^2 = 0.88$ $\bar{R}^2 = 0.85$ F = 28.3

Changes in nominal producer prices (significant at the 0.5 per cent level) and inflation (0.05 per cent level) were approximately equally important in influencing marketed quantities. This explains why during the post-1978 period the rapid rate of inflation more than cancelled the influence of the modest producer price increases.

Short-run supply functions were also estimated for the two key food grains, paddy and maize, regressing desired marketed quantities on expected prices, using the Nerlove model where desired production is a function of expected prices.[51] Officially marketed quantities were used as the dependent variable for both crops. In the case of paddy, only the quantities marketed by smallholders were used. The price variables include the own price, the price of cotton, the national consumer price index and the unofficial market consumer price (to capture market-switching effects). Weather was included as a dummy variable (1 = bad, 0 otherwise). The choice of cotton as the competing crop is due to the fact that cotton-producing areas (Lake Victoria zone, Tabora and Morogoro) account for the bulk of the official purchases of paddy,[52] the only other major supplying region being Mbeya. (State farms sell all their paddy in the form of rice and have therefore been excluded here.)

As for maize, the corresponding relevant prices have been used. However, in this case, the choice of competing crops is more difficult, since maize is grown all over the country, with varying competing crops. Here, tobacco and pyrethrum were chosen, since these are the main competing crops in the key surplus areas of Iringa and Ruvuma. A weighted average price was constructed for these two crops.[53]

The producer prices included in the supply functions are lagged one year. Although the government has increasingly been announcing prices prior to the production season,[54] constraints on the dissemination of information until recently and delays in the setting of area-specific prices by cooperatives, prior to the institution of pan-territorial pricing in 1973–74, made farmers rely on the previous season's prices in their formation of price expectations. In view of the relatively stable producer prices prior to 1973–74 and the unidirectional upward change thereafter, it has been judged reasonable to rule out distributed lags. The anticipated price should not fall short of the current one. Due to the information problem the anticipated future prices have been assumed to be equal to those actually prevailing currently. In terms of the Nerlove model, the coefficient of expectation is assumed to be equal to one.[55] The same goes for the consumer price index which is a weighted average of current official fixed prices. Hence, these have also been lagged one year.

In the case of unofficial prices, a different logic has been followed. *Ceteris paribus*, an increase in the unofficial price should have two effects. If an increase is anticipated at the time when the production decision is taken it stimulates production of the crop. Secondly, *ex post*, when the higher price has materialised, it shifts marketing away from official sources to unofficial ones. It is unlikely that the output increase induced by higher anticipated unofficial prices has found its way into official channels since the gap between unofficial and official prices has on average been widening during the period under consideration.[56] In the present formulation use has been made of non-lagged unofficial prices, since our primary concern is to examine the growth of the *marketed* surplus via *official* channels. This allows us to concentrate on the market-shifting effect.

On the quantity side, complete adjustment to desired quantities is assumed to take place within one season.[57] This is plausible both because the adjustment costs for annual crops are negligible and because the increases in producer prices have on average not been so high as to require substantial increases of desired quantities relative to current production. Moreover, Gerrard and Roe, as we have seen, estimated the Nerlovian partial adjustment coefficient for both maize and paddy to lie in the neighbourhood of one, which strongly supports our assumption regarding complete adjustment to desired quantities within the production season.

All equations were estimated in log-linear form, using the maximum likelihood iterative procedure.[58] The periods covered are 1965/66–1980/81 for paddy and 1965/66–1981/82 for maize. The results are presented in Table 8.1.

The independent variables in the paddy equation account for 99 per cent of the variation in marketed quantity. The signs of all elasticities are those expected. The own price-elasticity for paddy is quite high, 3.1, and is significant at the 0.05 per cent level. The consumer price index and the unofficial consumer price are statistically significant (0.5 and 1 per cent levels) indicating strong terms of trade effects and market switching. The price of the competing

Table 8.1 Short-run supply elasticities of paddy and maize

Crop	Own price	Competing crop price	National consumer price index	Unofficial price	Weather	R^2	$\bar{R}^2$	F
Paddy	3.10	−0.97	−1.75	−1.10	−0.25	0.99	0.98	135.9
t-stat.	(7.27)	(−1.35)	(−4.12)	(−2.75)	(−1.52)			
Maize	1.67	−0.82	−0.23	−0.96	−0.81	0.79	0.69	7.4
t-stat.	(2.42)	(−0.82)	(−0.25)	(−1.27)	(−2.61)			

crop is only weakly significant, at the 15 per cent level. The statistical significance obtains in spite of high collinearity among the price variables. However, when the equation is estimated without the unofficial price variable, all the remaining variables, including the price of the competing crop, are highly significant, which is a further indication of multicollinearity. Thus, probably the influence of the price of the competing crop is more important than indicated by our results.[59]

In the case of maize, the results obtained are weaker. As indicated previously, the difficulties of determining appropriate weights for competing crops as well as the constraints on the scale of unofficial trade in maize (due to the high proportion of transport cost in its value and to the poor infrastructure in some key surplus areas) weaken the relationships estimated. Nevertheless, all variables have the right signs, and the own price-elasticity is significant at the 2.5 per cent level. It is, however, lower than the one obtained by Gerrard and Roe (2.29). (The statistical insignificance of the other price variables — in spite of the high R^2, the included variables account for some 79 per cent of the variation in marketed quantity, though the adjusted R^2 value is only 0.69, and the significant F statistic — is probably explained by high collinearity among the price variables, especially with the consumer price index.)[60]

Thus, to conclude, there is nothing to indicate that the Tanzanian smallholder is not responsive to price incentives, regardless of whether these stem from changes of relative prices within the agricultural sector or from changes of the terms of trade of agriculture with the rest of the economy. This definitely seems to be the case for paddy. With regards to maize, the regression is more conclusive at the joint explanatory level than for each individual price variable, other than the own price. However, a pattern similar to that of paddy is likely to emerge if the maize equation is re-estimated on the basis of regional data thus reducing the problem of selecting the competing crop.

CONCLUSIONS: SOME POLICY IMPLICATIONS

Some important policy implications emerge from the above discussion of theory and empirical evidence. First, the recognition of self-interest in production decisions and the key role of economic motivation should constitute the micro-foundations of policies related to increasing agricultural production. Economic motivation should be emphasised more than hitherto has been the case. By the same token, there should be less reliance on central control measures and more on price incentives coupled with necessary supportive services (transport, extension, etc.), since this is likely to encourage increased production. Incentives to increase production will, however, have to focus both on increases in nominal producer prices and on improvements in the agricultural terms of trade via increased availability of basic consumer goods and control of inflation. The current efforts in this direction are encouraging and should be strengthened.

Our analysis also has strong implications for the institutional framework conducive to agricultural growth and development. Increased use of incentives and less central control of production decisions calls for a more flexible institutional structure that can respond to the complex and changing needs of the agricultural producers. Systems for distributing inputs and agricultural credit could be decentralised so as to more efficiently meet the needs and demands of the producers, based on the relative profitability of different crops as perceived by the farmers. Even though the overall supply of these factors is severely constrained today, the available quantities can be more efficiently distributed and used if the distribution system becomes more flexible and is directed towards the most profitable uses. In this context, the increased profitability of input use arising from more favourable agricultural *output* prices rather than from direct subsidies of a limited range of inputs that are centrally distributed would encourage the utilisation of locally available substitutes, like manure and compost, which are not subject to the distribution constraints that have hampered the use of manufactured inputs.

In the past, there has been a conflict between the two major goals for Tanzania's food policy: self-sufficiency and the maintenance of low food prices to the consumers. During the first one and a half decades after independence, the maintenance of low consumer prices entailed keeping producer prices down as well, using imports to bridge the gap between domestic demand and supply. During the following decade, with the increasing limitations on import capacity, producer prices were increased to enhance domestic supply, while at the same time low consumer prices were maintained through subsidies that were largely financed via a growing budget deficit. The consequent inflationary pressures coupled with imported inflation linked to the oil price shocks wiped out the effects of increased nominal producer prices which were themselves limited by the budgetary pressures.

The resultant shortages led to the dual market structure discussed above. The growing dominance of the parallel market forced the target group of low-income consumers into this market where prices were substantially higher than in the official channels. The recent removal of food subsidies was simply an official recognition of a *de facto* situation. Thus, the economy ended up in a situation where neither of the two objectives of food policy was achieved. This has served to bring home the message that in the long run, a simultaneous attempt to maintain low prices to consumers and self-sufficiency is possible only through increased productivity and improved efficiency in distribution and marketing. In the short run, the plight of the urban poor is a real problem that has to be tackled. However, ways should be sought to supplement the incomes of this target group directly without jeopardising the motivation of the smallholders to produce.

Finally, it must be emphasised that although price incentives are powerful instruments for achieving increased production, they require an adequate agricultural infrastructure to be effective. It is in the area of infrastructure that direct government action is most needed — in the form of expenditures for improvement and mobilisation of local efforts. Stimulation of these efforts and less emphasis on direct intervention and control of the micro production decisions would go a long way towards increasing agricultural production and efficiency. After all, the producers are aware of their micro level environment and of their own best interests. An appropriate use of a system of market related incentive signals could make use of the producers' self-interest for achieving national goals.

NOTES

* The research for this chapter was financed by a SAREC grant, which is gratefully acknowledged. The authors also received helpful comments from Jannik Boesen and Bo Sandelin during the discussion at Frostavallen.

1. Katz (1977), Nicholson (1978), Bergman (1983).
2. From an average of 4 kg per person to 10 kg (computed using food import data as reported by Ödegaard (1985), p. 150 and population data from URT, Central Bureau of Statistics (1984)).
3. Cook (1984), pp. 58–9.
4. Amani *et al.* (1984).

5. At least seven different series are available. None of these is completely reliable. The one that appears have the fewest defects is the one stemming from the Ministry of Agriculture (Kilimo) Statistics Section. (For details, see Hedlund and Lundahl (1984) and Cook (1984), Appendix A.)
    An independent estimate of the growth of food consumption can be obtained from the 1969 and 1976–77 household budget surveys (cf. Ödegaard (1985), p. 144). Using these, a figure of 2.9 per cent per annum is arrived at. Given a population growth rate of 3.3 per cent, this means that the total supply (domestic production plus imports) would have to increase at a rate of 5.2 per cent per annum. According to Kilimo figures, domestic food production grew by 7.4 per cent per annum over the period, while FAO data indicate a mere 0.8 per cent (figures in ibid., Appendix, Table A.3, p. 234). Even though the Kilimo series may be on the high side, it is much more in line with the household budget consumption figures than the FAO estimate. Moreover, taking into account that imports constituted a mere 2.3 and 3.5 per cent of estimated consumption in 1969 and 1976–77, respectively (ibid., p. 150) it is clearly evident that, on average, there was no immediate threat of hunger, except for during drought years.

6. Hedlund and Lundahl (1984); Cook (1984), pp. 49–50.

7. URT, Central Bureau of Statistics (1980). According to the household budget surveys, the most rapid growth of per capita consumption was in the so-called preferred cereals (maize, rice and wheat): 4.7 per cent per annum. The growth rate was much higher in rural areas (5.1 per cent) than in urban districts (1.2 per cent) (data from Ödegaard (1985), p. 144). This further constrained supplies in the cities. It is precisely in this category of foodstuffs that the import share of consumption was highest: 6.2 per cent in 1969 and 8.3 per cent in 1976–77 (ibid., p. 150).

8. Hedlund and Lundahl (1984).

9. Cf. e.g. the reasoning in Berg (1961).

10. Under the Village Act 1975, registration gave a village legal status and a village council that could enter into contractual obligations (business or otherwise) with other legal entities.

11. For an analysis, see Ödegaard (1985), Ch. 4.

12. Bank of Tanzania (1984), p. 98.

13. Leonard (1985), p. 5.

14. Bank of Tanzania (1984), p. 83.

15. Msambichaka, Ndulu and Amani (1983), p. 45.

16. Bank of Tanzania (1984), p. 82.

17. Leonard (1985), p. 5.

18. Bank of Tanzania (1984), p. 81.

19. URT, Central Bureau of Statistics (1984), Table 342.

20. Hydén (1982); Bates (1982, 1983).

21. URT, Marketing Development Bureau (1981), p. 22.

22. Bank of Tanzania (1984), Table 31, p. 303.

23. According to this principle a producer obtains the same price for a given crop regardless of where he is located in the country.

24. URT, Marketing Development Bureau (1981), Annex 1, Appendix 2.1, gives official purchase figures for the two regions for 1970/71–1980/81.

25. Ödegaard (1985), p. 65, provides some evidence based on studies

by Gottlieb (1973), indicating that some 500,000 people were hired for work on peasant farms during the mid-1960s; and Mbilinyi (1976), indicating that 25–30 per cent of the total labour used in the major coffee-growing areas was hired for the 1968–69 crop year. According to the 1977 World Bank Basic Economic Report (World Bank (1977), quoted in URT, Marketing Development Bureau (1980), Table 11, p. 28), agricultural wage labour contributed 7.7 per cent of total smallholder income and 15.7 per cent of smallholder cash income, respectively. Again, a study by Bo and Rasmussen (1982), p. 106, showed that wage employment contributed 19 per cent of the total incomes earned by smallholders in Iringa region. In addition, petty trade, handicrafts, etc. contributed 15 and 14.2 per cent of smallholder cash income in 1969 and 1975, respectively. (See URT, Marketing Development Bureau (1980), pp. 27–9.)

It should be noted that the above labour sales exclude labour swapping between rural households on a mutual help basis for certain production activities. These over a reasonable time span cancel each other in terms of the labour time expended.

26. We abstract from the use of such 'seasonal' inputs as fertiliser and pesticides. These may simply be interpreted as 'landesque' capital that acts as a substitute for land and can hence be included with land. (Cf. Sen (1962), pp 90–7.)

27. There are areas with high population pressure on the land, such as Kilimanjaro region. These are, however, not typical at present. In addition, the current resettlement programmes allow for movement from such areas to more land abundant areas.

28. The predominant implements in smallholder agriculture are hoes and machetes, although the use of ox-ploughs and hired tractor services has increased during the 1970s.

29. There is a vast literature on semi-subsistence agricultural household behaviour models, including the works by Krishna (1962, 1963); Tanaka (1962); Sen (1966); Hymer and Resnick (1969); Nakajima (1970); Winkelman (1972); and Barnum and Squire (1979). This family of models provides various extensions of pure labour allocation models, including wealth, labour markets, technological innovation and the production of non-marketed, non-agricultural goods and services. They, however, all have in common that they are centred on the problem of labour allocation by the peasant family household.

30. Cf. Frisch (1965), Ch. 8, on the ultra-passum law. The assumption receives some empirical support from the work of Cornia (1985) who, using farm level cross-section data for 15 developing countries, including Tanzania, found that in the land-rich countries of Africa both productivity per hectare and labour input per hectare declined as farm size increased. Moreover, the decline of productivity per hectare was proportionately higher than that of the labour input, which indicates decreasing marginal returns to labour as the scale of operations increased. In the case of Tanzania, the estimated elasticities of land productivity and labour input per hectare as farm size increased was -0.57 and -0.47, respectively (ibid., p. 525).

31. We also assume that the second-order conditions necessary for a utility maximum are fulfilled. For brief discussions of the problem of

finding plausible assumptions regarding the utility function that guarantee this, see Nakajima (1970), p. 183; and Barnum and Squire (1979), Ch. 3.

32. This curve is concave to the origin, as shown in the diagram. Successive equal decreases of cash crop output free less and less labour, due to the decreasing returns to labour. Thus, successively smaller amounts of labour will be transferred to the production of food. There, adding successively equal amounts of labour to food production will, due to decreasing returns to labour in food production, give rise to successively smaller additions to food output.

33. Cf. Barnum and Squire (1979), pp. 36–8.

34. The FAO has estimated income elasticities of demand in Tanzania to be 1.0 for wheat, 0.6 for rice and 0.4 for coarse grains and starchy roots (quoted in URT, Market Development Bureau (1981), Summary, p. 13).

35. If the wage rate also increases in terms of purchased goods, the slope of the segment corresponding to B_1A_1 in Figure 8.2 will increase, and if it becomes steep enough it will move the point corresponding to B_1 to the right of B, so that fewer hours are worked in agriculture even though the point corresponding to C_1 remains on the linear segment.

36. Ödegaard (1985), p. 156.

37. URT, Marketing Development Bureau (1983), Table 1, estimates that only 25 per cent of the maize surplus was being sold via official channels. (Cf. Ödegaard (1985), p. 156.)

38. URT, Marketing Development Bureau (1984, 1985).

39. Ödegaard (1985), p. 151.

40. The National Agricultural Food Corporation and other, smaller state farms accounted for 51.6 per cent of all officially marketed paddy between 1975–76 and 1980–81 (URT, Marketing Development Bureau (1981), Annex 1, Appendix 3.1).

41. Ellis (1982).

42. Gwyer (1971); Malima (1971). For the Nerlove model, see e.g. Nerlove (1956, 1958a, 1958b).

43. Ndulu (1979).

44. Gerrard and Roe (1983).

45. Ibid., p. 120.

46. Ödegaard (1985), pp. 167–73. The unofficial market premium was defined as the excess of the consumer price in the unofficial food market over the official consumer price, measured as a share of the latter.

47. Rasmussen (1985).

48. Coffee, cotton, sisal, tobacco, pyrethrum, tea, cashew nuts, maize, paddy, wheat, millet and sorghum, cassava and beans. Data for marketed quantities were obtained from URT, Marketing Development Bureau (1981), Table 4.1 (preferred cereals 1972/73–1980/81), Table 4.5 (drought staples 1972/73–1980/81), Table 4.8 (domestically consumed oilseeds 1972/73–1979/80), Table 4.11 (export crops 1972/73–1980/81); URT, Ministry of Planning and Economic Affairs (1984), Table 45 (official purchases of food crops 1979/80–1982/83).

49. See URT, Marketing Development Bureau (1981), Table 5.1 for average producer prices 1971/72–1981/82 of food and export crops.

50. Cf. note 22, above.

51. No simultaneous equation bias will arise, since producer prices are administratively set and are not market-clearing prices. Consumers and producers face different prices because of consumer subsidies. In addition, the total market supply (inclusive of imports and unofficial sales) generally exceeds the marketed quantities dealt with in this chapter.

52. See URT, Marketing Development Bureau (1981), Annex 1, p. 22 and Appendix 3.1.

53. Data sources for the short-run supply functions: Paddy: (1) Official purchases of paddy (by NMC and NAFCO) for the period 1965/66–1969/70 were obtained from Ödegaard (1985), Table 5.5, p. 150; 1970/71–1980/81 from URT, Marketing Development Bureau (1981), Annex 1, Appendix 3.1, which distinguishes paddy purchases from rice purchases, beginning in 1975–76. Prior to 1975–76 only paddy was purchased. (2) Official producer prices for paddy and cotton (national average) and unofficial consumer prices were obtained from Ödegaard (1985), Appendix Tables B.1 and B.2, covering 1965/66–1981/82 (producer prices) and 1965/66–1981/82 (unofficial consumer prices). (3) The national consumer price index comes from URT, Ministry of Planning and Economic Affairs (1984), Table 33, for 1969–83. Extrapolation of the series backwards to 1966 was undertaken by using the Dar es Salaam minimum wage earners' index, since the national consumer price index did not exist at that time. (4) The weather dummy variable (1 = bad) 1969–70, 1974/75–1976/77, 1980–81 as indicated in URT, Ministry of Agriculture, *Bulletin of Crop Production Statistics* and URT, Marketing Development Bureau, *Price Policy Recommendations, Summary, Annexes*, various years, complemented with personal judgement for years with large deviations from trend quantities. Maize: (1) Official purchase data 1965/66–1980/81, from Ödegaard (1985), Table 5.5, 1981–82, from URT, Ministry of Planning and Economic Affairs (1984), Table 4.1 (2) Official producer prices for maize, tobacco, pyrethrum and unofficial consumer prices 1964/65–1981/82 from Ödegaard (1985), Table B.1 and B.2. (3) National consumer price index as above. (4) Weather dummy (1 = bad) for 1969–70, 1971–72, 1973/74–1974/75, 1980–81, based on the same sources as for paddy.

54. See e.g. Gerrard and Roe (1983), pp. 110–11; and Ödegaard (1985), p. 110.

55. Nerlove's equation for adjustment of the expected price reads

$$P_t^* - P_{t-1}^* = B(P_{t-1} - P_{t-1}^*)$$

where asterisks denote expected prices and no asterisks actual prices (Nerlove (1958a), p. 53). With B, the coefficient of expectation, equal to one, the expected price in period t equals the actual price in period $t-1$.

56. Ödegaard (1985), p. 156, contains the relevant information.

57. In Nerlove's formulation (1958a, p. 62), the quantity adjustment equation reads

$$q_t - q_{t-1} = D(q_t^* - q_{t-1})$$

meaning that with the coefficient of adjustment D, less than one (but greater than zero) farmers do not adjust their output perfectly when they perceive a difference between what they produced during period $t-1$ and what they want to produce during period t. If, as is assumed, D equals one, however, adjustment is perfect.

58. OLS estimates yielded Durbin–Watson statistics of 2.25 and 2.35 for maize and paddy, respectively. This in both cases places the Durbin–Watson statistic in the inconclusive range. As the possibility of autocorrelation could not then be excluded, the maximum likelihood procedure described in Beach and MacKinnon (1978) was employed.

59. In the specification of the regression equation we have used what on *a priori* grounds appears as the most relevant formulation. This formulation entails multicollinearity problems. To check this the formulation where the unofficial price was omitted was tried. Omitting the unofficial price reduces multicollinearity, but its omission would lead to misspecification of the model, and a consequent specification bias. There is no way of establishing which of these two is the lesser evil (cf. e.g. Koutsoyiannis (1977), p. 253). In the present case, however, the unofficial price should be retained in the regression. As explained in the main text, 75 per cent of all scheduled food crops are marketed outside the official channels. Consequently there are strong *a priori* grounds for suspecting that the unofficial price is an important determinant of the officially marketed surplus.

60. A specification with all price variables deflated by the national consumer price index was attempted:

$$\text{LQNMZ} = 3.71 + 1.68 \, L \, \frac{\text{PM}}{\text{NCPI}} - 0.28 \, L \, \frac{\text{PC}}{\text{NCPI}}$$

$$(0.73) \quad (2.53) \qquad\qquad (-1.02)$$

$$- 0.97 \, L \, \frac{\text{PMU}}{\text{NCPI}} - 0.72 \, W$$

$$(-1.32) \qquad\quad (-3.06)$$

and

$$R^2 = 0.77, \quad \bar{R}^2 = 0.69, \quad F = 9.8.$$

A slight improvement in the significance of the coefficients results, which should be an indication of multicollinearity in the original price variables.

REFERENCES

Amani, Haidari K.R., Mabele, Robert, Rugumisa, Salvatore and Msambichaka, Lucian A. (1984), 'Agriculture in Economic Stabilization Policies', Paper presented at the Workshop on Economic Stabilization, Dar es Salaam.

Bank of Tanzania (1984), *Tanzania; Twenty Years of Independence (1961– 1981): A Review of Political and Economic Independence*, Dar es Salaam.

Barnum, Howard N. and Squire, Lyn (1979), *A Model of an Agricultural Household*, Baltimore and London.
Bates, Robert H. (1982), *Markets in Tropical Africa*, Berkeley.
—— (1983), *Essays on the Political Economy of Rural Africa*, Cambridge.
Beach, Charles M. and MacKinnon, James G. (1978), 'A Maximum Likelihood Procedure for Regression with Autocorrelated Errors', *Econometrica*, vol. 46.
Berg, Elliott J. (1961), 'Backward-Sloping Labor Supply Functions in Dual Economies: The African Case', *Quarterly Journal of Economics*, vol. 75.
Bergman Kenneth (1983), 'Climate Change', *International Journal of Environmental Studies*, vol. 20.
Bo, Per and Rasmussen, Torben (1982), 'Peasant Economy and Rural Credit: The Study of Maize Production, Tanzania', Research Report, Centre for Development Research, Copenhagen.
Cook, Kristy D. (1984), 'Dimensions of Food Security/Insecurity: Tanzania, A Case Study', MA thesis, Department of Economics, University of Dar es Salaam.
Cornia, Giovanni Andrea (1985), 'Farm Size, Land Yields and the Agricultural Production Function: An Analysis for Fifteen Developing Countries', *World Development*, vol. 13.
Ellis, Frank (1982), 'Agricultural Price Policy in Tanzania', *World Development*, vol. 10.
Frisch, Ragnar (1965) *Theory of Production*, Dordrecht.
Gerrard, Christopher D. and Roe, Terry (1983), 'Government Intervention in Food Grain Markets: An Econometric Study of Tanzania', *Journal of Development Economics*, vol. 13.
Gottlieb, Manuel (1973), 'The Extent and Characterization of Differentiation in Tanzanian Agricultural and Rural Society', *African Review*, no. 3.
Gwyer, G.D. (1971), *Perennial Crop Supply Response: The Case of Tanzanian Sisal*. University of London, Wesley College, London.
Hedlund, Stefan and Lundahl, Mats (1984), 'The Present State of Food Production in Tanzania', mimeo, Department of Economics, University of Lund.
Hydén, Göran (1982), *Beyond Ujamaa in Tanzania, Underdevelopment and an Uncaptured Peasantry*, London.
Hymer, Stephen and Resnick, Stephen (1969), 'A Model of an Agrarian Economy with Non-Agricultural Activities', *American Economic Review*, vol. 59.
Katz, Richard W. (1977), 'Assessing the Impact of Climate Change on Food Production', *Climate Change*, vol. 1.
Koutsoyiannis, Anne (1977), *Theory of Econometrics*, 2nd edn, London.
Krishna, Raj (1962) 'A Note on the Elasticity of the Marketable Surplus of a Subsistence Crop', *Indian Journal of Agricultural Economics*, vol. 18.
—— (1963), 'Farm Supply in India–Pakistan: A Case Study of the Punjab Region', *Economic Journal*, vol. 73.
Leonard, David K. (1985), 'Developing Africa's Agricultural Institutions: Putting the Farmer in Control'. Background paper for the Committee on

African Development Strategies, January, 1985 Session, New York, Council on Foreign Relations, New York and Overseas Development Council, Washington, D.C.

Malima, Kighoma A. (1971), 'The Determinants of Cotton Supply in Tanzania', Economic Research Bureau Paper, No. 69.14, University of Dar es Salaam.

Mbilinyi, Simon (1976), *Economics of Peasant Coffee Production in Tanzania*, Nairobi.

Msambichaka, Lucian A., Ndulu, Benno J. and Amani, Haidari K.R. (1983), *Agricultural Development in Tanzania: Policy Evolution, Performance and Evaluation. The First Two Decades of Independence*, Bonn.

Nakajima, Chihiro (1970), 'Subsistence and Commercial Family Farming: Some Theoretical Models of Subjective Equilibrium', in Clifton R. Wharton, Jr. (ed.), *Subsistence Agriculture and Economic Development*, London.

Ndulu, Benno J. (1979), 'The Role of Transportation in Agricultural Production Decisions in Tanzania', PhD thesis, Northwestern University, Evanston.

Nerlove, Marc (1956), 'Estimates of the Elasticity of Supply of Selected Agricultural Commodities', *Journal of Farm Economics*, vol. 38.

────── (1958a), *The Dynamics of Supply. Estimation of Farmers' Response to Price*, Baltimore, MD.

────── (1958b), 'Distributed Lags and Estimation of Long-Run Supply and Demand Elasticities: Theoretical Considerations', *Journal of Farm Economics*, vol. 40.

Nicholson, Sharon E. (1978), 'Climatic Variations in the Sahel and Other African Regions during the Past Five Centuries', *Journal of Arid Environments*, vol. 1.

Ödegaard, Knut (1985), *Cash Crop versus Food Crop Production in Tanzania: An Assessment of the Major Post-Colonial Trends*, Lund.

Rasmussen, Torben (1985), 'The Private Market for Maize in Tanzania — A Preliminary Analysis', mimeo, Centre for Development Research, Copenhagen.

Sen, Amartya K. (1962), *Choice of Techniques. An Aspect of Planned Economic Development*, 2nd edn, Oxford.

────── (1966), 'Peasants and Dualism with or without Surplus Labor', *Journal of Political Economy*, vol. 74.

Tanaka, Osamu (1962), 'Labor Supply and Farm Output', *Kobe University Economic Review*, no. 8.

URT (United Republic of Tanzania), Central Bureau of Statistics (1980), *1978 Population Census, A Preliminary Report*, Dar es Salaam.

────── Central Bureau of Statistics (1984), *The 1976/77 Household Budget Survey*, Dar es Salaam.

────── Marketing Development Bureau (1980), *A Profile of the Agricultural Sector*, Dar es Salaam.

────── Marketing Development Bureau (1981), *Price Policy Recommendations for the 1982-83 Agricultural Price Review, Summary, Annexes 1-13*, Dar es Salaam.

────── Marketing Development Bureau (1983), *Price Policy Recommendations for the 1984-85 Agricultural Price Review, Summary*, Dar es Salaam.

―――― Marketing Development Bureau (1984, 1985), *Monthly Market Bulletin*, May 1984–March 1985, Dar es Salaam.
―――― Ministry of Agriculture (1983), *The New Agricultural Policy*, Dar es Salaam.
―――― Ministry of Planning and Economic Affairs (1983), *The Economic Survey, 1982*, Dar es Salaam.
―――― Ministry of Planning and Economic Affairs (1984), *The Economic Survey, 1983*, Dar es Salaam.
Winkelman, Don (1972), *The Traditional Farmer: Maximization and Mechanization*, Paris.
World Bank (1977), *Tanzania Basic Economic Report*, Washington, D.C.

9

Kibbutz Efficiency and the Incentive Conundrum

Haim Barkai*

INTRODUCTION

Common ownership of property, self-labour and collective control over the disposal of manpower are among the distinguishing characteristics of the kibbutz. However, the identifying feature *par excellence* of this group of collective entities, which has the most direct bearing on efficiency-*cum*-incentive issues, is the Principle of Equality. This guiding rule on the distribution of real income is manifested in a complete severance of the nexus between a member's contribution to production and the benefits accruing to him. It has often been suggested that abiding by this rule blunts incentives and induces inefficiency, which ultimately leads to the demise of the collective as an economic and social entity.

In what follows we shall explore the various facets of the case against collectives, which apply to the kibbutz. The first section, which analyses the impact of the Principle of Equality on the labour/leisure option, on effort, on factor allocation and output composition, on the choice between present and deferred consumption, and on the composition of consumption expenditure, describes the nature of the issues involved. These are followed up in the next section by a survey of kibbutz performance. The following sections offer some insights on the reasons for kibbutz survival (in 'defiance' of its predicted demise) and hopefully identifies the *sine qua non* of this genus of social entity.

THE INEFFICIENCY AND INCENTIVE CASE AGAINST THE KIBBUTZ

Consumption sector inefficiencies

a. Suboptimal use of consumption expenditures. The commune is said to waste resources due to the (socially) suboptimal composition of its consumption basket. This argument can be presented in terms of conventional microeconomic analysis, as follows: The income generated in the kibbutz production sector, Y, allows the distribution of an *equal* amount of consumption expenditure ('token income') to each community member such that per capita (token) income, I, is

$$I^i = Y/N$$

where N is the number of members. An individual member's problem of optimal choice of a consumption basket can thus be presented as a two-goods formulation as in Figure 9.1, where the horizontal and vertical axes represent the two goods. The market prices (or their real marginal production cost) to the community of each good are P_x and P_y. From the per capita income and price information we derive the budget line I_1I_1, representing the constraints on each member's expenditures and whose slope represents the relative cost to the community of x in terms of y. Its intercepts are given by the individual's endowment, I^i. Suppose now that the commune's distribution technique is to hand out an equal endowment of tokens to each member, allowing freedom of choice between x and y. Now consider two members whose different preferences can be described in terms of ordinal utility functions $U^i(x,y)$. Figure 9.1 accordingly shows the two intersecting indifference curves (drawn from the corresponding 'maps') of members M_1 and M_2. Since both members are subject to the same relative prices and receive the same endowment, their choice of optimal baskets must differ — the optimal basket of M_1 is at A_1 whilst that of M_2 is at B_1.

This would seem to suggest that striving for economic equality and real-life situations which involve diverse tastes can be reconciled. Thus, with freedom of choice, each kibbutz member reaches his or her highest feasible indifference curve so that the community at large can reach a Pareto-optimum at a given level of total income. But this is far from being the case. By present-day practices, only 25 per cent of total consumption expenditures (not of total income)

Figure 9.1

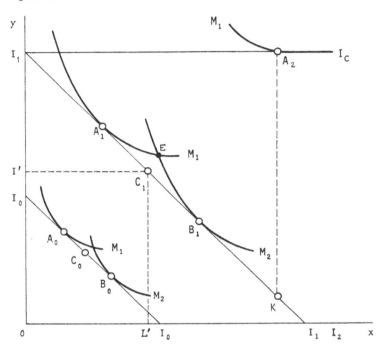

are distributed in the form of equal endowments.[1] Most kibbutz real income earmarked for consumption has always been and still is distributed as 'free goods' (e.g. child care, education, specific personal services, and food), and as 'personal allocations' (in particular housing), by means of quotas.

The significance of an equal-ration distribution technique can easily be shown in terms of the simple model in Figure 9.1. Assuming knowledge of the preference sets of individual members, the community is obviously in a quandary: by setting A_1 as the basket of goods distributed to all members, it would abide by the requirements of the budget constraints and allow member M_1 to reach the highest preference level consistent with that constraint. But A_1 obviously differs from member M_2's preferred basket, B_1, at the same 'budget'. It is also quite obvious that splitting the difference by setting the basket at C_1 would not do, as both M_1 and M_2, though on the budget line, would be pushed to lower levels on their preference scales. A basket such as E would, of course, leave both on the same level of utility as the initial free choice situation, with baskets A_1 and B_1, but E can only be reached by exceeding budget I_1 — say, at budget I_2. Critics would thus maintain that the difference between the value of these two budgets $(I_2 - I_1)$, measures the inefficiency inherent in the system of distribution applied by the kibbutz.

The 'inefficiencies' involved in applying a 'free good' distribution technique can also be demonstrated in terms of Figure 9.1.[2] Suppose x (say, food) is freely distributed. Since application of this technique does not affect the real cost borne by the community, the I_1I_1 budget line represents the economic constraint, and its slope — the cost to the community of the forgone alternative. Yet once x items are freely distributed, the relevant budget line for the individual member rotates counterclockwise to I_1I_c, parallel to the x axis. The zero slope (with respect to x) indicates the zero cost to the individual member of an increase in the consumption of x. Thus, member M_1 settles for a basket of, say, A_2 located at a higher indifference curve, at which his marginal rate of substitution of y for x is close to zero.[3] A_2K in Figure 9.1, which reflects the alternative cost to the community of basket A_2 chosen by M_1 subject to the 'free good' distribution technique applied to item x, is a measure of (Paretian) inefficiency generated by the use of that technique. The kibbutz must, of course, provide the resources required to allow members to move from basket A_1 to basket A_2.

The fact that different members would reach zero marginal utility of item x at differing quantities, and the very size of the fraction of income distributed by means of the free goods technique suggests that the A_2K gap in Figure 9.1 signifies substantial inefficiency in the use of resources earmarked for consumption. Since the rationed items and those distributed as free goods make up about 70–80 per cent of real consumption, the rules of the game applied in the kibbutz presumably involve tremendous waste in its *use* of wealth.

Critics of kibbutz distribution techniques maintain that applying the alternative technique of equal (token) endowments and individual choice of consumer goods subject to the relative prices facing the community would allow both members and the community as a whole to reach higher levels on the preference scale without compromising the equality tenet. Hence the desire of many kibbutz members to extend the 'comprehensive budget' technique of distribution.[4]

b. Stifling the inducement to save. The capital required by kibbutzim for setting up production and consumption facilities can be acquired by borrowing from the non-kibbutz environment. However, as equity capital is also necessary for the acquisition of additional resources through financial and capital markets, kibbutzim must save. Common ownership of property excludes not only the keeping of any kind of personal accounts with non-kibbutz entities, it also implies the exclusion of interest as an income paid out to members for the balance of their annual equal (token) cash endowment. This goes beyond the technical issue of whether members' balances with the community bear any interest. It means, in effect, that interest is excluded from the set of factors that affect individual behaviour in choosing between current or deferred consumption.

The significance of this constraint for the attitude toward, and therefore the technique of saving in kibbutzim can be presented in terms of a conventional Fisherian diagram (Figure 9.2). This represents some of the dimensions implicitly suppressed by the two-dimensional features of Figure 9.1. Present and future income and consumption of an individual kibbutz member are measured along the horizontal and vertical axes respectively.

Suppose each member's present income endowment is X_0, and that his expected next-period endowment is Y_0. At zero interest, the budget line through C is bX_1 with a slope of unity. Thus, if kibbutz members were free to choose between present and deferred consumption, they would choose a corner solution at X_1 (unless they have no subjective time preference, which is unlikely). This corner solution involves negative saving, to the tune of the total value of future income.

The dilemma created by the rational behaviour of members facing the consumption/saving option with zero-interest is underlined by the realities facing the community at large. When total kibbutz income is distributed among members, this is expressed in Figure 9.2 as the ac ('per capita') budget constraint passing though C. Its slope is, of course, greater than unity, reflecting the fact that the kibbutz operates in financial markets where interest rates are positive, and in an environment in which the marginal rate of return to capital is positive. Inspection of Figure 9.2 highlights the inconsistency between an individual's behaviour and that of the community as a whole. Obviously, the community cannot allow its members a current consumption level at X_1; this would mean that total consumption expenditures exceed the present value of its current and future incomes. Even if the commune adopts a corner solution approach, the interest rate constraints would only allow it

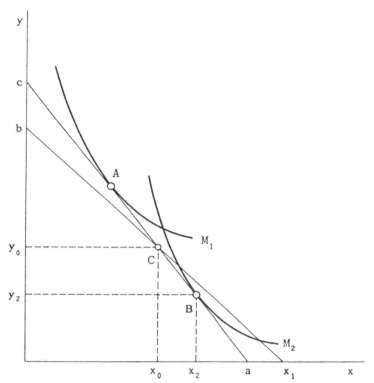

to go up to a point like a (per member), so that X_1 (and indeed the whole section CX_1 along the member's budget line) would be beyond the communal budget constraint.

This 'overspending' feature means that if total current income (product) were distributed in equal endowments, and if members had free choice, the community would generate negative saving. This, in turn, means that the decision on the level of saving cannot be left to the individual member in his capacity as a consumer.

The artificial 'zero interest' environment in which members operate, prescribed by the *modus operandi* of the kibbutz, is, however, not the only factor leading to the exclusion of the consumption/saving option from the realm of the individual in the kibbutz. The heterogeneity of tastes would generate another dilemma even if kibbutzim were to pay interest on members' positive balances with the community treasury and charge interest on their debts (if any).[5] If this was so, and if the imputed rate to members equalled the relevant market rate (or the internal rate of return to capital assets in the kibbutz production sector), the budget line through C in Figure 9.2 would be the 'community line', ac. The indifference curves of members M_1 and M_2 are tangential to ac at A and B. Thus, at the cost of abandoning one of its basic tenets, the zero-interest rate in intra-commune dealings enables the commune to avoid the inherently unstable dissaving corner solution. With an internal rate of return on assets identical to the market rate, a rate of dissaving per member of $X_2 - X_0$ (assuming all members have identical M_2-type preference scales), is a steady-state solution, since the community could borrow at market rates and invest in activities that offer at least the same return.

In practice, however, this issue is one in which tastes do differ. Figure 9.2 suggests that the optimal solutions at A and at B imply that member M_1 forgoes current consumption from his endowment of x_0 — current income. Yet the resources he provides by abstaining from consumption are transferred to member M_2, whose consumption expenditure at B exceeds x_0. This transfer of resources implies a stable equilibrium only if members M_1 and M_2 are directly or indirectly engaged in capital transactions where the market price for 'waiting' sets the margin of individual choice. Since this is a breach of kibbutz tenets — the ac budget line, which reflects options facing the *community*, is irrelevant to individual members. With a unity-sloped bx_1 budget line they would drift toward the corner solution on the bx_1 budget line, eventually leading to the demise of the commune's production capacity. It is probably this feature that led so many collectives to dire straits.

The only escape from this dilemma is obvious, and was adopted long ago by the kibbutz movement: saving decisions are made at the plane of the community by majority vote.[6] But the adoption of this rule of the game on saving apparently supports the lack-of-incentive case against the commune. Obviously, the elimination of individual inducement to save shifts the saving decision onto the 'political plane'. The political environment, however, has a notorious preference for the present; in the corridors of power 'the future has no constituency'.[7] Critics of the kibbutz claim that the stifling of individuals' incentive to save, an inherent feature of kibbutz rules, indirectly pushes the community onto a track of low saving levels, slow expansion of capacity, and thus sluggish — if any — income growth.

Production-sector inefficiencies

The 'waste of resources' case, and the argument of stifled propensity to save, refer to the distribution of a *given* level of income. Yet kibbutz income is not a given quantity; it has to be produced, and this involves inputs of labour and capital. The level of output that can be derived from any given quantity of primary inputs depends on the efficient combination of the specific set of factors used in the production process: labour, and the heterogeneous set of non-human inputs (land, raw materials, machinery, equipment, etc.). Maximising income under objective constraints thus requires both readiness of members to perform at the limit of their ability and the choice of an optimum input combination and output composition.

The claim that the kibbutz is an inefficient production entity is thus made on two levels. On one, it refers to motivation and the exertion of effort, and is pegged on to the incentive argument; the other is the Von Mises–Hayek proposition, that the exclusion of wages from the factor price set inevitably leads to inefficient factor and output composition. In what follows I propose to focus on the first of these two lines of criticism; the second line, which is extensively treated in the 'market socialism' literature, will be dealt with only in passing.[8]

a. The labour–leisure option. The labour–leisure option is usually the prime exhibit in the case against collectives. Critics claim that the Principle of Equality, which severs the link between a person's contribution to production and his material reward, penalises the industrious worker and the enterprising manager and cannot but retard effort and dull human drive.

Even observers more favourable to what was considered 'an interesting socio-economic experiment' — the attempt to establish kibbutzim in Palestine in the 1920s — admitted the force of this 'muzzling-of-incentives' argument.[9]

In a paper on the workings of the Soviet *kolkhoz*, Israelsen (1980) presented a formal variant of the muzzling-of-incentives argument. This formulation was used by Putterman (1983) as a stepping stone to a more comprehensive model of incentives in a kibbutz.

Writing H for total labour input of a commune, and specifying h^i as the labour input of a kibbutz member, we have

(1) $$H = \sum_{1}^{N} h^i.$$

Now specify a production function for given (and implied) non-labour inputs:

(2) $\quad Y = F(H) \quad$ and $\quad F'(H) > 0$

The equality condition requires equal distribution of income between commune members. Hence, writing y^i for per-member income, we have:

(3) $\quad y^i = \dfrac{Y}{N} = \dfrac{1}{N} F(H)$

Differentiating (3) with respect to h^i yields an expression for the marginal change of a member's income due to an increase in *his own* labour input. This is:

(4) $\quad \dfrac{\partial y^i}{\partial h^i} = \dfrac{1}{N} F'(H) \dfrac{\partial H}{\partial h^i}$

Israelsen's formulation implies, for member i:

(5) $\quad \dfrac{\partial H}{\partial h^i} = 1$

which holds if all the other members of the commune do not respond at all to a change in the labour input of one of its members. In this case, (4) reduces to the apparently simple expression:

(4*) $\quad \dfrac{\partial y^i}{\partial h^i} = \dfrac{1}{N} F'(H)$

the marginal increase in a commune member's income in response to an increase in his input of labour is equal to the Nth fraction of his marginal product. Hence, the larger the collective the smaller the reward to an increase in a member's effort.

Note that (4*) is essentially a symbiotic expression integrating the production facet with the commune's rule on income distribution. It demonstrates the 'muzzling-of-incentives' case against the kibbutz: the marginal product of labour is obviously $F'(H)$, which is N times larger than the marginal income accruing to a kibbutz member subject to the same capacity and technology constraints and having identical skills. Hence, if the quantity of labour and the degree of effort depended on material incentives, the commune member would prefer more leisure and presumably put in less elbow grease than his 'identical twin' operating in a market environment.

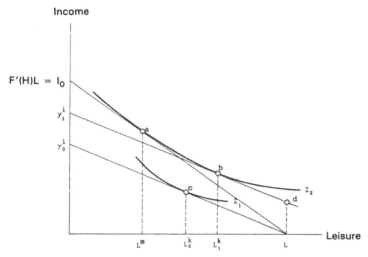

The Israelsen Theorem can be presented in terms of a conventional labour–leisure option model (Figure 9.3). Measuring leisure and income on the horizontal and vertical axes, respectively, the budget line linking the leisure and income options of an individual worker in a competitive labour market is LI_0. The slope of this line is the wage rate, which equals $F'(H)$, marginal product. A similar budget line, Ly_0^i can be drawn for the commune member. Its intercept on the income axis is, however, only 1/Nth of I_0. Thus, whatever point on his budget line the commune member chooses, the relevant sections of the two budget lines indicate that it would always involve a lower income. Thus, a worker in the (perfect competition) labour market would choose an income–leisure basket a, where the LI_0 budget line is tangent to a relevant indifference curve, whereas the commune member's choice would be, say, c on the Ly_0^i budget line, involving a lower labour input (L_2^k) (and a lower income) than the labour input at L^m and the corresponding income of the 'identical (labour market) twin'.

This result stems from an implied comparison of the subjective rates of substitution, the slopes of the indifference curves at relevant points, and the objective rates — the slopes of the two alternative budget lines. The more moderate slope of the commune member's budget line implies tangency at a lower rate of substitution of income for leisure. Hence, given 'regular' (say, Cobb–Douglas) utility functions, this would be to the right of L^m on the Ly_0^i budget line, at a lower labour input than that of his non-commune twin.

Inspection of (4*) shows, however, that this result does not follow explicitly from the Israelsen formulation. The relevance of the income–leisure rate of substitution does not appear at all, though it is implied by some statements in the supporting text. The advantage of the more comprehensive Putterman model lies in its explicit integration of utility and production dimensions, thereby allowing more insights on the labour incentive dilemma.

The Putterman formulation of the equilibrium conditions of the individual is spelled out in (6) below:[10]

(6) $\quad -\dfrac{U_h^i}{U_y^i} = \dfrac{1}{N} F'(H)$

Accordingly, in equilibrium, the marginal rate of substitution of income for leisure (the subjective cost of a unit of leisure in terms of income) of the member of a collective is equal to the marginal product of labour multiplied by a coefficient which is the reciprocal of the number of members.[11] The equivalent equilibrium condition for an individual in a competitive market inevitably involves a higher rate of substitution of income for leisure, since the right-hand side of the equilibrium condition would be N times greater.

The main virtue of the Putterman formulation is its focus on what he labelled 'the behavioural interdependence' of commune members. Its significance can be shown by following the implications of the Israelsen assumption to their logical conclusion. The assumption in (5) above, spliced with the commune income distribution rule, implies that if the ith member reduces his labour input, his income would fall only by a fraction, N, of the corresponding reduction in the (product) income of the community. This means that were one commune member to offer no labour at all (assuming his fellows keep on working), his income would still be a positive amount.

This shows up in Figure 9.3 as point d on the Ldy_1^i budget line. The distance dL measures the level of income which an individual commune member would enjoy even if he does not contribute any labour at all. Note that the slope of the Ldy_1^i budget line is identical to that of the Ly_0^i budget line, which reflects the marginal income per unit of forgone leisure of a commune member. In other words, it reflects the same marginal condition spelled out on the right-hand side of (4*) and of (6). The difference between these two budget lines is in their location in the plane, reflecting a 'consistent' application of (5), the implied Israelsen condition, at its very limit — zero input of labour.

The equilibrium condition of the commune member in (6) is described in Figure 9.3 as the tangency of an indifference curve, say, Z_2, to the budget line dy_1^i at b. The optimal basket of the commune member involves a labour input of $L - L_1^k$ and a somewhat higher income than the one he could have enjoyed if his labour input had been zero. The significance of this choice is revealed in Figure 9.3 by comparison with the optimal basket of an individual with the preference system of an identical twin in the (competitive) labour market, whose reward is equal to $F'(H)$, the marginal product of labour, and whose budget line is therefore I_0L. The identity of tastes implies that the same indifference curve, Z_2, represents the level of preference of both individuals. The tangency of Z_2 with the I_0L budget line is at a, while the tangency with the budget line of the commune member is lower: b. This offers dramatic proof of the claim that the muzzling of incentives (due to the lower rewards to commune members) lowers labour input, effort, product and income.

But this reflects only the substitution effect due to the lower 'cost' of leisure to the commune member. The income effect due to the equal income distribution rule, which reduces the marginal income of a commune member to the Nth fraction of his identical twin, works in the opposite direction. This can be shown by referring to Figure 9.3. Suppose a worker starts out in the non-commune environment, with an equilibrium basket at a; suppose now that he joins a commune, which of course means that his reward is reduced to 1/N of its former level. His relevant budget line would be the 'Israelsen' budget line, Ly_0^i, and his equilibrium income–leisure basket would drop to c on the Z_i indifference curve. This move from a to c is the familiar sum of substitution and income effects. The move from a to b is the substitution effect due to the lowering of the price of leisure, and the move from b to c (assuming leisure is a normal good) is the positive income effect which, owing to the reduction in income, works in the opposite direction. The substitution effect reduces the amount of labour offered when moving from a market environment to a commune, while the income effect reduces the quantity of leisure demanded, i.e. increases the amount of labour offered.

If the 'equal income' rule applies — that is, if by joining a commune the worker can enjoy an income of dL even if his labour input is zero — the $Ly_1^i d$ budget line and not the lower $y_1^i L$ line is the relevant one. Therefore the equilibrium basket would be at b and not at c, and hence the equal income distribution rule can be visualised as *negating* the income effect of lower income on the supply of labour. This rule involves not only a reduction in labour supply from $(L - L^m)$, supplied by the 'individual market twin', to $(L - L_2^k)$ it actually leads to an even smaller quantity of labour supplied by the commune member $(L - L_1^k)$ and to a correspondingly lower production level.

All this assumes, of course, that other commune members do not react to the leisure-*cum*-income choice of each individual member. Being 'rational', any collective member could be expected to choose his optimal basket along the $Ly_1^i d$ budget line. If too many members chose the low-income maximum-leisure (hence almost zero labour) basket (d in Figure 9.3), the collective could not survive even in the short run. Even if the preferences of commune members placed them at, say, point b, the low material income feature of communes compared with the alternatives open to 'identical market twins' would eventually lead to their demise.

This seems to clinch the argument that by muzzling incentives the commune environment discourages effort and production. *Quod erat demonstrandum.*

b. Inefficiency in factor allocation. The last argument in the case against the economic rationale of the kibbutz relates to the efficiency of factor allocation. Optimal use of resources in the Paretian sense requires a combination of factors and outputs in which rates of transformation between products at the margin are equal to their (relative) prices. Like many socialist thinkers, Von Mises interpreted the abolition of the 'wage system' to mean the disappearance of wages as an economic category, denying the feasibility of rational economic calculation in the socialist commonwealth. The socialist planning debate initiated by Barone (who anticipated Von Mises in formulating the problem) had settled this issue by the mid-1930s. Taylor, Dickinson, Lange and Lerner had the better of the argument with Von Hayek and Robbins by showing that scarcity prices can be consistently imputed to intermediate products and to primary factors. These scarcity prices would then simultaneously serve to identify optimal factor allocations and product composition in a socialised sector.

The Barone–Lange proof, however, does not apply directly to the kibbutz, since it assumes a wage nexus between the socialist firm and its workers. This is, of course, inconsistent with the kibbutz rules of the game, which completely sever the connection between an individual's contribution to production and his reward. Under these circumstances the claim that the kibbutz production sector does not allocate factors rationally, and hence that its choice of output combination might not be optimal, has apparent plausibility.[12]

KIBBUTZ PERFORMANCE

Muzzling work incentives, blunting the propensity to save, inefficiency in production and in the use of consumption expenditures, which combined to make up the inherent malaise of communes, bode ill for this kind of social organisation. Nor does historical experience provide much comfort. Yet the Israeli kibbutz movement, which had a population of about 120,000 in 1984 in 275 settlements, is now in the eighth decade of its sometimes turbulent history. A survey of the relevant data may therefore serve to test the various dimensions of the case against the commune, set out above.

An attempt to summarise some of the quantitative evidence is made in Tables 9.1 and 9.2. Consider first the data on population. The indexes (column (1)) and the ratios (column (2)) underline the nature of this social group — kibbutz membership is (and has always been) a minority phenomenon. Average annual growth rates of about 2 per cent since 1951 are undoubtedly comparatively high in an industrial society such as Israel's. Furthermore, although the ratio of kibbutz members to total Jewish population has fallen from its all time high in 1945 (6.7 per cent), kibbutzim have held their own, even in ratio terms, in the past quarter of a century. They may even have gained in ratio terms, if the social milieu to which they belong, which is far smaller than the Jewish community as a whole, is defined differently.

Finally, recent data on internal migration, first published in Israel in 1985, show that in 1980–85 kibbutzim had an annual net positive migration balance of close to one per cent. In the same period other rural settlements had a net loss of population.[13] This means that kibbutzim are not only able to hold their own demographically — namely, to grow by their full rate of natural increase — they can even withstand the prevailing trend towards urbanisation.

This demographic pattern can be attributed partly to the comparatively high living standards in kibbutzim. Israel's rapidly rising level of per capita income (about 5 per cent per annum in the 30 years ending in 1973) was more than matched by kibbutzim. The substantial slowdown in this increase since 1973 affected kibbutzim too, but no more — nor presumably less — than the effect on the country as a whole. Estimates for the 1960s put the mean per capita disposable income of kibbutzim in the 6th decile of Israel's income

Table 9.1 Selected indicators for kibbutz performance (AGR = agriculture; MFG = manufacturing)

	Population Index 1951 = 100 (1)	Ratio[a] (%) (2)	Labour: marginal product (1958 IL per manyear) AGR[b] (3)	MFG[c] (4)	Capital: % real rate of return AGR[c] (5)	MFG[c] (6)	Total factor productivity (1958 = 100) AGR (7)	MFG (8)
1931	7	2.5						
1945	41	6.7						
1951	100	4.9						
1954			3,016	6,318[e]				
1958	129	4.7	5,305	6,422	6.6	—	76.3	82.2[e]
1965	133	3.8	11,128	14,013	10.8	26.6	100.0	100.0
1971	154	3.8			10.9	19.6	134.9	162.0
1975	164	3.6			(4.2)[d]			
1983	185	3.6			(5.7)[d]			

a. Ratio of kibbutz to Jewish population.
b. The marginal product figures for agriculture were derived from a single-equation production-function model specified by the Cobb-Douglas equation $Y = AL^a K^b V^c$, where Y is gross product, L is labour input, K is agricultural gross capital stock, V is land, and A is a constant. The estimate is based on cross-section data for about 200 kibbutzim.
   The coefficients of determination for the regressions are within a range of 0.72–0.82; all the coefficients for labour and capital are significant at the 5 per cent level, most of them at 1 per cent.
c. The marginal product figures for manufacturing were derived from a single-equation production function model, $Y = AL^a K^b$, where Y is gross product, L is labour input, and K is gross capital stock in manufacturing (excluding workshops; see note a to Table 9.2). The number of observations is substantially smaller than in agriculture. The estimate is based on data for all manufacturing establishments in kibbutzim: just over 50 in the mid-1950s and about 100 by the mid-1960s; this is adequate for purposes of conventional regression analysis.
   The coefficients of determination are about 0.60, all the labour coefficients are significant at the 1 per cent level, and almost all the capital stock coefficients are significant at 5 per cent.
d. Sadan-Shaskin estimate: Applies to a subset of the movement — 47 settlements established in 1936 or earlier. The figure for 1971 applies to 1970.

Table 9.1 contd.

The whole series of real rates of return estimated by Sadan and Shaskin for this group is as follows (per cent):

1936	1940	1950	1955	1960	1965	1970	1975
6.5	4.8	7.6	5.8	6.6	6.6	4.2	5.7

e. Refers to 1956.

Source: Barkai (1977), as follows: p. 198, Table 10.6, for column (4); p. 203, Table 10.7, for columns (1)–(3); p. 214, Table 11.1, for column (7); and p. 219, Table 11.3, for columns (5)–(6). The data presented here refer only to one of a set of alternative models used to estimate kibbutz production functions. For details of the others see Barkai (1974) and Barkai (1979). For a discussion of the simultaneity issue and the use of the single-equation technique in the kibbutz context see Barkai and Levhari (1973). Barkai (1974), pp. 3–6, and Barkai (1979). Figures for rates of return on capital in agriculture for 1971 and 1975 and the whole series presented in footnote d is from Sadan and Shaskin (1980), Table 5, p. 169.

distribution.[14] But it is not only the reality presented by the data that counts in this context; the public image of 'rich' kibbutzim is common knowledge that featured prominently in the election campaigns of the 1970s and 1980s.

The entries in Table 9.1, derived from a larger series and a more comprehensive body of data, reveal that both the high growth rates and the levels of living standards reflect performance in production. The total factor productivity indexes (whose weights were derived from production function analysis) display rapid growth of the *residual*, largely due to innovation and rapid technological change. The available factor productivity figures give the annual rates of increase in the overall efficiency of kibbutz farming and manufacturing in the 1950s and 1960s. Although comparable figures for the 1970s are unavailable, it is unlikely that the high rates of the 1950s and 1960s were matched in the latter decades; however, the partial data available do not suggest that growth slowed down to almost zero.

What contributed to the vigour of kibbutz performance was obviously the rapid increase in marginal (!) labour productivity in farming and manufacturing. This was coterminous with reasonable real rates of return to capital in farming and with very high rates in manufacturing. The labour productivity figures in Table 9.1 (taken from a longer series) indicate that marginal labour productivity in kibbutz farming grew by a factor of 3.5 from 1954 until the mid-1960s, while rates of return were stable (and at any rate were not falling). This, of course, refutes a facile explanation of this performance in terms of excessively high capital and land intensities. Note further that the marginal product of labour in kibbutz farming exceeded the highest rate paid to Israeli farm workers by 20–30 per cent in the 1950s and by 60 per cent in the 1960s. Comparative data for the 1970s and 1980s are unavailable, but rough estimates suggest that the gap could not have been much smaller in these decades.

Labour productivity in kibbutz farming thus compares quite favourably with the non-kibbutz environment, and this applies to manufacturing too, where marginal labour productivity more than doubled, according to our production function estimates, from the mid-1950s to the mid-1960s. Comparable figures for Israeli manufacturing as a whole show that the value of marginal productivity of kibbutz labour was 1.5 times the average wage in Israeli manufacturing in the mid-1950s, rising to about three times this (by then much higher) wage in the 1960s. Indirect indicators for the 1970s and 1980s do not suggest a very substantial closing of the productivity gap in manufacturing.

This impressive performance is matched by comparative efficiency in kibbutz utilisation of capital. Our estimates for the 1950s through the mid-1960s, supported by the Sadan series (which extend the direct information on capital productivity in kibbutz farming to the mid-1970s; see Sadan and Shaskin, 1980), indicate that real rates of return in farming were not lower than, say, 4.5 per cent.[15] At these rates kibbutzim could easily borrow in the financial markets, suggesting that the use of capital in this line of production was hardly 'inefficient' by conventional market criteria. Until 1975 Israel could borrow abroad at these (or even lower) real rates. This means that until that year kibbutz utilisation of capital was fully consistent with the real cost of capital to the economy.

The rates of return to capital in kibbutz manufacturing, which were higher than those in agriculture (Table 9.1), lead to the selfsame conclusion: capital utilisation in this line of activity was not inefficient by conventional market criteria. Though the capital–labour ratio in kibbutz manufacturing was comparatively high and rising through the 1980s, real capital input did not exceed the limits warranted by its cost to the community and to the country as a whole.[16]

The gap between factor productivities in kibbutz farming and manufacturing begs the question. The higher marginal productivities of labour and higher rates of return to capital in manufacturing suggest inefficiency in factor allocation and output composition, which may, of course, be warranted in a static context. In a dynamic context, however, the existence of gaps between rates of return and/or marginal productivities of labour in different lines, at a given point in time, does suggest that an optimal allocation of factors requires reallocation. In this case, the productivity figures presented in Table 9.1 do suggest the profitability of reallocation from farming to manufacturing.

The figures in Table 9.2 suggest that this was indeed the consistent policy of kibbutzim from the late 1950s through the early 1980s. The data on ratios of factor inputs, investment (some of which are available through 1983), and gross product reveal the industrialisation policy endorsed and supported by the central organs of the kibbutz movement and consistently pursued by almost all the settlements. These figures show that kibbutzim responded vigorously to the pull of market forces, undergoing an industrial revolution which, within an interval of one generation, transformed them from predominantly mixed farming enterprises into industrial farming entities.[17]

Table 9.2 Factor input, investment, and gross product — ratios of manufacturing[a] to agriculture (per cent)

	Employment (1)	Capital stock (2)	Gross investment (3)	Gross product (4)
1954			5.7	
1956	13.8	6.2		7.3
1957	13.5	5.8		7.3
1958	15.2	6.3	11.2	8.8
1959	15.9	6.1		7.5
1960	18.6	6.9		9.6
1961	21.8	7.3		11.5
1962	22.6	7.9		15.4
1963	24.0	7.9		17.7
1964	30.6	9.5		18.1
1965	33.1	12.1	28.5	22.9
1970	54.0		95.4	(30.4)[b]
1972	65.3		111	
1973	66.4		120	(39.4)[b]
1980	81.7		128	
1983	89.0		(142)	

a. Since separate investment series for manufacturing proper are not available before 1965, the gross investment ratios are applied to the manufacturing and the workshop sector, and therefore understate the relative decline of agriculture in terms of capital formation and as the dominant industrial branch in the kibbutz. For the period after 1965 the manufacturing investment data are adequate and have been spliced to the manufacturing and workshop series on 1965: i.e. the ratios for 1970–73 represent the pattern of gross investment in manufacturing proper.
b. Extrapolated from 1965 on the basis of output data.
Source: Barkai (1977) as follows: p. 114, Table 6.2, for column (3); p. 190, Table 10.1, for column (1); p. 191, Table 10.2, for column (2); p. 192, Table 10.3, for column (4). The post-1965 data in columns (1), (3) and (4) are from Kibbutz Industries Association, *Reports* (various issues through September 1984; in Hebrew).

THEORY AND REALITY — A CONFRONTATION?

How can the success of the kibbutz as an economic entity be reconciled with the predictions of standard microeconomic theory? Specifically, does the case against 'collectives' — allocative inefficiency, stifling the propensity to save, and muzzling incentives — really hold when it comes to the case of kibbutzim, or do the unique historical context and the specific social milieu render these theoretical considerations inapplicable to kibbutzim?

Efficiency in factor allocation

The elimination of wages, which serve as the price parameter for labour services in private (and nationalised) firms, is said to make efficient factor allocation impossible at the firm level. This argument rests on the fallacy that eliminating wages as income payment also means that a relevant wage rate cannot serve as a price signal. This is obviously not so: a 'shadow' wage, properly calculated, can serve as the required price signal. The issue therefore boils down to the problem of estimating an 'equilibrium' shadow wage.

At the theoretical plane, this is similar to calculating efficient shadow prices for the fixed factors of competitive firms. In the case of the kibbutz this can be done in the short run by substituting a *quantity* constraint on the size of labour instead of a wage parameter within a general equilibrium framework involving production functions, product prices, and non-labour factor prices. For the long run, a supply curve of labour as a function of, say, comparative per capita income and demographic factors can be substituted for the quantity constraint.[18] Such a model yields efficient equilibrium solutions for factor combinations and product choices in the Paretian sense, for the kibbutz as a production entity. Non-price rules are then used to allocate the income generated between consumption and saving, and to distribute the share allocated to consumption among members.

This is not merely an academic exercise. Kibbutzim have always attempted to identify the most efficient production configuration in this manner. At first they used rule-of-thumb techniques to identify the proper pricing of their labour, while for product and non-labour input prices they had (and have) exogenous information (as do private firms). Later they adopted more sophisticated techniques such as linear programming to seek optimal solutions.[19]

The non-hiring tenet does create a theoretical problem, which has a significant empirical counterpart. If the kibbutz shadow wage is lower than the comparable market rate, efficiency considerations would require the kibbutz to hire out its labour force, a fairly common practice, fully consistent with kibbutz tenets and with the equilibrium criteria of both the kibbutz as a microeconomic entity and the system as a whole. But if the kibbutz shadow wage exceeds the market wage, as is often the case,[20] conventional market considerations require hiring non-kibbutz labour, which is a breach of kibbutz tenets. Although many kibbutzim do hire labour at market rates, they deliberately never satisfy their labour shortage (at the given level of shadow wages) by hiring.

The labour shortage caused by adhering to the 'non-hiring' rule need not be inconsistent with Paretian efficiency from the viewpoint of the kibbutz. Obviously, individuals and groups may have utility functions in which hired labour is a disutility, to be avoided even at a cost. By refraining from hiring labour at a market rate lower than the shadow wage, kibbutzim forgo the producer rent that would have increased their per capita income. This forgone income is a quantitative expression of the disutility of employing hired labour. The case of a corner solution — the kibbutz never hires any labour — might be interpreted as a case in which the marginal benefit from the forgone income is lower than the marginal disutility of hiring. This is, of course, fully consistent with the condition for the efficient use of resources from the kibbutz point of view. Charging the kibbutz with inefficiency on these grounds is therefore quite unfounded, though still applicable to the economy as a whole.

Under these circumstances (a positive gap between kibbutz shadow wages and market rates) efficiency considerations suggest higher capital intensities in kibbutz production than in similar sectors in the economy as a whole. This is indeed a well-known feature of kibbutz farming, manufacturing, and service sectors. Kibbutzim are constantly substituting more capital for labour in given production lines, and have been phasing out labour-intensive branches and activities (vegetable and fruit-growing are points in case).

The Israelsen muzzling-of-incentives argument

The merit of Israelsen's argument, a by-product of a model of the Russian *kolkhoz*, is in its pinpointing the crucial assumption on which the 'feeble motivation' argument depends, and thus affording a clear-cut test of its relevance in any specific context.

According to the Israelsen formulation (see equation (4*) above), the marginal income of a commune member is only $1/N$ of 'his' marginal product. An identical market twin who earns his full marginal product, has an incentive to exert a given effort that is N times larger. Hence, the erosion of the incentive to perform is a (proportionally) rising function of the size of the commune.

The Israelsen result, however, depends crucially on the hypothesis spelled out in equation (5) above, namely, that a given change in the quantity of labour offered by a commune member is *identical* to the change in the labour input of the commune as a whole. But as Putterman pointed out, this implies a crucial hypothesis on the nature of the reaction of other members of a commune to a given change in the labour input of the ith member. If (5) holds, it actually implies

(7) $\quad \dfrac{dh^j}{dh^i} = 0$

no response by other members of a collective entity to a change in the size of labour (effort) offered by any given member. This 'zero response' hypothesis is a formal expression of what we may call the case of the *reluctant* commune member. It is equivalent, as Putterman points out, to the 'non-reaction' assumption applied by Cournot in his classical duopoly model. Alternative duopoly models, which assume different types of reaction, have also surfaced in the past century. In modern duopoly theory, the 'no reaction' assumption is only one of many options. Similarly, the Israelsen 'zero-response' hypothesis, too, is only one of a set of feasible reactions, though it is probably a fair approximation of the practice in the Russian *kolkhoz* and in similar entities forced upon reluctant peasants in other 'socialist' countries.

The zero-response hypothesis is, however, almost diametrically opposed to the very nature of the kibbutz as such. Both the explicit and implicit rules of the game actually call for a 'unity response' hypothesis, namely:

(7*) $\quad \dfrac{dh^j}{dh^i} = 1$

— a kibbutz member expects that other members will emulate his change in labour input. Thus, differentiating equation (1) and substituting (7*) into the expression we have:

(8) $\quad \dfrac{dH}{dh^i} = 1 + (N-1)\dfrac{dh^j}{dh^i} = N$[21].

The substitution of (8) into (4) yields what may be labelled the Kibbutz Theorem or the relation between effort and reward:

(4**) $\quad \dfrac{dy^i}{dh^i} = F'(H)$

— the marginal income of a kibbutz member, *given the behavioural framework of the community*, is equal to his marginal product — exactly as in the case of the identical market twin. The Israelsen theorem, which imputes an inevitable erosion of the material incentives of commune members, thus falls to the ground.[22]

The behavioural framework of the community

This line of reasoning depends on the relevance of the proviso — *the behavioural framework of the community*. This framework, which emerged in the early 1920s, after a period of soul-searching and groping — when its very survival was at stake, involved the adoption of a strict labour code whereby 'kibbutz manpower is at the disposal of the community'. In everyday practice this means that the allocation of a member's time between work and leisure is determined by the community. It is hence the unity response (7*) that *should* call the tune with respect to the labour–leisure option and not the zero-response (7). If indeed kibbutzim did practise what they preach, the dread 'muzzling of labour incentive' syndrome formally expressed in (4*) could not rear its ugly head.

Do theory and practice really square? And if so, what mechanism makes practice a good approximation of kibbutz theory on labour? One way to bring these questions into focus is to suggest, as Putterman did, that other values, between zero and unity response, are quite feasible.[23]

The work *norm*, which is the operational rule in the kibbutz, is indeed a simple control device designed to push the system towards the expected 'unity' response. But not only prescribed *quantity* counts in this context. Even in the private sector, where incentives have a clear-cut quantitative definition, it is obvious that punching a clock does not necessarily mean that workers pull their full weight. Ensuring that kibbutz members put in 'an honest day's work' — their 'attitude to work' in kibbutz parlance — is a major problem in the kibbutz.

The issue here is one of work ethics and motivation. A clearer perception of the significance of this notion in our context can be gained by relating performance and motivation in formal terms. Performance could be specified as a product of two variables, say,

$$(9) \quad \begin{bmatrix} \text{Level of} \\ \text{performance} \end{bmatrix} = \begin{bmatrix} \text{Degree of} \\ \text{motivation} \end{bmatrix} \times \begin{bmatrix} \text{Level of personal} \\ \text{capacity} \end{bmatrix}.$$

The degree of motivation can be defined as a pure number between zero and unity. Personal capacity can be defined in value terms by applying the human capital approach, which approximates the cost of this variable.[24]

The product form of this expression was devised to suggest that when motivation is low so is performance, whatever the level of personal capacity. If motivation were merely a response to material incentives, it would have been relatively easy to devise a technique to measure the degree of motivation. Since this is not so, motivation might be considered a hybrid involving both pecuniary and non-pecuniary components.[25]

The message of the Israelsen formulation, when specified exclusively in terms of material incentives, as in (4*), is that the motivation of kibbutz members is closer to the lower limit. Our analysis suggests that the operating rule of the kibbutz — the labour *norm* — cancels 'the Israelsen effect', to a substantial extent.[26] The labour norm, however, provides only the *necessary* condition for the expected 'proper' reaction of other members to an individual member's extra effort. It is not a necessary and *sufficient* condition to ensure the high degree of motivation required to push the index close to unity.

Kibbutzim attempt to satisfy the sufficient condition for high motivation through informal social control and the practice of voluntary membership. Social control relies on community respect and approval — often intangible — for a good day's work; social opprobrium has a very powerful effect on behaviour, as anyone who has spent some time in a kibbutz rapidly learns from personal experience. Voluntary membership means that whereas membership in the commune is subject to majority consent, any member who cannot adjust to the formal rules and informal control mechanisms of the kibbutz is free to leave.

An outstanding description of these informal control devices, never formally codified, but that nonetheless somehow 'emerged', recently appeared in A. Lieblich's book, *Kibbutz Makom*, based on a series of interviews with kibbutz members by a Gestalt psychologist. Towards the end of a long interview with one of the kibbutz veterans who, at the age of 70, was at that time the commune's cost accountant, he strikingly underlines the relevance of the informal controls and their inherent linkage with the principle of voluntary membership:

> I repeatedly asked myself . . how can we live without any formal law enforcement? My conclusion is that in the kibbutz the disciplinary tool is the atmosphere which is created by the total community. If a person cheats me once or twice, I don't care. But I wait until it becomes known and then the social atmosphere will take care of the matter, and the individual will either have to change his behaviour or leave.[27]

The strength of these informal controls has been found to depend considerably on the size of the community; thus, N is indeed a relevant variable in the context of the incentive-efficiency conundrum. Note, however, that in the early years of the movement a population of, say, 100 was considered the upper limit in which social control could be effective. Yet in 1978–79, when these interviews were held, the population of Kibbutz Makom had long since passed the 1000 mark and still the veteran member concludes his story of the settlement's economic success with the observation: 'I don't think that our economic intuition is our secret charm; it's our social spirit which preserved us.'[28] This suggests that the impact of public opinion on behaviour, and specifically on the 'work ethic', is reinforced by specific characteristics of the self-selected population of kibbutz members, one of whose unique features is the nature of its response to non-pecuniary stimuli.

Reference to the age-old Smithian hypothesis concerning effort may clarify this point. Economic effort of most, though not *all* people does indeed depend to a very large extent on material incentives. This need not preclude the possible existence of a small group of people who are willing to function at full stretch as operatives, managers or entrepreneurs without any direct *differential* pecuniary reward.

If such a group were to form a collective, there is no reason why their motivation index (equation (9)) should not be close to unity, even though income is equally distributed and nobody receives a productivity-related reward. They might join a collective in the belief that material benefits are of minor importance, and if they realise that it still makes a difference to them, the error made by joining can be corrected by leaving, assuming voluntary membership.

The same rationale applies to members born in kibbutzim who for some reason choose to leave. It is *voluntarism* that makes the difference, building up populations with a built-in bias with respect to one or more specific relevant characteristics — response to non-pecuniary stimuli and the sensitive issue of work discipline. The latter involves the authority of the community not only to set the work norm but also to determine the specific occupations and functions of individual members.[29]

The work 'norm' and work discipline, informal social control over quality of performance, and a mechanism of self-selection can explain the high degree of motivation pushing kibbutz members to the frontier of feasible performance. What may have led critics astray on the matter of incentives was probably the false attribution of behavioural norms, which by and large may indeed apply to large 'normal' populations, to this self-selected group with a different preference scale, in which everyone may elect to move to greener pastures.

This is not to say that past successes scored by kibbutzim can be projected into the future. The growth in the absolute size of the movement involved some erosion in the quality of kibbutz manpower. The 'coming of age' of Zionism, expressed in the establishment of Israel, and the world-wide crisis of socialism inevitably muted some of the movement's ideological ardour, leading to some relaxation of self discipline. The growing number of kibbutz members who were born into the system, whose revealed preference for staying is substantially affected by the psychic and economic cost of leaving, may have a similar effect. Many of them may be more passively committed to the kibbutz ideal than those who deliberately chose this way of life by abandoning the non-kibbutz environment. All this might prevent the system from approaching as close to the 'unity response' and unity of 'motivation' as it did in the past, carrying in its wake lower standards of performance.

The work norm quandry

The work norm gives rise to another variant of the kibbutz 'inefficiency' argument. The significance of the argument that the imposition of a standard work norm violates efficiency criteria can be clarified by reverting to Figure 9.1. This time, however, the horizontal and vertical axes measure leisure and current income, respectively. Given a wage rate that reflects marginal labour productivity in the kibbutz production sector, we draw a budget line I_1I_1 whose slope reflects the relevant shadow wage.[30] Given freedom of choice and diverse tastes, represented by the two intersecting indifference curves drawn from M_1's and M_2's maps, the optimal income–leisure baskets are A_1 and B_1, respectively.

'Income' — defined to exclude the value of both leisure and the fraction that the community earmarks for saving — is equally distributed, and the work norm implies equal allocation of leisure. Equality considerations thus force the community to set a income–leisure basket of, say, C_1, corresponding to the equal I' 'income' and L' 'leisure' endowments of each member. The resultant length of the working day $(I_1 - L')$ thus calls for less labour input than member M_1 was willing to offer, for a higher endowment than I'. Setting the work norm at C thus forces him onto a lower level on his scale of preferences. At the same time the C_1 basket means that the work norm requires member M_2 to offer more labour units than he would have preferred if he were free to choose. Thus pushes him, too, onto a lower ladder on his preference scale.

Granting that the quantitative work norm does violate Paretian optimality, it does not differ much from the rules of the game in industrial society at large: the 45-hour week is an accepted norm in many lines of activity, and workplace conventions often involve overtime which employees might prefer to forgo. The kibbutz work norm thus does not interfere with the efficient allocation of time much more than do similar accepted conventions in non-kibbutz environments.

On the other hand, by severing the direct link between an individual's contribution to production and his real income, the principle of *equality* provides an important mechanism for productivity in the dynamic sense. It is well known that the introduction of new technologies must usually overcome the objections and resistance of the workforce due to the economic and psychic costs of changing an existing set-up — moving to other lines of activity, learning new work processes, etc. The psychic cost of changing activities is also a well-known feature in the kibbutz environment, but in terms of real income the cost of switching activities to the individual kibbutz member is *zero*. Closing down one line of production and diverting manpower to another is therefore that much easier than in the non-kibbutz environment.

Feasible productivity gains of this feature (the much greater interbranch mobility of the labour force) may be enormous. The 'industrial revolution' of the kibbutz, which in the past generation was one of the most important factors contributing to its economic success, is a case in point. The rapid transformation of occupations and composition of employment proceeded relatively smoothly. The absence of economic friction undoubtedly contributed to success.

The consumption-saving option

It is impossible to deny the relevance of the argument that 'quota' and 'free good' distribution techniques lead to suboptimal allocation of consumption expenditures. This is of particular importance in the dynamic context. Rising per capita income increases the distortions due to the application of quota and 'free good' techniques of distribution. Inspection of Figure 9.1, comparing the C_0 and C_1 ratios for corresponding I_0 and I_1 income endowments along the same expansion path, underlines the nature of the problem. On the other hand, one may note the continuous rise in the share of the 'cash endowment' allocated to members, and the fact that most of the items of the 'free good' list are what one nowadays might describe as welfare state items — education and health care are the most important amongst them. In this respect kibbutzim are now little different from the system in general.

The consumption-saving option may still be the Achilles heel of long-term kibbutz viability. The majority vote, which determines the level of saving in kibbutz settlements, might be strongly influenced, as are electorates in all democratic countries, by the craving for the good life here and now. Indeed, kibbutz leaders keep complaining about the present-day bias for the present.[31]

Yet the data on saving, available through 1975, do not indicate that kibbutzim are spendthrifts. On the contrary, kibbutzim, once past their infancy (say, past their first decade), have high saving rates. The averate rate for the movement as a whole was over 25 per cent in the 1960s — much higher than the ratio for Israel, twice as high as the ratio of employees, and about 50 per cent higher than the ratio of the self-employed. Furthermore, by one estimate the net saving/investment ratio in the 1960s was 63 per cent, while the gross saving/investment ratio reached 75 per cent. These figures are supported by the Sadan/Shaskin findings for the 1970s, though these apply to the older group of settlements. Some indicators suggest that in the first half of the 1980s saving ratios were much lower, and in some settlements (even mature ones) have recently been very low indeed, an economy-wide phenomenon.

How do these findings square with the image of low savings ratios when in the throes of a political process? One possible explanation could be the fact that kibbutzim are essentially composed of self-employed persons. It is well known that the self-employed, who plough back their savings into their own businesses, have higher saving ratios than wage-earners. Yet we note that kibbutzim performed even better on this score than their private sector counterparts.

The most likely explanation rests once again on the specific characteristics of these self-selected communities. The available data indicate that the value of their stock of human capital is much higher than average, and it is well known that the perception of the relevance of the future rises sharply with education and enterprise.

This could also explain an interesting and characteristic feature of kibbutz consumption and saving functions. Several estimates have shown a rather weak association between income and consumption. Thus, the rapid rise in production and income through about 1974 was indeed followed by a substantial (but slower) rise in consumption expenditures. Rapid growth through this period thus involved a rapid rise in savings and in saving rates.[32] The nation-wide deceleration of growth since 1973–74 affected the kibbutzim, too, but in this case the rather loose link between consumption and income worked in the reverse direction. Very slow income growth therefore left less room for saving, thus the lower saving rates featuring of the 1980s. The three-digit inflation of the late 1970s and early 1980s is another (short-run) factor which helps to explain the recent low rates.

The *non-failure* of kibbutzim on this score, too, does not disprove the hypothetical impact of politics on the overall propensity to save. This hypothesis, which might hold true for a democratic electorate as a whole, need not apply to a sample of this electorate distinguished by its bias favouring saving. Such a group is considerably more open to persuasion that substantial saving ratios are a necessary for *long-term* increases in income and consumption.

THE MESSAGE (IF ANY) ON INCENTIVES AND EFFICIENCY

Equity is a major consideration in running democratic economic systems. Since the economic significance of the term implies the distribution of (some) income without reference to involvement and contribution to production, considerations pertaining to equity have a direct bearing on incentives. In more than one sense, one might describe the ongoing debate and political struggle over economic policy in democratic countries as a running engagement between policies designed to bolster incentives and those striving for equity. The successful economic performance of the kibbutz, while maintaining the most equitable income distribution conceivable, would *prima facie* suggest a technique of reconciling the two imperatives of the last quarter of the twentieth century — production and 'social justice'.

The equal income distribution rule is indeed applied within each kibbutz. However, since every kibbutz is an independent economic entity, the equality rule does not apply in inter-kibbutz relations. Substantial differences in real per capita income between kibbutzim have already emerged.[33] The movement does employ redistributive devices (mostly in the form of aid to young settlements) that reduce short-run differentials and are mainly designed to reduce differentials in the long run (learning-by-doing training and coaching by experienced members of older settlements are the main form of this inter-kibbutz aid). This means that the kibbutz experiment bears no tidings on the reconciliation of the incentive–equity quandary at the macroeconomic plane.

Things might look different at the microeconomic level. Efficiency and incentives in public sector firms are an obvious case in point, and the very size of this sector, even in non-centrally planned systems, make incentives a major issue. The vicious circle of low incentives, low production, low income on the farm in centrally planned countries, undoubtedly due to inappropriate incentive mechanisms at the grassroots level, is another area in which kibbutz experience could offer a contribution. This might also apply to attempts to build up cooperative producer entities in the rural areas of developing countries.

Kibbutz experience in promoting effort and efficiency suggests that it is hardly relevant to the running of a public sector firm. The *modus operandi* of such a firm is based on the wage nexus: *pay and differentials* are the relevant stimuli. The 'public opinion' device used by kibbutzim to promote effort is not a feasible mechanism in the public sector environment. The effectiveness of public opinion in the kibbutz is due to several conditions: an ownership attitude towards the entity, which involves the perception of the linkage between production and income, and the understanding that the 'firm' has to face competition; in addition, personal contact, which means living in a tightly-knit community where people are in close touch not only as operators in production but in all other spheres of life, is almost a *sine qua non* for public opinion to have a significant effect. These conditions do not prevail in public enterprises — large entities only remotely subject to market push-and-pull discipline in which 'ownership' identification is practically non-existent. (Postwar experience proves this point: the attitude of workers and their representatives did not change after their firms were nationalised.)

The shadow-pricing device gave kibbutzim an appropriate planning tool, enabling them to overcome the absence of information on labour costs available to every firm. Yet the efficient running of this complex set-up requires an elaborate system of information, the capacity to analyse its significance, and the ability to make on-the-spot decisions. All this presumes a highly articulate, well-educated pool of manpower, which includes a high ratio (say, 50 per cent or more) of people capable of running the show, in managerial and entrepreneurial roles. These conditions do not obtain in the farming sector of developing countries, where the need to maintain even a most rudimentary form of accounting can usually not be satisfied. In centrally planned systems it is presumably no problem to set up a properly informed and run accounting system. The 'command economy' feature, which grants very little authority to the grassroots production entity is evidently the main source of trouble. The *kolkhoz* management has very little authority in operational decisions on the mix of inputs and the composition of output. Indeed, where devolution of authority in these matters was introduced, as in Hungary, farm productivity improved rapidly. This, of course, suggests that an important factor in the success of Israeli kibbutzim was the pushing and prodding of markets, and the discipline imposed by the product and (non-labour) factors markets to which they were subject from the very beginning.

Kibbutzim overcame the incentive dilemma by means of 'informal social control' over the work ethic and thanks to the specific (biased) nature of its composition, which is undergoing a continuous process of self-selection. In such a milieu members could expect their extra effort to be emulated by other members of the community. The behavioural feature (which rests on the understanding that the viability of the community depends on abiding by accepted norms), the power of public opinion, and self-selectivity — all require people with considerable powers of abstraction who are strongly motivated by ideology.

These conditions are hard to find in developing countries, nor, I believe, amongst the farming population in centrally planned systems. In the latter, though, what accounts most for the flagging of effort is undoubtedly the 'Israelsen effect' — the muzzling of incentives due to the relevance (in this social environment) of the fairly certain knowledge held by individuals that extra effort will *not* be emulated by others. This scenario describes the *reluctant* commune member, who is held in this type of organisation by government fiat. Only free choice of commune membership could overcome this inherent 'incentive' handicap. This is indeed a pipe-dream not only because of the relevant politics but also because the kibbutz-type social and economic organisation is likely to remain a small, minority phenomenon in the foreseeable future. Thus, although the kibbutz is indeed alive and well, its message on the role of incentives may, after all, be quite limited.

NOTES

* The first draft of this paper was presented at the Arne Ryde Symposium on 'Incentive Mechanisms and Problems in Major Economic Systems', held at Lund University, Frostavallen, 26–27 August 1985. I am indebted to Alec Nove and to other participants for their enlightening remarks. I also benefited from Stefan Hedlund's detailed criticism. All remaining errors of substance and presentation are mine alone.

1. In kibbutz parlance this is the 'comprehensive' budget technique. See data and discussion in Barkai (1977), pp. 17–22.
2. 'Free' items account for about 60–65 per cent of kibbutz consumption expenditure, and food for about 30 per cent. See Barkai (1977), p. 20, n. 16.
3. The definition of the marginal rate of substitution implies that at this point the marginal utility of x to the member is zero.
4. Barkai (1977), pp. 17–22.
5. Members usually have credit balances with the community treasury; a 'debit' balance is the exception to the rule.
6. The location of I_1I_1 in Figure 9.1 is accordingly specified by the fraction of income allocated to consumption expenditure, and not by total current income, say, X_0, in Figure 9.2. The difference is determined by the fraction of income channelled into saving by communal decision. Note that the exclusion of saving from the set of options of the individual member places a question-mark on the significance of Pareto-optimum in the kibbutz environment even if the whole fraction of income allocated for consumption were distributed in the form of equal token endowments, and if members were free to choose their consumption baskets.
7. Particularly in modern (populist) democracies, where politics depends so much on media exposure and on the power of the fourth estate.
8. A detailed technical treatment of the second argument is given in Barkai (1977), pp. 267–89. See also Barkai (1980), pp. 243–4.
9. Ruppin (1936), pp. 162–3, 155–9, 131–41.
10. Though our notation is somewhat different, equation (6) is, for all practical purposes, identical to eq. (1) in Putterman (1983), p. 158.
11. The right-hand side of (6) is identical with (4*), while the left-hand side reflects the individual's preference set-up. The underlying model, which yields the reduced form of (6), thus involves the production dimension specified above by (1) and (2) and the income distribution rule spelled out in (3).

The preference dimension is introduced by specifying a commune member's conventional utility function in terms of the income-leisure option:

(I) $\quad U^i = U^i(y^i, h^i)$, where $u^i_y > 0$, $u^i_h < 0$, $u^i_{yy} \leq 0$

$\quad$ and $u^i_{hh} \geq 0$

Equations (I), (2) — the production function, and (3) — the income distribution rule, can be combined into a conventional Lagrangian form

(II) $\quad Z = U^i(y^i,h^i) + \lambda[y^i - F(H)/N]$

The first order conditions for the maximum utility of the individual subject to the production constraint is obviously:

(III) $\quad \partial z/\partial y^i = U^i_y + \lambda = 0$
$\quad\quad\quad \partial z/dh^i = U^i_h - \lambda(1/N)F'(H)(\partial H/\partial h_i) = 0$

Assuming $\partial H/\partial h_i = 1$, as in (5) above, moving terms to the right-hand side of (III), and dividing, yields (6). This is the reduced form of the utility maximisation model of a commune member subject to a per capita income (production) constraint.

The equilibrium condition for the identical twin operating in a capitalistic labour market, which does not involve 1/N as in equation (6), can be derived from the same premises by eliminating the (equal) income distribution rule (3) and reformulating the second term of the Lagrangian (II) above.

12. This dimension of the 'inefficiency case' is treated more extensively in Barkai (1980), pp. 243–4, and Barkai (1977), pp. 284–9.

13. C.B.S. (1985).

14. The figure for kibbutzim is much more representative than the mean for the economy as a whole. Comparative data on per capita income and consumption are presented in Barkai (1977), pp. 157–8 and Table 8.8.

15. The Sadan–Shaskin series apply only to about 50 older kibbutzim (specifically, settlements founded before 1936). In view of their higher-than-average (for the movement) capital intensities, rates of return in this group should be expected to be lower than those of the entire population of settlements.

16. Some qualification is called for with reference to the developments since 1973. The unprecedented leap in real interest rates in world capital markets substantially increased the marginal cost of credit to Israel, though their full impact was not transferred to local borrowers. Thus, even if kibbutz performance on this count did not deteriorate as compared with the marginal productivity of capital in the 1950s and 1960s, the gap between the cost of foreign funds and the productivity of capital was undoubtedly lower through the 1980s. Accelerating inflation at three-digit rates from 1979 on could not but have negative effects on factor allocation, and thus on productivity. The squeeze on profitability, noted by many kibbutzim especially since 1983, reflects this narrowing and perhaps even (temporary) closure of the gap between the real cost of capital and its marginal productivity. Note, however, that this squeeze applies to economic activity in Israel's private sector too.

For a comprehensive and detailed empirical treatment of factor productivity in kibbutzim see Barkai (1974); for a shorter and partially updated version see Barkai (1979). The comparisons with the economy as a whole are from Barkai (1980), pp. 6–14, and references cited there.

17. Labour input in kibbutz farming hardly rose from the late 1950s through 1984. Output and value added did, however, grow substantially. On the other hand, labour input in kibbutz manufacturing in 1983 was more than five times larger than in 1958, and output, which more than doubled

between 1970 and 1983, rose more rapidly than labour input in the same period. Output and investment data for kibbutz manufacturing from Kibbutz Industries Organization (1980 and 1984).

18. See Barkai (1977), pp. 266–89; and Barkai (1980), pp. 243–44.

19. Since 'labour' is a heterogeneous factor, the efficient equilibrium configuration requires proper pricing of its various grades and types. Labour market information is therefore an important source of data for the pricing of labour services of members with specific skills and training.

20. By now this applies to most settlements except those in their early infancy. The theory and practice of the hired labour dilemma is treated in Barkai (1977), pp. 217–22, 287–9.

21. The substitution of (7) — the zero-response hypothesis — into the differential yields the 'Israelsen expression' (5): $dH/dh^i = 1$, which is a (latent) building block of the Israelsen theorem (4*) above.

22. Israelsen did not attribute his result to the kibbutz. He refers to the commune in general in the context of, and as an alternative type of organisation to the Russian *kolkhoz*. See also Putterman (1983), pp. 166–8 in particular. Although I have adopted Putterman's original and felicitous notion, which he labelled *behavioural interdependence*, the reasoning above follows a somewhat different track.

23. The zero-response hypothesis and its unity counterpart are not the only ones conceivable. Early critics of the commune suggested the feasibility of 'free-rider' effects (cf. basket d in Figure 9.3) which, of course, involves the presumption $dh^j/dh_i < 0$, and an even smaller effect on incentives than the one in (4*): Similarly, it is unwarranted to reject the possibility of $dh^j/dh_i > 0$ or, what may be more relevant, any value between zero and unity.

24. In the case of persons with high entrepreneurial abilities, a cost measure which reflects cost of education and training does, of course, understate the value of 'personal capacity'. A demand measure would have been preferable, but is unfortunately an elusive notion for quantification purposes. Specification of performance level (9) as a funciton of these two variables is due to Liviatan (1977).

25. Israelsen admits the possible relevance of other factors: he maintains, however, that in the specific context of his analysis (the Soviet *kolkhoz*), 'economic reward would seem the most obvious measure of work incentives' (Israelsen, 1983, p. 103).

26. The cancellation of the 'Israelsen effect' on material incentives can be visualised in terms of Figure 9.3 as a clockwise rotation of the $(y_0^i L)$ budget line towards congruence with the $(I_0 L)$ line, whose slope represents a full marginal product of labour. An inspection of Figure 9.3 suggests that this also signifies the cancellation of the 'free rider' feature, Ld (the income of the commune member at zero labour).

27. Lieblich (1981), p. 182. Another outstanding description of the nature and workings of the informal controls is presented in an interview with the kibbutz secretary (pp. 189–92). Only a small section of this book is devoted to 'Administration', with an emphasis on the economic dimension of the workings of the kibbutz. This section, and also Chapter 11, 'Individualists', offer enlightening empirical information on this matter.

28. Lieblich (1981), p. 193. It is amusing to note that an average

Russian *kolkhoz*, with a labour force of about 500, is no larger in terms of population and manpower than Makom or scores of other Israeli kibbutzim. Yet the *kolkhoz* has obviously not solved the motivation issue to this very day, in spite of the fact that material incentives are not an ideological issue. On the size of the *kolkhoz* see Nove (1983), p. 87.

29. The psychic cost of submitting to kibbutz authority should not be underestimated, as shown by the number of kibbutz-born members who leave the movement. About 40-45 per cent of kibbutz-born children leave before reaching the age of 30.

30. The *shadow* wage rate can be derived for the given real capital at the disposal of the settlement, the technology applied, and the condition of efficient factor allocation and output composition. The consistent derivation of a 'shadow wage' rate is analysed in Barkai (1977), pp. 46-8, 269-71.

31. See Lieblich (1981), p. 177.

32. See estimates of consumption function and (implied) propensities to save in Barkai (1977), pp. 154-66; see also Gan (1975) and Helman (1976). The estimates for the 1970s are from Sadan and Shaskin (1980), Table 3, p. 167.

33. Differences in per capita income are widespread, as are differences in per capita consumption expenditures. Lorenz curve estimates show, however, that they were relatively small in the 1950s through the early 1970s (see Barkai, 1977, pp. 154-7).

REFERENCES

Barkai, Haim (1974), 'An Empirical Analysis of Productivity and Factor Allocation in Kibbutz Farming and Manufacturing', Jerusalem: Falk Institute Discussion Paper No. 74.8.

—— (1977), *Growth Patterns of the Kibbutz Economy*, Contributions to Economic Analysis 108, North-Holland.

—— (1979), 'Productivity and Factor Allocation in Kibbutz Farming and Manufacturing', *Revue Economique*, 30 (No. 1, January): 144-61.

—— (1980), 'The Kibbutz: Incentives, Efficiency and Social Control', in W.J. Baumol (ed.), *Public and Private Enterprise in a Mixed Economy*, London: I.E.A. and Mcmillan.

—— and David Levhari (1973), 'The Impact of Experience on Kibbutz Farming', *Review of Economics and Statistics*, 55 (No. 1, February): 56-63.

Central Bureau of Statistics (C.B.S.) (1985), *Press Release* No. 86/85. June 13.

Gan, H. (1975), *Consumption Patterns in Kibbutzim*, unpublished M.A. thesis, Tel Aviv University (in Hebrew).

Helman, A. (1976), 'The Association of Consumption and Income in the Kibbutz', *Economic Quarterly* (No. 91, January): 389-93 (in Hebrew).

—— and Krol, Y. (1979). 'Resources, Uses and Economic Decisions in the Kibbutz', *Economic Quarterly*, No. 100: 94-101 (in Hebrew).

Israelsen, L. Dwight (1980), 'Collectives, Communes and Incentives', *Journal of Comparative Economics*, 4 (no. 1): 100-5.

Kibbutz Industries Organization (1980, 1984), *Annual Report* (in Hebrew).
Lieblich, A. (1981), *Kibbutz Makom, Report from an Israeli Kibbutz*, New York: Pantheon. Hebrew version, Jerusalem: Schocken.
Liviatan, U. (1977), 'Work Motivation of Kibbutz Members', *Hakibbutz ve-Hata'asiya* (No. 2): 13–21 (in Hebrew).
Nove, A. (1973), *The Economics of Feasible Socialism*, London: Allen and Unwin.
Putterman, L. (1983), 'Incentives and the Kibbutz: Toward an Economics of Communal Work Motivation', *Zeitschrift für Nationalökonomie (Journal of Economics)*, pp. 157–88.
Ruppin, A. (1936), *Three Decades of Palestine*, Jerusalem: Schocken.
Sadan, E. and E. Shaskin (1980), 'Capital Formation and Financing in the Older Kibbutz Settlements: 1936–1975', in M. Bruno and Z. Sussman (eds), *Proceedings of the 1979 Conference of the Israeli Economic Association*, Jerusalem (in Hebrew).

Part Four

Incentives and the Welfare State

10
The Share Economy: Plausibility and Viability of Weitzman's Model[1]

D. Mario Nuti

INTRODUCTION

The persistence and apparent intractability of both large-scale unemployment and inflation coexisting in advanced capitalist countries over the last decade have stimulated a number of new or revamped policy proposals, mostly altering the terms of employment contracts, in an attempt to cure one illness without aggravating the other. These proposals range from the introduction of wage indexation formulas at times of accelerating inflation to their abolition when inflation decelerates; from the collectivisation of unemployment (i.e. 'work-sharing') to synchronised collective bargaining; from tax-based incomes policy to direct wages and prices control — with or without formal or informal stipulations of neo-corporatist social pacts to make them acceptable to workers as part of a package.

The latest proposal in this vein is from M.L. Weitzman (1983, 1984a, 1984b, 1985), advocating the replacement of the fixed wage contract by a form of generalised (i.e. economy-wide) sharing contract whereby at least a substantial component of workers' earnings is made of a stake in their enterprise performance. The idea is not new: forms of income-sharing or performance-related payments abound in modern capitalism (cooperatives, productivity bargaining, workers' shareholdings), in pre-capitalistic formations (share-cropping, sliding-scales) and post-capitalistic experiments or projects (like the Yugoslav system, the labour-managed firm theorised by Ward, 1958 and Vanek, 1970; or Hertzka's Utopia, 1891). What is new in Weitzman's proposal is the specific rejection of workers' participation in decision-making as a necessary feature of income-sharing; the wide scope of envisaged implementation, since the proposal is expected to apply to the bulk of employment in all sectors of the economy in order to produce the desired macroeconomic benefits; and the emphatic enthusiasm, to the point of exaggerated assertiveness, with which the proposal is put forward as the total and miraculous answer to *the* major economic problem of our time: stagflation. Weitzman's evangelism has infected others[2] and received wide press coverage.[3]

In this chapter a summary of the proposal and a comparison with other share formulas are followed by a number of critical reflections. First the plausibility of Weitzman's assumptions is challenged, for the implicit neglect of Keynesian and classical unemployment and of the persistent inflationary feedbacks of full employment and, above all, the lack of workers' participation in enterprise decision-making under continued full employment. Then the viability of Weitzman's model is questioned even within the framework of its own assumptions; it is argued that the model has systemic instability because of its proneness to mergers in the short run, the entry of non-income-sharing new firms in the medium run, and above all, a built-in tendency to revert to the wage economy in the long run. The last section sums up the arguments and assesses their impact on the proposal. It should be stressed that the objections raised do not refer to income-sharing as such, only to its miraculous properties as postulated by Weitzman, and to its introduction in isolation without the parallel progress of workers' participation in decision-making.

WEITZMAN'S MODEL

The model proposed by Weitzman is the macroeconomic extension of enterprise behaviour in conditions of monopolistic competition in the product market, replacing wage labour by net revenue-sharing workers. The formulation presented here is slightly modified, without loss of generality, to allow for the comparison of alternative labour contracts.

The monetary revenue of the firm, R, net of all non-labour costs, is a function of output and, therefore, indirectly of the employment L necessary to obtain that output for the given amount of fixed capital at the firm's disposal:

(1) $R = R(L)$, at L_0, $R' = 0$ and $R'' < 0$

Net revenue per worker R/L is a function of employment; at first it will rise because of the presence of overhead costs, up to the employment level L_c, then it will fall with output increases because of falling marginal revenue (which will dominate even the possible presence of increasing returns to scale as long as total revenue beyond some point falls faster than costs, with respect to output; a sufficient condition is demand saturation at some level of output, which is a standard feature of monopolistic competition models). For simplicity, inputs other than labour and fixed capital are ruled out. Therefore:

(2) $\quad R/L = f(L), \; f' \gtreqless 0 \text{ for } L \lesseqgtr L_c \text{ (at } L_c, f = R')$

Money earnings e per worker, in their general form, are defined as composed of a fixed component a and a share b of net revenue per worker R/L after the deduction of a:

(3) $\quad e = a + b(R/L - a), \text{ where } a \geqslant 1; \; 1 > b \geqslant 0$

The actual values of a and b define alternative labour contracts, namely wage labour corresponds to $a = w$, $b = 0$; income-sharing corresponds to $a \geqslant 0$ and $1 > b > 0$.

Profit-maximising firms employing wage labour under the postulated monopolistic competition will employ labour up to employment level L_w where $R' = w$; those paying labour under a mixed (fixed/sharing) contract for $a > 0$ and $1 > b > 0$ will employ workers up to a level L_s at which $R' = a$; while with profit maximisation under pure income-sharing ($a = 0$, $1 > b > 0$) workers will be employed up to the point where $R' = 0$, i.e. up to the level L_b.

On the basis of this simple analysis Weitzman puts forward the following propositions:

1. For any level of workers' earnings $e = a + b(R/L - a)$ the revenue-sharing enterprise will offer more employment than the wage labour enterprise facing $w = e$ (since $a = w - b(R/L - a) < w$), so that the switch from a given wage to a formula initially yielding the same level of earnings in the economy as a whole will lead to a higher demand for labour, i.e. that corresponding to $w = a$, as if wages had fallen by $(w - a)/w$ (under pure sharing, i.e. $a = 0$, the same labour demand will obtain that in a wage economy would correspond to zero wages).

2. Money earnings per worker would fall, but the impact on employment would be greater than the effect of wage flexibility (which is 'desirable *per se*'; Weitzman 1984a, p. 143), because of

the decoupling of trends in average versus marginal labour cost, the first (= e) not having to fall as much as the second (= a) as is the case, instead, for wage labour. Workers' total money earnings in the economy, however, would not necessarily fall, while *real* earnings (and real incomes all round) in the economy as a whole would actually increase, if the switch to a sharing contract was economy-wide, since the proportional price fall would be greater than the fall in earnings in the transition from wage to income-sharing (because the elasticity of the R' function is smaller than that of the net revenue per worker curve over the relevant range).

3. The labour demand expansion resulting from the economy-wide switch from wage contracts to income-sharing is expected, by Weitzman, to be greater than existing unemployment. Thus the switch would generate not only full employment of labour, but a sizeable permanent excess demand for labour, which would absorb all or part of occasional or cyclical demand falls in the economy without inducing firms to pay inflationary wage rises because these would violate profit-maximisation conditions; indeed, higher employment would have a deflationary impact on prices via greater output.

4. In the long run, the same level of employment, output, prices and earnings would prevail as in a wage economy, earnings gradually settling down at the full-employment marginal revenue product of labour and prices following suit. Excess demand for labour, however, would be maintained because the presence of a sharing component in full-employment earnings will maintain the marginal labour cost to the firm (= a) below the full-employment marginal revenue product of labour ($w^* = e^* = a + b(R/L - a) > a$, where the asterisk indicates values at long-run full employment).

Weitzman considers, in passing, alternative sharing formulas, all linking workers' pay to firm-specific indicators including the price of output, revenue, value added or profit per worker, gross or net. Strangely, he regards profits as more stable over time (1984a, p. 137) as well as a truer measure of the firm's economic condition. He favours revenue because it is 'inherently a more precise concept than profits and might be better to use for that reason' (ibid.). The essence of the sharing contract is that 'if workers are laid off or quit, the remaining employees are paid more, whereas if new workers are hired, all employoyss are paid less' (1984a, p. 83); thus 'a *share* contract is defined to be any compensation function' such that 'the level of workers' pay is inversely related to the level of firm's employment' (1983, p. 768). Weitzman refers to share contracts as involving a change in the 'numéraire' of the wage contract (1984a, pp. 763–4) but this is a misnomer since there is normally a difference between a *fixed* payment (denominated in whatever units) and a *performance related* payment; the two are the same thing only for sliding-scale contracts in which the money wage is indexed to product price, and the notion of a change in numéraire is misleading for the general class of sharing contracts as defined above.[4]

The switch from wage to income-sharing would then produce the costless and simultaneous achievement — hitherto believed impossible — of full employment, stability in the face of sudden demand shocks and the control of inflation (which could then be delegated to monetary policy without fear of adverse effects on employment).

A share system looks very much like a 'labour shortage' economy. Firms cruise around like vacuum cleaners on wheels, searching in nooks and crannies for extra workers to suck in at existing compensation parameter values. Such an economy is inherently recession resistant. Every share firm wants to hire more workers at the equilibrium parameter rates, making temporary additional profits by absorbing any incipient pockets of unemployment that arise or can be found (1983, p. 777).

It is especially difficult . . . for cost-push inflation to get even a toehold in a share firm. Any raising of labor's pay above the going level is a temporary effect that the firm will automatically offset, over time, by hiring new workers attracted to its higher compensation and by flooding its product market with low-priced output (1984a, p. 117).

Moreover, 'There is another, more subtle benefit of permanent excess demand for labour: it gives dignity to the working man and woman, the sense of being significant, useful members of society' (ibid., p. 121), due to non-price competition for workers by firms; 'gain sharing . . . can boost employee morale, increase worker participation, improve labor-management relations, foster a sense of partnership, raise productivity and so forth' (ibid., p. 142). If the whole world were to adopt sharing schemes we would get 'strong export-led growth in an enduring world economic boom' (ibid., p. 120). Wage labour is a 'perilous anachronism' (ibid., p. 46) while the proposed system is 'The superior profit-sharing variant of capitalism' (1985, p. 44).

Why, then, is this wondrous institution not used more widely in economies plagued by precisely the problems which it is alleged to cure? Because, Weitzman explains, the achievement of full and more stable employment with lower inflation depends on the *nationwide* (or at any rate, large-scale) diffusion of sharing schemes, which have no attraction for the individual firm and its employees: 'The firm and its workers do not have an incentive to consider the macroeconomic implications of the contract form they are selecting' (1984a, p. 124); there is an 'externality', a 'public good' or a 'market failure' involved (ibid., p. 123). Therefore it is necessary to undertake 'a high priority, vigorous national program stressing awareness, education and information to infuse a sense of social responsibility into the collective bargaining process' (ibid., p. 128); to introduce fiscal incentives lightening the tax burden on the share component of earnings (ibid., p. 130) and to protect firms and unemployed workers from restrictive employment practices favoured by employed workers (ibid., p. 133). In Weitzman's own words: 'This is supply-side economics *par excellence*' (ibid., p. 132).

A COMPARATIVE ANALYSIS

It is interesting to compare Weitzman's analysis of sharing contracts' properties with the standard treatment of income-sharing enterprises in order to understand both the specific features of Weitzman's proposal and the ultimate source of its originality. Two models are relevant for comparison since they both replace wage with a net revenue share: the dominant Ward–Domar–Vanek model of the labour-managed cooperative (Ward, 1958; Domar, 1966; Vanek, 1970) and the Hertzka–Breit–Lange model of workers' free access to employment in the firms of their choice (Hertzka, 1891; Breit and Lange, 1982; for an up-to-date bibliography on labour-managed firms and employee participation see Bartlett and Uvalic, 1985).

Both models envisage enterprises operating in market economies and replacing labour wage with shares in net revenue; indeed workers' earnings from labour are derived exclusively from share income ($a = 0$) and the whole net revenue of the enterprise can be distributed ($1 \geqslant b > 0$). The share b of net revenue to be distributed to workers is decided by employees through self-management organs (in Hertzka's model always $b = 1$). In the

Hertzka–Breit–Lange model any worker has the legal right to be employed by any firm of his choice at its average distributed net revenue per worker; in the Ward–Domar–Vanek model, on the contrary, the size of employment is decided exclusively by those already employed.

Optimising behaviour in the Ward–Domar–Vanek model takes the form of net revenue per worker maximisation through workers' control over the size of employment, or rather membership, of the cooperative. The result is the opposite of Weitzman's and consists of a restrictive employment policy stopping recruitment, in equilibrium, at L_c (where $f = R'$); therefore, in the short run, employment is lower and full employment can only be reached, in the long run, through the entry of new and the exit of old firms. The short run is characterised by, instead of stability, perverse response to output price (because a price rise starting from equililbrium raises average above marginal net revenue thus encouraging a reduction instead of an increase in membership and vice versa) and to fixed capital rental (though there are a number of mitigating factors; see Vanek, 1970). Thus a small cooperative sector behaving in this fashion will have an anticyclical influence but, if extended to the whole economy, the system will be highly unstable. Unlike Weitzman, the whole literature on workers' income participation schemes has postulated that these are paralleled by at least some workers' voice in decision-making, expressing concern directly or vicariously for the level of R/L and exercising restraint on the size of employment (see also the section below, 'Lack of codetermination').

The Hertzka–Breit–Lange model ensures the elimination of involuntary unemployment through workers' access to any form of their choice as does the later Weitzman model. However in Weitzman's 'labour shortage' scenario workers have *de facto* access to any firm because of the postulated permanent excess demand for labour, whereas in the Hertzka–Breit–Lange model it is their access *de jure* that is the source, and not the consequence, of full employment. In both models the actual level of net earnings per man is equalised in the economy as a whole by workers' mobility across firms, whereas marginal products (and marginal revenue products) of labour are bound to differ across firms (but see the section below 'Systemic mergers'; and Nuti, 1983). On the contrary, in the Ward–Domar–Vanek model average revenue per worker will be equalised only slowly through the entry and exit of firms, while within each firm marginal and average revenue per worker will tend to be in equilibrium (save for possible limits to the cooperative's ability to reduce membership in the short run).

PLAUSIBILITY

Neglect of Keynesian and classical unemployment

Throughout Weitzman's analysis there is an assumption that unemployment is neither Keynesian nor classical implicit in the notion that lower wages are sufficient to ensure full employment. Classical unemployment, here, is understood as a state in which the marginal product of labour reaches zero before full employment because fixed equipment is not sufficient to provide employment for everybody, regardless of the wage level. Keynesian unemployment is a state in which the marginal *revenue* product of labour reaches zero before full employment in spite of positive physical productivity of labour because aggregate demand — whether in money terms or, worse, in real terms — is insufficient.

The very notion of firms facing a given demand curve unrelated to the overall employment in the economy is a totally inadequate micro-foundation for *any* kind of macroeconomics, though Weitzman makes an occasional reference to possible multiplier effects elsewhere of the higher level of employment reached in firms switching from wage to sharing.[5] These effects would actually strengthen Weitzman's case for sharing contracts, but the impact of a switch to those contracts on aggregate demand would also be partly negative, at least in the short run, through investment behaviour. In the long run, we can accept Weitzman's contention that the opportunity cost of labour would be the same under both types of contracts and, therefore, the same techniques would be favoured (1984a, pp. 90–1; investment is not considered in any of his other writings on the subject); but in the short run, the essence of the sharing contract is precisely the lowering of the opportunity cost of labour below the equivalent wage for the same level of earnings; thus equipment will be scrapped later, formerly obsolete equipment might be reinstated if available and new techniques, embodied in new equipment which would have been introduced under wage contracts, will not be for equivalent sharing contracts. Empirical evidence on the relationship between employment and wage levels, whether in the short or the long run, is inconclusive, and it cannot be taken as a matter of course that higher employment will be generated by a lower marginal cost of labour.

It is true that the fall in average earnings associated with lower marginal cost of labour under sharing contracts is not as large as the fall which would be necessary under wage contracts to reach the same effect and, therefore, the adverse impact of lower money earnings on consumption monetary expenditure is not as great as it would be if the same marginal cost of labour was to be achieved in a wage economy. It is also true that in an economy of universal monopolistic competition *à la* Weitzman higher employment is associated with lower prices (as long as it is not achieved through the upward shift of demand curves as would be so in the case of greater government expenditure) and, therefore, lower money earnings would represent higher real earnings and actually boost real consumption demand. Nevertheless it still remains a matter of assumption and, therefore, of faith that the postulated position of demand curves for all of the enterprises in the economy — whether these curves are fixed or move as a result of the switch to sharing contracts — is such that aggregate demand for labour is at least as large as supply (which in turn might also be affected, either way, by a change in money and real earnings associated with the switch), at least as long as $a > 0$ and the marginal cost of labour is not actually zero. Besides, it is sufficient to postulate kindred demand curves (for instance, *kinked* demand curves) to open the possibility of discontinuities in marginal net revenue per worker and a zero response of employment, even for $a = 0$.

It is also a matter of assumption that there is enough equipment in the economy to provide full employment of labour. This used to be a standard assumption in the Keynesian approach, likely to be satisfied for relatively short-lived fluctuations of output and employment; but now, after over a decade of protracted and drastic recession, the closure, dismantling and demolition of plant on a large scale openly visible, for instance, in the landscape of the West Midlands or northern France, it is unlikely that an expansion of labour demand would find matching equipment on the required scale.

It might be retorted that these objections invalidate Weitzman's claim that sharing contracts can deliver full employment, but not the claim that they lead to *higher* employment than equivalent earnings under a wage regime, within the bounds set by either Keynesian aggregate demand or the availability of plant. But aggregate demand is not necessarily invariant with respect to the kind of labour contract prevailing in the economy and the adverse impact on investment might more than offset the expected boost of real consumption demand. And, if capital equipment is a binding constraint before full employment is reached, then public policy should encourage investment, instead of promoting measures, like sharing contracts, which are acknowledged to discourage it.

Persistent inflationary trends

In the sharing model three factors are expected to keep inflation under control. First, firms refrain from raising prices because this leads to the equiproportional increase in the sharing component of earnings, thus reducing the advantage obtainable from price rises. Second, firms refrain from raising wages because this would go against profit-maximisation: if they can get the labour they want they have no incentive to raise wages, while if they are labour-constrained they would lower their profit by offering more than the going earnings rate to workers already employed as well as workers attracted from other firms. Third, if they did pay higher earnings than the going rate and managed to ease their employment constraint, the concomitant output expansion would cause a fall in output price, turning a potentially inflationary move into a deflationary one and teaching firms not to bid up earnings in the labour market in spite of overfull employment.

Suppose that the switch from a wage to a sharing contract does lead to an expansion of employment and real output of both consumption and investment up to full employment (i.e. the objections raised in the previous section do not apply). *Any* feedback of real income on demand of the kind contemplated by Weitzman (1983, p. 747; quoted here in note 5) through multiplier effects, or accelerator effects, or both interacting in the familiar way, will shift upwards the firms' demand curves, unless all demand is totally income-elastic. This recreates the possibility — if not the certainty — of output and employment expansion being inflationary, recreating the unemployment/inflation dilemma which sharing contracts are expected to eliminate. The actual terms of this dilemma would be somewhat improved by sharing formulas because output expansion *along* a given demand curve would not be inflationary but any upward shift of demand curves due to feedbacks of real income on demand would be just as inflationary as any other shift of that kind, including that obtained through increases in government expenditure.

If the sharing scheme is successful in reaching full employment without inflation it is unlikely to maintain this achievement in the face of the postulated persistent excess demand for labour at full employment. Persistent overfull employment is bound to raise the bargaining power of workers as well as their militancy regardless of the official policy of trade unions. Although an individual firm will not have an incentive to bid up wages in spite of labour shortages, overfull employment conditions are bound to force all firms to concede higher money wages, which will push up prices through the uplift of demand curves and/or through firms' mark-up pricing, without any restraining impact of output on prices because aggregate real income is labour-constrained. Indeed at overall full employment firms may well collude between themselves or with workers at the expense of consumers, to raise money wages for the sake of industrial peace, triggering off the earnings–prices spiral only too familiar from the wage system. (See Tyson (1977) who suggests this as an explanation of Yugoslav inflation.)

A further inflationary impact of over-full employment — if the sharing formula functions as envisaged by Weitzman — is due to its inescapably adverse effect on workers' discipline, supply of effort and labour turnover. We know, from the experience of the Soviet and Soviet-type economies characterised by precisely the permanent state of excess demand for labour which Weitzman recommends for the capitalist system, that these adverse effects of over-full employment are endemic and their cost, though difficult to measure, is by no means negligible. (The lesson is two-way: Soviet-type economies should learn that without the parallel introduction of workers' participation in decision-making the introduction of sharing components or other firm-performance-related payments, of a kind often recommended and implemented in reform projects in these economies, by itself is bound to exacerbate their labour shortage and all the problems associated with its persistence). Like any other factor lowering labour productivity, these adverse effects of overfull employment will be inflationary.

It is worth stressing that while full employment is a most desirable objective there is no virtue in permanent disequilibrium even of a benign kind like overfull employment. The only advantage is the instantaneous adjustment to a sudden unexpected demand downturn, but there is a continuous price to pay in terms of productivity and anyway, if the world was as Weitzman paints it, and if one could persuade economic agents of it, probably if demand dropped from full employment it would be no more difficult to enforce generalised wage restraint by workers or price restraint by firms than to replace the wage contract altogether.

Lack of codetermination at overfull employment

The specific rejection of workers' participation in enterprise decision-making (including employment and income distribution) is essential to Weitzman's model (see the comparative analysis presented above). This is well understood by commentators: 'if it is to work on the Weitzman model, management must retain and even strengthen its right to hire and fire. This gives the whole idea a more astringent flavour and separates it from the workers' cooperative idea' (Brittan, 1985, p. 12). Lack of codetermination is the ultimate source of the divergence of Weitzman's results from those of conventional theory of income-sharing and his only claim to originality. If that assumption is relaxed his results fall; since the whole analysis stands or falls with it, it deserves closer scrutiny.

All Weitzman says here is that he takes 'as given the age-old hallmark of capitalism: private ownership of the means of production, where the decisions on output, employment and pricing are essentially made by capitalists' (1984a, p. 132); 'I can see no compelling reason why a capitalist firm should be more prone to allow increased worker participation in company decision-making under one contract form than under another' (ibid., p. 133); 'The bargaining power of labor unions is not a natural right' (ibid., p. 109); 'In law and in custom, hiring new workers is a management prerogative, not a mandatory [sic] subject to bargaining. . . . The share system is a better game than the wage system, but played with strict rules; and one of them is that new workers are welcome to join a share firm' (ibid., p. 110). This is neither evidence nor analysis, it is assertion without foundation in economics or political economy.

Freedom of association *is* a natural right, or at any rate it is enshrined in law and custom, and the bargaining power of associated labour just as naturally rises, with its relative scarcity, when full employment is approached. If this is not regarded as a compelling reason at full employment, it must become compelling when excess demand for labour arises, let alone when it becomes a permanent, and not just an occasional, feature.

Whether or not trade unions exist, and whatever are workers' legal rights, a permanent labour shortage will give workers an *informal* bargaining power which they can exercise within the enterprise, regardless of their formal position. If and when managerial decisions should disregard substantially the interests of employed workers as they perceive them, workers can retaliate with appropriately graded responses ranging from lower work effort to absenteeism to strike and industrial sabotage; the simple tacit threat of response, in the absence of the disciplining and intimidating effect of unemployment, should be enough to assert workers' views of what is good for them as opposed to the views of others, no matter how enlightened. In Poland in 1980–81, workers' informal powers at overfull employment almost brought down a highly centralised power system and could only be stopped by the use of military power and, in spite of this, forms of self-management have been introduced and are now thriving. Surely overfull employment strength should be sufficient to obtain self-management in a capitalist society with a liberal and democratic tradition.

Considerable pressure towards an expansion of workers' participation in decision-making would also come from the general participatory climate established by the educational and promotional campaign envisaged by Weitzman. It does not go against the essence of capitalism, on the contrary, it is an integral part of the capitalist spirit, that risk-taking should be associated with reward and with power; thus equity shares, unlike preference shares which are more protected from risk, carry a voting right. Weitzman is proposing not the 'share economy' but a 'non-voting share economy'. Why ever should reward and penalty be separated from responsibility? Why ever should workers be exposed to the income risks resulting from decisions in which they have no part, more than they are already exposed in the wage system with respect to employment risks?

Weitzman argues that:

> a wage system does not offer labor as a whole a less risky compensation than a share system. It is not true that in a share economy workers are bearing the risk, while in a wage economy firms are bearing the risk. . . . The relevant issue is not whether the firms pool of workers should put all their eggs in one basket — they each did that already when they went to work for a single company — but rather which type of basket is more crush-resistant for whom (1984a, pp. 139–40).

Paradoxically, Weitzman here rehearses the best case for workers' participation in decision-making in the enterprise — a case that holds both under wages and sharing systems. Whatever the relative riskiness of wages and income shares, there is an underlying risk due to practical limits on the divisibility of the labour services offered by a worker who, unlike the owner of capital, *must* put all his eggs in only one (or sometimes two) baskets. The case for workers' participation is already there before the introduction of sharing contracts; certainly it is not weakened in any way by the introduction of sharing. It is a case for the 'labour-equity economy', recognising that in practice the employment contract involves an investment decision (and a fairly illiquid investment at that) on the part of both workers and firms.

Unless there is a substantial measure of participation in decision-making, Weitzman's remarks on income-sharing giving 'dignity to the working man and woman, the sense of being significant, useful members of society' (ibid., p. 121) sound paternalistic and hollow. There can be no dignity or fulfilment or sense of belonging in being passive objects of other people's decisions; if those feelings were aroused by income-sharing, they would certainly promote the demand for codetermination.

It is no accident that the path taken by Weitzman has been neglected: there are excellent reasons for the conventional association of income-sharing with at least a measure of workers' decisional power. That power might be exercised selfishly, or even short-sightedly, but this remains to be shown: there is no empirical evidence of the short-term inefficiency and instability of the labour-managed firm and economy. One thing is sure: once employed workers have a say, income-sharing will not have the effects expected by Weitzman.

Partly for the sake of argument, suspend now all the objections to the plausibility of Weitzman's model, in order to consider the viability — in the sense of systemic stability — of the model on its own terms.

VIABILITY

Systemic mergers

Weitzman briefly refers to the possibility that his model might have systemic instability:

> there is always a temptation for the individual share firm to become a free rider. . . . If one share firm converts to a wage contract paying the prevailing level of compensation, it loses nothing and gains the added short-run flexibility of being able to lay off workers freely when its business is bad and take on more of them when business is good. Nor do the workers care that much because there are always jobs available in a share system. . . . A share system

thus has some tendency to be an unstable social institution under individualistic decision-making (ibid., p. 126).

If one accepts Weitzman's version of how a share economy would function it is hard to see why this should be the case. Contrary to Weitzman's contention, firms confronted with the choice between a wage contract and a sharing agreement yielding equivalent earnings would be wise to adopt the sharing agreement. The firms' ability to 'lay off workers' whenever they wish is presumably identical in both systems. There is no suggestion in Weitzman that share contracts are tenured and if they were there would be far-reaching implications which would drastically alter the system and would have to be analysed; Brittan stresses that 'management must retain and even strengthen its right to hire and fire' (1985, p. 12). Before full employment, firms would actually have a positive incentive to introduce sharing contracts with parameters initially set to match the current wage, because they would lower the marginal cost of labour below the average cost and be able to expand output and profits; if they do not, it is because of worker resistance to the possibility of resulting lower money earnings; in any case workers are risk-averse, so that they would require higher average earnings with a sharing agreement than with the wage contract. At full employment, neither firms nor workers would gain anything from reverting to a wage contract and, if they have already experienced the external economies of sharing contracts, there is no reason to be found in Weitzman's analysis why they should want to disturb current practice. The sharing system would not be introduced spontaneously but, if Weitzman was right, once established would be happily maintained.

The sharing economy *à la* Weitzman is, as it turns out, 'an unstable social institution' and this systemic instability manifests itself in the short, medium and long run, in different forms, to the point of destroying the viability of the system — but not for the reasons Weitzman thinks.

In the short run, the system is subject to a concentration process, due to the appearance of system-specific mergers, which makes the system more monopolistic than its capitalist twin. In the Hertzka–Breit–Lange model and in Weitzman labour mobility across firms ensures the equalisation of average earnings throughout the economy. Given differences in the elasticity of net revenue per worker f-curves at those points in different firms, marginal net revenue per worker R' (and marginal product of labour) will also differ throughout the economy. The divergence of marginal net revenue per worker is made possible by the decoupling of the marginal and average cost of labour together with the maintenance of a uniform average cost. This causes a short-term inefficiency in labour allocation which, in the longer run, might be eliminated by investment replacing labour up to a uniform rate throughout the economy but which, in the short and medium run, cannot be eliminated by labour redeployment across firms, because sharing firms push employment to the point where net marginal revenue per worker is equal to the basic element of pay, a, and this is said to be firm-specific and vary across the economy (though the process determining the relative weight of basic and variable elements of pay is not satisfactorily clarified in Weitzman's writings). If full employment is reached before firms reach the equilibrium point at which $R' = a$, as long as there are sharing components in workers' earnings (i.e. unless we have $e = a = w^*$ for all firms, in which case sharing would come to an end — see below) there is no reason why any particular value of a should prevail and establish itself throughout the economy; hence net marginal revenue per worker would differ. This short-term micro-inefficiency could be overlooked, in view of the claimed victory over macro-inefficient unemployment and inflation; but an opportunity for the internalisation of the potential gains from redeployment of labour is offered by enterprise mergers.

By merging, share firms starting with different marginal net revenue per worker can redeploy workers from that with lower to that with higher marginal revenue, thus raising joint revenue, altering pay parameters to a new uniform scale corresponding to workers' earnings at least as large as before the merger. The increment in net revenue can be distributed to shareholders, retained, used to raise the earnings of existing employees, or to raise average earnings slightly less but sufficiently to attract more labour to the new firm arising from the merger. Profits from this operation may be temporary but, as Weitzman argues about some other profits said to be 'transitory and fleeting', 'they are none the less real for that' (1984a, p. 120).

The systemic instability generated by mergers of this kind consists in the fact that, in principle, unless we introduce restrictive assumptions on static or dynamic diseconomies of size and growth, or other rigidities, the merger process can continue until the whole economy is encompassed by, if not a single firm, at least a small handful of them. (For the analysis of this process in the Hertzka–

Breit–Lange model; see Nuti, 1983.) The more monopolistic nature of the economy could alter significantly the resulting output, pricing and employment decisions, at least partly offsetting the expected advantages of the share economy.

Entry of non-share firms

In the medium run (i.e. over the timespan when productive capacity may change and new firms enter) another threat to the systemic stability of the share economy must come from the entry of non-share firms. Weitzman acknowledges that 'it may be unreasonable to suppose that a new firm would be able to attract labour by offering to pay share income'; such a firm, like others with 'inherently greater variability may offset more volatile share income by paying higher than average compensation, or they may just choose to offer wages alone and forgo the tax advantage of the share contract' (1984a, p. 139). Since workers hired by a new firm have no way of assessing prospective pay they would have to be hired on a wage contract, thereby reducing the relative size of the sharing sector in the economy, the more the higher the weight of new firms operating wage contracts.

In the presence of tax advantages of share incomes, however, there is another class of firms at an advantage over Weitzman's share firms, namely cooperatives. The entire distributed income of cooperatives is share income and certainly they would be boosted by tax privileges and the envisaged educational campaign. However, cooperatives are not share firms in Weitzman's sense for member/workers themselves are in charge and decide the size of membership/employment. Cooperatives' members do not regard shared income as cost (see above) and in so far as they maximise anything at all, they will be concerned with net revenue per capita, i.e. restrict employment instead of promoting it.

Now look at the population of firms after the generalised introduction of share contracts: some will remain wage firms because of revenue volatility; cooperatives will stay as they are; some firms will merge to redeploy labour efficiently and enjoy stronger monopolistic power; new entrants will be wage firms or, more likely, cooperatives. Unless the relative size (appropriately weighted by employment) among new firms of new wage firms later to be transformed into share firms other than cooperatives is greater than half (assuming identical mortality rates among all kinds of firms), in due course the economy will revert to a mixed cooperative/wage/share firm economy in which Weitzman's share firms (weighed by employment) are a minority, even if the initial drive towards the new system originally had succeeded.

Full employment reversion to the wage economy

In the long run, Weitzman argues, the share economy will settle down to a state of full employment characterised, *mutatis mutandis*, by the same level of earnings per worker, output, price level and of course employment that would prevail in a wage economy. Contrary to Weitzman's conviction, however, at full employment the share economy would also revert to the wage contract; not, as he fears, because of the adoption of a 'free-riding' strategy on the part of the firms, but because of the competitive elimination of the sharing element in workers' pay due to firms correctly pricing the opportunity cost of labour at full employment, which is something they do not do, though they should, in Weitzman's model. He says that 'the best the share firms can do in the long run is to hire labour to the point where its marginal value equals the prevailing pay' (1984a, p. 90), whereas he should have said to the point where its marginal value equals *its marginal cost*.

Inexplicably this elementary piece of neoclassical theory is neglected: that a firm whose purchase of a production factor is rationed at the ruling price or pricing formula must be willing to incur a marginal cost for its acquisition equal to the marginal net revenue obtainable from it. In spite of excess demand for labour at full employment, firms are expected not to raise labour earnings over labour marginal productivity at full employment, because otherwise their profit would fall. Given the premises this is, of course, correct. What is not correct is the inference that, in view of a sharing component of workers' earnings, basic pay must be lower than the full-employment marginal productivity of labour (= full employment equilibrium wage) and therefore there must remain a chronic labour shortage. The assumption of basic pay remaining below the full-employment marginal product of labour is simply incompatible with optimising behaviour on the part of firms; the marginal cost of labour to firms is the basic pay and any competent MIT-trained manager will most certainly try, before giving up his search for more workers, offering *a higher basic pay, without raising the level of total (basic plus sharing) earnings*, knowing that workers are risk-averse and that, therefore, they will gratefully accept, in their pay packet, the substitution of any amount of contractually fixed pay for an identical claim to share income. Put in another form, there are cost savings to be made for a firm offering a contractually fixed sum of money to workers instead of what is to them its certainty-equivalent. But even if workers were risk-neutral any self-respecting manager will have to experiment with alternative pay parameters and not rest unless the marginal cost and marginal revenue per worker are equalised, in which case only can he rest assured that he is not missing a profitable opportunity.

As a result of this process basic pay a, which is the marginal cost to firms of acquiring new workers, will be made to coincide with full-employment marginal revenue product of labour w^* throughout the economy. At that point, the sharing element of workers' earnings vanishes and with it Weitzman's share economy. This is a far more fundamental systemic instability than that contemplated by Weitzman, i.e. the attraction for firms of retaining the 'short-run flexibility of being able to lay off workers' (1984a, p. 139) — a flexibility which they neither lose nor, if the share economy worked as Weitzman expects, in any case would need. Even if none of the objections raised in the previous sections applied, and the diffusion of share contracts were able to deliver full employment, in the long run (which is not even very long, since Weitzman assumes that sharing coefficients are revised 'once a year'; 1983, p. 769), the system would revert to a wage economy. At best, therefore, Weitzman's model is one of a soft-landing on full employment through initial reductions in the money earnings of workers, not as drastic as would be necessary under wage contracts and, therefore, more likely to be acceptable to workers, though eventually full-employment money and real earnings would be the same under either system.

But suppose money wage flexibility was sufficient to obtain full employment, and full employment obtained through lower money wages was associated with lower prices and higher real earnings and real incomes all round, and no other objections held, and the government had to make substantial tax concessions to introduce the new system and reap a most desirable external effect or 'public good'. Then why not simply use the same fiscal resources to introduce a wage subsidy instead, first on a small scale and afterwards, as employment rises and prices fall boosting real incomes, on an ever-increasing scale financed out of the taxation of resulting real income increases, up to full employment? Neither firms nor workers could possibly object, the public good would be purchased, as it should be, out of the public purse but at no real cost to the public under the postulated assumptions. This proposal would have all the advantages of Weitzman's scheme, without many of the disadvantages such as the drawbacks of overfull employment, or the inefficient deployment of labour, or monopolistic tendencies — if, of course, the underlying assumptions are correct, while if not correct this would become apparent at the first round of wage subsidies which then would be stopped without having done any harm, without the dangerous frustration that would follow the (probable) failure of the economy-wide introduction of share contracts.[6]

CONCLUSIONS

Workers' participation in enterprise revenue or profit has been introduced in modern capitalism, historically, 'as a way of building employee loyalty, thus avoiding industrial unrest and unions' as well as 'a way of putting the employee on the side of management, thereby boosting production and efficiency', thus being unpopular with trade unions (Mitchell, 1985, p. 38). Weitzman proposes the economy-wide diffusion of sharing contracts relating at least a substantial part of workers' earnings to the performance of their enterprise. In economies characterised by sufficient plant to employ the whole workforce and by generalised monopolistic competition, the large-scale introduction of share contracts in place of wages is expected to rapidly lead to full employment, lower prices and permanent excess demand for labour which is not inflationary and absorbs partly or wholly the shocks of demand recession (Weitzman, 1983, 1984a, 1984b, 1985).

But the plausibility of Weitzman's assumptions and the model's viability — understood as the system's capacity to reproduce its institutional features once it is introduced — are doubtful on several grounds. Usually one good reason for rejecting a case is sufficient, but the strength of conviction with which the scheme has been put forward, the importance of its claims and the favour it has received justify the extensive treatment of both the model's assumptions and functioning.

Weitzman's model implicitly assumes the absence of classical unemployment (i.e. marginal product of labour reaching zero before full employment is reached) and Keynesian unemployment (i.e. marginal revenue of firms reaching zero before full employment). Income-sharing, at least initially, will discourage investment by lowering the incentive to replace labour which is being made marginally cheaper, thereby slowing down the absorption of classical unemployment and possibly offsetting the positive impact of income-sharing on consumption demand).

If share contracts did succeed in raising employment and output, multiplier and accelerator effects might revamp inflation in spite of sharing; while, if full employment were reached and the envisaged excess demand for labour established and maintained, firms facing the ensuing bargaining pressure of labour might collude between themselves or with workers at the expense of consumers to raise prices and earnings. Moreover, persistent excess demand for labour will lower productivity through higher labour turnover and absenteeism and lower discipline and supply of effort, pushing up costs and prices.

It is neither feasible nor desirable to expose workers to the risks of income-sharing without parallel expansion of their participation in enterprise decision-making. The formal and informal bargaining power of workers at full employment with excess demand for labour will demand and obtain forms of codetermination, which will bring share contracts closer to the cooperative model, well known for its restrictive employment and output policies.

Even if none of these objectives applied, the model would not be viable, i.e. would not maintain its distinguishing institutional features, whether in the short, the medium or the long run.

In the short run, the equalisation of earnings per worker through labour mobility will lead to diverging marginal product or marginal net revenue per worker; this inefficiency in labour deployment cannot be eliminated other than through enterprise mergers, which raise considerably the monopolistic character of the share economy.

In the medium run, new firms will be either wage firms (because workers hired by a new firm have no way of assessing prospective pay) or cooperatives (which can take fuller advantage of the proposed privileged tax treatment of share income). Unless specific conditions are satisfied concerning the proportions of various kinds of firms entering, changing or dying, the weight of share firms will gradually dwindle.

In the long run, at full employment, average earnings are pegged to the full-employment marginal revenue product of labour but competing firms have an incentive to raise the fixed component of pay — which is the marginal cost of labour to firms — up to the marginal net revenue product of labour, thus reducing the share component of earnings to zero. At best (i.e. if none of the other objections counted) the proposal would allow full employment to be reached through the downwards flexibility of labour earnings offered by the share system, but with smaller cuts in money earnings of workers than would be required to obtain full employment through money wage cuts, thereby raising the probability of cuts being accepted.

Is there any alternative way of defeating both unemployment and inflation? If we are to believe Weitzman's account of how the economy works, there certainly is: a wage subsidy would have the same effects on employment, output and prices, and if it were introduced at first on a small scale, it would boost real incomes enabling the government to expand the scale of wage subsidies financed out of additional tax revenue until full employment was reached; any displacement from full employment would be dealt with in the same way if and when it occurred, without the drawbacks of permanent labour shortage.

None of what precedes should be understood or construed as a criticism of income-sharing *per se*, but of its introduction on a substantial scale without the parallel expansion of workers' participation in enterprise decision-making without which substantial income-sharing would involve a regress to pre-capitalistic conditions, and of the gross overclaims for its expected achievements put out by Weitzman. The dependence of the smaller part of workers' earnings from their enterprise performance, or better still *from the overall economy's performance*, accompanied by forms of workers' codetermination, can have — if the terms are right — beneficial effects on productivity and be an attractive counterpart for workers' acceptance of the austerity policies which may be necessary to reach and maintain full employment without excessive inflation.

NOTES

1. Acknowledgements are due to Will Bartlett, John Cable, Pierre Dehez, Jacques Drèze and Saul Estrin for helpful comments, though of course they are not responsible for errors and opinions contained in this chapter. This research is part of an EC-funded project on 'The impact of workers' participation schemes on enterprise performance in Western Europe', conducted by the author at the EUI.

2. Pre-publication comments on Weitzman's book (1984a) by R.M. Solow, J.E. Roemer and J.E. Meade, printed in the book's cover, uncharacteristically depart from the usually sober style of these authors: '. . . marvellous book . . . daring . . . practical' (Solow); 'One of the most

exciting books in economics . . . the most profound intervention in unemployment policy of capitalist countries since Keynes's' (Roemer); 'Important, stimulating . . . persuasive . . . should be read and inwardly digested by every concerned economist, administrator and politician' (Meade).

3. See, for instance, S. Brittan in the *Financial Times*, Monday, 25 February 1985, p. 12; C.P. Alexander in *Time Magazine*, 20 May 1985.

4. Weitzman refers to wages as sometimes 'rigidly indexed to money' (1983, p. 780), whereas money is the one thing to which money wages or any other money payments cannot be indexed by definition.

5. 'Now as each firm expands, its new workers spend their wages on the products of other firms creating new demand . . . and encouraging further expansion' (Weitzman, 1983, p. 764). This implies upward shifts of demand curves, with possible inflationary implications.

6. For alternative institutional innovations, which do not require but are compatible with the assumptions underlying Weitzman's model, see Nuti, 1985.

REFERENCES

Alexander C.P. (1985), 'Search for a miracle cure', *Time Magazine*, 20 May.
Bartlett, W. and Uvalic, M. (1985), 'Bibliography on labour-managed firms and employee participation', EUI Working Paper no. 85/198, Florence, November; Presented at the IV International Conference on the Economics of Self-Management, CIRIEC, Liège, 15-17 July.
Breit, M. and Lange, O. (1982), 'Un modello di economia socialista di mercato autogestita con garanzia di pieno impiego e di uguaglianza distributiva', *Rivista internazionale di Scienze sociali*, XC, no. 3, pp. 301-4.
Brittan, S. (1985), 'Profit sharing: the link with jobs', *Financial Times*, Monday 25 February, London.
Domar, E.D. (1966), 'The Soviet collective farm as a producer cooperative', *American Economic Review*, LVI, no. 4, pp. 737-57.
Hertzka, T. (1891), *Freeland: a Social Anticipation*, Chatto & Windus, London.
Lane, D. (1985), *Employment and Labour in the USSR*, Harvester Press, London.
Mitchell, D.J.B. (1985), 'Wage flexibility in the United States: lessons from the past', *American Economic Review*, Papers and Proceedings, LXXV, no. 2, May, pp. 36-40.
Nuti, D.M. (1983), 'Fusioni di imprese ed efficenza nei modelli di economie autogestite', *Rivista internazionale di Scienze sociali*, XCI, no. 4, pp. 487-94.
——— (1985), 'Economic planning in market economies: scope, instruments, institutions', EUI Working Paper no. 85/180, Florence, July; also in *The Socialist Register 1985-86*, Merlin Press, London.
Tyson, L. (1977), 'The Yugoslav inflation: some competing hypotheses',

Journal of Comparative Economics, I, no. 2, pp. 113–46.
Vanek, J. (1970), *The General Theory of Labor-Managed Market Economies*, Cornell University Press, Ithaca, New York.
Ward, B.M. (1958), 'The firm in Illyria: market syndicalism', *American Economic Review*, XLVIII, no. 4, pp. 566–89.
Weitzman, M.L. (1983), 'Some macroeconomic implications of alternative compensation systems', *Economic Journal*, XCIII, no. 4, pp. 763–83.
―――― (1984a), *The Share Economy*, Harvard University Press, Cambridge, Mass.
―――― (1984b), 'The simple macroeconomics of profit-sharing', MIT Working Paper no. 357, December, Cambridge, Mass.
―――― (1985), 'Profit-sharing as macroeconomic policy', *American Economic Review*, Papers and Proceedings, LXXV, no. 2, May, pp. 41–5.

11
An Economic Theory of Workfare

Richard S. Toikka and William L. Dreifke*

INTRODUCTION

In the United States the relationship between work and welfare has received much attention in recent years from scholars and policy-makers alike. Much of the attention has been focused on the growth of the Aid to Families With Dependent Children Program (AFDC) which is the largest of the welfare programmes financed through a mix of federal and state funds. When the programme was originally established in 1935 to provide income to single parents and their children, most recipients were viewed as not especially employable. Many changes have altered the public perception of the programme and its reality since then. These have included the growth and changing composition of the programme (away from the widows, towards divorced and never married women), increasing labour force participation of women and changing societal attitudes, the expansion of the programme to include two-parent households, and, recent evidence that there is substantial turnover in the welfare population.

Emphasis came to be placed increasingly on assuring adequate incentives for welfare recipients to look for and accept jobs. In 1967 the Work Incentive Program (WIN) was established to increase the employability of welfare recipients. Recent initiatives in WIN have centred on providing job-search instruction rather than on providing employment and training services. In 1981 major changes in the AFDC programme provided states with the option to restrict the WIN programme and to establish Community Work Experience Programs (CWEP) which required recipients to work in government-provided jobs in exchange for their benefits. This type of programme has been called 'workfare' as contrasted with the politically less attractive 'welfare'. A few years earlier Congress had mandated a demonstration of workfare in the Food Stamp Program which aims to assure adequate diets for the poor. It is likely that work-for-benefit programmes will continue in the United States since there is strong political pressure to require welfare recipients to work. However, some very difficult questions remain about the feasibility of such programmes and their effectiveness in reducing welfare costs. At the present time many states are experimenting with various forms of work-for-benefit programmes.

A primary objective of workfare is to distinguish individuals who need public assistance and are willing to work, from individuals who need public assistance due to a preference for leisure or an unwillingness to work. Appropriately structured, workfare creates an incentive for individuals who could accept an adequate paying private sector job to leave the workfare programme. At the same time however, benefits continue to be available for individuals who are willing to work but are unable to obtain adequate paying private sector jobs. While there are a number of studies which estimate the impact of workfare, there is little or no discussion of an underlying theoretical model describing how workfare influences behaviour. In this chapter, a theoretical model of workfare is developed using the neoclassical theory of consumer choice.

In the next section, after briefly reviewing the labour supply effects of a public transfer programme, the effects of a generalised workfare programme are analysed under the assumption that the rules regarding reduction in benefits for cause are strictly enforced. The model suggests that individuals' market wage rate plays a key role in determining whether participation in workfare is preferred. An important implication not widely recognised is that labour supply (in market work) may actually decrease if the individual participates in workfare. Then, the effects of expectations by participants regarding programme sanctions in the event of non-compliance with the work requirement are considered. It is shown that with imperfect sanctions, programme participation may be selected by individuals who would not choose to participate if sanctions were perfect. Thus, expectations regarding sanctions replaces the market wage as a key determinant of programme participation.

AN ECONOMIC THEORY OF WORKFARE

INCENTIVE EFFECTS WITH PERFECT SANCTIONING

Income–leisure choice

Incentive effects may be examined using an income–leisure framework from the theory of consumer choice.[1] In Figure 11.1 the income and leisure opportunities for a welfare recipient are shown without workfare. The family budget constraint without the welfare benefit is

(1) $Y = \Sigma W_i(T_i - L_i) + NEY$

where T_i is total hours, W_i is the hourly wage rate, L_i is leisure hours (i indexing family members) and NEY is income other than wages and salaries. A welfare programme alters the family budget constraint by adding an income conditioned benefit (B) defined to be

(2) $B = \begin{cases} 0 & \text{for } Y \geqslant \frac{A}{r} + D \\ A - r(Y - D) & \text{for } D < Y < \frac{A}{r} + D \\ A & \text{for } Y \leqslant D \end{cases}$

where r is the benefit reduction rate, Y is family income without the benefit, D is deductions from income, and A is the maximum benefit (payable to a family with income less than or equal to total deductions).

Holding earnings of other family members constant, the line defined by equation (1) represents income and leisure available to an individual (i = 1) with a market wage of W_1. The slope of the line is $(-W_1)$; a person trades leisure for income by moving up and to the left. This movement represents an increase in the number of hours of labour supplied to the market. Redefining the income constraint to include welfare benefits gives

(3) $Y' = Y + B$

$= \begin{cases} \Sigma W_i(T_i - L_i) + NEY & \text{for } Y \geqslant \frac{A}{r} + D \\ A + rD + (1 - r)[\Sigma W_i(T_i - L_i) + NEY] \\ \qquad\qquad\qquad \text{for } D < Y < \frac{A}{r} + D \\ A + \Sigma W_i(T_i - L_i) + NEY \\ \qquad\qquad\qquad \text{for } Y \leqslant D \end{cases}$

293

AN ECONOMIC THEORY OF WORKFARE

Figure 11.1 Income–leisure opportunities

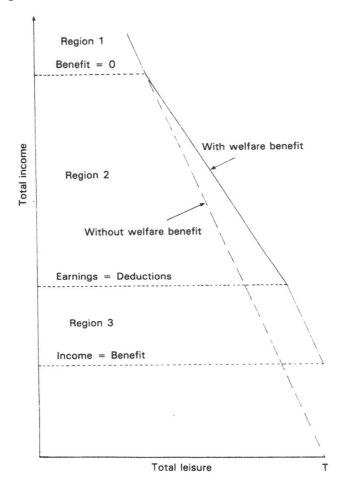

The three regions of the constraint (as shown in Figure 11.1) may be described as follows: (1) income exceeds the eligibility cut-off and the income–leisure choice is represented by a line whose slope is $(-W_1)$; (2) income is above the deductions but below the eligibility cut-off and the income–leisure choice is described by a line whose slope is $[-(1 - r)W_1]$; and (3) income is below the deductions and the slope of the budget line is once again the negative of the wage rate $(-W_1)$.

Potential influence of workfare

A fairly general representation of the work requirement in workfare is to assume some sensitivity to household earnings, that is the work requirement is reduced as earnings rise. The number of hours required (g) is determined by

(4) $\quad g = g(E) \quad g' < 0$

The income constraint is modified to become

$$(5) \quad Y' = \begin{cases} \Sigma W_i(T_i - L_i) + \text{NEY} & \text{for } Y \geq \dfrac{A}{r} + D \\[6pt] (1-r)[\Sigma W_i(T_i - L_i) - W_1 g(E) + \text{NEY}] + A + rD & \\ & \text{for } D < Y < \dfrac{A}{r} + D \\[6pt] \Sigma W_i(T_i - L_i) - W_1 g(E) + \text{NEY} + A & \\ & \text{for } Y \leq D \end{cases}$$

where the work requirement is arbitrarily imposed on the family member (i = 1) with wage W_1 and family earnings are

(6) $\quad E = \Sigma W_i(T_i - L_i) - W_1 g(E)$

In what follows, income–leisure frontiers are derived under the assumption that welfare benefits are received only if the workfare obligation is completely satisfied.[2] Workfare will never be preferred if both more income and more leisure are available without participation in workfare. An analysis of the circumstances under which workfare may be preferred will be conducted by comparing the income–leisure frontier under workfare with that defined solely by the market wage. Three specific forms of the work requirement which have been used in previous or current workfare programmes will now be examined.

The first is a constant number of hours to be worked regardless of earnings, that is,

(7) $\quad g = g_0$

This is an extreme form of workfare since it does not discriminate in its requirement between those who receive different levels of income support.

A second form of the work requirement is where the participant must 'work off' all the benefit. The requirement may be stated algebraically as

(8) $\quad g = \dfrac{B}{W^m}$

where W^m is the statutory minimum wage. The workfare obligation is phased out at the same point as the welfare benefit. This form of the work requirement is part of the current Food Stamp Program legislation.

A third case is a rule in which a participant is required to 'work off' only that portion of the benefit that exceeds earnings. The formula is

(9) $\quad g = \dfrac{B - E}{W^m}$

where W^m is again the statutory minimum wage. This rule was in effect during the evaluation of the Food Stamp Workfare Demonstration.

Each of the three types of workfare requirements may be represented by a linear function with different parameters.

(10) $\quad g = \beta_0 + \beta_1 E$

$\quad\quad$ Case 1: $\beta_0 = g_0;\ \beta_1 = 0$

$\quad\quad$ Case 2: $\beta_0 = \dfrac{A - r(NEY - D)}{W^m};\ \beta_1 = \dfrac{-r}{W^m}$

$\quad\quad$ Case 3: $\beta_0 = \dfrac{A - r(NEY - D)}{W^m};\ \beta_1 = \dfrac{-(1 + r)}{W^m}$

The implication of each type of programme for work incentives will now be considered.

Constant obligation

If the workfare obligation is constant ($g = g_0$), the income–leisure frontier in the range of workfare eligibility (that is, for $Y < A/r + D$) becomes

(11) $\quad Y' = \begin{cases} (1 - r)[\Sigma W_i(T_i - L_i) - W_1 g_0 + NEY] + A + rD \\ \quad\quad\quad\quad\quad\quad\quad\quad\quad\quad\quad\quad \text{for } D < Y < \dfrac{A}{r} + D \\ \\ \Sigma W_i(T_i - L_i) - W_1 g_0 + NEY + A \quad\quad \text{for } Y \leqslant D \end{cases}$

Figure 11.2 Constant obligation

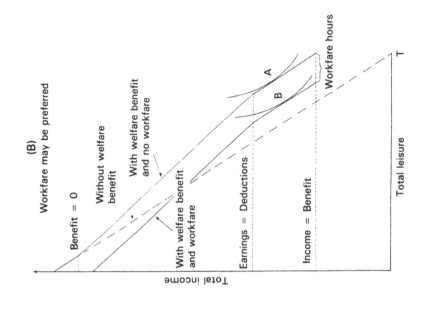

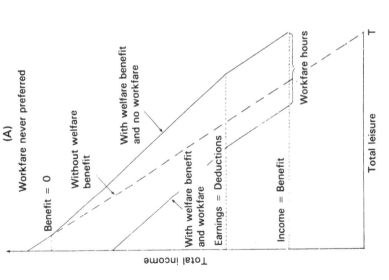

The modified frontier is displayed in Figure 11.2 along with the frontier prior to the imposition of the work requirement.

In the case of a constant work requirement, the income–leisure frontier shifts to a left by the amount of time spent in a workfare job. Using Figure 11.2, several implications of the model can be demonstrated which also apply to the other forms of workfare. First, if the market wage rate (W_1) exceeds the implicit wage rate in the workfare programme (A/g_0) as shown in Figure 11.2A, then participation in workfare will never be preferred. The effect of workfare is essentially the same as taking away the welfare benefit. Any work disincentive effects caused by the welfare benefit are reversed by the work requirement. Assuming leisure and consumption goods (income) are both normal goods, labour supply will increase or may remain unchanged.

A considerably different result occurs when participation in workfare is preferred. This can occur when $W_1 < A/g_0$ in which case the income–leisure frontier lies partially above the frontier for market work alone (as shown in Figure 11.2B). When workfare is preferred, the work requirement is basically a fixed cost required in order to receive the welfare benefit (i.e. an income effect). What is special here is that it is a fixed *time* cost of participation rather than a fixed money cost. As noted by Cogan (1981), an increased in fixed time costs of work results in a decrease in labour supply. Similarly, the work requirement in workfare results in a reduction in leisure, income and labour supply (in market work). An example of this effect is shown in Figure 11.2B by the movement from point A to B. The possibility of a negative impact of labour supply such as this has generally been ignored in previous studies on workfare.

Benefit-based obligation

A more common form of the work requirement is a benefit-based obligation where time spent in a workfare job is simultaneously determined with time spent working outside of workfare and leisure. The workfare requirement as a function of leisure time is obtained by substituting the earnings equation (6) into the workfare determination equation (10) and solving for g, the workfare obligation. For the benefit-based case (that is, $g = B/W^m$) when income without the welfare benefit (Y) is above allowed deductions but below the eligibility cutoff (that is, $D < Y < A/r + D$), the resulting equation is

AN ECONOMIC THEORY OF WORKFARE

$$(12) \quad g = \frac{r\Sigma W_i(T_i - L_i) - (A - rNEY + rD)}{rW_1 - W^m}$$

for $rW_1 \neq W^m$. If $rW_1 = W^m$, the condition reduces to

$$r\Sigma W_i(T_i - L_i) - (A - rNEY + rD) = 0$$

and leisure is constant for all values of g.

The resulting income–leisure frontier is derived by substituting (12) into the budget constraint (5) to get

$$(13) \quad Y' = \frac{-(1-r)W^m[\Sigma W_i(T_i - L_i) + NEY]}{rW_1 - W^m} + \frac{W_1 - W^m}{rW_1 - W^m}(A + rD)$$

It will be useful to restate the expression for the frontier using the ratio $k = W^m/W_1$. So stated, the frontier becomes

$$(14) \quad Y' = \frac{-(1-r)[\Sigma W_i(T_i - L_i) + NEY]}{r/k - 1} + \frac{1-k}{r-k}(A + rD)$$

Finally, for the region where $Y \leq D$, the income–leisure frontier under benefit-based workfare is

$$(15) \quad Y' = \Sigma W_i(T_i - L_i) + NEY + \left(1 - \frac{1}{k}\right)A$$

The income–leisure frontier for the benefit-based workfare obligation is shown in Figure 11.3A. In the region above the deductions level, as earnings increase the workfare obligation decreases until the point at which both the workfare obligation and the benefit equal zero. The sign of the frontier is determined by the size of rW_1/W^m. This expression represents the *increase in the workfare* obligation resulting from *withdrawing one unit of labour* from the market. If it exceeds unity, leisure actually falls as labour is withdrawn from the market indicating a positively-sloped frontier. For values less than unity the frontier is negatively sloped and for a value of unity the frontier is vertical.

The income–leisure frontier is shown in Figure 11.3B for three different values of the participant's market wage (W_1). If the wage used to determine the workfare obligation (W^m) is less than the market wage (W_1), the income–leisure frontier lies below and to the left of the price line representing the income–leisure

Figure 11.3 Benefit-based obligation

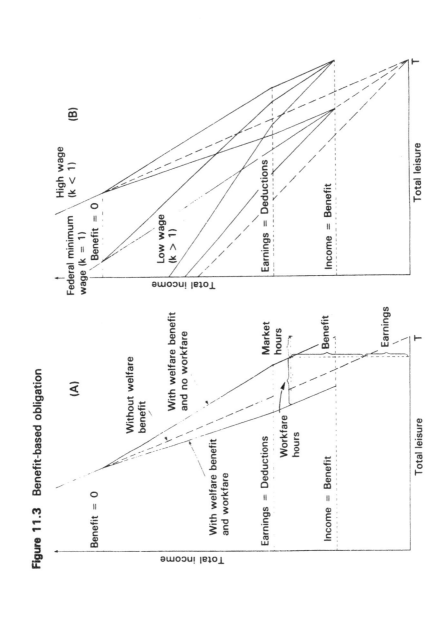

opportunities available by working at the market wage. If $W^m = W_1$, then the income–leisure frontier under workfare is identical to the price line representing the market wage. Finally, if $W^m > W_1$, then the income–leisure frontier under workfare lies above the market wage frontier, but below the frontier with the welfare benefit and no workfare.

With some modification, the effect of workfare on labour supply with a benefit-based obligation is similar to the effects with a constant obligation. In this case the implicit wage rate in workfare is W^m and therefore workfare is never preferred if $W_1 \geqslant W^m$. For these individuals, the work requirement has the same effect on labour supply as taking away the welfare benefit. If $W_1 < W^m$, then workfare may be preferred in which case there is again a fixed time cost (income effect) of participation in the welfare programme. In the region above the deductions level, the effective wage rate in market work is increased as a result of workfare causing a substitution effect. Since these two effects work in opposite directions, the impact of workfare on labour supply is ambiguous; labour supply (in market work) could either increase or decrease.

Excess benefit-based obligation

The third case is similar to the second except that the workfare obligation is phased out while the participant is still receiving welfare benefits. For excess benefit-based workfare (that is, $g = (B - E)/W^m$), the workfare obligation as a function of leisure time obtained by substituting (6) into (10) for the region where earnings are above the deductions is

$$(16) \quad g = \frac{(1 + r) \Sigma W_i(T_i - L_i) - (A - rNEY + rD)}{(1 + r)W_1 - W^m}$$

for $(1 + r)W_1 \neq W^m$. If $(1 + r)W_1 = W^m$, then the condition is

$$(1 + r) \Sigma W_i(T_i - L_i) - (A - rNEY + rD) = 0$$

and leisure is constant for all values of g.

The modified income–leisure frontier in the range of the workfare obligation is obtained by substituting (16) into (5) to get

$$(17) \quad Y' = \frac{-(1 - r)W^m \Sigma W_i(T_i - L_i)}{(1 + r)W_1 - W^m} + \frac{(1 - r)(W_1 - W^m)}{(1 + r)W_1 - W^m} NEY + \frac{2W_1 - W^m}{(1 + r)W_1 - W^m} (A + rD)$$

Restating (17) in terms of the ratio $k = W^m/W_1$ gives the modified expression

(18) $\quad Y' = \dfrac{-(1 - r) \Sigma W_i(T_i - L_i)}{(1 + r)/k - 1} +$

$\dfrac{(1 - r)(1/k - 1)}{(1 + r)/k - 1}$ NEY $+ \dfrac{2/k - 1}{(1 + r)/k - 1}$ (A + rD)

For earnings below the deduction level, the income–leisure frontier is given by

(19) $\quad Y' = \dfrac{\Sigma W_i(T_i - L_i)}{1 - 1/k} +$ NEY $+ \dfrac{2/k - 1}{1 - 1/k}$ A

The resulting income–leisure frontier is shown in Figure 11.4A. When market earnings are greater than the welfare benefit level the workfare obligation is zero. As earnings fall below the welfare benefit level the workfare obligation becomes positive, and the slope of the income–leisure frontier depends on the ratio $k = W^m/W_1$. In Figure 11.4B the income–leisure frontiers for three values of k are shown. When earnings are less than the welfare benefit and greater than the deduction, the slope of the frontier will be negative (positive) when k is less (greater) than $1 + r$. Finally, for earnings below the allowed deduction, the slope of the frontier will be negative (positive) when k is less (greater) than 1.

The effect of workfare on labour supply is somewhat different for this form of the work requirement since it is possible to have a zero obligation and a positive welfare benefit. This occurs in the region where earnings exceed the welfare benefit. If the individual would locate on this part of the budget constraint when there is no work requirement, then workfare has no effect on labour supply.

If, on the other hand, the individual would choose a point where $E < B$ in the absence of a work requirement, then workfare may have a positive, negative or no impact on labour supply. As before, there is a critical value, W* (which depends on W^m and other variables) such that if $W_1 \geq W^*$ workfare is never preferred and therefore has a positive or no impact on labour supply. If $W_1 < W^*$, then working in a workfare job may be preferred in which case the impact on labour supply is ambiguous. An important difference from the previous cases is that the substitution effect is greater, making it more likely that labour supply (in market work) will increase.

Figure 11.4 Excess benefit-based obligation

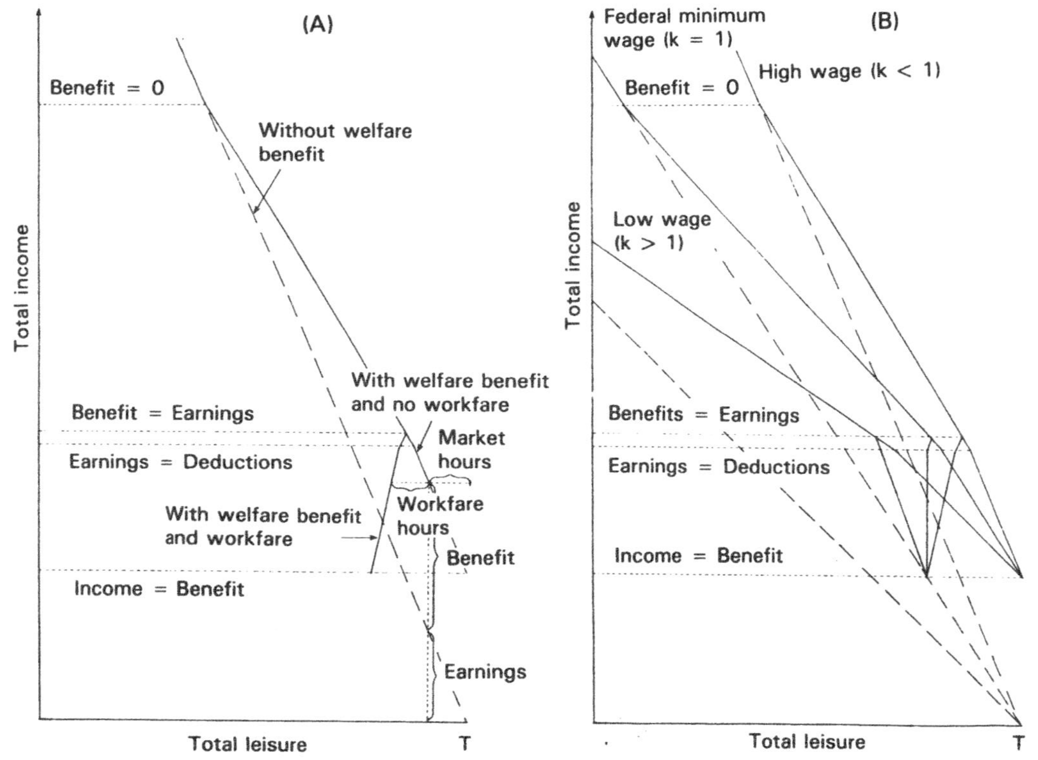

Policy implications

To summarise the policy implications of the preceding analysis, two questions can be addressed: first, what is the impact of workfare on labour supply; and second, how does the impact differ for different forms of the work requirement? As the analysis shows, the impact of workfare on labour supply (in market work) is ambiguous. If the participant's wage rate exceeds a critical value, then workfare is never preferred and the impact on labour supply is positive or zero. On the other hand, if the wage rate is less than this critical value, then labour supply (in market work) could decrease instead as a result of the work requirement.

Comparing the three forms of the work requirement suggests that there are some very important differences. For the excess benefit-based obligation, it is possible to stay on the welfare programme with no work obligation regardless the value of the participant's wage rate. With this form of the obligation if earnings are initially less than the welfare benefit it is more likely that labour supply (in market work) will increase as a result of workfare. With the constant or benefit-based obligations, the substitution effect is less important and thus it is more likely that the income effect will dominate and labour supply will decrease as a result of workfare. That is, time spent in a workfare job may actually draw hours away from both market work and leisure.

SANCTIONS

Theory

The analysis in the preceding section was based on the assumption that programme benefits are withheld if the workfare obligation is not met. In this section, participant behaviour is examined under the assumption that the sanctioning process is imperfect, that is, the probability of having benefits withheld when the full workfare obligation is not satisfied, is less than unity.

A critical concept will be the 'sanction expectation curve'. The expected probability of the benefit being withheld (p) is related to actual hours worked in the workfare programme (g^A). If the programme is expected to operate according to its rules, the sanction probability will be unity for all values of $g^A < g$, where g is the

Figure 11.5 Sanction expectation curves

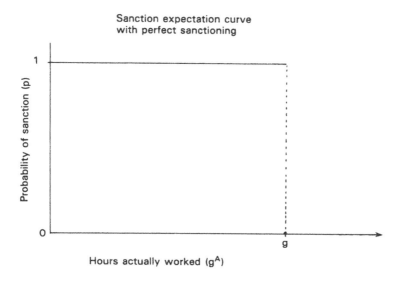

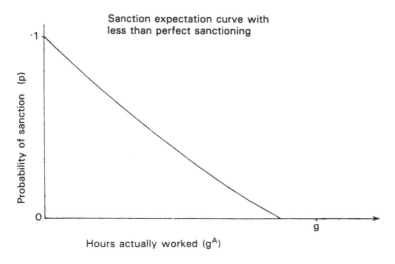

workfare obligation, and will be zero for all values of $g^A = g$. This curve is shown in Figure 11.5. However, if sanctioning is expected to be less than perfect, the curve may indicate a sanction probability of less than unity for $g^A < g$, as also shown in Figure 11.5.

Sanctions are likely to be important determinants of programme participation for individuals whose wage exceeds the implicit wage in workfare. As shown in the preceding section such individuals will never prefer workfare to market work alone when sanctions are perfect. However, if sanctions are imperfect, some of these individuals may prefer workfare. The decision will depend on the relation between the likelihood of sanctions and the labour supplied to workfare. Expectations regarding the sanctioning process replaces the market wage as a determinant of participation in workfare. The conditions under which workfare is preferred will now be derived.

For any sanction expectation curve which has a value of $p < 1$ for any $g^A < g$, there may be a rational temptation to cheat. Whether cheating can be expected to pay off depends on whether the expected utility from a violation of the rules exceeds the utility from both market work alone (i.e. non-participation in the programme) and compliance with workfare regulations. For market wage rates greater than the implicit workfare wage, the utility of market work alone exceeds the utility of compliance with workfare, therefore the decision to cheat depends on a comparison of the expected utility of cheating with the utility of market work alone.

The individual's decision may be stated in terms of the following inequality:

Participate in workforce if $V^E > V$ where,

$$V^E = \max_{L_1, L_2} [pU(L_1, L_2, Y) + (1 - p)U(L_1, L_2, Y + B)]$$

$$\text{subject to } L_1 \leq T_1 - g^A; \; L_2 \leq T_2$$
$$Y = \Sigma W_i(T_i - L_i) - W_1 g^A + NEY$$
$$B = A - r(Y + NEY)$$

$$V = \max_{L_1, L_2} U(L_1, L_2, Y)$$

$$\text{subject to } L_1 \leq T_1; \; L_2 \leq T_2$$
$$Y = \Sigma W_i(T_i - L_i) + NEY$$

and $i = \begin{cases} 1 = \text{workfare participant} \\ 2 = \text{other household members} \end{cases}$

For $V^E = V$, an individual will be indifferent between

AN ECONOMIC THEORY OF WORKFARE

participating in workfare and not participating, since the expected utility of each alternative is the same. An indifference curve relating the sanctions probability to hours of work at a workfare job may be derived for any given value of V. Such an indifference curve may be shown to have the following properties: (1) to pass through the point ($p = 1$, $g^A = 0$), (2) to be negatively sloped, (3) to have a slope that increases (in absolute value) with time spent in workfare,[3] and (4) to have a slope that varies directly (in absolute value) with the participant's wage rate. These points are proved in the Appendix.

The indifference curve indicates how much of a reduction in the probability of being sanctioned would be necessary to bribe an individual to release one more unit of time to the workfare programme. Since both the probability of being sanctioned and hours worked in workfare have a negative impact on utility, one is traded off against the other to maintain the same level of expected utility. An example of an indifference curve is shown in Figure 11.6.

Figure 11.6 Sanction indifference curve

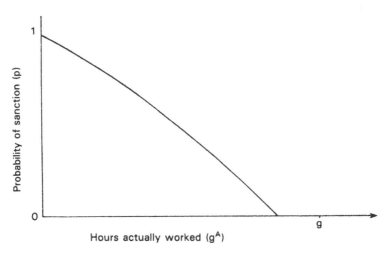

By combining the sanction expectation curve and the indifference curve, the conditions under which an individual would choose to participate in workfare may be examined. The sanction expectation curve is simply a menu of all possible combinations of values of the sanction probability and time in workfare that an individual thinks

AN ECONOMIC THEORY OF WORKFARE

Figure 11.7 Programme participation is preferred

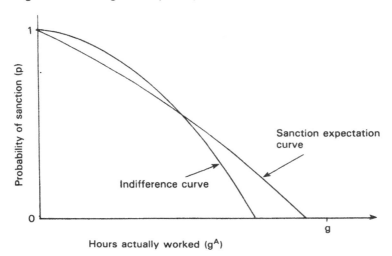

are available. If any of these available combinations lie inside the indifference curve (for which $V^E = V$), a higher expected utility is obtained by participating in the programme. This curve is illustrated in Figure 11.7.

The indifference curve derived from the equality of V^E with V represents the lower bound of achievable utility. If programme participation is preferred, the actual utility level will exceed V. In fact one could define a family of indifference curves representing higher and higher levels of utility above V, with utility increasing as the curve and the indifference curve approaches the origin. The preferred point would then be represented by a tangency of the sanction expectation curve closest to the origin.

One implication of this analysis is that if the expected sanction probably is less than unity at the point $g^A = 0$, workfare will always be preferred. For example, see the case shown in Figure 11.8. This suggests that for sanctions to be effective, a participant must believe that benefits will be withheld if he does not work at all in workfare.

However, sanctions may be completely effective in deterring cheating with $p < 1$. As long as the sanction expectation curve lies outside the indifference curve, participation in workfare is not preferred. With a steeply sloped indifference curve the expectation curve may fall more rapidly without encouraging participation in

AN ECONOMIC THEORY OF WORKFARE

Figure 11.8 Constant probability of sanction

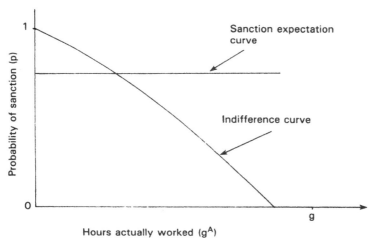

Figure 11.9 Indifference curves for different wage rates

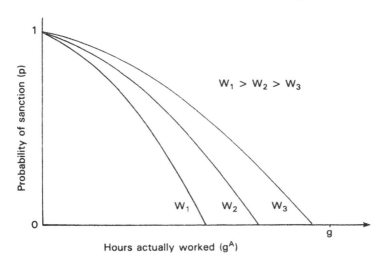

309

workfare. One determinant of the slope of the indifference curve is the market wage of the workfare participant. The greater the participant's wage, the lower the value of p for any g^A, as shown in Figure 11.9. This fact implies that the sanction probability necessary to discourage cheating is lower for high wage workers.

To demonstrate the potential implications of this analysis, assume a sanction expectation curve for the following form:

$$p = \begin{cases} 1 \text{ if } g^A < g^* \\ 0 \text{ otherwise} \end{cases}$$

This function is based on an expected threshold of cheating beyond which sanctioning is assumed to occur with certainty. With such an expectations function, the individual will always choose to work g^* units in workfare. Since there is no perceived risk of sanction for $g^A \geq g^*$, an optimising individual would reduce workfare participation to level g^*. In other words, individuals will behave as though the workfare requirement is actually g^* and sanctions are perfect. Under these circumstances the analytical models developed in the preceding section to predict participation when sanctions are perfect may be directly applied by substituting g^* for g in the equations. If g^* is constant, then the results of the constant obligation apply. Alternatively, in the case of a proportional relation such as $g^* = \alpha g$, the results of the preceding section directly apply. The proportionality constant enters the inequality affecting participation so that, for example, in the benefit-based case workfare is never preferred if $\alpha W_1 > W^m$.

CONCLUSIONS

To summarise the implications of this analysis, the following conclusions can be drawn. First, the participant's market wage rate and expectations concerning sanctions are key determinants of the decision to participate in workfare. As the market wage increases relative to the implicit workfare wage, participation in workfare decreases. Similarly, as the probability of being sanctioned for noncompliance increases, participation in workfare decreases. A second conclusion is that if participation is preferred, then the impact of workfare on labour supply in market work may be negative. Finally, different forms of the work obligation can have very different effects on labour supply.

In a dynamic framework where wage rates are endogenous,

participation decisions may change over time if workfare provides investment in human capital or job-search instruction. If adequate investment is provided, workfare participants may leave the programme as market wages increase. However, if no investments are made in the workfare participants, a larger fraction are likely to remain on the programme indefinitely or for long periods of time. Hence policy makers face a trade-off. A workfare programme with limited investments will lead to higher benefit costs but lower investment costs, while a programme with extensive investments will have lower benefit costs but will cost more in terms of investments. Thus, some investment in training and job search instruction can be justified by the resulting saving in benefit costs.

APPENDIX

In this appendix certain properties of the indifference curve relating the sanction probability to actual time in workfare are demonstrated. The indifference curve is defined by the equality between expected utility of participating in workfare (V^E) with a sanction probability p and utility derived from market work without welfare (V). Formally, V^E and V are defined by

(1) $\quad V^E = \max_{L_1, L_2} [pU(L_1, L_2, Y) + (1 - p)U(L_1, L_2, Y + B)]$

$\quad$ subject to $L_1 \leq T_1 - g^A; L_2 \leq T_2$
$\quad\quad Y = \Sigma W_i(T_i - L_i) - W_1 g^A + NEY$
$\quad\quad B = A - r(Y + NEY)$

(2) $\quad V = \max_{L_1, L_2} U(L_1, L_2, Y)$

$\quad$ subject to $L_1 \leq T_1; L_2 \leq T_2$
$\quad\quad Y = \Sigma W_i(T_i - L_i) + NEY$

and $\quad i = \begin{cases} 1 = \text{workfare participant} \\ 2 = \text{other household members} \end{cases}$

An indifference curve relating to p to g^A under the constraint that $V^E = V$ may be shown to have the following properties: (1) to pass through a point defined by (p = 1, g^A = 0), (2) to be negatively sloped, i.e., dp/dg < 0, (3) to be convex, i.e. $d^2p/dg^2 < 0$ and (4) to have a slope which varies directly with the participant's wage (W_1). These properties are derived below.

Statement 1: The indifference curve passes through a point defined by $(p = 1, g^A = 0)$.

Proof: Substituting $p = 1$ and $g^A = 0$ into (1) and (2) yields an equality $V^E = V$, therefore, such a point lies on the indifference curve.

Statement 2: The indifference curve is negatively sloped.

Proof: To show that the slope is negative, impose the constraint $V^E = V$ and differentiate the two expressions with respect to p and g^A to get the expression:

$$(3) \qquad \left.\frac{dp}{dg^A}\right|_{V^E = V} = -\frac{V^E_g A}{V^E_p}$$

Evaluating $V^E_g A$ and V^E_p separately gives:

$$(4) \qquad V^E_g A = -[pU_{1T_1} + (1-p)U_{2T_1}]$$

where U_{jT_1} represents the marginal value of the participant's time when sanctions occur $(j = 1)$ and when they do not occur $(j = 2)$ (i.e. $U_{iT_1} = -U_{ig}A$, since $T_1 = L_1 + g^A$).

$$(5) \qquad V^E_p = U_1 - U_2 + p(U_{1L_1}L_{1p} + U_{2L_2}L_{2p} + U_{1Y}Y_p)$$
$$+ (1-p)(U_{2L_1}L_{1p} + U_{2L_2}L_{2p} + U_{2Y}Y_p)$$

where subscripts denote derivatives with respect to the variables in subscripts. The last two terms in (5) sum to zero if expected utility is maximised. To verify this fact, substitute the identity $Y_p = -(W_1L_{1p} + W_2L_{2p})$ and the following first-order conditions for utility maximisation into (5).

$$(6) \qquad W_i [pU_{1Y} + (1-p)U_{2Y}] = [pU_{1L_i} + (1-p)U_{2L_i}]$$
$$\text{for } i = 1, 2$$

This substitution reduces the expression to:

$$(7) \qquad V^E_p = U_1 - U_2$$

The expression for the slope becomes

$$(8) \qquad \left.\frac{dp}{dg^A}\right|_{V^E = V} = -\frac{V^E_g A}{V^E_p} = \frac{pU_{1T_1} + (1-p)U_{2T_1}}{U_1 - U_2} < 0$$

The slope is negative since the marginal utilities of time are positive and since $U_1 - U_2 < 0$.

Statement 3: The indifference curve is concave.

Proof: The indifference curve is concave because the second derivative is negative, as shown below.

AN ECONOMIC THEORY OF WORKFARE

(9) $$\frac{d^2p}{dg^2} = -\{(U_1 - U_2)[pU_{1T_1T_1} + (1-p)U_{2T_1T_1}]$$
$$+ [pU_{1T_1} + (1-p)U_{2T_1}](U_{1T_1} - U_{2T_1})\}/$$
$$(U_1 - U_2)^2 < 0$$

The expression is negative as long as $U_{1T_1} < U_{2T_1}$, which is satisfied if the marginal utility of time rises with unearned income.

Statement 4: The absolute value of the slope of the indifference curve varies directly with the participant's wage rate.

Proof: The expression for the slope is

(10) $$\left.\frac{dp}{dg^A}\right|_{V^E = V} = \frac{pU_{1T_1} + (1-p)U_{2T_1}}{U_1 - U_2}$$

This expression simplifies under the assumption utility is maximised. The numerator, the expected marginal utility of time may be written as:

(11) $$pU_{1T_1} + (1-p)U_{2T_1} = [pU_{1L_1} + (1-p)U_{2L_1}]L_{1T_1}$$
$$+ [pU_{1L_2} + (1-p)U_{2L_2}]L_{2T_1} + [pU_{1Y} + (1-p)U_{2Y}]Y_{T_1}$$

Since income is defined by

(12) $$Y = (T_1 - L_1)W_1 + (T_2 - L_2)W_2$$

The following differential identity holds:

(13) $$Y_{T_1} = W_1 - W_1L_{1T_1} - W_2L_{2T_1}$$

In addition, if expected utility is maximised the following first-order conditions hold:

(14) $$pU_{1L_i} + (1-p)U_{2L_i} = W_i[pU_{iY} + (1-p)U_{2Y}]$$
for $i = 1, 2$

Substituting (13) and (14) into (11) yields the following simplified expression for the expected marginal utility of income:

(15) $$pU_{1T_1} + (1-p)U_{2T_1} = W_1[pU_{1Y} + (1-p)U_{2Y}]$$

The resulting expression for the slope of the indifference curve then becomes:

$$\left.\frac{dp}{dg^A}\right|_{V^E = V} = \frac{W_1[pU_{1Y} + (1-p)U_{2Y}]}{U_1 - U_2} < 0$$

Thus, the slope varies directly with the level of the participant's wage, W_1.

313

NOTES

* Deputy Area Manager, Applied Management Sciences, 962 Wayne Ave., Silver Spring, MD 20910, and, Economist, KETRON Inc., 350 Technology Dr., Malvern, PA 19355. We gratefully acknowledge the cooperation and assistance of Abigail Nichols, Mike Temple, Gloria Gambone, and two anonymous referees. Parts of this research were performed persuant to Contract No. 53-3198-2-71 from the US Department of Agriculture. The views expressed herein are those of the authors and do not necessarily represent the official position or policy of the government of the United States.

1. The assumptions of this model include: this is a one-period (static) model; utility is maximised subject to the budget constraint; and individuals can freely choose their desired hours of work at the fixed market wage rate. These assumptions are described more completely in Killingsworth (1983).

2. The term 'frontier' is used here rather than constraint since in some cases there are income–leisure combinations above and to the right of the frontier which could be chosen. The frontier is intended to describe income–leisure combinations when the full obligation is worked.

3. That is,

$$\left. \frac{d^2 p}{(dg^A)^2} \right|_{U=U_0} < 0.$$

REFERENCES

Cogan, J.F. (1981), 'Fixed Costs and Labor Supply', *Econometrica* 49 (July): 945–63.

Killingsworth, M.R. (1983), *Labor Supply*, Cambridge: Cambridge University Press.

12

British Work Incentives and the IR/DHSS Effective Tax System: An Essay Designed to Provoke Discussion

Tom Kronsjö*

Some years ago a mother with a young child explained to me her personal experience of the British unemployment situation as follows: 'I was offered £45 per week by my former employer, but when I discovered what I would lose in benefits, I decided not to take the job as we are better off on social security.'

That unemployment in Britain has reached quite substantial proportions is a well-established fact, although it may not be recognised in all quarters as a major problem. In January 1986 we were stuck with 3,407,729 jobless, with an end-September 1985 additional 671,000 employed under the Manpower Services Commission,[1] all of whom are presided over by 114,800–171,990 civil servants (see Appendix, Table 1). Together, these people exceed the unemployment of the Great Depression.

An issue of considerable controversy is how this unemployment arises, that nourishes the sectarian violence of Northern Ireland, the hopes of political overthrow by the miners, and the rampages of youth. Needless to say, there are many explanations, not all of which are mutually exclusive. The villain of the piece may be seen as insufficient demand, as the government wanting to discipline the trade union movement, or in terms of the Marxist thesis that capitalism requires a large army of unemployed in order to depress wages and so increase profits.

It is not our aim here to contribute further along those lines. Instead, we shall direct our interest at some of the negative side-effects that are produced by the palliatives distributed to those hurt by joblessness. That the social security system can create unemployment is well known in the literature, and we shall not add to these writings here. Instead, we shall attempt to quantify the disincentive effects that are created by the British system in particular, and the results obtained are so startling that we have deemed it necessary to present them in a rather provocative way.

In the UK, the benefit system of the Department of Health and Social Security (DHSS) has grown steadily over time, as have Inland Revenue (IR) progressive tax rates, assisted by large doses of inflation. Our aim in this chapter is to study the combined effects of these two factors (progressive tax rates and income-related benefits) on the decision-making of the unemployed. We shall treat the DHSS as a regular employer for the unemployed, and ask ourselves what possibilities other employers have of competing for that labour. A worthwhile net earning from working, above that provided by the DHSS benefit level, will be seen to require a gross wage that exceeds by three to nine times the worthwhile net amount. As will be evident from the following Figures and Tables, the UK tax/benefit system deprives the unemployed of incentives to work by requiring low-income earners to pay marginal effective taxes in the range of 70–90 per cent. This can in some sense be seen as a new type of poverty-trap.

Critics may say that this trap is largely irrelevant because the replacement wage (at which net income in work equals net income out of work) has been effectively unchanged, while unemployment has been increasing. One of the important conclusions of this study, however, is that, for all practical purposes, the replacement wage is utterly misleading. Its proposed successor is the concept of an acceptable gross wage (AGW), and if instead we study the movement over time, in real terms, of this concept, for any particular type of household we find that it has been increasing. This upward movement seems to offer a partial explanation to the paradoxical situation of rising average wages for manual work at a time of increasing unemployment.

In order to bring home the seriousness of the disincentive effects of the benefit *cum* marginal tax system, apparent from the data presented below, we shall pursue the argument that a reduction in unemployment requires a reversal of DHSS–IR growth, thus ensuring that the acceptable gross wages are brought down.

THE SUPPLY OF LABOUR

The unemployed complain that there are no jobs. The employers' experience is that few unemployed persons turn up for job interviews and that it is very difficult to find anybody willing to work.

Who's telling the truth here? Let us take a closer look at the supply side.

A person will be prepared to take a job if the remuneration and the working conditions and prospects are more attractive than those he can get elsewhere. Among possible 'jobs', we shall include one as being at home doing whatever he fancies on the payroll of the DHSS. If that is better than the low-paid jobs which are available, he will sign on for unemployment/social security benefit until he either finds a more remunerative job, or until — while being unemployed — he has increased his skills to a level where he can successfully apply for a job for which he was previously not qualified.

Any income gained from a 'proper' job must be compared with the loss of income from unemployment and other benefits. The position is clearly seen when an unemployed person increases his income from a 'proper' job. With every additional pound of gross earnings there are associated deductions for PAYE (Pay As You Earn) tax and employee national insurance, but also losses of rent and rate rebates, family income supplement, free welfare milk and free school meals for children, and a number of other benefits for the unemployed. The total sum of these deductions constitute his or her *marginal effective income tax*.

The marginal effective income tax may be plotted for various types of households, of varying numbers of adults and children of different ages. The DHSS calculates such tables biannually for households consisting of one to two adults and 0–4 children of specified ages.[2] These tables indicate the gross wage at which the working head of a household earns exactly the same net income as he/she would receive from unemployment and other benefits. The appropriate rounded figures have been specifically indicated in each of the figures that follow. It is unlikely, however, that many unemployed persons would accept such a wage offer, as they then lose the net value of the relinquished free time.

When a person takes a full-time job, he/she gives up the alternative use of 40 hours and additional travelling time. That time might have been spent boosting unrecorded GNP in the black economy, at a gain of maybe a few pounds per hour (risking detection by the DHSS–IR). Alternatively, one may perfectly legally spend time decorating one's house to sell at a profit and reinvest most of the proceeds in another dwelling for restoration. Further, one may look after one's children at a saving of perhaps £1.00 per hour (equivalent to £40 per week). Some unemployed may spend their time in gardening, providing free untaxed food with an average value of, say, 50p per hour (£20 per week). Yet others may do nothing — just sit around feeling bored and value their free time at £0.00 per hour.

So we conclude that some people attribute a zero cost to giving up 40 hours of free time, i.e. would be prepared to work for the same net pay as received from the DHSS in benefits. Others, with a lost opportunity cost of 50p per hour, will expect a net income increase (after all deductions) of £20 more from employment (e.g. to compensate for forgone garden produce) than what they receive net from the DHSS. Again others, with an opportunity cost of £1.00 per hour, expect to have a net income increment of £40 from employment (to compensate for the do-it-yourself achievements forgone).

THE ACCEPTABLE GROSS WAGE

The acceptable gross wage (AGW) depends on benefits, on the opportunity cost of the potential employee's surrendered free time, and on taxes, national insurance and the rules for reduction of benefits as income increases. The DHSS implicitly assumes that an unemployed person values his free time at £0.00 per hour, shown by the W'(B' + 0) curve in Figure 12.1, where B' is benefit and 0 the opportunity cost. It looks agreeably low, for all of the representative households, and one wonders why the 3.4 million unemployed are not chasing any £13.20–£62.03 jobs in the country.

The position is radically different if an 'honest' unemployed person (that is, one who does not enter the black economy) rationally calculates that an acceptable gross wage should not leave him worse off than social security benefits plus the modest value of, say, £20.84 per week gained from his gardening and other do-it-yourself activities. (£20.84 in April 1985 prices corresponds to £20.00 in November 1984 prices, which were used in the original calculations made for this chapter.) If so, only jobs with a gross wage above £38.21–£180.82 are now worth taking, shown by the W'(B' + 20.84) curve.

Still worse, if the unemployed person becomes very skilled in his 'home' activities and produces an untaxed £41.68 product per week, we would only find him taking a job which pays above £133.13–£214.98, shown in the W'(B' + 41.68) curve. From the two top curves in Figure 12.1 we can see clearly how the same pattern

BRITISH WORK INCENTIVES

Figure 12.1 The acceptable gross wage for an unemployed person, with different family responsibilities, who considers his free time worth £0, £20.84, £41.68, etc.[3]

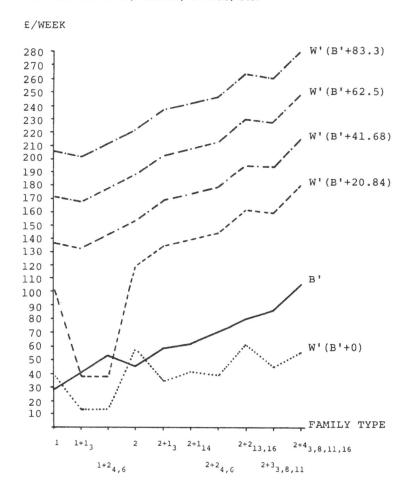

continues. As the unemployed become more and more productive in the use of their free time, the requirements of the AGW rise correspondingly.

Unemployed with the modest forgone opportunity cost of the order of £41.68 for single parents and of £20.84 for all others, find that due to the marginal effective tax system of the DHSS–IR they do not derive sufficient gain from jobs paying less than £103–£182,

319

depending upon their family situation and housing benefit. This should be compared to the present manual average weekly wage of £97.34 for women and £159.30 for men.

In our scenario, we find a very conspicuous correlation between UK unemployment and the DHSS-IR tax/benefit system. The objection may be raised, that the DHSS-IR have kept the replacement wages largely constant and nevertheless unemployment has dramatically increased. This must therefore be due to a Keynesian demand shortfall. The replacement wage, however, is of interest only to unemployed persons with zero domestic productivity or zero enjoyment of 40 hours of leisure. They probably comprise a minute fraction of Britain's unemployed population. The overwhelming majority of unemployed may be expected to have an AGW far in excess of the replacement wage. This is of crucial importance as DHSS-IR policies have caused a steady rise in this concept.

The simplest way to study the relationship between benefits, the replacement wage, the AGW and unemployment is to use the DHSS tax/benefit model (first published for November 1980) in conjunction with the DHSS and Department of Employment statistics on unemployed social security receivers, on retail price index and on average wages.[4] This is shown in Figure 12.2. On the vertical axis financial amounts are shown, in November 1984 prices for the beginning of each period, and on the horizontal we have the corresponding unemployment rates, measured at the end of each period by the number of recipients.[5]

The following conclusions emerge for the available time series: the benefit, B, and the replacement wage W(B) curves are roughly constant over time. The AGW for £20, £40, etc. additional earnings has been rising, thereby causing an increase in unemployment, as reflected in the positive slope of the W(B + 20), the W(B + 40) and higher curves. The average manual male and female wages have increased slightly in spite of increased unemployment. This result may be attributed to the increase of the AGW W(B + 20) — and higher curves — for single people and married couples, and W(B + 40) — and higher curves — for one-parent families.

The deviations from a smooth curve may be due to (a) cyclical fluctuations; (b) the introduction or discontinuation of additional benefits like low-cost travel, leisure activities, etc. for the unemployed; (c) sample errors in measuring the average council housing benefit; (d) a movement by the unemployed away from council housing into more expensive owner-occupied dwellings; (e) possible change in the domestic productivity/enjoyment of leisure by the unemployed.

Figure 12.2 The benefit (B), replacement wage W(B), acceptable gross wage for different net earnings W(B + 20), ..., W(B + 80) averaged for the representative households, average earnings of manual workers (at the beginning of each period) against total unemployment (at the end of each period) from November 1980 to November 1985. (Weights used are proportional to the number of unemployed supplementary benefit receivers of the corresponding type in January 1982.)

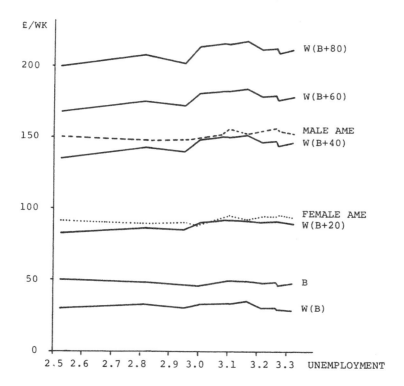

THE UK MARGINAL EFFECTIVE INCOME TAX

The marginal effective income tax graphs that are presented in the following figures are given for the DHSS representative households as of April 1985. They are understatements, because they do not include employer's National Insurance payments, which are presumed to be paid by the employers. National Insurance contributions on earnings are sometimes defended as being not a tax but an insurance premium. This argument, however, is undermined by the operation of Supplementary Benefit, which means that most people not paying their 'premium' will still get insurance (whether in unemployment or in pensionable age or sick). Only those whose non-wage income is above the Supplementary Benefit ceiling would not be so insured. Hence the gross wage should be defined as the present gross wage plus the employer's National Insurance contribution.[6]

As of 6 October 1985, a system of graduated rates was introduced for employees. The tax scale used below is based on using the allowance for single person (and wife's earned income) election, i.e. separate taxation for husband and wife. The loss of social security benefits with increasing income is not included. As we can see from Appendix Table 2, the adjusted marginal tax rate rises from 0 per cent for incomes below £35.50, to 44.77 per cent for the £130.00–264.99 income bracket, falling to 36.62 per cent for incomes of £265.00–352.99, finally rising to 63.78 per cent for incomes of £813.27 and up.

In addition to disregarding employer National Insurance payments, there is another reason why the tax picture is an understatement. It will only be accurate if a person can spend his money on goods exempt from value added tax (VAT). Accuracy would thus require adjustment for indirect taxes, as shown in Appendix Table 3. The disposable incomes of low-income earners, for example, are subject to an additional indirect taxation of about 7.64 per cent. The resulting total of marginal taxation is not unimportant, because tax-payers may be smarter than the tax-gatherers. They may find it advantageous to retire from the Adam Smith world of wealth-creation by specialisation, to the tax haven of a Robinson Crusoe existence of do-it-yourself, thereby escaping the Inland Revenue and Customs and Excise tax inspectors, accepting instead the benefits granted by the DHSS welfare officials.

Let us now proceed to study the empirical evidence of what has been said above.

REPRESENTATIVE HOUSEHOLDS

The following ten figures depict the situation for each of the DHSS representative households, from the single person to the married couple with four children. On the horizontal axes we have plotted

Figure 12.3 The marginal effective income tax of a single person

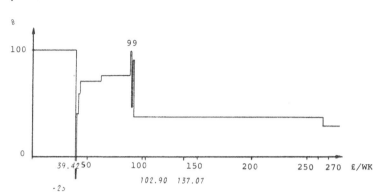

gross weekly wages, and on the vertical the corresponding marginal effective tax rates, as defined above. For completeness we have included the full set of households, but a reader who finds the data repetitious after, say, half a dozen may turn directly to Table 12.1, where the principal results are summarised.

A single person living on social security (Figure 12.3) is unable to derive any financial benefit from a job which offers less than £39.42, as his/her earnings would be deducted from the social security benefit. Above that, for every £1.00 of gross pay, he would be taxed at the rate of 42–99 per cent. If he persists in increasing his skills so that he can earn a gross income above £92, then his additional earning is taxed at 39 per cent, up to £265 where it again reduces to 30 per cent. If the unemployed person evaluates his 40 hours of free time at £0.50 per hour (i.e. proceeds from gardening, servicing, do-it-yourself and any moonlighting jobs, the equivalent of an after-tax income of £20.84 in April 1985 prices), he would be a fool to accept any job paying less than £102.90. The gross wage is 4.94 times the net wage and the average tax rate is about 80 per cent.

The single parent with one child aged three (Figure 12.4) derives no financial benefit from any work paying less than £13.20. A net earning of £20.84 is obtained from a gross earning of £38.21. The situation improves with increasing gross wage up to £67 where the net earning reaches £29.67. From then on, up to a gross wage of £103.57, further efforts only give financial losses. After that the

Figure 12.4 The marginal effective income tax of a single person with one child aged three years

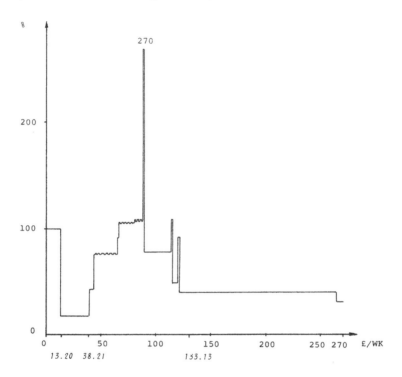

financial position improves though with an occasional setback. To get a net increase in income of £41.68, that may be sufficient to compensate for the loss of free time and employing an occasional childminder, the single-parent has to earn a gross wage of £133.13. The gross wage is 3.19 times the net wage and the average effective tax rate is about 69%.

A single-parent with two children aged four and six (Figure 12.5) derives no financial benefit from any work paying less than £13.95. A net earning of £20.84 requires a gross wage of £38.12. The family position improves up to a gross wage of £67.00 which gives a net earning of £31.73. From then on increased efforts are rewarded by financial losses. The gross earning of £116.83 gives the single-parent the same earning as that provided by the gross earning of £67.00. Still further efforts result in a sequence of financial ups and

Figure 12.5 The marginal effective income tax of a single person with two children aged 4 and 6 years

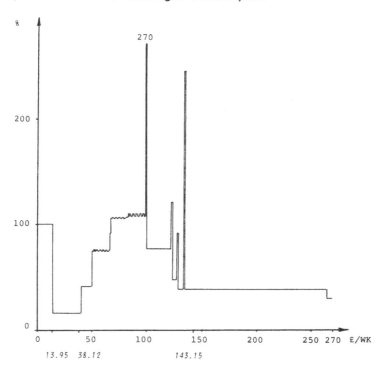

downs. A net earning of £41.68 requires a gross wage of £143.15. The gross wage is 3.43 times the net wage and the average tax rate is about 71 per cent.

For a married couple with no children (Figure 12.6), any job offer at a gross wage of less than £58.44 is not worth considering, thereafter the financial position improves with occasional financial setbacks. A net £20.84 increment from working is achieved at a gross wage of £119.77. The gross wage is 5.75 times the net wage and the average tax rate is about 83 per cent.

The married couple with one child agred three (Figure 12.7) encounter financial loss from a job with a gross wage less than £34.95. Thereafter the position improves so that a net earning of £9.32 is achieved from a gross wage of £67.00. From there onwards up to the gross wage of £102.57 increased efforts are in vain. A net

Figure 12.6 The marginal effective income tax of a married couple with no children

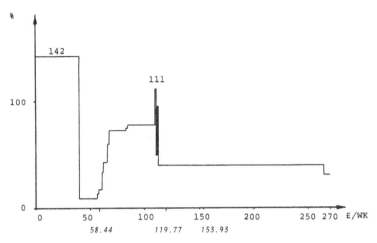

earning of £20.84 requires a gross wage of £134.62. The gross wage is 6.46 times the net wage and the average effective tax rate is about 85 per cent.

A married couple with one child aged 14 (Figure 12.8) work in vain for any wage less than £41.91. A gross wage of £67.00 will provide them with a net earning of £6.67. Improved vocational skills will only result in losses or gains between −£1.18 and +£1.48, until a gross wage of £104.52 is reached, which yields no improvement upon the gross wage of £67.00. Earning an additional £20.84 above the benefit level requires a gross wage of £139.70. The gross wage is 6.7 times the net wage and the average effective tax rate is about 85 per cent.

A married couple with two children aged four and six (Figure 12.9) derive no financial gain from any job with a gross wage less than £39.20. Thereafter the position slightly improves and a net earning of £11.38 is derived from a gross wage of £67.00. Increased skill will pay 4p when a gross income of £116.00 is reached. Any intermediate position is a waste of talent. A net earning of £20.84 requires a gross earning of £144.64. The gross wage is 6.94 times the net wage and the average effective tax rate is about 86 per cent. At £265 the marginal effective tax rate drops to 30 per cent.

A married couple with two children aged thirteen and sixteen

Figure 12.7 The marginal effective income tax of a married couple with a child agred three years

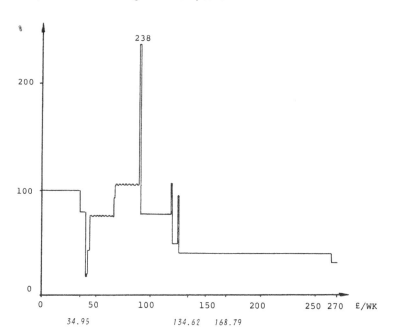

(Figure 12.10) derive no benefit from working for a gross wage under £62.03 or between £86.00 and £104.80. Efforts to locate a gross wage of £67.00 will be crowned by a net earning of £1.03. Thereafter increased skills are rewarded by financial loss until the gross wage of £108.83 will have been reached, which gives the same net earning of £1.03 as £67.00. A net earning of £20.84 requires a gross wage of £162.34. The gross wage is 7.79 times the net wage and the average effective tax rate is about 87 per cent.

A married couple with three children aged three, eight and eleven (Figure 12.11) can only derive a financial benefit from a gross wage exceeding £45.54. A net earning of £9.21 is achieved from a gross earning of £67.00. Thereafter increased effort results in less earnings up to the gross wage of £129.09. Another net £3.49 will have been earned by the gross wage of £147.00. A net income of £20.84 is reached at a gross wage of £160.31. The gross wage is 7.69 times the net wage and the average effective tax rate is 87 per cent.

BRITISH WORK INCENTIVES

A married couple with four children aged three, eight, eleven and sixteen (Figure 12.12) can only derive some financial benefit from a gross earning exceeding £56.76. A net earning of £4.09 is obtained from a gross wage of £67.00. After that increased efforts are punished by net losses up to £135.35. Thereafter follow ups and downs until the gross wage of £161 is reached which gives a net improvement of £4.66 above that yielded by the gross wage of £135.35. A net earning of £20.84 requires a gross wage of £180.82. The gross wage is 8.68 times the net wage and the average effective tax rate is about 88 per cent.

THE NEW STYLE POVERTY TRAP

The evidence presented in the Figures 12.3–12.12 above indicates rather forcefully the impact of the combined DHSS/IR tax and benefit systems on incentives for the unemployed to accept job offers. Table 12.1 summarises two of the most salient features.

Table 12.1 Ratios between acceptable gross and net wages (G/N) for the DHSS representative households, and corresponding marginal effective tax rates (MET), in percentages

Adults:	1	1	1	1	1	2	2	2	2
Children:	0	1	2	0	1	2	2	3	4
Ages:	—	3	4,6	—	3	14	4,6	13,16	3,8,11	3,8,11,16
G/N:	4.94	3.19	3.43	5.75	6.46	6.70	6.94	7.79	7.69	8.68
MET:	80	69	71	83	85	85	86	87	87	88

Source: Figures 12.3–12.12.
Calculations are based on a net wage of £41.68 for single parents and of £20.84 for all others.

From Table 12.1 we can see that a low income-earner wishing to achieve a worthwhile net earning from work is forced to pay an effective marginal tax ranging from 69 to 88 per cent, depending on the type of household. In consequence, the acceptable gross wage will exceed the worthwhile net earning by between three and nine times. In our opinion, this comes very close to a new-style poverty-trap, barring the unemployed from taking up low-paid jobs, and thus condemning them to permanent unemployment, as job offers

Figure 12.8 The marginal effective income tax of a married couple withone child aged 14 years

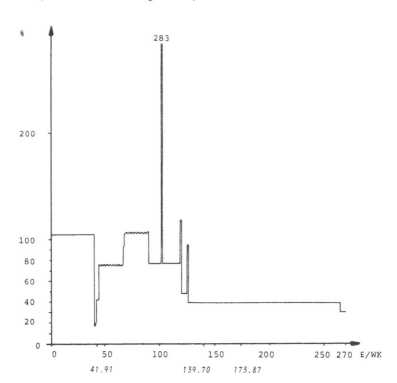

meeting the acceptable gross wage will be scant indeed. Let us now proceed to see how the system could be revamped, in order to free the unemployed from their trap.

THE LOGIC OF A NON-TRAP SYSTEM

We shall now proceed to outline how a system could be devised that avoids this trap and instead confronts the unemployed with tangible incentives to work. The basic propositions are:

1. a person with no income and no capital should have a guaranteed minimum;

Figure 12.9 The marginal effective income tax of a married couple with two children aged 4 and 6 years

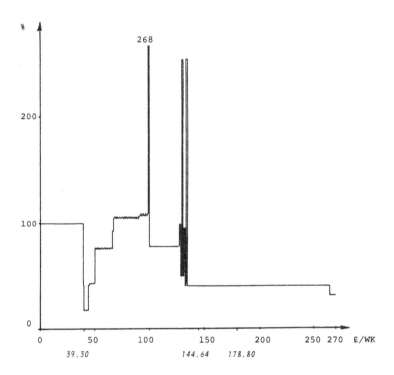

2. a person with a certain (unspecified) income or capital should neither pay tax nor receive benefits;
3. any increase in earnings from work or capital should give a net gain to stimulate effort and thrift;
4. the marginal tax at low earnings should not exceed that at high earnings;
5. the tax on low-paid jobs should leave a net earning after tax large enough generally to exceed the value of domestic productivity or the enjoyment of leisure, here assumed to be around £20 per week.

The satisfaction of Propositions 1-4 requires the award of a fixed payment (tax credit or basic income) to everybody, and a constant or increasing marginal tax of less than 100 per cent on income and

Figure 12.10 The marginal effective income tax of a married couple with two children aged 13 and 16 years

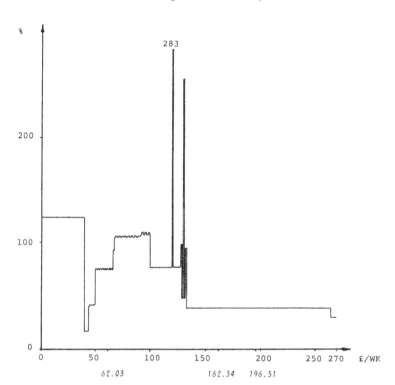

earnings from capital. Proposition 5 is satisfied as long as the gross wage is above or equal to £20/(1 − a), where a is the tax rate (e.g. £32.13 at 30 per cent basic tax and 7.75 per cent national insurance). Should the remuneration of low-paid jobs begin to approach this level, as may be the case for the 16 year olds, then a further tax reform could be considered, viz. the institution of zero marginal tax for gross earnings up to £20 per week. Such a reform would be rather expensive, as it would cost £7.55 per week in lost tax revenue per income-earner.

However, as currently 90 per cent of all male manual workers (excluding overtime and absences) earn more than £94.10 and female workers more than £62.00,[7] the manual wage level may move downwards for some while without violation of Proposition 5

Figure 12.11 The marginal effective income tax of a married couple with three children aged 3, 8 and 11 years

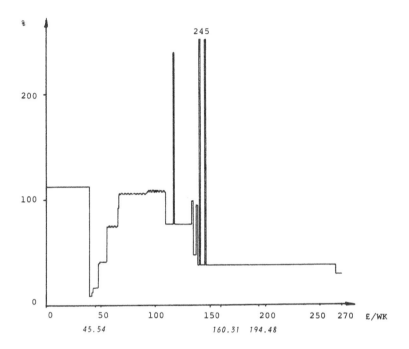

(except for some youngsters who may have to be dealt with by special measures).

When the problem is seen in this way, the multitude of benefits, rules, queuing and surveillance can be scrapped and replaced by a simple system administered by the Inland Revenue, with most people never noticing the change. The important exceptions are the unemployed, who are faced with incentives to improve their lot by taking up low-paid jobs, or by self-employment, and the employers, who now find takers for jobs at low wages.

THE NO FRILLS EGALITARIAN WELFARE STATE

Having considered the marginal effective tax schedules of the DHSS–IR, it may be of interest to estimate the total expenditure on

Figure 12.12 The marginal effective income tax of a married couple with four children aged 3, 8, 11 and 16 years

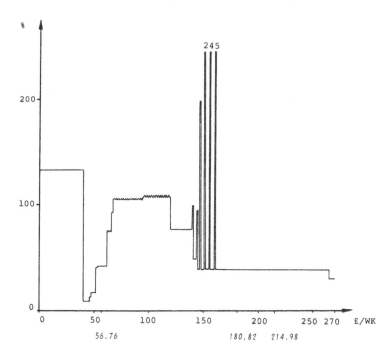

the present social security policies (excluding the cost of the pensioners). This is done in Appendix Table 4 and it comes to a round figure of £48 billion. To estimate the financial effects of the proposed reform, we also need to know the market clearing gross wages of the unemployed. These have been assumed to average at £60.00, with a token spread of earnings as given by Appendix Table 5. The corresponding tax revenue is calculated in the same table at £5.070 billion.

The general consequences of a low, middle and high tax credit, respectively, to adults of working age and to children are then explored and presented in Appendix Table 6. It is assumed that the previously unemployed take up low-paid jobs with a total gross wage of £60 per week. Under these assumptions, a *low* tax credit of £7.00–£10.50 (depending on age) would cost a mere £15.371 billion (20.441–5.070).

In the *medium* case, a £10 credit to every adult of working age and to every child would cost £20.011 billion (25.081–5.070), or less than half the estimated expenses of £48 billion for the present social-industrial policy. Using the representative households of the DHSS model, only the largest (with four children) would be worse off financially, and then only marginally so. In practice, the psychological benefit the children derive from growing up in an average working family might adequately compensate.

Finally, a *high* tax credit of £20 to every adult of working age, and £10 to every child, would cost £36.937 billion (42.007–5.070), or around three-quarters of the expenditure of the present social policy. All the representative households of the DHSS would be better off.

In practice there would be winners and losers depending on current housing benefits. People with low housing benefits would gain, and people with high benefits would lose. As the reform would be introduced gradually, however, there would be time for families to adjust, by moving from regions with fewer overall advantages to those with greater. Winners and losers would similarly arise from the differential ability of families to advance their vocational skills and to find the appropriate jobs or become self-employed.

REDIRECTED SPENDING

Fixed payments are currently paid for all children. All people paying income tax are implicitly getting a fixed payment equal to the allowance × the tax rate. Raising the tax allowances would thus be equivalent to raising the fixed payment. An employee earning the assumed gross wage of £60 would be liable to a tax, inclusive of employee national insurance, of £22.65 and to a tax credit of e.g. £10.00. His or her net income would be equal to £60.00 – 22.65 + 10.00 = £47.35. A person due less tax than £10.00 would receive a cheque from the Inland Revenue for the difference.

Changing from one system of payment to another should not present unsurmountable problems, provided it takes place at e.g. 1 per cent per fortnight over 200 weeks, i.e. nearly four years. In the first fortnight the DHSS payment is decreased to 99 per cent of its original value, and everybody receives an earnings-unrelated payment of 1 per cent of its final value. In the second fortnight the DHSS payment is decreased to 98 per cent and the earnings-unrelated payment is increased to 2 per cent of its final value, and so on. As benefits are reduced, the earnings-*cum*-credit option becomes more and more attractive, relative to the unemployment benefit-*cum*-credit option.

The cuts will be felt in the budgets of the spending departments, as these are cut by approximately 1/4 of the desired final cut per year. For a planned final cut of 20 per cent at the end of four years, an annual cut of 5 per cent is implied. The spending departments would have to seek new markets for their services or goods, or cut their wage levels. Removing some of the wild undergrowth of benefits of the DHSS–IR system should improve the performance of the UK economy and hasten the transition of the beneficiaries from unemployment to employment.

THE UPSIDE DOWN WORLD

Suppose that a £10.00 credit to every adult of working age and to every child is approved by Parliament. The consequences of this are explored in Table 12.2. The currently awarded (April 1985) DHSS total income support is tabulated in Column B for Benefit. The total income support that a £10 per capita credit would provide to the DHSS representative families is tabulated in Column C for Credit, and the shortfall in conventionally defined welfare is then listed in Column D = B − C for Difference.

The gross wage (assuming 30 per cent taxation and 7.75 per cent employee national insurance contribution) that would have to be earned in order to compensate for the difference D is listed in Column GW(D) = D/0.6225. Some people with a preference for an alternative life-style maintain that dairy milk and overeating are health hazards. Therefore, an alternative lifestyle shortfall, A, may be defined by disregarding the value of the free welfare milk and the free school meals, V, to provide the column A = D − V. The so-defined shortfall in alternative lifestyle welfare requires the earning of a lower gross wage, as listed in the column GW(A) = A/0.6225.

The required gross wage figures are astounding. At the local Job Centres, vacancies seem to abound at this range of low pay. Though perhaps none of the unemployed may have fully fathomed the profound depths of DHSS benefit or IR tax instructions, the average unemployed person seems to have a good understanding of the consequences of the net payment received from the dole office and the proposed net payment, after deducting travel expenses, from the

Table 12.2 The gross weekly wage that would compensate for the shortfall in income support under a credit system of £10 per child and per adult of working age

Size child age(s)	B	C	D = B − C	A = D − V	GW(D)	GW(A)
1	28.05	10.00	18.05	18.05	29.00	29.00
1 + 1 3	41.36	20.00	21.36	19.75	34.31	31.73
1 + 2 4 6	53.02	30.00	23.02	19.35	36.98	31.08
2	45.55	20.00	25.55	25.55	41.04	41.04
2 + 1 3	58.86	30.00	28.86	27.25	46.36	43.78
2 + 1 14	61.96	30.00	31.96	29.90	51.34	48.03
2 + 2 4 6	70.52	40.00	30.52	26.85	49.03	43.13
2 + 2 13 16	81.32	40.00	41.32	37.20	66.38	59.76
2 + 3 3 8 11	86.93	50.00	36.93	31.20	59.33	50.12
2 + 4 3 8 11 16	106.29	60.00	46.29	38.50	74.36	61.85

prospective employer. He quickly grasps that those low-paying job offers on the notice boards are best disregarded, unless he has more than £3000 in (declared) savings or has a working spouse. Employers tell the opposite story, that it is almost impossible to find somebody willing to work for a wage under £150.

THE FOUR-YEAR TRANSITION

Economic forecasting models usually give a pessimistic assessment of the possibility of abolishing unemployment within the relatively short period of four years. Such models are built upon fitting curves to scattered observations, showing small variations. For the evaluation of the effect of decisive changes, they usually require extensive reconstruction and tend to become very tentative, because of the missing practical observations of the effect of large changes.

Hence, in contemplating the necessary path ahead it may be best to get the broad conceptions outlined, not being bound by the mathematical constructs of such models, which presently incorporate the labour market behavioural relationship appropriate to the high effective marginal taxation of the DHSS–IR system. Getting rid of 13.5 per cent unemployment over four years would in this perspective require generating about 3.4 per cent, or 851,932, more low-paid jobs per year.

During recent years, the DHSS–IR benefit-tax system has deprived the unemployed of reasonable incentives to take up menial jobs at low wages supported by a fixed, (age-) graded egalitarian payment, thereby forcing employers to use expensive capital as a substitute for labour, to the detriment of wage-earners, taxpayers and the prosperity and profitability of the companies and regions. This shedding of workers is visible in the rise of notified redundancies, from 158,000 in 1977, to a peak of 532,000 in 1981 and a subsequent drop to 238,000 in 1984.[8] These figures, moreover, only give part of the picture, as redundancies involving less than ten workers per firm are not included. Statistics on the total number of redundancies are not readily available. Evidence that a developed industrial economy can adjust on the required scale, however, is indicated by the decrease in US unemployment by about 20 per cent in one single year, between the third quarters of 1983 and 1984.

The problem of transition can be conceptually simplified into the phasing-out of the old system and the phasing-in of the new. This allows us to calculate the overall savings (revenues) from the phase-out. Their details are left undefined, a proportional reduction being one of the possibilities. The pace of the rundown is chosen to be four years, so that it may go relatively slowly. Hence the phase-out fraction is 1/4 per year, and it is assumed to take place continuously. Taking the initial expenditure on social security in year 0 as unity, and in year 5 as zero, it follows that the average social security expenditure fraction in an intermediate year i will be $((5 - i) + (4 - i))/8 = (9 - 2i)/8$, which comes to 7/8, 5/8, 3/8 and 1/8 of the normal annual expenditure, here taken to be the total of £48 billion given above.

By taking the initial level of taxes and unemployment as well as the final level of tax credit and additional tax income from increased employment for any age group as unity, the progress of the reform can be described in terms of fractions. During the first transition year, the 16–19 year olds are given a full tax credit and become ineligible for social security benefits. As all reforms are assumed to take place continuously, the yearly cost is only half of the final cost. All other age groups are increasingly being given a tax credit, which at the end of the first year amounts to 1/4 of its final value. The average tax credit over the year for these groups is thus $(0 + 1/4)/2 = 1/8$. For simplicity it is assumed that the unemployed age groups stay unemployed proportionally to the remaining unemployment related social security payments.

The additional tax revenue fractions follow the increase in employment (decrease in unemployment). The difference between the fractions used is due to the fact that the unemployment one refers to the end of each period, while the additional tax revenue refers to an average for each period. In the year of the full extension of the tax credit to any particular age group, the corresponding annual expenditure fraction becomes $((i - 1) + 4)/8$. The reform aims in the first instance to get the young into work. Simultaneously a gradual change is applied to all remaining unemployed, in order to make a gentle transition into work. Hence in each of the four years the age groups 16–19, 20–24, 25–34, 35–64 and 0–15 (denoted by 35–15) is in turn given the full tax credit, thus becoming ineligible for the remaining unemployment related benefits.

The formerly unemployed are supposed to earn gross wages and pay tax and national insurance (including employer's contribution) according to Appendix Table 2. Table 12.3 then lists the actual costs involved for the three tax credit variants, as specified by Appendix Table 6.

The middle variant is preferred, as it provides a basic existence minimum as well as reasonable incentives for further improvement by work and study, all at a moderate cost that leaves some surplus for possible reductions of the tax schedules, particularly to the low income-earners. The conversion of a further tax reduction into an equivalent credit is probably undesirable as the resulting higher marginal taxation in the lower income bracket may take away work incentives to those who need them most.

CONCLUSION

Needless to say, the argument presented in this paper suffers greatly from the ambition of attempting to present a simple panacea for a complicated problem. Yet, our defence against such criticism shall be that the evidence presented above on the disincentive effects of the DHSS–IR benefit *cum* tax system are of such a magnitude that a rather provocative formulation of the argument may be necessary, in order to attract the desired attention.

The starting point for our programme to reduce UK unemployment can be stated very simply: To the employers the gross wage (plus employer national insurance) is important, while to the employee it is the net earning — consisting of the tax credit and the net wage (less employee national insurance) — that is relevant.

It is evident from the acceptable gross wage figures shown above that the UK social security system currently sets a floor on gross

Table 12.3 The expenditures and revenues of the reform calculated for the three variants, in £bn

Year	ssb + ia policy	Tax credit low	Tax credit mid	Tax credit high	Orig. tax	Add. tax	Surplus low	Surplus mid	Surplus high
0	−48.000	0.000	0.000	0.000	48.000	0.000	0.000	0.000	0.000
1	−42.000	−3.063	−3.862	−5.977	48.000	0.817	3.754	2.955	0.840
2	−30.000	−8.936	−11.221	−18.174	48.000	2.385	11.449	9.164	2.211
3	−18.000	−14.274	−17.817	−29.810	48.000	3.780	19.506	15.963	3.970
4	−6.000	−18.622	−22.998	−38.618	48.000	4.747	28.125	23.749	8.129
5	0.000	−20.441	−25.081	−42.007	48.000	5.070	32.629	27.989	11.063

Source: Own calculations.

wages, depending upon family size, actual family housing cost and its domestic productivity. This sloping floor begins at about £100 and ends at about £200 per week, which should be compared to the average weekly manual wage of about £160 for men and about £100 for women. The proposals made above would remove this artificial floor on UK gross wages. It would lead to a fall in wages particularly for unskilled labour but with repercussions through the entire wage range due to substitution effects.

Net earnings to labour consist of any tax credit, like the child benefit, plus net wages excluding employee national insurance contributions. The net wages are determined by the gross wages and the tax and national insurance rates. The fall in gross wages does not necessarily imply a fall in net earnings to labour due to the simultaneous changes in tax credits, tax and national insurance rates. Table 12.4 summarises the main effects of the proposed transition to a non-trap system.

Table 12.4 The transition years in summary

Year	Full credit phased in to age	Surplus £bn low	middle	high	Unemployment (000s)
0	none	0.000	0.000	0.000	3276.9
1	16–19	3.754	2.955	0.840	2041.1
2	20–24	11.449	9.164	2.211	1015.9
3	25–34	19.506	15.963	3.970	316.2
4	35–64, 0–15	28.125	23.749	8.129	0.0
5	all	32.629	27.989	11.063	0.0

Job creation may require some further discussion in this framework, but our ambition has not really been to proceed much beyond a simple demonstration of the disincentive effects of an important part of the current British social and labour market policies. It is to be hoped that others will realise the gravity of the situation and make their contributions towards its rectification.

NOTES

* The author gratefully acknowledges the helpful suggestions of the Editor, Professors Patrick Minford and Prasantha Pattanaik, Drs Hans Aage, Rosemary Clarke, Lydia Kronsjö and Steven Tupper, and students Simon Pegg, Tim Sprackling and Robert Thomson.
1. *The Daily Telegraph*, 31 January 1986, p. 1.
2. DHSS (1985c).
3. These tables suffer from the shortcoming that they do not begin their listings from £0 but start at £40. It has therefore been necessary to average or extrapolate in that range, when such values have been required. A request was made to the DHSS that the model be tabulated from £0 instead of from £40 but that request was turned down. Whatever those values might be, they do not affect our main conclusions.
4. DHSS (1985b), Tables 34.81, 34.85, DE (1986), Tables 5.4, 6.4.
5. For each point, the financial figure refers to the beginning of a period, the unemployment figure to the end of the same period.
6. Minford (1984), p. 6.
7. DE (1984), Table 38, p. B42.
8. DE (1986), Table 2.30 and footnote.

APPENDIX

Table 1 Civil servants involved directly or indirectly with the current social security *cum* industrial aid programme in 1985

DHSS	81,000	
Department of Employment	26,000	
Local Authorities housing benefit	7.800	
Total official estimate		114,800
Manpower Services Commission	20,802	
Trade and Industry	7,989	
Ulster Defence Regiment	6,500	
British Army in N. Ireland	9,500	
Police force increase (1978–83)	12,399	
		57,190
Total unofficial estimate		171,990

Sources: DHSS (1985a), Vol. 1, p. 7. H.M. Treasury (1985a), Table 1, Department of Trade and Industry 12, 620. HM Treasury (1985b), Class IV, Department of Trade and Industry, non-unemployment related staffing deductions, Votes 4c(1/3), 6a1(4), 6e, 17b at 1 April 1985 totalling 4,630.5 civil servants. Macdonald (1985). CSO (1985a), Table 4.2, by strength excluding Scottish Central Service and Seconded as elsewhere included.

Table 2 The marginal income tax and national insurance rates (exclusive of the loss of social security and other benefits)

Weekly earnings £	Income tax %	Employee NI contribution %	Employer NI contribution %	Marginal tax rate %
0.00– 35.49	0	0	0	0.00
35.50– 42.28	0	5	5	9.09
42.29– 54.99	30	5	5	38.10
55.00– 89.99	30	7	7	41.12
90.00–129.99	30	9	9	44.04
130.00–264.99	30	9	10.45	44.77
265.00–352.99	30	0	10.45	36.62
353.00–410.52	40	0	10.45	45.68
410.53–510.25	45	0	10.45	50.20
510.26–661.75	50	0	10.45	54.73
661.76–813.26	55	0	10.45	59.26
813.27–	60	0	10.45	63.78

Source: The marginal tax rate was calculated out of a gross wage enlarged by the employer national insurance contribution, on the basis of the income tax and national insurance schedules from 6th of October 1985 given in H.M. Treasury (1985c), pp. 26–8.

Table 3 Indirect taxes paid by all households (per cent)

Increasing gross income % of observations	% of gross income	Indirect tax % of disposable income	% of household expenditure
0–10	9.59	7.64	7.41
10–20	8.34	9.72	8.80
20–30	9.86	11.24	10.34
30–40	10.80	13.12	12.32
40–50	9.38	12.11	11.67
50–60	9.42	12.31	12.40
60–70	9.25	12.11	12.57
70–80	8.54	11.43	12.36
80–90	9.07	12.19	13.38
90–100	7.26	10.14	12.17
Total	8.80	11.39	11.95

Source: Todd and Hamilton (1981), p. 18.

Table 4 An estimate of the cost of the 1984–85 tax/benefit *cum* industrial aid system

Expenditure	£bn
DHSS: unemployed people	6.400
families	7.540
DES: meals	0.524
IR: Income tax allowances & relief	25.768
Industry, Energy, Trade, Employment	6.316
Ministry of Defense: Ulster ops	0.121
Home Office, etc. riots-notional[a]	1.331
Total to the order of	48.000

a. An estimate of the cost of the policing of riots and of the associated destruction was requested from the Home Office. In the absence of an official figure, a notional figure was used based upon an estimate of the cost of the miners' strike at £6bn. This sum spread over six years gives £1bn per year. The notional figure of £1.331bn was used as it gives a round figure to the total.

Sources: DHSS (1985a), Vol. 3, Table 5.5. CSO (1985a), Table 3.4 meals in 1983–84 £0.499bn with relative RPI 0.9529.BIR, (1984) Table 1.5 for 1983–84, Income tax allowances less exemption for first £7,100 of investment income and Blind Person's Allowance; Relief less Losses on unquoted shares of trading companies, Expenditure of property managed as one estate, Foreign pensions: 10 per cent deduction; in total in 1983–84 £24.555bn with relative RPI 0.9521. H.M. Treasury (1985b), Class IV Industry, Energy, Trade and Employment, Class IV total less 1C3 & 6, 2C6/7, 2E, 4B1, 4C, 5G, 6A1(4), 6E, 9C5, 10, 11, 12B, 13B/D, 14, 15B, 16A1(3/4), 16A4, 17B, 20; in total in 85–86 £6.627bn with relative RPI 1.0493. Macdonald (1985), in 1985–86 £0.127bn with relative RPI 1.0493.

Table 5 Different age groups of unemployed (000s), assumed gross wages after the reform and corresponding tax revenues calculated at the pre-6 October 1985 rates; basic tax 30%, employee national insurance 9% and employer national insurance 10.45%

Age	Unemp	£gw/wk	£bn/yr
16–17	211.2	32.75	0.178
18–19	344.2	35.00	0.311
20–24	689.8	40.00	0.711
25–34	766.9	65.00	1.285
35–44	475.6	85.00	1.042
45–54	425.4	80.00	0.878
55–59	287.8	75.00	0.557
60–65	76.0	55.00	0.108
Total	3276.9	60.00	5.070

Source: DE (1986), No. 1, Table 2.7, unemployment age, entry October 1985.

Table 6 An estimate of the cost of a tax credit system by age group

Age group	£bn/yr £1/wk	Low variant £/wk	Low variant £bn/yr	Middle variant £/wk	Middle variant £bn/yr	High variant £/wk	High variant £bn/yr
0-4	0.1874	7.00	1.312	10.00	1.874	10.00	1.874
5-9	0.1748	8.00	1.399	10.00	1.748	10.00	1.748
10-14	0.2112	9.00	1.900	10.00	2.112	10.00	2.112
15-19	0.2421	7.00	1.694	10.00	2.421	10.00	2.421
20-24	0.2421	7.00	1.694	10.00	2.421	20.00	4.841
25-29	0.2076	7.00	1.454	10.00	2.076	20.00	4.153
30-34	0.1981	7.00	1.387	10.00	1.981	20.00	3.962
35-39	0.2136	8.00	1.708	10.00	2.136	20.00	4.271
40-44	0.1740	8.50	1.479	10.00	1.740	20.00	3.479
45-49	0.1645	9.00	1.481	10.00	1.645	20.00	3.290
50-54	0.1602	9.50	1.522	10.00	1.602	20.00	3.204
55-59	0.1618	10.00	1.618	10.00	1.618	20.00	3.236
60-64	0.1708	10.50	1.793	10.00	1.708	20.00	3.416
Children & working adults			20.441		25.081		42.007

Source: CSO (1985b), Table 2.2 age distribution of estimated population at 30 June 1984.

REFERENCES

BIR (1984), *Inland Revenue Statistics*, (1983-84), HMSO, London.
CSO (1985a), *Annual Abstract of Statistics*, No. 121, HMSO, London.
⸻ (1985b), *Monthly Digest of Statistics*, No. 476, HMSO, London.
DE (1984), *New Earnings Survey*, HMSO, London.
⸻ (1986), *Employment Gazette*, Vol. 94, No. 1, HMSO, London.
DHSS (1985a) *Reform of Social Security*, HMSO, London.
⸻ (1985b), *Social Security Statistics*, HMSO, London.
⸻ (1985c), *Tax/Benefit Model Tables April 1985*, London.
H.M. Treasury (1985a), *Civil Service Statistics*, HMSO, London.
⸻ (1985b), *Supply Estimates 1985-86*, 239-IV, HMSO, London.
⸻ (1985c), *Budget Report 1985-86*, HMSO, London.
Macdonald, W. (1985), *Letter D/GS Sec/66/3/1 of 28 October 1985*, General Staff Secretariat, Ministry of Defence, London.
Minford, Patrick (1984), 'Twilight of the Union Bosses', *University of Liverpool Quarterly Economic Bulletin*, Vol. 5, No. 4.
Northern Ireland (1979), *Northern Ireland Education Statistics*, No. 27, HMSO, Belfast.
Todd, Douglas and Hamilton, Vivien (1981), *The Impact of Indirect Taxes on Households*, Government Economic Service, Working Paper No. 44.

Part Five

A Final Note

13
'Productive' and 'Non-productive' Economic Activities: A Note on Haavelmo

Björn Thalberg

The idea that the economic activities of a person who strives to maxmise his or her utility may take a 'non-productive' as well as a 'productive' form is explicit or implicit in the writings of a number of economists from Adam Smith onwards. Smith's view on the concept of 'non-productive' economic activity, i.e. activities which do not have a positive impact on the total flow of goods and services but may affect distribution, may be exemplified by references to the familiar dictum that whenever businessmen gather together they as a rule start conspiring against free competition. For an early example where the idea is expressed very explicitly, we may look at Pareto's *Manuale di economia politica*: 'We can assert', Pareto writes,[1] 'as a uniformity revealed by history, that the efforts of men are utilised in two different ways: they are directed to the production or transformation of economic goods, or else to appropriation of goods produced by others.' 'This division of human activity', he continues, 'is not peculiar to the division which results from free competition, it is one of general applicability.'

In the same passage Pareto also criticised the optimistic view of Say, who implied that the phenomenon of non-productive economic activities might gradually vanish as a result of the diffusion of economic knowledge. It was, in Say's view,[2] 'education which we lack, and especially education in the art of living in society'. Pareto, however, argued that economic knowledge or theories 'have only a very limited effect in the determination of man's actions, self-interest and passions play a much greater role, and some obliging theory is always found in the nick of time to justify them.'[3]

The idea of the dual directions of the economic efforts of men is also, to mention an example from Swedish literature, explicit in Göran Nyblén's book *The Problem of Summation in Economic*

349

Science. Nyblén distinguishes on the one hand between the 'pure production aspect', or 'Man versus Nature', and on the other the 'pure distribution aspect', or 'Man versus Man'. 'We find', he writes, 'that under certain circumstances the production aspect dominates the life of a social economy . . . under other circumstances the production aspect is remarkably absent . . . but a conflict of interest is quite evident to the observer, although the traditional economics and the political speeches sometimes try to obliterate it.'[4]

The distinction between 'productive' and 'non-productive' (or 'unproductive') economic activities is sometimes found, as in the above examples, in introductory considerations or in discussions of a very general type. But it has also been the subject of more specific and formal types of analysis, a prime example being Jagdish Bhagwati's analysis of DUP activities.[5] A review of this literature is, however, outside the scope of this chapter. We shall instead concentrate our interest on a model suggested by Trygve Haavelmo in a series of lectures at Oslo University in 1950. The aim of Haavelmo was, *inter alia*, to analyse how the relation between total 'productive' and total 'non-productive' economic efforts may tend to change during the development of a 'welfare state'.[6] Unfortunately, Haavelmo's ideas and suggested analysis appeared only in Norwegian, and then only in the form of mimeographed notes from his lectures.[7] It has, as far as I know, never been discussed or referred to in the literature. His analysis, however, represents an interesting early attempt to illuminate, in a very suggestive and aggregative way, the question as to whether peoples' efforts will, in changing circumstances, tend to go in a more 'productive' or in a 'non-productive' direction. It remains, I think, of considerable interest even today.

HAAVELMO'S MODEL[8]

Let us use the following symbols:

y_i' 'productive' input from individual i (measured for example in working hours of a certain standard)
y_i'' 'non-productive' economic activity from individual i (measured in some standard unit)
X total flow of goods and services in the economy

By y"-activity is meant efforts which do not increase X, but are intended for distributional purposes only. We may, for example, think of activities which take place within trade unions and employers' associations, within political parties, within various kinds of organisations which promote particular group interests, and finally some specific activities within private firms and even within public institutions. The activities of these organisations do, of course, contribute to total production, but in varying degrees they also feature components which benefit their own distributional interests only.[9] With respect to private firms, we may mention 'excessive' advertising as an illustrative example. To defend their market shares firms may feel that they have to keep up with the advertising volume of their competitors, implying that the industry as a whole may expend more money on this account than is justified for purely informational purposes. In respect of public institutions, we learn from the public choice literature that y"-activities may take place in this sector as well.

A further important factor is of course taxation. We know from observation and introspection that people and organisations often make great efforts to keep their tax liabilities low and, if possible, to increase their subsidies, allowances and/or compensations of various kinds. In fact, private persons as well as firms often pay specialists for such purposes.

The level of y"-activities obviously depends, as the above examples imply, upon the design and working of the economic system. The less an economic system works through simplifying devices (the main and most celebrated simplifying 'device', of course, being a smoothly working market price mechanism),[10] and the more the economy develops towards a 'bargaining society',[11] and the more complicated and confused the tax system becomes, the greater will be the level of unproductive, as compared to productive, activity.

We assume that the total flow of goods and services depends on the sum of the productive inputs y'_j, $j = 1, 2, \ldots, N$.[12]

(1) $\quad X = \phi(\Sigma\, y'_j)$

Moreover, we also assume that the income of individual i depends upon his individual efforts y'_i and y''_i, as well as upon the levels of total productive and unproductive activity in the economy.

(2) $\quad x_i = k\, \dfrac{y'_i}{\Sigma\, y'_j}\, \phi + \dfrac{1-k}{N}\, \phi + h\left(y''_i - \dfrac{\Sigma\, y''_j}{N}\right) \dfrac{\phi}{\Sigma\, y''_j}$

where $0 < k < 1$, $0 < h$, and ϕ is given by (1).

According to (2), x_i varies positively with y_i' (as seen from the first term on the right-hand side). However, it is assumed that only a fraction of total income is distributed according to people's productive inputs. A person can, as is described by the second term, also count on a 'fixed' income, independently of his or her productive efforts. The relationship between how much of X is distributed according to, or independently of, the individual's productive input, is expressed by the parameter k. The greater the levels of various kinds of social transfers and public consumption, the lower the value of k.

Furthermore, (2) also expresses the possibility that a person can boost his or her income by means of y''-activity. The marginal effect of these kinds of activity depends, according to the last term of (2), on the parameter h, on total y''-activity,[13] and on ϕ, the total quantity to be shared. A value of h close to zero implies that the scope for y''-activities is very limited, while a value close to or above unity implies that such activities are a matter of vital importance.

Taking the sum over $i = 1, 2, \ldots, N$ on both sides of (2) we get $\Sigma x_i = \phi$, i.e. total income equals total production. Thus, the remuneration function (2) satisfies this basic requirement. A specific and somewhat questionable property of (2), however, is that the personal marginal income of y_i' and y_i'', respectively, are both approximately constant; i.e. independent of y_i' and y_i''. A constant marginal income may, however (within relevant limits), be fairly realistic regarding y'-activities, since hourly wages will as a rule be independent of the number of hours worked. For y''-activities though, decreasing returns might seem a more plausible alternative.

Incidentally, the simplifying assumption of (near) constant marginal productivities may in certain situations imply that an individual either concentrates on y'- or on y''-activities, a tendency which does not seem realistic and which may cause analytical difficulties regarding questions of stability. In a more extended analysis, it might therefore be relevant to operate with an institutionally given floor on y_i'.

A general formulation of the individual utility function is:

(3) $\quad U_i = U_i(x_i, y_i', y_i'')$

However, for our purposes it may be justifiable to operate with a simplified version of (3). The effects on U_i of the two types of activity, y_i' and y_i'', may seem symmetrical in the sense that they are, and perhaps to about the same degree, a strain on the nerves and strength of the individual. Certainly, the marginal disutility of y_i' depends on the level of y_i' as well as on y_i'', and vice versa. We may therefore, as Haavelmo did, assume that the disutility of economic efforts depends on the sum $(y_i' + y_i'')$ instead of on y_i' and y_i'' separately, granted that the two types of activity are measured in suitable units. For example, one hour spent on a lobbying mission, or one hour of queuing, may — in disutility terms — be equivalent to one hour of 'ordinary' y'-activity. Or we may imagine that one hour's y"-activity is equivalent to, say, 1½ hour's y'-activity, which, however, we can (in principle) account for by means of a system of weights in the quantification of y".

A particular problem is that the y"-activity may be illegal, which may have a bearing on disutility per se. However, we shall not go into such complexities here. Thus, we may write:

(3b) $\quad U_i = U_i(x_i, y_i)$, where

(4) $\quad y_i = y_i' + y_i''$

We now imagine that the individual maximises his utility U_i with respect to y_i' and y_i'', given (2), (3b), and (4), i.e.:

(5) $\quad [U_i(x_i, y_i) - \lambda_i(x_i - k\dfrac{y_i'}{\Sigma y_j'}\phi - \dfrac{1-k}{N}\phi - h\dfrac{y_i''}{\Sigma y_j''}\phi + \dfrac{h}{N}\phi)]$

$= \max$

We imagine that the individual considers the total levels of y_j'- and y_j''-activities as constants, i.e. independent of his or her own adjustment. We then get the following necessary conditions for a maximum:

(6) $\quad \dfrac{\partial U_i}{\partial x_i} - \lambda_i = 0$

(7) $\quad \dfrac{\partial U_i}{\partial y_i} + \lambda_i k \dfrac{\phi}{\Sigma y_j'} = 0$

(8) $\quad \dfrac{\partial U_i}{\partial y_i} + \lambda_i h \dfrac{\phi}{\Sigma y_j''} = 0$

From (7) and (8) we get:

(9) $\quad \dfrac{\Sigma y_j'}{\Sigma y_j''} = \dfrac{k}{h}$

Since only the sum of y_i' and y_i'' enters the utility function, i.e marginal disutility is always the same in both directions, then the individual marginal income of y'_i and y''_i must, in a possible equilibrium situation, be the same in both directions. This leads us to question (9).

By (9) Haavelmo has arrived at a seemingly simple and intuitively quite plausible result. The relative size of total unproductive inputs, $\Sigma\, y''_j$, compared to total productive inputs, $\Sigma\, y'_j$, depends on the relationship between the two structural parameters h and k. The greater the value of h, in relation to that of k, i.e. the greater the possibilities to improve one's lot by y''-activity (or in other words the more urgent the necessity to fight for one's share), and the less people are remunerated according to their productive inputs, the greater is the proportion of a person's effort which goes in an unproductive direction.

A possible equilibrium situation of the sort displayed in (9) may, however, be unstable. The income of extra effort is, for each individual, the same in both directions, and so is marginal disutility. If, therefore, the relationship between k and h changes, the conceived marginal incomes of all persons would, according to the model, change in the same direction, i.e. there would be a rush towards increasing either productive or unproductive activities, whereby the relationship between $\Sigma\, y'_j$ and $\Sigma\, y''_j$ may, at least temporarily, shift dramatically.

Haavelmo deduced the result (9) from, *inter alia*, the specific formulation of the utility function (3b) and not from the more general formulation (3). However, even when (3) is applied, the model implies that the relative size of $\Sigma\, y''_j$ rises with h/k. Maximising (3) with respect to y'_j and y''_j, subject to (2), gives the following result:

(10) $$\frac{U'_{i3}}{U'_{i2}} = \frac{h}{k} \cdot \frac{\Sigma\, y'_j}{\Sigma\, y''_j}$$

Here U'_{i2} and U'_{i3} denote the derivatives of U_i with respect to y'_i and y''_i, respectively. If, from an equilibrium situation where (10) is satisfied, the ratio h/k increases, e.g. the individual will adjust his activities such that the marginal disutility of y''_i increases in relation to that of y'_i, i.e. a person's economic efforts go in an increasingly unproductive direction. But $\Sigma\, y''_j$ thus increases in relation to $\Sigma\, y'_j$, which again has a bearing upon the relationship between the marginal incomes. Hence, if h/k increases by, say, 10 per cent, the emerging new equilibrium would be characterised by relatively more y''-activity, but the relationship between the marginal disutilities of the two forms of activities does not increase by as much as 10 per cent. Furthermore, depending upon the form of the utility function, we may not in this case encounter a stability problem.

We assumed above that an individual, when maximising his utility (as given by (3) or (3b)), acts as if variations of his own economic activities do not affect the aggregated totals $\Sigma\ y_j'$ and $\Sigma\ y_j''$. Whilst this is not strictly true, it may seem plausible that people act in this way. In fact, the average participant supplies only 1/N of total input, which may seem insignificant. We are concerned here with a psychological phenomenon which is sometimes referred to as the '1/N-problem'. This phenomenon is, incidentally, quite central to discussions of environmental problems, as it may explain why people neglect (on the individual level minor) negative secondary effects of their actions. But it may, in certain circumstances, be important also in connection with people's supply of labour.[14]

However, Haavelmo also considered the case where individuals do take into account the fact that variations in their own inputs affect the aggregated totals $\Sigma\ y_j'$ and $\Sigma\ y_j''$. Maximising (3b) with respect to x_i, y_i' and y_i'', subject to (4) and the remuneration function (2), we obtain:

$$(11) \quad \frac{k\ (\phi/\ \Sigma\ y_j')\ [1\ -\ (y_i''/\ \Sigma\ y_j')\ (1\ -\ \varepsilon)\ +\{(1\ -\ k)/kN\}\ \varepsilon]}{h\ (\phi/\ \Sigma\ y_j'')\ (1\ -\ y_i''/\ \Sigma\ y_j'')} = 1,$$

$$\text{where } \varepsilon = \frac{d\phi}{d\Sigma\ y_j'} \frac{\Sigma\ y_j'}{\phi}$$

The order of magnitude of the two last terms in the bracket of the numerator is probably close to zero (at least if k is not extremely small). The same is the case with the term $y_i''/\Sigma\ y_j''$ of the denominator. Taking this into account we may write:

$$(12) \quad \frac{\Sigma\ y_j'}{\Sigma\ y_j''} \sim \frac{k}{h}$$

Thus, we find that the relationship between total productive and unproductive efforts depends upon the relationship between the two 'possibility' parameters k and h, i.e. more or less the same result as above. This is also what we would expect, at least if N is large. It is interesting to note, however, that ε (i.e. the elasticity of total production X with respect to $\Sigma\ y_j'$) now enters the picture. The individuals' possible underrating of the marginal income of their y'-activities (because they ignore the effect of their own input on $\Sigma\ y_j'$, and thus on the size of the total cake to be shared), may seem small, but it is, according to (12), larger the larger the value of the elasticity ε.[15]

It is assumed above that the individuals, when adjusting their inputs, consider the other persons's inputs as independent of their own. This assumption may, as suggested, not be realistic regarding y''-activities. Haavelmo, therefore, lastly and briefly, suggests an extension of his analysis by introducing a 'retaliation parameter'. When people decide to increase their 'elbow activities', they expect, he assumes, some increased y''-activity (counteractions) from other people. To simplify, we make the assumption that the derivative of y_j'' with respect to y_i'' is equal to a constant m, $0 < m < 1$.[16] The conceived marginal income of an increased y''-activity is, according to (2), in this case:

$$(13) \quad \frac{\partial x_i}{\partial y_i''} = h \frac{\phi}{\Sigma y_i''} [1 - \frac{y_i''}{\Sigma y_j''}(1 + (N-1)m)]$$

Thus, the conceived advantage of dy_i'' is, *ceteris paribus*, lower the higher the value of the retaliation parameter m.

Maximising utility, as expressed by (3), with respect to y_i' and y_i'', subject to (2), and assuming that the individual takes into account the effects of variations in his own inputs on the aggregated totals, and that the derivatives of y_j'' with respect to y_i'' are equal to m, we get an expression for U_{i3}'/U_{i2}' which looks quite complicated. However, to study the order of magnitude of the expression, we assume that $\varepsilon = 1$ (i.e. constant returns to scale) and moreover, that N is large, k not very close to zero, and y_i'' about average. In this case we get:

$$(14) \quad \frac{U_{i3}'}{U_{i2}'} \sim \frac{h}{k} \cdot \frac{\Sigma y_j'}{\Sigma y_j''} (1 - m)$$

Thus, the relative level of non-productive efforts depends, as above, on the relationship between the two possibility parameters h and k. However, a change in the economic system such that m rises could serve to contain potential y''-activities.

A BRIEF COMMENT

With his model Haavelmo was able to sketch, in a very aggregated and simplified way, how the direction of people's economic efforts may tend to shift as a result of changes in the economic system. By its emphasis both on incentives, i.e. individual (net) marginal remuneration from the two different kinds of economic efforts, and on the level of economic transfers and public consumption, his model represents a formalisation of thoughts which are quite common in discussions of the recent developments in major economic and social systems. In particular, his analysis has, one may claim, a bearing upon the development of modern western economies such as Norway and Sweden. These are rich countries with so-called 'mixed' economies, and which strive to develop the 'welfare state'. Looking at equation (2), a characteristic feature of this development may be described by a falling value of the parameter k, implying a net income which owes less and less to productive inputs and more and more to social transfers and public consumption.

The fall in k has naturally been accompanied by a rise in h, i.e. the parameter which describes the possibility, or necessity, to increase or defend one's share by means of non-productive economic activities. At the beginning of the era the levels of public consumption and social transfers were low, as was taxation, which was built on a few clear-cut principles such as taxation according to the household's ability to pay. Hence the value of h was relatively low. In recent decades, the volume of taxation, as well as the complexity of the rules, and thus the possibilities for individual agents to exploit assymmetries and loopholes, have increased substantially. In various other respects the legal system, which regulates and controls the economy, has also grown in complexity, leaving considerably more scope for people to engage in various types of 'zero-sum games'.[17]

Consequently the ratio h/k has clearly increased, which according to the above model would imply a tendency for people's economic efforts to go in a less productive direction.[18] But are there (e.g. in Sweden) signs that people have in recent decades increasingly turned to more non-productive economic efforts? Or is Haavelmo's suggested analysis too simple? Certainly, the level of people's engagement in y''-activities seems considerable in Sweden today, but this does not necessarily mean that the ratio $\Sigma y_j''/\Sigma y_j'$ has increased more or less constantly. Direct observations on this matter are of course largely lacking, but a thorough study of the working of the central legal system and of reforms, and the subsequent development of the main incentive mechanisms, might help give an answer. Here we shall, however, limit our consideration to only two important reforms connected with the tax system.

First, we may mention the introduction of individual taxation around 1970. Before the reform, a household was treated as a unit, paying tax based on its aggregate income. A housewife who considered entering the labour market had to take into account the often high taxation rate on additions to the family's income. After the reform this was all changed, i.e. the incentive to enter the labour market was stronger. Moreover, average personal taxation increased markedly from around 1970, implying that it became harder and harder for a family within normal income brackets to live on *one* income. Thus, both increased pull and push mechanisms were at work. Not surprisingly, the participation rate of married women began, at about the same time, to rise markedly. Moreover, the reproduction rate declined, attitudes towards jobs outside home changed, and facilities for the care of children outside the home increased, which again had positive effects on the female participation rate.

Thus, along with a rising h/k ratio, in Sweden there has been a tendency for relatively more members of the family to want a job, which tends *per se* to increase the total labour supply. However, the higher participation rate of women has, to a considerable extent, meant that some kinds of productive inputs, e.g. child care, have been transferred from the non-market to the market sector with little effect on the total flow of goods and services. So the introduction of individual taxation and the subsequent developments described have here probably not after all affected the $\Sigma y_j'' / \Sigma y_j'$ ratio significantly.

A second reform to be stressed is the introduction, around 1970, of what have subsequently become very high (social) taxes on wages, paid by the employers. These payroll taxes have strongly contributed to boosting activities within the so-called 'black' or 'grey' sectors. The order of magnitude of the payroll taxes is by now some 40 per cent of gross wages received by the workers, i.e. such taxes obviously comprise a large part of the price of goods and services. Naturally, many people are looking for opportunities to avoid paying this high tax, thereby getting goods and (particularly) services cheaper, i.e. the payroll taxes stimulate demand on the black market. On the supply side, people are, because of the high marginal taxation, strongly tempted to provide black sector services, which as a rule are paid much better, net of income tax, than ordinary taxed work.

Efforts provided in or for the black or grey markets are, of course, y'-activities, which contribute to the total flow of goods and services in the economy. Since working hours and working routines at a person's ordinary (white sector) job are to a large extent institutionally determined, extra black market jobs may, as a rule, not reduce his or her time or total productive effort on the ordinary job. Thus, the development of the type of incentive structure provided by the high payroll taxes combined with very high marginal income taxes may have stimulated many people to increase their total productive efforts. Much work now accomplished in the black sector would never have been undertaken without this particular incentive structure, and the aggregate flow of goods and services would most certainly shift downwards with a possible introduction of 100 per cent effective control on black market activities. Thus, one may claim that the development of very high payroll taxes, together with high marginal income taxes, has contributed in keeping the level of aggregate productive inputs rather high in Sweden and thus strongly counteracted the potential negative effects of a rise in the h/k ratio as discussed above.

NOTES

1. Pareto (1971), p. 341.
2. Say (1828), pp. 9–11.
3. Pareto (1971), p. 342. The matter of the old Pareto–Say controversy, i.e. individuals' social and economic behaviour, has of course been more or less constantly debated. However, while we may find many examples where people behave in accordance with social and moral norms and signals *irrespective* of economic incentives, such examples are, we may argue, more the exception than the rule. Basically, people's decisions are, as Pareto suggested, guided by self-interest (as we ordinarily assume when we base our explanation of the consumer's behaviour on utility maximisation). This is, of course, one main reason why the structure of economic incentives is so important in all economic systems.
4. Nyblén (1951), p. 49.
5. Bhagwati (1982).
6. That is, an economy where, for one thing, people are, through publicly organised social security systems, guaranteed a fairly high consumption standard irrespective of their productive input. Cf. equation (2).
7. Haavelmo (1950).
8. The model below is a slightly elaborated version of the model in Haavelmo (1950).
9. In this simple analysis we disregard possible interdependence between distribution and production.
10. For example, in a system where goods and services are rationed more through *queues* than through the wallet, the level of y''-activites is, as a rule, relatively high. Incidentally, this example also suggests that the

average y''-level may be abnormally high in periods dominated by 'sellers' markets'.

11. Cf Johansen (1978).

12. We may, more specifically, operate with X as a function of both $\Sigma\ y'$ and $\Sigma\ y''$, imagining that unproductive activities have, *per se*, a negative effect on X (through 'distortions' of various kinds). However, in this study we concentrate on the 'zero-sum-game' of the y''-activities.

13. The higher the level of total y''-activity, the greater is the struggle for income shares, and the stronger is the opposition an individual encounters when seeking to boost his share by means of y''-activity.

14. Cf. equation (11), and note 15.

15. In an article Frisch (1947) argued that total (productive) labour input tended to be too low at that time in Norway, as people tended to underrate the effects of their marginal productive efforts on production and income. In the postwar years, the value of ε was, Frisch asserted, extraordinarily high, so an all-out effort to get the economy on track again could be beneficial to all. To break the attitude usually connected with the '1/N-problem', i.e. the feeling that it does not matter if only I take into account some minor secondary effects of my actions, Frisch advocated a national campaign.

16. Haavelmo considered the case where m = 1 for all j = 1, 2, . . ., N, or, alternatively, a subgroup (coalition) of N.

17. Cf. Myrdal (1978).

18. The analysis above builds on utility-maximisation at the individual level. In addition, one may argue that at the institutional level the scope for y''-activities has increased as various public or semi-public units of the growing bureaucracy strive, at least to some extent, to keep or expand their own employment as an aim *per se*.

REFERENCES

Bhagwati, Jagdish (1982), 'Directly Unproductive Profit-seeking (DUP) Activities', *Journal of Political Economy*, vol. 90, no. 5.

Frisch, Ragnar (1947), 'Den samfunnsmessige optimale arbeidsinnsats', *Stimulator*, vol. 1, no. 7.

Haavelmo, Trygve (1950), 'Teorier om produktiv innsats', Lecture notes from Professor Haavelmo's lectures in the autumn 1950, by Björn Thalberg, Institute of Economics, Oslo University, mimeo.

Johansen, Leif (1979), 'The Bargaining Society and the Inefficiency of Bargaining', *Kyklos*, vol. 32, no. 3.

Myrdal, Gunnar (1978), 'Dags för ett bättre skattesystem', *Ekonomisk Debatt*, vol. 6, no. 7.

Nyblén, Göran (1951), *The Problem of Summation in Economic Science*, Lund.

Pareto, Vilfredo (1971), *Manual of Political Economy*, London.

Say, Jean Baptiste (1828), *Cours complet d'économie politique pratique*, Paris.

Index

Aage, Hans 7-8, 10, 92(n32), 96(n45), 99(n56), 106(n3), 109(n19), 116(n38), 117(n39), 119(n48), 120(n49), 121(n53), 122(n), 128(n5), 343(n)
absent successes 4-5, 36-7, 44, 45, 47-8
absenteeism 128
acceptable gross wage (AGW) 21-2, 316, 318-34
accounting 258; *see also khozraschet*
Adam, J. 84(nn12,13), 91(n26), 116(n37)
advertising 351
Africa, food production in 191, 193-6; *see also* Tanzania
Aganbegyan, S. 94
agriculture
   in China 14, 182, 186
   in Tanzania 15-16, 191-6, 197-9 (*see also under* households)
   in USSR 186-7
   skills in 17
   subsistence 192, 193, 194, 198-9
   supervision in 130-1
   technology in 187, 195, 198, 248
AGW (acceptable gross wage) 21-2, 316, 318-34
aid 15, 191-2
   among kibbutzim 257
Aid to Families with Dependent Children Program 291
Alchian, A.A. 33(n14)
Alexander, C.P. 268(n3)
alienation 3
allocative actions 33, 35
allocative preferences 41
altruism 49; *see also* commitment
Amani, Haidari K.R. 192(n4), 195(n15)
anti-social behaviour 8, 98
Aoki, Masahiko 5-7, 60(n1), 61(n2), 65(n4), 69(n10), 70(n13)
apathy 98-9
Arzumanjan, A. 140(n26), 171(n115)
Asanuma, B. 61(n3), 64, 68
assessment 34-5, 67, 93-4
associative actions 32-3
associative preferences 41

attestation, workplace 110-11, 120-1
Avdakov, Yuri K. 154(n11)
Axelrod, R. 60

Bachurin, A.V. 108(nn13,15), 116
Bailes, Kendall 154(n13)
Baka, W. 94(n43)
bankruptcy 65, 69-70, 129, 137
banks 69, 70
bargaining 351
Barkai, Haim 16-17, 129(n7), 230(n1), 231(nn2,4), 235(n8), 241(n12), 244(n14), 245(n16), 247(nn18,20), 253(n30), 256(n32), 257(n33)
Barnum, Howard N. 199(n29), 200(n31), 204(n33)
Barone, Enrico 141(n29), 240
Bartlett, W. 272, 288(n)
Baryshnikov, Yu. 109
Bates, Robert H. 197
Baumol, W.J. 44(n25)
Beach, Charles M. 215(n58)
Bebel, August 153
behaviour 8, 98-9; *see also* rationality
Belkin, M.I. 91(n27)
Belousov, R.A. 167(n85)
benefits *see* welfare benefits *and under* Britain
Berg, Elliott J. 193(n9)
Bergman, Kenneth 191(n1)
Bergson, A. 94(n40)
Berliner, Joseph 10, 92(n32), 94(n40), 98, 105(n1), 111(n25), 113(n27), 133, 135(n17), 156
Bhagwati, Jagdish 22, 136, 350
biology 31(n9), 33(n14), 36(n19)
biotechnology 72
Birbraier, M. 166-7, 168
Birman, A. 171
Birman, Igor 141(n30)
Birman, S. 162
black economy *see* second economy *and* black markets
black markets 15-16, 196-7, 207-11
Bo, Per 199(n25)
Boesen, Jannik 219(n)
Boev, I. 160-1

361

INDEX

Bogdanov, 153
Bogomazov, G.G. 151(n2), 155(n18), 156(nn19,20), 159(n40), 166(n82)
Bonin, J.P. 84(n14), 86(n18)
bonuses
   in Japan 6-7, 65
   in USSR 7-8, 81-2, 83-6, 91-2, 112-18, 121
      analysis 81-3, 84-6, 88-9, 91-2, 95-6
      complexity 97
      problems with 184
      size of fund 112
Boot, Pieter 122(n)
Borilin, B. 165-6, 169(n101)
Bornstein, M. 79-80, 84(n15), 91(nn27,28), 92(n30), 97(n47)
Borodin, V.V. 154(n11)
Bradley, Michael 131(n11)
Branson, Philip 67(n9)
Breit, M. 272-3, 281, 282-3
Brezhnev, Leonid 79, 183
brigades
   contract 93, 94
   work 14, 91, 156, 166-7, 183, 186-7
Britain
   tax system see under taxation
   welfare benefits 21-2, 315-34
      as 'disincentive' 315-16, 319-34, 339
      costs 335-6
      proposals for reform 334-43
Brittan, S. 268(n3), 278, 281
Buchanan, J.M. 27(n2), 31(n8)
Bukharin, N. 153-4
Bukovski, Vladimir 142-3
Busjatskaya, L. 93(nn34,37)
Butaev, K. 162(nn59,61), 163

Cable, John 288(n)
Cameron, Norman 129(n7)
capital 48, 106, 245, 248
capital productivity 80, 84, 86, 89, 248
capitalism see market economies
car manufacture 60
Carlsson, Eva 122(n)
Carr, E.H. 154(n12)
Cave, M. 97(n49)
centralised entrepreneurship 44-50
change, costs of 254
Chapman, J. 111(n24)

cheating 20, 41, 306-10
Chen Yu 189
Chernichenko, Yuri 131(n12)
Chevrier, Yves 183, 185, 189
childcare 317, 358
China 13-14, 181-9
   Cultural Revolution 182
   Great Leap Forward 13-14, 182
   incentives in 186, 187-8
   inequality in 187-8
   private enterprise in 184-5
   reforms in 13-14, 184, 188-9
   relations with USSR 14, 189
   wages in 184, 187
Chinese people 185
Chinn, David 128(n6)
choice 126-7
Chrysler 69
Clark, Gardner M. 131(n11)
Clarke, Rosemary 343(n)
class identity 41
climate 191
Cogan, J.F. 298
Cohen, Stephen F. 154(n10)
Cohn, S. 80, 107(n6)
Cole, R.E. 60(n1)
collectives 252
   criticisms of 228, 246
   see also kibbutzim
collectivisation 13, 181; see also decollectivisation
command economies 5, 27-8, 30, 44-5, 46; see also individual countries
commitment 252-3, 258; see also motivation
communes 228, 241; see also kibbutzim
communication 33-4
communication skills see contextual skills
communism 153, 165-6; see also socialism
Community Work Enterprise Programs see workfare
companies 28, 30, 65
competence 34-5; see also skills
competition 5, 34-5, 45, 49-50, 70-1, 138
complaint books 11, 142
Conn, D. 84(n14)
constraints 33
consumer goods, availability 184; see also rationing

362

consumers 15, 141–2, 196–7; *see also* households
consumption, in kibbutzim 16, 229–31, 256
'contestable private enterprise' 5, 44–50
contests *see* competition
contextual skills 6, 65, 66
contract brigades 93, 94
contracting, relational *see* relational contracting
contracts 83
  employment 39, 267
control 131(n12), 132, 140, 144, 145–6, 157
  in African agriculture 193–6
  of prices 196–7, 207–8
  social 251–3, 257, 258
  see also supervision
Conyngham, W.J. 83(n11)
Cook, K.D. 192(nn3,5,6)
cooperation
  in Japan 59–64, 66, 71
  see also cooperatives and kibbutzim
cooperatives 257, 267, 272–4, 278, 283
coordination 30, 59
Cornia, Giovanni Andrea 200(n30)
corporate groupings 60–1, 63, 69–71
costs 2, 59, 62, 106, 111, 355
credit 194, 195

Dadashev, A.Z. 113(n28)
Davies, R.W. 151(n2), 154(n12), 155(nn15,16), 160, 163, 165, 167(n84), 168, 171, 172(n117)
Day, Richard B. 154(n10)
decision-making, workers' participation in 268, 277, 278, 279–80
decollectivisation 14, 185
Dehez, Pierre 288(n)
demoralisation 128, 132
DHSS (Britain) *see* welfare benefits *under* Britain
Directly Unproductive Profit-seeking Activities 22, 136, 350
discipline *see* sanctions *and* supervision
Dmitriev, Y. 94(nn42,44)
do-it-yourself 317–18, 322
dogcatching 126
dogma 143–4

Domar, E.D. 272–3
Dreifke, William 19–21
Drewnowski, J. 98(n50)
Drèze, Jacques 288(n)
Drize, I.D. 119(n45)
drought 191, 192
Dukor, G. 161
DUP (Directly Unproductive Profit-seeking Activities) 22, 136, 350

economic systems
  and 'rational' behaviour 2–3
  and social welfare 42–3
  and socio-cultural environment 40–1
  as mixtures 28
  change in 31–2
  comparisons between 4, 27–31, 38, 44–50
  likenesses 27–9
  strain on 3
  voluntary membership *see* voluntarism
  see also institutitional rules *and* organisation structures
economic theory, in USSR 140–1, 151–2, 157–72
education 34, 349
  effects 17, 255–6
efficiency, attainable 39, 99, 106
effort, measurement of 128
Eliasson, Gunnar 50(n)
Ellis, Frank 211–13
Ellman, M. 118(n44)
Elster, Jon 1, 2, 127(n1)
employers 278, 316–17, 335
employment
  contracts 39, 267
  full, effects of 276–7, 278–9
  guaranteed 137
  'lifetime' 63, 72
  see also unemployment
entrepreneurs and entrepreneurship 36–7, 39–42, 45, 185–6
  as variable 43
  centralised 44–50
  'exit' 46
  incentives for and costs of 38, 40, 41–2
  needs 50
entry
  costs 143
  see also hiring *under* labour
environmental problems 2, 355

363

INDEX

equality 228, 229
equilibrium 36, 37, 42
equipment
  obsolete 107, 110
  see also technology
errors and error-elimination 4–5, 44, 45–8
Estrin, Saul 288(n)
ethics 2, 41, 42, 137
evaluation *see* assessment
exit 10–11, 46, 47, 138–9, 144–5
  costs 143
  'soft' 11, 139–40, 141, 145
experiments 89; *see also* Shchekino experiment

factories, Japanese 58–64
Faijersson, Margit 51
failure 4–5, 44, 45–8, 70
famine 13, 182, 191
farm households *see under* households
farming *see* agriculture
fertilisers 187, 194, 195
finance, company, in Japan 65
flexibility 58–9, 105–6, 254
Folmer-Hansen, Anne-Maj 122(n)
food-processing 72
Food Stamp Program 291–2, 296
food supply
  in China 13
  in Tanzania 15, 191–2, 197–8, 218–19
  see also agriculture, famine *and* rationing
Forte, F. 45(n26)
France 46
free time, value of 21, 204, 238–9, 293, 295, 317–18, 319, 320
freedom 140, 251, 258, 278
Freris, A. 84(n13), 85(n16), 86(n18), 91(n29), 92(n30), 97(n49), 120(n50), 134(n14)
Frey, Bruno 50(n)
Frisch, Ragnar 200(n30), 356(n15)

Gambone, Gloria 314(n)
games 31, 40
Gan, H. 256(n32)
gardening 318
Gatovskii, L. 157(+n26), 160(+n49), 164, 165, 166, 168, 169(n100), 170(n106), 171
Gerrard, Christopher D. 211–13, 214(n54), 215, 217
Ginzburg, L. 155(n17), 162(n59), 166, 168
Godson, J. 111(n25)
Gomulka, S. 80(n8)
Gorbachev, Mikhail 79, 127, 138, 146, 185, 186, 189
Gorelov, N. 110(n22)
Gosplan 83, 91
Gossnab 83
Gottlieb, Manuel 199(n25)
Gould, S. 33(n14)
government 43, 45, 49–50; *see also* centralised entrepreneurship *and* state
Granick, David 133(n13), 156
Greblis, A. 162(n59), 164, 166(n81)
Greffe, X. 28(n3)
Grossman, Gregory 7
Groves, T. 28(n4), 38(n20)
growth 5, 9
Gubareva, O. 168(n95)
Gwyer, G.D. 211–13

Haavelmo, Trygve 22–3, 350–6
Hanson, P. 91(nn27,28,29), 92(n30), 94(n40), 106(n3), 109(n19), 110(nn20,23), 120
Hare, P. 97(n49)
Hayek, F.A. 31(n8)
Hedlund, Stefan 10–11, 50(n), 122(n), 129(n8), 192(nn5,6,8), 259(n), 343(n)
Helman, A. 256(n32)
Hertzka, T. 267, 272–3, 281, 282–3
hierarchies 27–8, 30, 36–7, 39, 49, 62
hiring *see under* labour
Hirschman, A.O. 10, 44(n24), 46, 50(n), 138, 139, 142, 143–5, 146(+n)
hoarding 105; *see also* labour hoarding
Holliday, G.D. 80(n8)
household responsibility 14, 186
households, farm, in Tanzania 198–9
  model of 199–206
housing 317, 319, 320
Hungary 44, 137, 185, 258
Hurwicz, L. 27(n1), 29, 31(n8)
Hydén, Göran 197
Hymer, Stephen 199(n29)

364

ideology
  of kibbutzim *see under* kibbutzim
incentive(s) 1, 11–13, 21–2, 37–42, 66–7, 258, 358
  and quality 250
  comparisons between 27
  for acquiring skills 6, 65
  for information-sharing 64–7
  for long tenure 6, 65, 66
  in China 186, 187–8
  in kibbutzim 235, 240–1, 248–53, 257
  in large firms 28
  in Tanzania 16, 192–3, 195, 218, 219
  in USSR *see under* USSR
  social 17, 41, 67, 248–54, 258
  socialist 12–13, 151, 153, 158–72
  workfare as 292
incentive funds 80, 93, 97
  see also bonuses
income
  forgoing 248
  guaranteed minimum 334
  social 230, 254–5 (*see also* welfare benefits)
  token 17, 229–31, 238
income-sharing 85, 94, 267–8, 288; *see also* bonuses *and* 'share economy'
indexation 267
individuals 30, 32, 49
  see also rationality *and* responsibility
industrial action 278–9
inflation 18, 188, 197, 256
  and taxation 316
  and unemployment 267, 268, 276–7
  controlling 276, 288
information
  assumptions about 33–4
  in USSR 10, 133–6
  mechanisms 57
  sharing 6, 7, 57–64, 66, 71–3
  and research 72–3
  and shirking 67
  see also tacit knowledge
institutional rules 31, 35, 36
  and incentives 38, 40
  limitations 40–1
insurance, company, in Japan 69–70
integration of supplies 6, 59

interest 232–4
intervention, effects of 2–3
investment 107–8
  in training 21, 311
IR *see* institutional rules
Ireland, N.J. 81(n9), 84(n14), 86(n17)
Ishikawa, T. 65(n5)
Israel 241–5, 253, 256; *see also* kibbutzim
Israelsen, L. Dwight 128(n3), 235–40, 248–51, 258

Japan
  industrial organisation in 6–7, 57–64, 67–71, 72
  Post-War Reform 61
  trade dispute with USA 7
  wages in 6–7, 64–7
job classifications 58
Johansen, Leif 351(n11)
judgement 34–5, 45, 46, 67

kanban 6, 59
Kats, V. 160(nn46,47)
Katz, Richard W. 191(n1)
Kautsky, Karl 152, 153
Kenney, M. 72(n17)
Khavin, I. 162(n59)
khozraschet 12–13, 160–72
  attempts to reform 79
  definitions 12, 79, 152, 158
  history 79, 155
Khrushchev, Nikita 141, 145, 182–3
kibbutzim 16–17, 129, 228–58
  capital in 245
  criticisms of 228, 231, 234–5, 240–1, 246, 248, 253, 255
  distribution in 229–31, 254–5
  economic analysis 229–50, 253–6
  history 235, 241–5, 250, 252–3, 254
  ideology 17, 228, 249–53, 255–8
  'industrial revolution' 254
  'irrationality' 16–17
  membership 17, 241, 251, 252, 255–6, 258
  planning in 17, 247, 257–8
  rules 234, 240, 247, 249–51, 254
  success 16–17, 241–6, 252–3, 255–6, 258
Killingsworth, M.R. 293(n1)
Kirsch, L.J. 115(n34)
Kirzner, I.M. 37

365

INDEX

knowledge *see* information *and* tacit knowledge
Koike, K. 58
kolkhozy 128(n3), 129(n9), 182–3, 235, 249, 252(n28), 258
Kornai, J. 98(n51), 137
Kostin, L.A. 107(nn11,12), 108(n17)
Kosygin, Alexei 7, 14, 79, 83(n11), 112(n26), 115
'Kosygin reforms' 7, 79, 83–4, 112–13, 115
  and China 14, 184
Kotylar, A.E. 107(nn4,5), 112, 114(nn31,32)
Koutsoyiannis, Anne 217(n59)
Kozlov, G. 160
Kravel, I. 160(n47)
Krishna, Raj 99(n29)
Krivitskii, M. 160(n46), 166, 171
Kronrod, Y. 169–70
Kronsjö, Lydia 343(n)
Kronsjö, Tom 21–2
Kulagin, G. 97(nn46,47)
Kunelskij, L.E. 84(n13), 118(nn42,43)
Kuznetsov, A. 160(nn48,50)

labour 107–8, 128
  control 13
  costs 115, 117–18
  demand 9–10, 108–9, 110
  hiring 106, 111, 247–8, 278
  in Tanzanian farm households 200, 201
  laws 90, 111
  lay-offs *see* lay-offs
  supply *see under* USSR *and under* USA
  tax on 117–18, 122
labour exchanges 111
labour hoarding 105–6, 108, 110–11, 116, 120–2
labour productivity 7–10, 80, 127–32, 184
  analysis 80–6, 87–9, 92, 95–6
  and equipment 107
  and freedom 140
  and plan targets 113, 117, 120(n51)
  and unemployment/redundancy 80(n7), 86–7, 99
  in kibbutzim 235–40, 244–6
  measuring 91, 186
labourers *see* workers

Lampert, Nicholas 154–5, 157(n23)
land 199, 200
Lange, Oskar 133, 141, 240, 272–3, 281, 282–3
language(s) 33
Law, P.J. 81(n9), 84(n14), 86(n17)
laws, labour 90, 111
lay-offs 67, 90, 278, 281
  and labour productivity 80(n7), 86–7, 99
  costs 106, 111
  figures, for Britain 339
Lazear, E.P. 67(n8)
Leibman, Y. 167(n89)
leisure *see* free time
Lenin, V.I. 14, 152, 153, 154, 167, 189
Leonard, David K. 195(nn13,17)
Leontyev, A. 168(n91)
Lerner, Abba 141, 240
letters to newspapers 11, 142
Levontin, R. 33(n14)
Lewin, Moshe 157(n25)
Lieblich, A. 251–2, 255(n31)
littering 2
Liviatan, U. 250(n24)
Loeb, M. 28(n4)
loyalty 143–4, 286
Lundahl, Mats 14–16, 192(nn5,6,8)

Mabele, Robert 192(n4)
McAuley, A. 115(n34)
MacKinnon, James G. 215(n58)
Magat, W.A. 28(n4)
maintenance 58, 107
Malima, Kighoma A. 211–13
Malmygin, I. 107(n8), 109
management 59, 257–8
Manager's Fund 156
managers
  in China 13, 181, 188–9
  in USSR 9–10, 83–5, 97
    and soft options 136–7
    incentives to distort information 133–6
    problems of 10, 127
    rationality of labour hoarding 105–6, 108, 110–11, 116, 120–1
    scope for response 142
  power 278
Mao Tse-Tung 181–2, 185
marginal tax rates 21–2, 316, 317, 321–34, 359

366

INDEX

market economies
  and social efficiency 27-8
  arguments for 43
  hierarchies in 28, 30
market mechanism 64
market socialism 47-50
markets
  development of 36-7
  in China 14, 185, 188-9
  in Tanzania 194, 195, 208-11
  see also black markets
Markov, V.I. 117(n40)
Martin, J.M. 84(n14), 85(n16), 86(n18), 119(n48), 120(n49)
Marx, Karl 152, 153, 158, 165, 167
Maschak, J. 31(n8)
Material Incentive Fund 112, 113, 114
  analysis 118-20
Mbilinyi, Simon 199(n25)
Meade, J.E. 268(n2)
mechanisation 9, 106, 107; see also technology
Meerzon, D. 167(n90), 168(n93)
Mekhlis, L. 159, 160(n46)
mergers 19
MIF see Material Incentive Fund
Minford, Patrick 322(n6), 343(n)
Miroshnikov, I. 170(n106)
Mitchell, D.J.B. 286
Miyazaki, Y. 71(n14)
mobility 72-3, 111, 254, 273
Molotov, V.M. 161, 171
monitoring, mutual 67
monopolies 19, 195
moonlighting see second economy
morals see ethics
motivation 252-3, 257
  in kibbutzim 17, 235, 250-3
  measuring 250-1
Msambichaka, Lucian A. 192(n4), 195(n15)
mutual help 199(n25)
mutual monitoring 67
Myrdal, Gunnar 357(n16)

Nakajima, Chihiro 199(n29), 200(n31)
Nakatani, I. 70
Nalebuff, B.J. 35(n18)
Narkhoz, 106(n2), 117(n41)
national characteristics 185
National Insurance 321-2

Ndulu, Benno 14-16, 195(n15), 211-13
needs 33, 41-2
negotiation 64
Neiman, G. 157(n26)
Nelson, R.R. 34, 42, 44(n23), 47(n28), 50(n)
NEM 137
NEP (New Economic Policy) 12, 79, 154-68
  compared to Chinese reforms 14, 185, 188, 189
Nerlove, Marc 211, 214, 215
net normative output 91-2
new technology 7, 69, 72
  in USSR 8, 91, 93
newspapers, letters to 11, 142
Nichols, Abigail 314(n)
Nicholson, Sharon E. 191(n1)
Nigeria, state railway system in 138
Niskanen, W.A. 27(n2)
NNO (net normative output) 91-2
non-productive activities see Directly Unproductive Profit-seeking Activities and productive/non-productive activities
North, Douglass 1-2
Norway 357
Notkin, A. 169(n104)
Nove, Alec 10, 13-14, 30(n7), 79(n1), 80(n8), 83(n11), 97(n49), 127(n2), 146(n), 252(n28), 259(n)
Novosibirsk report 98-9(+n52)
Nuti, D. Mario 18-19, 122(n), 273, 283, 286(n6)
Nyblén, Göran 349-50

Ödegaard, Knut 191(n2), 192(nn5,7), 194(n11), 199(n25), 207(nn36,37), 208(n39), 212-13, 214(nn53,54), 215(n56)
Ohsawa Shokai 70
Okuno, M. 67
opportunism 27-8; see also rationality
organisational activity 351, 353
organisational dynamics 31-2, 36-7, 38-40, 42-50
organisational processes 35-7, 43-50
organisational statics 31, 32, 42
organisational structures (OS) 4, 29-35
  and incentives 38

367

failures in 4–5, 44, 45–8
individuals in 30, 32
tacit knowledge in 34–5
Ostrovityanov, K. 162, 163(n66), 164(n69), 165(n73)
overtime 254
Oxenstierna, Susanna 8–10, 84(n14), 128(n4)

Pachomov, J.N. 107(n7), 114
Panzar, J.C. 44(n25)
paperwork 59
Pareto, Vilfredo 141(n29), 349
Pascale, R. 70(n12)
passivity 98–9
Pattanaik, Prasantha 343(n)
Pavlov, A. 160(n51)
pay *see* wages
pay-offs 128–32
Pazychuk, E. 91(n27)
peasants, assumptions about 193, 198
Pegg, Simon 343(n)
Pelikan, Pavel 4–5, 28, 33(n12), 43, 47(n28), 50, 122(n)
pensions *see* retirement
People's Court (USSR) 111
personal responsibility *see* responsibility
Petrov, A. 91(n27)
plan targets
  in Tanzania 196
  in USSR 83–4, 105, 112–18, 121–2
    and individuals 126, 134–5
    defects 184
    indicators 83, 90–1, 93–4, 120(n51), 121
    method of setting 105
    see also khozraschet
Plotnikov, K. 170(n105)
Poland 94, 279
Polanyi, M. 34
Pomanskij, A.B. 91(n27)
Popov, G. 90
Postanovlenie 92(n32), 93(nn33,36,39), 94(nn40,41)
poverty trap 21–2, 315, 316, 321–34
Pravda 142
preferences 33, 41, 42
Preobrazhensky, E. 12, 153–4, 158
President Clubs 61
prices 64, 68, 351
  and black markets 16, 196–7, 209–11
  in China 184, 188
  in Tanzania 15–16, 196–8, 199, 206–17
  in USSR 8, 91, 93–4, 122, 157, 168–9, 170–1, 188
  shadow 247
prisoners 142–3
Prisoner's Dilemma 1, 10, 67, 127, 128–9, 131
  and second economy activities 132
problem-solving 58, 62, 63, 105–6
productive/non-productive activities 22–3, 349–59
  economic analysis 351–6
  see also DUP
productivity *see* capital productivity *and* labour productivity
profit-sharing 65, 286; *see also* 'share economy'
property rights 38, 40
psychology 355; *see also* motivation *and* rationality
Putterman, L. 235, 238, 248–50

quality 93–4, 130, 250
queueing 351(n10), 353

Rabinovich, Ts. 165(n77)
Raisov, A. 167(n89)
Rajkhelson, E. 94(nn42,44)
Rasmussen, Torben 199(n25), 212–13
rationality 1–2, 10, 27–8, 33, 126–8, 355
  and kibbutzim 232, 240
  as bounded 38
  differences in 49
  of labour hoarding 105–6, 108, 110–11, 116, 120–1
rationing 12, 155, 157, 196, 351(n10)
recruitment 106, 111, 129
redundancy *see* lay-offs
regulations *see* rules
relational contracting/subcontracting 6, 7, 60–1, 63–4
  and risk 68–71
  as trade barrier 73
remuneration *see* wages
reports 120–1
repression *see* control
research 61, 72–3, 93
Resnick, Stephen 199(n29)

368

resource allocation, incentives for 38–40
responsibility 8, 79, 98–9
  and efficiency 99
  household 14, 186
  see also rationality
retirement, payments on 65, 66
reward versus punishment 1, 3
rights 278
risk(s)
  and black market prices 16, 196, 209, 210–11
  and power 279
  sharing 7, 68–71
  workers' attitudes to 19, 281, 285
risk capital 48
Roe, Terry 211–13, 214(n54), 215, 217
Roemer, J.S. 268(n2)
Rohlen, T.R. 70(n12)
Ross, S. 38(n20)
rotation of tasks 6, 58
Rozenberg, D. 168(n94)
Rugumisa, Salvatore 192(n4)
rules 10, 31, 99; see also institutional rules and under kibbutzim
Ruppin, A. 235
Russia
  and kibbutzim 16, 235
  see also USSR
Russian people 185–6
Rutland, P. 80(n7), 87(nn19,20), 89(nn21,22), 97(n47), 113(n28), 114(n30), 116(n38)
Ryabushkin, T.V. 113(n28)
Rylskii, M. 159(n38)

Sadan, E. 245, 255, 256(n32)
safety-valves 11, 138–46
salaries see wages
sanctions
  against unemployment 20, 291, 292
  in USSR 9, 98, 99, 137, 157
  in workfare programs 292, 304–10
Sandelin, Bo. 219(n)
Sätre, Ann-Mari 122(n)
saving 16, 17, 231–4, 255–6
Saxonhouse, G. 72(n16)
Say, Jean Baptiste 349
Schroeder, G.E. 107(nn9,10), 108(nn14,16)
Schumpeter, J. 29(n5), 37, 39(n22), 44(n23)
second economy 20, 128, 131–2, 139–40, 146, 185, 317, 358–9; see also black markets and productive/non-productive activities
security 98
Selden, Mark 182
self-employment 255
self-help 317–18, 322
self-organisation 33, 35–6, 39
Sen, A.K. 83(n10), 199(nn26,29)
serfdom 140
Shapiro, A.D. 91(n27)
'share economy' 18–19, 267–72, 274–88
  compared with cooperative models 272–4
  criticisms of 274–88
shares 69, 70, 279
sharing of information see under information
Shaskin, E. 245, 255, 256(n32)
Shchekino experiment 8, 86–7, 88, 90, 94, 116, 167
  analysis 87–9
  influence 89–90
Shchekinskij combine 86–7
shirking 10, 66–7, 126, 130
  incentives for 127–32
Sidorova, Zh.I. 119(n45)
Simon, H. 39(n21)
single parents 291, 315, 319, 323–7
Širokorad, L.D. 151(n2)
size of units 39, 182, 252
skills 17, 254, 317
  and task rotation 58
  and wages 6, 64–5
  contextual 6, 65, 66
slavery 140
smallholders 15, 16, 193–6, 197–206
Smith, Adam 349
social approbation 17, 251–3, 257
social control see under control
social efficiency 27–8
social incentives 17, 41, 67, 248–54, 258; see also social approbation
social income 230, 254–5; see also welfare benefits
social needs 33, 41–2
social welfare 42–3
socialisation 144

INDEX

socialism 133, 141, 152-4
   achievements 98
   and kibbutzim 240, 253
   and NEP 189
   and wages 240
   disillusionment over 128
   see also command economies *and* socialist incentives
socialist economies/states *see* command economies *and individual states*
socialist ethics 137
socialist incentives 12-13, 151, 153, 158-72
socio-cultural environment 30
soft options 126, 127, 132, 136-46
Solow, R.M. 268(n2)
specialisation 6, 58, 62, 67, 106
   and markets 73
spot contracting 60
Sprackling, Tim 343(n)
Squire, Lyn 199(n29), 200(n31), 204(n33)
Stalin, Joseph
   economic and wages policies 12-13, 156, 159-60, 162, 164, 167, 168-9
   on economic theory 140, 172
   on socialist incentives 12-13, 165, 167, 168-9
   policy of terror 144, 145
   quarrel with Tito 181
state, viability of 2
status 41; *see also* social approbation
Stiglitz, J.E. 35(n18)
stock *see* shares
Strazhevskii, B. 170, 171
stress 352-3
subcontracting, relational *see* relational contracting
subsidies 194, 195, 196, 207-8
   wage 288
successes, absent 4-5, 36-7, 44, 45, 47-8
Sumitomo Group 70, 71
supervision 10, 110, 120-1, 130-1, 140
   mutual 67
   see also control
suppliers 6, 60-1
Suslov, I. 129(n9), 183(n2)
Sutela, Pekka 11-13, 79(n4), 140(n26), 141(nn28,30), 151, 163(n64), 164(n70)

Sweden 46, 357-8, 359

tacit knowledge 4, 33-5, 38, 39-40, 43
   and competition 45
   and incentives 49
talent 34-5
Tanaka, Osamu 199(n29)
Tanzania 14-16, 191-219
   exports 192
   imports 191-2
   model of farm households in 199-206
   policy suggestions for 217-19
   prices, food 15-16, 196-8, 199, 206-17
   regional differences 207-8
   urban poor 196-7
tariffs 73
task rotation 6, 58
taxation 351, 357
   complexity 351, 357
   effects 3
   efforts to minimise 351
   in Britain 21-2, 316, 317, 321-34
      proposals for reform 334-43
      relation to welfare benefits 316, 318-34
   in Poland 94
   in Sweden 357-8, 359
   in USSR 155
   labour 117-18, 122
   marginal rates 21-2, 316, 317, 321-34, 359
   payroll 321-2, 359
technology
   agricultural 187, 195, 198
   innovation in 37
   in USSR 9, 106, 107, 135
   new *see* new technology
Temple, M. 314(n)
Thalberg, Björn 22-3
Thomson, Robert 343(n)
Tito (Joseph Broz) 181
Toikka, Richard 19-21
Tollison, R.D. 27(n2)
Toyo Kogyo Co. 69-70
trade barriers 7, 73
trade disputes 7, 73
trade unions 111, 278, 286
   and unemployment 315
training
   collective 58, 66
   in kibbutzim 257

investment in 21, 311
transactional analysis 30(n6)
Trapeznikov, V. 97(n48)
Tretyakova, Albina 141(n30)
trial and error 4–5, 44, 45
   in forming groups in Japan 61
truthfulness, incentives for 38
Tullock, G. 27(n2)
Tupper, Steven 343(n)
Turetskii, Sh. 169, 170–1
Turner, S. 50(n)
Tyson, L. 277

Ueda, K. 65(n5)
Uekusa, M. 71(n15)
UK *see* Britain
unemployment 18, 22, 80(n7), 274, 275
   absent successes and 5, 37
   and inflation 267, 268, 276–7
   and poverty trap *see* poverty trap
   as job 317
   British figures 315, 339
   controlling 288
   explanations of 315
   frictional 106, 109
   in USSR 106–7, 108, 109
   in Yugoslavia 48
   models for elimination 273
   sanctions against 20, 291, 292
unemployment benefits, suggestions for, in USSR 90
urbanisation 196, 207
   and kibbutzim 241
USA
   auto industry 60
   labour supply 20–1, 298, 301, 302, 304
   mobility of researchers 72
   trade dispute with Japan 7
   union-negotiated rights in 67
   welfare system 19–21, 291–2
      costs 21, 311
      perception of 291
      see also workfare
USSR 7–13, 79–172
   and kibbutzim 16, 235
   consumers in 141–2
   economic reforms in *see* reforms *below*
   economic situation 138
   economic system 12–13, 48
   economists in 140–1, 151–2, 157–72

incentives in 79–80, 83–9, 115, 151–2, 156–72, 186–7
   analysis in 80–3, 91–2
   criticism of 183
   effects 105, 126, 132
   limitations 98–9, 105
influence 13, 181
labour laws 90, 111
labour productivity in *see under* labour productivity
labour shortages and overstaffing in 9, 90, 105–18, 120–2
   effect 277
   see also labour hoarding
managers *see under* managers
nomenklatura 139, 143–4, 145
planning systems 9–10; *see also* plan targets
prices in *see under* prices
prisoners in 142–3
private plots in 139
reforms in 7, 79, 83–4, 90–4, 112–22, 146, 184
   seriousness questioned 138
response to China 14, 185, 186, 188
safety-valves 11, 138–46
sanctions in 157
   lack of effective 137
   problems with 9, 99
second economy 139–40, 146
service organisations 183, 185
social benefits 156, 157
Stalin era 11, 12–13, 132, 140–1, 145, 155–6, 182
   economists in 151–2
   Mao's response to 181, 182
   see also NEP
technology in 9, 106, 107
unemployment in 106–7, 108, 109
wage levels 90
wage systems 7–8, 9–10, 81–2, 112–18, 130
   analysis 81–3, 84–6, 95–6
   development 12–13, 154–72
   problems 186, 187
utility, maximising 353–5
Uvalic, M. 272

value-added 91
Vanek, J. 267, 272–3
voice 10–11, 46, 138, 143, 144–5
   'soft' 11, 140–3, 145

371

Volkonskii, V.A. 91(n27)
voluntarism 17, 241, 251, 252-3, 258
Voznesenskii, N. 157, 158(n27), 161, 163(n67), 164, 166(n81)

Wadensjö, Eskil 122(n)
wages
   acceptable gross 21-2, 316, 318-34
   and effort 115-16
   and inflation 276
   and unemployment 274
   as incentive 12-13
   as sub-organisational structures 30
   bases for 6, 64-7; *see also under* USSR
   bonuses *see* bonuses
   in Britain 319, 320, 335
   in China 184, 187
   in Israel 244
   in Japan 6-7, 64-7
   in USSR 90 *see also under* USSR
   piece-rates 130
   'right to' 90, 99
   shadow 17, 247, 253
   sharing systems 19, 267-88
   subsidies 288
   see also income
Ward, B.M. 267, 272-3
waste 126
Weitzman, M. 18-19, 109, 267-88
welfare 42-3
welfare benefits
   costs 21, 311, 335-6
   see also social income *and under* Britain *and* USA
welfare economies 50
welfare state
   development of 350, 357-8
   kibbutzim compared to 255
   labour in public services 115
Werin, Lars 112(n)
Wihlborg, Claes 50(n)
Wiles, P. 85(n16)
Wilhelm, J.H. 135(n19)
Williamson, O. 4, 27(n1), 28, 30(nn6,7), 32(n10), 33(n13), 38-9, 50(n), 60
Willig, R.D. 44(n25)
WIN 291
Winkelman, Don 199(n29)

Winter, S.G. 34, 44(n23)
women, married 358
work brigades *see under* brigades
work, hours of 254
Work Incentive Program 291
work teams
   in Japan 6
   in USSR *see under* brigades
workers
   apathy 98-9
   assignment to tasks, in Japan 6, 58
   assumptions about 81, 82
   grading, in Japan 58
   incentives for working/shirking 10, 127-32
   participation in decision-making 268, 277, 278, 279-80
   power 278-9
   pressure from, in USSR 84
   proportion in auxiliary functions 107-8
   rotation of tasks, in Japan 6, 58
   security 98
   see also labourers, managers *and* peasants
workfare 19-21, 291-311
   and market labour supply 20, 298, 301, 302, 304
   costs 21, 311
   different forms 295-6, 298, 304
   economic analysis 293-302, 306-10
   sanctions 304-10
   suggestion for similar scheme in USSR 90
working conditions 254
workplace attestation 110-11, 120-1

Yakushiji, T. 60(n1)
Yampolskii, M. 167
Yanov, A. 130(n10), 131(n11)
Ysander, B.C. 34(n17), 50(n)
Yugoslavia 48, 181, 267

zaibatsu groups 61
Zajkauskas, B.A. 93(n35)
Zaleski, E. 135
Zaslavskaya, T.I. 186; *see also* Novosibirsk Report
Zeleny, M. 32(n11), 50(n)
zero inventory method 59